Contents

1.1 Merger control under prior Community law 1.2 The commercial context 1.3 A new era of merger control

2.1 Definition of concentration 2.2 The Community dimension 2.3 Concentrations not having a Community dimension 2.4 Derogations from exclusive application 2.5 Entry into force

3.1 Prior notification 3.2 Evaluation of the notification 3.3 Suspension of the merger 3.4 Referral to Member State authorities 3.5 Substantive appraisal

4.1 Initiating proceedings 4.2 Commission investigations 4.3 Jurisdsiction 4.4 Time-limits 4.5 Due process 4.6 Enforcement 4.7 Relations with Member States 4.8 Supervision by the Court of Justice 4.9 Relations with third countries

5 Control of Joint Ventures in the Economic Community   133

5.1 Scope of control   5.2 Common types of joint venture   5.3 The application of article 85 EEC to cooperative joint ventures   5.4 Conclusion

6 Merger Control in the Coal and Steel Community   162

6.1 The scope of merger control under the Treaty of Paris   6.2 The application of article 66   6.3 Procedure in respect of article 66

7 The 'One-stop Shopping' Principle and Articles 85 and 86 EEC   178

7.1 Introduction: the 'one-stop shopping' principle   7.2 Potential derogations from the 'one-stop shopping' principle   7.3 The residual scope of article 85 EEC

8 The Interface of Community Law and National Law   198

8.1 Community law in national courts   8.2 Community law and national supervision of the bid process   8.3 Community supremacy in matters of merger control   8.4 Conclusions

Appendix I   Council Regulation 4064/89   223

Appendix II   Commission Regulation 2367/90   242

Appendix III   Commission Notice (90/C 203/06)   272

Appendix IV   Commission Notice (90/C 203/05)   281

Index   287

Preface

The adoption in December 1989 of Regulation 4064/89 on the control of concentrations between undertakings brought to an end an inordinately long period of gestation, during the last years of which both child and midwife did their share of kicking. On more than one occasion there were grounds for very serious fear that a successful delivery would not be achieved, and there is still a tendency to watch the child closely to see if it has been irreparably harmed by the traumas of birth. And if we have already been able to observe the first teetering steps, it is too soon to predict in what direction they will eventually lead.

The writing of this book has been among my list of projects for more than ten years, although for a long time it awaited the catalyst that would translate it from the germ of an idea to a concrete proposal. That came with the decision of the European Court of Justice in *BAT & RJ Reynolds* v *Commission*. Consequently, much early work has been discarded or radically reworked as the text of Regulation 4064/89 crystallised and was implemented. Since the book was inevitably to appear during a period of significant transition in Community control of mergers and acquisitions, some strategic decisions had to be taken about what could properly be covered, and should most usefully be included in a single volume on the subject. Of these, two must be stressed. First, although the supervision of Commission decisions in the field of competition law by the Court of Justice, and the investigative procedures of the Commission (which under Regulation 4064/89 are modelled on and similar to those under Regulation 17), are well-documented elsewhere, it was felt that treatment of the topic of merger control would not be complete without proper coverage of these important practical matters. Secondly, although it was recognised that the criteria for control under article 2 of the Regulation, and especially the notion of significantly impeding competition on the common market, are imprecise and offer little by way of guidance to undertakings and their legal advisers, it was decided that it would be idle speculation to attempt to predict how these concepts would be employed by the Merger Task Force or interpreted by the Court of Justice (and it is important that the latter should not be forgotten amid the flurry of Guidance Notes issued by the Commission). Before very long, there will be a body of decisions from which Commission policy can be distilled, and at that point a more useful commentary will be provided.

The law is stated as of 31 January 1991, although occasionally it has been possible to include later material in the footnotes. It has not been possible to include reference to either the first full clearance (with stringent conditions attached) in *Alcatel/Telettra*, or the first Commission refusal to a Member State request for transfer of the matter to its authorities for a distinct market investigation under article 9 (*Varta/Bosch*).

The greatest and perhaps only pleasure in writing a preface is in the opportunity it affords to thank publicly all who have contributed to the writing of the book. My former colleagues at Durham gave generously of their time so that I might take research leave, for which I must also thank the University's Research and Initiative's Committee. My new colleagues at Reading have been understanding about my need to complete this task while also finding my feet in new surroundings. The Department has also generously supported my collaboration with Julian Ellison in Brussels. Officials at the Merger Task Force, elsewhere in the Commission, and at the Department of Trade and Industry, have been very helpful in providing advice and documentation. The Appendices are reproduced with the permission of, and with due thanks to, the Publications Office of the Commission. I must also thank Andrew Soundy, Roger Finbow and Nigel Parr of Ashurst Morris Crisp, each of whom made a significant contribution to the publication. I would also like to thank all at Blackstone Press for their encouragement, and for being constantly cheerful, helpful and tolerant of an author's foibles.

I have reserved a separate paragraph to record my thanks and my indebtedness to Julian Ellison. He has been an unfailing source of enthusiasm and critical rigour, of moral support and practical advice. He has contributed a practical element wherever necessary, and in particular his expertise and experience in handling mergers and acquisitions made sense of the difficult question of the identification of concentrations, which is addressed in the first section of Chapter 2. His contributions to the book have been invaluable.

My final words are for my wife Barbara, and our children Thomas and Sophie. Their patience has been great, and their support immeasurable. They are the very best inspiration anyone could wish for.

T. Antony Downes
Reading

Table of Cases

Court of Justice of the European Communities

Cases have been arranged in chronological order by case number and year. See page xii for alphabetical list of European Court of Justice cases.

Court of Justice of the European Communities

Cases have been arranged in alphabetical order. See page ix for chronological list of European Communities Court of Justice cases.

Belgian Courts

United Kingdom Courts

Table of Commission Decisions

Table of UK Legislation

Table of European Legislation

Bibliography

The works listed below have been referred to several times in the text, and are cited by author's name only:

Bellamy & Child   *Common Market Law of Competition*, by C.W. Bellamy and G.D. Child, 3rd edition, 1987, Sweet & Maxwell

Goyder   *EEC Competition Law*, by D.G. Goyder, 1988, Clarendon Press, Oxford

Hartley   *The Foundations of European Community Law*, by T.C. Hartley, 2nd edition, 1988, Clarendon Press, Oxford

Kerse   *EEC Antitrust Procedure*, by C.S. Kerse, 2nd edition, 1988, E.L.C., London

Whish   *Competition Law*, by R. P. Whish, 2nd edition, 1989, Butterworths

ONE
The climate for merger control

Competition policy was one of the first areas of sustained legal and judicial activity in the European Communities, and by the early 1970s there had developed a substantial body of case law and subordinate legislation, in addition to the main Treaty provisions. A notable omission from the Treaty of Rome was any provision in Title III, Chapter 1 (Competition Policy) on the legal control of mergers.[1] Such provision had been included in the earlier European Coal and Steel Community Treaty (of Paris), but it was not repeated in the EEC Treaty. In addition, the Member States were far from uniform in their approach to mergers: some had no legal controls, while others (including the United Kingdom) had quite sophisticated mechanisms in place.[2] The omission of merger control from the Rome Treaty has now been remedied by the adoption in December 1989 of Council Regulation 4064/89, which is the principal subject-matter of this book. The Regulation applies to 'concentrations' which have a 'community dimension'. A 'concentration' may consist of either a merger, a takeover or a joint venture where the effect is to make a permanent or at least indefinite change in the corporate structure, rather than simply to co-ordinate competitive behaviour.[3] Because the new Regulation has to operate within the framework of the prior competition law, which had come to address the question of mergers, if only obliquely, it will be necessary also to consider the operation of articles 85 and 86 EEC, and for the sake of completeness, article 66 ECSC. In particular, the omission of an express merger control provision led to attempts to achieve some control under articles 85 and 86 to which the European Court of Justice gave at least limited approval. As a result

[1] The Community term of art to describe all such activity is concentration: in the text the more familiar merger has been used loosely to describe a number of different types of dealing, including complete acquisitions, acquisitions of minority shareholdings and joint ventures. The forms of merger activity are considered in more detail below (at 2.1 et seq.); where a specific type of activity is referred to that will be made clear in the text.
[2] For a good, English language survey of merger control in the majority of member States (excluding Greece, Luxembourg and Portugal) see: *Merger control in the EEC*, London, Kluwer, 1988 prepared by a syndicate of firms established in Brussels.
[3] For more precise definitions see 2.1 and 2.2.

there is some difficulty in the relationship between the prior law and the new Regulation.

1.1 MERGER CONTROL UNDER PRIOR COMMUNITY LAW

In order to appreciate the background against which the new Regulation has developed, it is important to understand the limits of existing Community law as an instrument of merger control. It is not easy to identify a convincing explanation for the absence of express provision for merger control in the Treaty of Rome. It has been suggested that in the mid-1950s, when the Treaty was drafted, the threat from mergers was not perceived to require control.[4] The argument is far from compelling in the light of the provision made in the earlier Treaty of Paris (considered below), and the fact that within 10 years the Commission issued a Memorandum regretting, but accepting, that article 85 EEC did not apply to mergers.[5] At about the same time, the United Kingdom, not then a member of the Communities, introduced merger control via the Monopolies and Mergers Act 1965. These factors, of course, make an explanation on the basis of simple oversight even less compelling. The only alternative explanation, however, appears to be that the original intention was that article 85 should apply to mergers, and that the more difficult obstacles to its application which led to the 1966 Memorandum derive not from the wording of article 85 itself but from Regulation 17, passed by the Council under powers conferred by article 87 EEC in order to implement the substantive law established by articles 85 and 86. Commission attempts to achieve a form of merger control through the medium of articles 85 and 86 EEC have met with some success, but cannot be regarded as a satisfactory basis for a comprehensive system of control.[6]

1.1.1 Merger control under article 66 of the Treaty of Paris

The Treaty of Paris establishing the Coal and Steel Community contains merger control powers. Article 66(1) introduces a system of prior notification where a concentration occurs, which the article equates with the fact of one undertaking acquiring control of another. The Commission must authorise any merger falling within the terms of the provision provided it does not allow the undertakings concerned to hinder effective competition in the market for the products in question, nor allow them to establish an advantageous position in relation to access to supplies and markets.[7] Merger

4   *Merger control in the EEC* (*op. cit.* at note 2 above), p.222.
5   *Memorandum on the problem of concentration in the common market*, Competition Series, Study No. 3, Brussels 1966.
6   See 1.1.3.4 below.
7   Art. 66(2).

control under the Treaty of Paris remains unaffected by the new Regulation, and is treated in outline in Chapter 6.

1.1.2 Merger control under article 86 of the Treaty of Rome

Article 86 of the Treaty of Rome prohibits any abuse of dominant position by undertakings. It is, therefore, primarily concerned with the misuse of 'monopoly' power rather than the creation of monopoly power which may come about through the process of merger, acquisition or joint venture. However, no other means of merger control was thought to exist under the Treaty, and the Commission's desire in the late 1960s to achieve some form of control over mergers led to the identification of article 86 as the provision most amenable to an interpretation which would enable the Commission to exert such control. As a result, it became the vehicle for the Commission's first venture into merger control within the ambit of the main Treaty of Rome. The case in question was *Continental Can*,[8] which then became the first Treaty of Rome merger case to come before the Court of Justice. Although the absence of formal decisions by the Commission should not be taken as conclusive evidence of inactivity on its part, it is of some significance that *Continental Can* remains the only fully argued example of proceedings under article 86 formally concluded by the Commission against an undertaking alleged to have abused its dominant position by participating in a merger.[9]

1.1.2.1 Article 86 EEC: general principles
Article 86 provides that:

'Any abuse by one or more undertakings of a dominant position within the common market or in a substantial part of it shall be prohibited as incompatible with the common market in so far as it may affect trade between Member States.'

Unlike article 85, the nature of article 86 does not allow for an exemption process which is independent of the finding of infringement. Under article 85, a course of conduct might be held to be subject to the basic prohibition in article 85(1) but nevertheless qualify for an exemption under article 85(3) on the basis that its positive effects outweigh its negative effects, and that consumers will receive a fair share of such positive benefits. Under article

[8] Cf. 6/72 *Europemballage and Continental Can v Commission* [1973] ECR 215; see below 1.1.2.3.
[9] In *BAT and RJ Reynolds v Commission* (142 & 156/84; see below 1.1.3.4) the Court did express an opinion on the applicability of article 86, but the reasoning was essentially reliant on the reasoning in relation to article 85, and adds little to the understanding of article 86 in merger control proceedings.

86 no such independent analysis is possible. Infringement depends upon the existence of **abuse**. Conduct by a dominant firm which might be thought worthy of exemption would not fall within the definition of 'abuse' in the first place.

The Court of Justice identified[10] five issues to be examined in the assessment of abuse of a dominant position:

(a)   whether there is a dominant position within article 86?
(b)   which market must be considered?
(c)   whether there has been any abuse?
(d)   whether the abuse affects trade between Member States?
(e)   whether the alleged abuser is an economic unit?

Article 86 thus requires as a first step the identification of a relevant market both in terms of 'product' and in terms of a geographical area. For the purpose of identifying the relevant product market, the Court of Justice has developed a test of 'reasonable substitutability' which is a practical application of the notions of cross-elasticity of demand and supply used by economists.[11] It may not be sufficient to establish that there is only limited substitutability in demand if it can be shown that there is a reasonable level of substitutability on the supply side. That is to say that, where there is only a narrowly defined range of goods within the apparent product market, it may be that producers of goods not within the market but involving reasonably similar processes can switch their production to competing goods. In *Continental Can*,[12] the Court found against the Commission's ruling that there had been abuse of a dominant position on the ground that the Commission had failed to take into account the possibility of producers of similar products making a 'simple adaptation'[13] of their production processes and thus entering into competition with the undertaking in question. In this case the relevant market was assessed, therefore, not in terms of products but in terms of the range of potentially competing producers. The Court thus requires the Commission to take considerable care in the identification of relevant markets, and may refuse to uphold the Commission's decision on the ground that the relevant market was too narrowly defined and failed to take into account potentially competing products.[14] In practice the

---

[10]   6 & 7/73 *Commercial Solvents* v *Commission* [1974] ECR 223, [1974] 1 CMLR 309.
[11]   Cf. 85/76 *Hoffman-La Roche* v *Commission* [1979] ECR 461 at 516.
[12]   [1973] ECR 215; see below 1.1.2.3.
[13]   [1973] ECR 215 at 248.
[14]   Other attempts to attack Commission decisions on the ground that supply substitutability was not taken into account have failed, because the Commission's reasoning was more careful on this issue; cf. 322/81 *Michelin* v *Commission* [1983] ECR 3461 (car tyre production could not easily be switched to truck and bus tyre production); 22/78 *Hugin* v *Commission* [1979] ECR 1869 (other manufacturers of cash registers unlikely to switch production capacity to manufacture spare parts suitable for Hugin machines).

Commission has to steer a careful course between defining the market so widely that there is no prospect of ever establishing the existence of a dominant position and defining it so narrowly that any substantial market share can be described as a dominant position. It must also avoid attempting an analysis of the market which is economically justified but perhaps beyond the practical limits of justiciability.

The Court of Justice has developed a general test of dominant position within the relevant market which was expressed in the following terms:

'a position of economic strength enjoyed by an undertaking which enables it to hinder the maintenance of effective competition on the relevant market by allowing it to behave to an appreciable extent independently of its competitors and customers and ultimately of consumers.'[15]

To this general definition must be added the Court's observation in the *Hoffman-La Roche* case to the effect that:

'such a position does not preclude some competition, which it does where there is a monopoly or quasi-monopoly, but enables the undertaking which profits by it, if not to determine, at least to have an appreciable influence on the conditions under which that competition will develop, and in any case to act largely in disregard of it so long as such conduct does not operate to its detriment.'[16]

So, as a matter of general principle it can be said that dominant position for the purposes of article 86 requires an ability to act independently of competitors in the relevant market, without there necessarily being a complete absence of competition for the allegedly dominant firm on that market.

In practice, dominance is determined by reference to a combination of market share and the competitive structure of the market. In all but extreme cases the competition authorities are unwilling to regard the fact of high market share alone as an indicator of dominance.[17] A more significant factor contributing to the establishment of a dominant position is the market share of the firm in question viewed in relation to the share of other firms competing in the market. Thus, even a quite low absolute market share may take on far greater significance if the firm is the only sizeable undertaking in the market.[18]

[15] 322/81 *Michelin* v *Commission* [1983] ECR 3461 at [30].
[16] 85/76 *Hoffman-La Roche* v *Commission* [1979] ECR 461 at 520.
[17] One reason is that market share is a transient indicator of power; it is in the nature of markets to evolve, and for firms to respond to and drive that evolution, so that market share changes as new entrants join the market or existing competitors take the benefits of their relative efficiency. Consequently, absolute market share on a single date is not a good indicator of enduring market power.
[18] *United Brands* [1978] ECR 207, 282.

Even where relative market share indicates a *prima facie* position of dominance, other questions, in particular the cross-elasticity of supply test and the existence of barriers to entry, must be addressed in order to determine the existence of a dominant position. The underlying principle of the test of cross-elasticity of supply, in the context of assessing market power, is that no undertaking can be said to be in a dominant position unless it can be shown that, if it does act independently of its competitors, customers and consumers, there is no possibility of competition from a source not yet present in the market. In other words, an alleged dominant position is no such thing where inefficient behaviour would provide the incentive for new entrants to the market to attempt to take away some of the market share. A consideration of the possibility of new market entrants inevitably leads to a consideration of the extent to which there exist 'barriers' to such entry. Barriers to entry include access to technology,[19] access to finance,[20] access to advertising,[21] access to raw materials[22] and access to or control of outlets for products.[23] Where a substantial market share exists at the same time as significant barriers to entry[24] of new firms, the likelihood of there being a dominant position is significantly increased.

The simple possession of market power through a dominant position is not of itself an infringement of article 86.[25] Nevertheless, the existence of a dominant position without more does entail some consequences for the holder, since the Court has made clear that it regards a dominant position as an inevitable distortion of the normal conditions of competition on a market,[26] and as a consequence Community law imposes obligations of good behaviour on dominant firms which do not apply to non-dominant firms.[27] Thus, the primary concern of the Community authorities in controlling abuses of dominant position is to prevent behaviour which is prejudicial to the competitive structure of the market. The Court has confirmed the Commission's opinion that in appropriate circumstances a merger may be regarded as an anti-competitive abuse of this kind.[28] Although article 86 is expressed in terms of abuse of a dominant position, the Court has consistently held from the very earliest cases that there need be no causative link between the dominant position and the alleged abuse. The behaviour

---

[19] See *Hoffman-La Roche* at [48]; *United Brands* at [82] - [84].
[20] *Continental Can* at [30]; *Hoffman-La Roche* per A-G Reischl.
[21] *United Brands* at [91] - [94].
[22] *United Brands* at [72] - [77].
[23] *United Brands* at [70] - [81]; *Hoffman-La Roche* at [48].
[24] See Baden-Fuller, *Article 86 EEC: economic analysis of the existence of a dominant position* (1979) 4 ELRev 423.
[25] For an account of abuse of dominant position, see: Bellamy & Child 408 - 429; Whish 302 - 311; Goyder 304 - 316.
[26] *Hoffman-La Roche* at 541.
[27] *Michelin* at 3511.
[28] *Continental Can* see also *BAT & RJ Reynolds v Commission* 142 & 156/84 [1988] 4 CMLR 24; see 1.1.3.4 below.

classed as abusive need not be directly derived from the existence of the dominant position for the existence of an infringement to be established.[29] This reasoning reinforces the message emanating from the Court that, once a dominant position is shown to exist, the undertaking in question is subject to a higher standard of behaviour than might otherwise apply in all respects, not only in respect of the use made of the market power which goes with the dominant position.

1.1.2.2 Problems in using article 86 for merger control

The nature of article 86 is such that there are a number obstacles to its being used as an instrument of general merger control. The principal obstacle is that control is aimed exclusively at the behaviour of firms which enjoy dominant positions. Where the parties to a merger, or in the case of a takeover the acquiring company,[30] are not in a dominant position then the Commission has no formal power under article 86 to exercise control. Even where a merger or takeover between two non-dominant firms would create the size of company or group which the Commission might regard as *prima facie* dominant and so likely to distort the market, the Commission is powerless to intervene in the absence of evidence of abuse of any such dominant position. The Treaty of Rome does not seek to control corporate size, or its creation or acquisition, only its abuse. Under its article 86 merger control powers the Commission was powerless to control the creation of dominant positions through mergers or takeovers. As in *Continental Can*,[31] only the strengthening of an already existent dominant position was subject to control.[32]

A further obstacle is that under article 86 there is no effective mechanism of formal prior control of proposed mergers. In *Continental Can*,[33] the investigation took place at the Commission's own instigation. It is possible for the parties to seek a negative clearance by making application under article 2 of Regulation 17, but in practice such an application would be very unlikely to be processed within the time necessary to make the procedure suitable as a means of prior control. Commission investigations take anywhere between a few months and several years. Although it is true that negative clearance procedures are usually more quickly despatched than notifications for exemption, even a decision time of a few months would probably be too long for most proposed mergers. It is sometimes argued that such

---

29 *Continental Can* at 245; *Hoffman-La Roche* at 541.
30 Whether a dominant position held by a target company in a takeover would ever give jurisdiction under article 86 is questionable. It does not seem likely that to succumb to a hostile takeover could be classed as an abuse; but it might be that willing participation in a takeover, including recommendation of the offer to the shareholders, might constitute an abuse.
31 [1973] ECR 215.
32 See now article 2(2) Regulation 4064/89, which subjects both the creation and the strengthening of qualifying concentrations to Commission regulatory control.
33 *Supra* note 31.

objections to the control of mergers and takeovers under article 86 are misplaced because the Commission is always willing to entertain informal approaches from firms contemplating merger activity and anxious to be reassured that the Commission will not subsequently seek to pull the rug out from under their deal. On this view there is a system of informal prior control available. This willingness on the part of the Commission was certainly welcome during the period when article 86 was being pressed into service for merger control, in advance of purpose-built legislation, but it suffers from a number of drawbacks. The first is that an informal response by letter from the Commission to an informal approach is far from secure legal protection against subsequent proceedings against the merger. While the Commission may have seen itself 'morally' bound by its informally stated view (in the absence of a material change in the facts or circumstances) third parties would not be so bound, and the Commission would be obliged to give due consideration to any third party complaint. A second drawback is that it places control on an uncertain legal basis, beyond the scope of proper supervision by the Court of Justice (which requires a formal decision before it can exercise its appellate role),[34] and in a context in which a full economic analysis, which the Court usually stresses is essential in such cases,[35] cannot take place.

The absence of a positive clearance procedure under article 86 (since there is no possibility of an exemption such as might be obtained under article 85(3)) is a further disadvantage of using article 86 as an instrument of merger control. It has been suggested that the legitimacy of the application of national competition law to an issue which has received a clearance from the Commission under community law will depend upon the nature of the clearance given.[36] In particular, while a negative clearance is no more than a statement from the Commission that an agreement or practice is not regarded as harmful within the provisions of Community law, and so may be overridden by a stricter rule under national law, a positive clearance is a statement from the Commission that the agreement or practice is desirable in terms of Community policy, and as such should not be overruled by a decision of national competition authorities. Consequently, the absence of a positive clearance procedure might make mergers which were desirable in terms of Community industrial policy nevertheless subject to further control under national competition law.

Finally, it has been questioned whether Regulation 17 provides remedies for infringement of article 86 which are suitably adapted to the process of merger control. The imposition of fines is largely irrelevant to the assessment of whether mergers and takeovers, which are eventually matters

---

[34] 60/81 *IBM* v *Commission* [1981] ECR 2639, [1981] 3 CMLR 635.
[35] Cf. *Continental Can.*
[36] See 8.3 *et seq.*

of public knowledge, should be allowed to proceed. What is required are powers either to prevent the merger taking place or, in the last resort, powers to order divestiture. Both appear to be at least to some extent available in article 86 proceedings. Technically the Commission may, under article 3 of Regulation 17, order the firm in question to put an end to the infringement by not going through with the acquisition or merger. The problem with this apparently straightforward power to prevent the consummation of mergers is that the Commission could not, given the amount of time that article 86 investigations currently take, issue such an order early enough to prevent the merger. However, it may be possible, by taking or threatening to take interim measures, to achieve a functionally equivalent effect.[37] In *Camera Care*[38] the Court interpreted article 3(1) of Regulation 17 as giving the Commission power to take steps 'indispensable . . . for ensuring the effectiveness of any decisions requiring undertakings to bring to an end infringements which it has found to exist.' Until now interim measures have only been taken in cases where the infringement has already begun, but there appears to be no great obstacle to taking them in order to prevent the infringement beginning, especially where to do so would be a more effective response to the conditions of urgency and the prevention of irreparable damage which are said to justify the taking of the measures.

Whether the Commission has the power to order divestiture has never been tested, although the Commission clearly believed in the *Continental Can* proceedings[39] that it did have such power. Such power as there is must derive from article 3 of Regulation 17, which empowers the Commission to require undertakings to bring any infringements which it finds to an end. In *Continental Can*, the Commission simply ordered the undertakings to put an end to the infringement and gave them a period of time in which to submit proposals to the Commission. This was clearly intended to make provision for divestiture. Before the Court of Justice the Commission's case failed at the stage of assessment of dominant position;[40] the Court had however already approved the principle of using article 86 for merger control and, in so doing, had presumably considered the implications of a finding of infringement.

1.1.2.3 Article 86 merger control in practice

The only fully reasoned decision of the Court of Justice in this area is *Europemballage and Continental Can v Commission*.[41] Continental Can was a New York company manufacturing metal containers, other forms of packaging, and the machines for manufacturing such things. The company

---

[37] On interim measures more generally, see 3.3 and note 38 below.
[38] 792/79R *Camera Care* v *Commission* [1980] ECR 119, [1980] 1 CMLR 334.
[39] [1973] ECR 215.
[40] See 1.1.2.3 below.
[41] 6/72 [1973] ECR 215, [1973] CMLR 199.

was international in scale, operating in a number of different countries through locally based subsidiaries. In particular, it owned nearly 86% of the nominal capital of a German packaging company, SLW. In 1969 Continental Can proposed to a number of European companies, including Thomassen & Drijver Verblifa (TDV) of the Netherlands and Metal Box of the UK, that they should participate in the establishment of a European holding company for packaging. The plan was to establish a company, Europemballage Corporation, which, using funds provided by Continental Can, would purchase the shares of TDV. TDV agreed to this proposal, and by March 1970 the company had been set up and the Europemballage takeover bid for TDV had been announced. At that point the Commission drew the attention of the companies involved to its view that the takeover might be an infringement of article 86. Metal Box Company then withdrew from further dealings with Europemballage, in view of the financial risks raised by the Commission's statement. Nevertheless, in early April 1970 Europemballage went ahead with the purchase of the TDV shares then available, which gave it an immediate 91% stake in the company.

The Commission[42] immediately decided to commence proceedings against both Europemballage and Continental Can, with a view to ordering that the infringement be brought to an end under article 3(1) of Regulation 17, under the abuse of dominant position rule. The Commission found that Continental Can held a dominant position in the market for light metal packaging for preserved meat, fish and crustacea, and for metal caps for glass containers; and that its dominance, achieved through its subsidiary SLW, extended over a substantial part of the Common Market. The finding of dominance was based partly on market share and partly on other factors such as access to financial and technological resources not available to competitors. It also found that the purchase of the shares in TDV was an abuse of dominant position because it had the effect of practically eliminating competition in the markets in question. Continental Can was therefore ordered to put an end to the infringement.

Continental Can challenged the Commission's decision on a number of legal and factual grounds. It was argued that article 86 was not applicable to mergers, since it was concerned with conduct on the market which was directly prejudicial to consumers and not with structural changes in the market. The company relied on the existence of merger control provisions in the Treaty of Paris and their absence in the EEC Treaty in order to argue that the intention must have been to omit merger control from the scope of the competition rules of the EEC Treaty. It also argued that article 86 required the dominant position to be instrumental in the abuse, while in this case the dominant position was held through a subsidiary which played no part in the alleged abuse. It took this argument a step further

[42] OJ 1972 L7/25, [1972] CMLR D11.

to suggest that since Continental Can, the firm singled out by the Commission as addressee of its decision, was an American company the Commission had no jurisdiction over it. Finally, it argued that the Commission had got its facts wrong in finding that it occupied a dominant position in a substantial part of the Common Market.

The firm was successful with this last argument, and so the Commission's finding of abuse of dominant position and accompanying order to end the infringement were overturned. The Court found that the Commission had not sustained the burden of proving that the relevant market was the very narrow market it had defined, and not a more general market for light metal containers for all kinds of products. In particular, the Commission had failed to take into account the possibility that other metal container manufacturers might enter the market.[43] In other respects, however, the Commission's analysis prevailed, so that the legal basis of article 86 as a means of merger control was firmly established.

On the matter of jurisdiction, the Court proceeded on the basis of the now familiar argument that the activities of subsidiaries within the Community may be attributed to parents outside the Community where those activities are not independent but, as in this case, are directed by the parent.[44] The question of causative link between dominance and abuse is addressed earlier in this Chapter, and need not be returned to here.[45] The Court dismissed comparisons with the Treaty of Paris as irrelevant, finding instead that the answer to the question whether article 86 should apply to mergers lay in a consideration of the competition rules of the EEC Treaty, in their fullest context. This required a return to article 3(f) of the Treaty, requiring institution of a system ensuring that competition in the Common Market is not distorted, which the Court was quick to point out required *a fortiori* that competition must not be eliminated.[46]

The tests as to the necessary degree of distortion of the competitive structure for a finding of abuse of dominant position by merger proposed in *Continental Can* were strict. The conduct complained of must substantially fetter competition. This was taken to mean the virtual elimination of effective competitors. The minimum requirement for such an abuse in the case of a merger was reconsidered and set out briefly by the Court in *BAT and RJ Reynolds v Commission*:[47]

'An abuse of such a position can only arise where the shareholding in

---

[43]   [1973] ECR 215 at 248.
[44]   Ibid.
[45]   See 1.1.2.1 above.
[46]   The Court also argued that there must not be a gap between article 85 and article 86 which firms could exploit in order to turn behaviour prohibited under the one into behaviour not caught by the other. In this respect they were not entirely successful, since article 86 was found not to prohibit the creation of market power by non-dominant firms.
[47]   142 & 156/84 [1988] 4 CMLR 24; see 1.1.3.4. below.

question results in effective control of the other company or at least in some influence on its commercial policy.'

The true extent of the Commission's merger control activity under article 86 is revealed by examination of its informal practice in the years after *Continental Can*. During that period the Commission considered numerous proposed mergers in the light of the article 86 criteria established in that case; at times causing a change of conduct by the firms concerned;[48] at other times seeing fit to take no action.[49] These cases reveal a number of aspects of the Commission's use of article 86 as a means of informal merger control. In the first place, there is no particular pattern about the way in which such control takes place. The means of reference to the Commission is fairly evenly spread between Commission initiative, the acquiring company seeking assurances and third party complaints. Third party complaints divided between target companies using a complaint as a defence mechanism in the face of a takeover and companies who were not involved in the merger acting out of anxiety about the adverse impact of the merger on their competitive position on the market. Further, in a small but significant number of cases the Commission was able to exercise its influence in such a way as to change the behaviour of companies, although it is not clear whether this was because the companies accepted that the Commission's objections were wellfounded or because they did not want to have to face up to a long investigation in order to prove the case for allowing the merger to go ahead. Lastly, on one occasion the Commission has been willing to use the threat of interim measures to bring merger talks to an immediate halt.

---

[48] Cf. *Pilkington/BSN* [10th CP Rep (1980) para 152] Commission approved takeover on the receipt of undertakings from the firms as to their continuing mutual independence; *Amicon/Fortia/Wright* [11th CP Rep (1981) para 112] action to impose interim measures under the *Camera Care* formula to prevent the distortion of the market caused withdrawal from proposed merger; *British Sugar/Berisford* [12th CP Rep (1982) para 104] change of conduct caused by the institution of formal proceedings by the Commission; *BA/BCAL* [(1988) 21 Bull. of EC 3/37] merger had been scrutinised by UK Monopolies and Mergers Commission, which had imposed certain conditions - European Commission secured further undertakings from the companies which it believed were necessary to maintain competition on routes in and out of the United Kingdom. See also *Danish Fur Sales* [1989] 4 CMLR 353 (purchase of minority shareholding opposed by Commission); *Consgold/Minorco* [1989] 4 CMLR 323 (takeover approved after Commission obtained undertakings as to disposal of certain interests acquired).

[49] See also *Rhone Poulenc/Monsanto*; (1989) 22 Bull of EC 7-8/32. The Commission raised no objection under art.86 to Rhone Poulenc's acquisition of Monsanto's worldwide production capacity for analgesic and antipyretic compounds, on the ground that it did not hold a dominant position in the markets in question. And see similarly: *Ashland Oil Inc/Cabot Co* 14th Report on Competition (1984); *Pont-à-Mousson/Stanton & Stavely* 14th Report on Competition (1984); *Mecaniver/PPG* OJ 1984 L35/54; *Cap Gemini Sogeti* 1988 OJ C 86/50; *Pechiney/American Can* IP(89) 45; *Ibercore/Outokumpu* IP (89) 795; *Siemens/ Nixdorf* IP (90) 378. See further the cases listed in notes 50-54.

Of the cases in which no change of conduct resulted,[50] the most significant single reason was the Commission's finding that there was no dominant position. This conclusion reflected not only size,[51] but also the relevant product market,[52] the geographic market[53] and the existence of external competition.[54] The other significant ground[55] for the Commission's decision to take no further action was that the conduct of a dominant or potentially dominant[56] firm did not amount to an abuse because there was no significant impact on the competitive structure.[57]

1.1.2.4 The future of merger control under article 86

The Commission has achieved a measure of merger control under article 86. All the instances of informal control, however, fall within the framework of the *Continental Can* decision in the Court of Justice. The conceptual constraints on further development meant that the Commission had already turned to article 85 as an alternative means of control[58] well before the adoption of the new merger Regulation, which came into force in September 1990 and which heralded (in the great majority of cases) the end of this form of merger control under Community competition law. It may be that, notwithstanding the legal and political intent of the merger Regulation, scope remains for parties (most obviously target companies or third party complainants) to seek the application of the old article 86 merger control powers through national courts.[59] National courts can be expected to be reluctant to exercise such powers but would clearly be obliged to consider the issue (or at least refer it to the Court of Justice under the article 177 procedure) were it brought before them.

50 It should be noted that the *Coats Patons/Gutermann* takeover was dropped, but at the instance of the German Federal Cartel Office, not the Commission.
51 *Peugeot-Citroen/Chrysler UK* (8th Report); *Kaiser/Estel* (9th Report); *Coats Patons/Gutermann* (9th Report); in *Ashland Oil/Cabot* (14th Report) the undertaking certainly enjoyed a very substantial market share, but there was a competitor of similar size, and the company was caught between commercially strong raw material suppliers (oil companies) and commercially strong purchasers (tyre companies), and so there was no dominant position.
52 *AVEBE/KSH* (8th Report); *Pont-a-Mousson/Stanton & Stavely* (14th Report).
53 *Baxter Travenol Laboratories/Smithkline RIT* (10th Report).
54 *Peugeot-Citroen/Chrysler UK* (8th Report); *Fichtel & Sachs/Huret* (9th Report).
55 In one case the conduct about which enquiry was made was not a merger or acquisition at all, but simply an internal reorganisation within a group in which the subsidiary had no scope for action independent of the wishes of the parent: *Michelin/Kleber-Colombes* (10th Report).
56 In *Eagle Star/Allianz Versicherung* (12th Report) the Commission did not actually establish the existence of a dominant position, but proceeded on the assumption that it could be established, and dismissed the case on other grounds.
57 *Michelin/Actor NV* (8th Report); *AVEBE/KSH* (8th Report) - in relation to the separate market for industrial potatoes, on which a dominant position did possibly exist; *Eagle Star/Allianz Versicherung* (12th Report); *Berisford/Napier Brown* (13th Report).
58 See 1.1.3.4 below.
59 See 7.2.3.2 and 7.2.4.2 below.

1.1.3   Merger control under article 85 of the Treaty of Rome

Article 85 of the Treaty of Rome regulates agreements between undertakings. Although article 85 devotes some attention to the notion of 'agreement', there is no restriction on the application of the article to agreements under which property, such as company assets or shares, passes; nor any requirement that for the article to apply the undertakings involved remain independent after the time of the agreement. As a consequence, it might be thought that article 85 was a suitable vehicle to carry the Commission's aspirations of achieving a form of merger control at the Community (supra-national) level, operating independently of whatever merger control there might be under the law of some of the Member States. However, in 1966 the Commission issued a Memorandum on Concentrations,[60] in which it stated that:

> 'It is not possible to apply Article 85 to agreements whose purpose is the acquisition of total or partial ownership of enterprises or the reorganisation of the ownership of enterprises (merger, acquisition of holdings, purchase of part of the assets).'

Whatever the reasons behind the 1966 Memorandum, the Commission and Court's practice in relation to the application of article 85 to mergers was radically revised in *BAT and RJ Reynolds* v *Commission*.[61] The general application of article 85 is considered below.

1.1.3.1   Article 85(1)
Article 85(1) provides:

> 'The following shall be prohibited as incompatible with the common market: all agreements between undertakings, decisions by associations of undertakings and concerted practices which may affect trade between Member States and which have as their object or effect the prevention, restriction or distortion of competition within the common market.'

The article then lists what are no more than examples of anti-competitive behaviour falling within the scope of the article. The application of article 85(1) may conveniently be broken down into four parts.

---

[60]   *Memorandum on the problem of concentration in the common market*, Competition Series, No. 3, 1966, at para 58. For the distinction between concentrations (outside article 85) and agreements (within article 85) see 5.1.2 *et seq.*
[61]   142 & 156/84 [1988] 4 CMLR 24; see 1.1.3.4 below.

(a) Undertakings Article 85 applies to the activities of 'undertakings'. The most important meaning attributed to the term 'undertaking' is that of a person, legal or natural, carrying on independent economic or commercial activity. Where a parent company is able to dictate terms to a subsidiary, so that even where they have separate legal identities they operate as a single economic unit, they will be treated as a single undertaking for the purposes of article 85, and the conditions of applicability of article 85 will not be met.[62] The test of independent economic or commercial activity also results in article 85 applying to state-owned enterprises, provided they are not merely part of the administration of government, but actually carry on economic or commercial activities.[63] Further, an individual may be subject to article 85 if carrying out independent economic or commercial activity in his own right.[64]

(b) Agreements, decisions and concerted practices The concepts of agreement, decision by associations of undertakings, and concerted practice have presented only a little difficulty for the Commission and the Court of Justice, and for the most part it is unlikely that they will raise problems in the field of merger control. The intention of the draftsman was that the three concepts taken together should embrace all forms of mutual activity with a potential for anti-competitive effect, with the result that there is inevitably a degree of overlap between them. Agreement has been interpreted as including all forms of voluntary behaviour which are openly acknowledged, or which may be inferred from the conduct of the parties. In particular, there is no requirement that an agreement should amount to an enforceable contract.[65] A concerted practice has been held to consist of anti-competitive cooperation between firms (supposedly in competition with each other) which, without amounting to anything which might be recognised as a formal agreement, 'knowingly substitutes practical cooperation between them for the risks of competition'.[66] The concept is of little concern in the case of merger control, where the existence of formal agreements usually is a matter of public knowledge.

(c) Object or effect of preventing, restricting or distorting competition This key formulation provides the means of discriminating between permissible and impermissible agreements. The identification can only be of agreements

---

[62] See 15/74 *Centrafarm* v *Sterling Drug* [1974] ECR 1147; [1974] 2 CMLR 480. See also 170/83 *Hydrotherm* v *Compact* [1984] ECR 2999 at 3016.

[63] *British Telecommunications* OJ 1982 L360/36, [1983] 1 CMLR 457; confirmed on appeal 41/83 [1985] ECR 873, [1985] 2 CMLR 368.

[64] 258/78 *Nungesser* v *Commission* [1982] ECR 2015, [1983] 1 CMLR 278.

[65] 209/78 *Van Landewyck* v *Commission* [1980] ECR 3125, [1981] 3 CMLR 193.

[66] 48/69 *ICI* v *Commission* ('Dyestuffs') [1972] ECR 619 at 655.

which are *prima facie* impermissible because of the potential for exemption. The test depends upon two distinct sets of criteria.

In the first place there are the three criteria of 'preventing, restricting or distorting' competition. Prevention and restriction may be regarded as essentially similar, the difference reflecting the question whether the adverse effect on competition was total or partial. The third criterion of distortion has been interpreted by the Court of Justice,[67] as including causing competition to develop in a manner different from that which might have been expected in the absence of the agreement.

The second class of criteria within the test is that of having 'the object or effect' of affecting competition in the proscribed way. The Court has taken a restrictive view of what amounts to proof of the *object* of preventing, restricting or distorting competition, so that in most cases the issue cannot be determined on the basis of object alone. The Commission must conduct a full analysis of the economic circumstances of the agreement to determine whether it has the effect of preventing, restricting or distorting competition.[68] Such an analysis would be unnecessary only if it were apparent from all or some of the terms of the agreement that its effect would be so deleterious that it must be regarded as having the object of preventing, restricting or distorting competition. In practice, only certain types of agreement have been regarded as inevitably so deleterious that they may be classed as having such an object, most notably agreements which partition the internal market and agreements which fix prices.[69]

The object approach to preventing competition results in a limited number of agreements being *per se* illegal. They are by their very nature caught within the prohibition established by the legislation. However, at least in theory, under the Treaty of Rome, a finding that an agreement is *per se* subject to the prohibition in article 85(1) does not exclude it from consideration for exemption under article 85(3), although such a finding would no doubt considerably increase the burden of proof to be satisfied before any such exemption could be granted. The effect approach subjects all other agreements to detailed analysis under what may be termed a 'rule of reason'. It is a two-stage process involving a decision whether or not a practice is in fact a restriction of competition under article 85(1) (following the *Société Technique Minière* case),[70] and a decision whether or not a restrictive practice should nevertheless be allowed under article 85(3). In recent years the Court has caused some blurring of these stages by permitting national courts to rule that terms of an agreement which are themselves restrictive do not fall within

---

[67]   56 & 58/64 *Consten & Grundig* v *Commission* [1966] ECR 299.

[68]   *Société Technique Minière* v *Maschinenbau Ulm GmbH* 56/65 [1966] ECR 235, [1966] CMLR 357 (art. 177 reference).

[69]   For an example of the object approach in relation to price-fixing see: 8/72 *Vereeniging van Cementhandelaren* v *Commission* [1972] ECR 977, [1973] CMLR 7.

[70]   Supra note 68.

the prohibition of article 85(1) where they are indispensable and merely ancillary to the achievement of the main purpose of the agreement, which is not itself restrictive.[71] Finally under this heading, it should be noted that the requirement of having the object or effect of preventing, restricting or distorting competition is subject to a quantitative test or *de minimis* rule. The prohibition in article 85 will not apply where there is no 'appreciable' effect in preventing, restricting or distorting competition, or on trade between Member States.[72]

(d) Affecting trade between Member States The prevention, restriction or distortion of competition under article 85 is only prohibited in so far as it may affect trade between Member States. This jurisdictional test for article 85 (and article 86) has in practice proved relatively easy to satisfy, and accordingly is not unduly restrictive of the Community authorities' jurisdiction. Where the parties to the agreement are located in different Member States, or the subject-matter of the agreement is goods or services which are in international trade, an effect on trade between Member States is likely to be presumed. In the absence of such manifest cross-border elements, the determining factor will be the extent to which the agreement tends to partition the market. By such an approach the Court has been able to demonstrate that even agreements between undertakings within a single Member State and which are implemented solely within that state may affect trade between Member States.[73]

1.1.3.2 Article 85(3)

Article 85(3) provides for the exemption of agreements from the basic prohibition contained in article 85(1).[74] The power to grant such exemptions is restricted to the Commission by article 9 of Regulation 17. The first prerequisite of exemption is that the agreement produces some benefit which, in crude terms, makes the restriction on competition worthwhile.[75] The categories of benefits are widely drawn. Article 85(3) then provides that exemption will only be granted if a fair share of the benefit identified is

---

71 *Pronuptia de Paris* v *Schillgalis* 161/84 [1986] ECR 353, [1986] 1 CMLR 414. It is perceived by some (e.g., Kon (1982) 19 CMLRev 541; see also Steindorf (1983) 20 CMLRev 125) to be a weakness of article 85 that the grant of exemptions is exclusively reserved to the Commission by article 9 of Regulation 17. It may be this perceived weakness which has led to the blurring of stages noted above. See also: 26/76 *Metro* v *Commission (No 1)* [1977] ECR 1875, [1978] 2 CMLR 1; 258/78 *Nungesser* v *Commission* [1982] ECR 2015, [1983] 1 CMLR 278; 42/84 *Remia* v *Commission* [1987] 1 CMLR 1.
72 5/69 *Volk* v *Vervaecke* [1969] ECR 295, [1969] CMLR 273. See also the Notice on Agreements of Minor Importance (3 September 1986 OJ 1986 C231/2).
73 Cf. *Brasserie de Haecht* v *Wilkin (No 1)* 23/67 [1967] ECR 407, [1968] CMLR 26 - art.177 reference; *Vereeniging van Cementhandelaren* v *Commission* 8/72 [1972] ECR 977, [1973] CMLR 7.
74 See generally, Bellamy & Child, Chapter 3.
75 Cf. 25 & 26/84 *Ford* v *Commission (No 2)* [1985] 3 CMLR 528.

passed on to consumers by the undertakings participating in the agreement. The Court has not adopted a very precise definition of 'consumers'; nor has it been able to provide specific guidance as to what constitutes a 'fair share' of the benefit. The clear intention of the legislation is that where a restrictive agreement nevertheless produces benefits, an exemption will not be granted unless the Community as a whole can draw some benefit; the undertakings may not keep the whole of the benefit to themselves. In many cases the Commission can find no positive evidence and is left to rely on a presumption that where the undertakings remain exposed to healthy competition there will inevitably be a sharing of the benefit with consumers because the undertakings will be anxious to benefit from the competitive advantage it would give them. The Commission is not empowered to grant an exemption in conditions where the first two criteria are met unless it can be shown that the agreement does not impose restrictions other than those necessary for the attainment of the benefits and does not allow the parties to eliminate competition in a substantial part of the products in question.

1.1.3.3 Article 85(2)

Article 85(2) provides that any 'agreements or decisions prohibited pursuant to this Article shall be automatically void.' Although detailed treatment is not necessary here, this deceptively simple provision creates a number of quite difficult problems.

In the first place, it has been found to prevent the process of notification (which is the means of applying for an exemption under article 85(3)) operating as a stay of execution during the inevitable delay between notification and final decision.[76] Secondly, only those parts of the agreement which are anti-competitive will be automatically void; but where the offending parts cannot be severed from the agreement without rendering it meaningless, the whole agreement will be void. Clearly, automatic nullity, particularly in the case of mergers and takeovers, can fundamentally alter the relationship of, and the nature of the bargain between, the parties. Finally, an aggrieved third party may seek to argue that to continue to implement an agreement which is automatically void in such a way as to cause loss to that third party is tortious conduct for which damages are recoverable.

1.1.3.4 *BAT and RJ Reynolds* v *Commission*[77]

What Advocate General Mancini came to call 'l'affaire des cigarettes' involved four of the six largest cigarette manufacturers and marketers in the Community. The Rembrandt Group Ltd ('Rembrandt') is a South African based company which wholly owned Rothmans Tobacco (Holdings) Ltd

---

[76] 48/72 *Brasserie de Haecht* v *Wilkin (No 2)* [1973] ECR 77.
[77] 142 & 156/84 [1988] 4 CMLR 24.

('RTH'), which in turn had a controlling interest in Rothmans International ('RI'). Philip Morris Inc ('Philip Morris') is the largest American exporter of cigarettes and, according to the Advocate General, 'possibly the leading multinational in the industry'. British American Tobacco Company Ltd ('BAT') is the largest tobacco manufacturing company in the western world, as well as having diverse interests in other sectors, and is based in the United Kingdom. RJ Reynolds Industries Inc ('Reynolds') is an American company with interests in the tobacco and food industries. In April 1981 Rembrandt sold to Philip Morris 50% of the equity in RTH, for $350 million, and agreed with Philip Morris that the activities of RI should be managed on a joint basis. Rembrandt and Philip Morris had notified the agreement,[78] and, in addition, Reynolds and subsequently BAT complained to the Commission about the agreement, which in their view allowed Philip Morris the opportunity to influence the commercial conduct of RI which was supposed to be a direct and strong competitor on the Community market.

Figure 1 — Philip Morris acquisition of Rothmans

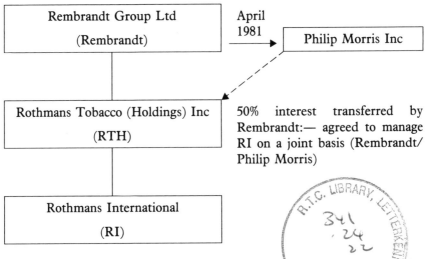

The Commission sent a statement of objections to the participants, who chose to enter into negotiations with the Commission for the restructuring of their agreement in order to obtain the Commission's approval. Agreement was reached in 1983 and signed in 1984. Philip Morris was to give up its 50% stake in RTH, and in return would take a 30.8% stake directly in RI, but with its voting share limited to 24.9%. Rembrandt would then have full control, through RTH, of RI (in which it had 43.6% of the voting rights)

---

[78] With a view to gaining exemption under article 85(3), which suggests that from the beginning the participants feared that article 85(1) might apply.

and would not be subject to influence by Philip Morris. The new agreement contained a number of terms relating to future disposals of shareholdings by either side. It gave each party a right of first refusal should the other wish to dispose of its shareholding. In the event of disposal to a third party, the agreement provided that a party's entire shareholding should be disposed of, for cash, either to a single purchaser, or to ten or more independent purchasers. Additionally, if Rembrandt were to dispose of its shareholding to a single purchaser, that purchaser must be required to make an identical offer for Philip Morris's shareholding. Finally, the agreement provided that in the event of a disposal of its shareholding by one of the parties there must be an adjustment of the voting rights in RI. For the parties it was argued that these terms were necessary to protect Philip Morris's investment in RI. The complainants argued that the cumulative effect of these terms was either to enable Philip Morris to gain a greater control in the future over RI than it had at present or to enable it to make acquisition of an interest in RI by another company most unlikely. The parties gave a number of undertakings to the Commission: that Philip Morris would not be represented in the management of RI; that information about RI which might affect competition between the two groups would not be communicated to Philip Morris; and that Philip Morris would inform the Commission of any amendment of the agreement, and of any increase in its shareholding, and of any circumstances in which it might obtain more than 25% or more of the voting rights in RI. The Commission took the view that the new agreement was compatible with article 85(1), and informed BAT and Reynolds of its intention to reject their complaints and the essentials of its reasons for so doing. Both complainants responded within the time allowed with submissions saying that the agreement had only changed in form and not in substance, and therefore maintaining their opposition. The Commission was not persuaded by these further submissions and gave formal notice that their complaints were rejected. The complainants then applied to the Court to have the Commission's measure (the formal letter of rejection) declared void.

The Court of Justice was clearly sensitive to the fact that these proceedings were regarded by many interested observers as a test case of the Court's attitude to the application of article 85 to agreements which have an element of concentration or merger in them, and made some statements which may be regarded as statements of principle. Certainly the Commission treated them as such, and did not hesitate to put its interpretation of those statements into effect.[79] The judgment begins with a consideration of matters of principle before proceeding to consider the particular facts of the case. For those seeking a major policy statement on the application of article 85 to mergers, the Court's consideration of the substance began unpromisingly, with what

[79] See 1.1.3.5 below.

appeared to be a limiting statement about the ambit of the Court's decision. It said:

'The main issue in these cases is whether and in what circumstances the acquisition of a minority shareholding in a competing company may constitute an infringement of Articles 85 and 86 of the Treaty. Since the acquisition of shares in Rothmans International was the subject-matter of agreements entered into by companies which have remained independent after the entry into force of the agreements, the issue must be examined first of all from the point of view of Article 85.'[80]

In some respects this statement conflicts with a broader approach later in the judgment, and so conceivably it was inserted in order to allow future limitation of doctrines emerging elsewhere in the judgment should they prove to be unworkable, or to be superseded by legislative developments in the Council. Three conceptual limitations can be identified. First, it would be possible to limit the precedent value of the decision to those cases where only the acquisition of a minority interest is involved, although at least in one respect that would be unusual since in terms of anti-competitive effect it is clear that acquisition of a majority interest will often be more serious than the acquisition of a minority interest. Secondly, it would also be possible to limit the doctrine to cases where the agreement or merger involved competing companies. Such a limitation might exclude various kinds of mergers from control under article 85. It could be used to exclude vertical mergers,[81] and such an exclusion would be welcomed in many quarters because such mergers are regarded as much more likely to introduce efficiency into an industry rather than to have an anti-competitive effect.[82] Alternatively, it might be used to exclude conglomerate takeovers where the acquiring company is not based in any single industry and simply markets its management expertise by buying companies through which it considers it is able to make profits, irrespective of their particular trading interests. Finally, it might be used to exclude mergers where there is no actual competition between the acquiring and the target company, although on the basis of an analysis of cross-elasticity of demand and production the potential for such competition can be shown to exist. The third potential limitation of the doctrine lies in the identification of the agreements in this case involving companies 'which have remained independent after the entry into force of the agreements'. The continuing independence of the companies after the time of the agreement might exclude full mergers from the scope of the

---

[80] Paras 30-31.
[81] I.e., a merger between undertakings in the same market but at different levels in the supply chain; e.g., between a supplier of raw materials or components and a manufacturer.
[82] See Korah, *The control of mergers under the EEC competition law* [1987] 8 ECLR 239 at 250

doctrine, since in such cases the independent companies are subsumed within the single entity which emerges at the end of the merger process.

The Court's main treatment of the legal issues is more expansive. The key passage is set out below:

'Although the acquisition by one company of an equity interest in a competitor does not in itself constitute conduct restricting competition, such an acquisition may nevertheless serve as an instrument for influencing the commercial conduct of the companies in question so as to restrict or distort competition on the market on which they carry on business. That will be true in particular where, by the acquisition of a shareholding or through subsidiary clauses in the agreement, the investing company obtains legal or *de facto* control of the commercial conduct of the other company or where the agreement provides for commercial cooperation between the companies or creates a structure likely to be used for such cooperation. That may also be the case where the agreement gives the investing company the possibility of reinforcing its position at a later stage and taking effective control of the other company. Account must be taken not only of the immediate effects of the agreement but also of its potential effects and of the possibility that the agreement may be part of a long-term plan. Finally, every agreement must be assessed in its economic context and in particular in the light of the situation on the relevant market. Moreover, where the companies concerned are multinational corporations which carry on business on a world-wide scale, their relationships outside the Community cannot be ignored. It is necessary in particular to consider the possibility that the agreement in question may be part of a policy of global cooperation between the companies which are party to it.'[83]

The most obvious comment is that here there is no mention of **minority shareholdings** or **companies remaining independent**, although the Court has retained its focus on mergers between **competitors**, without defining what that term means in the context. It seems clear, therefore, that this passage was intended as a broad statement of principle on the possible application of article 85 to a range of agreements including full mergers.

The necessary restriction on competition arises in such cases, according to the Court, from a number of potential sources. Most clearly it might come from the fact that the acquiring company would obtain legal or *de facto* control. It might arise out of subsidiary agreements which provided for or created a structure within the grouping which encouraged commercial cooperation between former competitors. Finally it might arise out of terms

---

[83]   Paras 37–40.

of the agreement which placed the acquiring company in a position to strengthen its holding or its influence at a later stage. Applying these principles to the facts, the Court took the view that the arrangements under the 1984 agreement left Rembrandt in secure control of RI's commercial policy by virtue of its voting share and its participation in the management of the company. Moreover, there were no ancillary agreements relating to commercial cooperation. As a result, viewed in isolation from the provisions as to future disposal of shares, the agreement did not restrict competition because Rembrandt and Philip Morris respectively had incentives to ensure the greatest possible profit from their 'own' cigarette companies and thus not to promote the other company's interests by some form of commercial cooperation.[84]

As far as the provisions as to the future disposal of shares were concerned, the Court did not take the view that they amounted to a present or a potential future restriction on competition.[85] For the future, the Court's view was that such risk as there was would be taken care of by the undertakings secured by the Commission, which would be effective in all but the least likely eventuality (in the Court's analysis) of Philip Morris gaining control of RI by Rembrandt's disposal of its shares to ten independent purchasers. As far as provisions having immediate effect were concerned the Court said:

> 'The fact that the provisions in question create obstacles to the purchase of an interest in Rothmans International by a third company cannot be regarded as a present restriction of competition on the market for cigarettes contrary to Article 85.'[86]

It is at this point that the Court's analysis differs most significantly from that of the Advocate General, and it is this aspect of the judgment which is most open to question. The only market considered was the market for cigarettes. It was surely important also to consider the wider question of the corporate control of RI, not least because Rembrandt, the present owners (through RTH) were not out-and-out cigarette manufacturers but rather were a broadly based industrial conglomerate. A competitive market for corporate control of RI might be regarded as an important element in maintaining an efficient management of RI; the absence of such a competitive market might lead to the risk of the RI management opting for the quiet life, to the detriment of competition in the European market for cigarettes. The provisions of the 1984 agreement, which on the Court's admission made sale of RI by Rembrandt to a third party very unattractive, would place a considerable dampener on the market for control of RI, and consequently have just such an effect on competition. It was the failure of the Commission

---

[84] Paras 46-51.
[85] Paras 55-58.
[86] Para 56.

to explain how the 1984 agreement and associated undertakings avoided this difficulty which led Advocate General Mancini to conclude that the Commission's decision was not properly reasoned.[87] The Court's narrow focus on the market for cigarettes, excluding the effect the agreement might have on managerial attitudes within the target company, fails to take account of the full economic context of the agreement.[88] Had such matters been taken into account it is not clear what the Commission's ultimate conclusion would have been.

1.1.3.5   Merger control under article 85 after *BAT & RJ Reynolds* v *Commission*

Whatever the merits of the individual decision in *BAT & RJ Reynolds* v *Commission*,[89] there are clear indications that the constraint upon the application of article 85 to mergers imposed by the 1966 Memorandum was threatened if not undermined by the Court's statements of principle. In the first place, the decision removed the significance of the distinction introduced by the *SHV/Chevron Oil* case[90] between collaborative joint ventures and joint ventures leading to a permanent change in the structure of the participating companies (so-called partial mergers) in respect of the ambit of article 85. That distinction has, however, reappeared in another guise in order to determine the scope of the new Regulation in respect of joint ventures.[91] Secondly, there could be little doubt that article 85 would apply to share transactions directly entered into between competitor companies for the acquisition by one of a minority shareholding in the other. It is possible that not every such transaction falls within the scope of the new Regulation.[92] It could further have been argued, by extrapolation from the decision, that article 85 would in future apply to share transactions between competitor companies leading to the acquisition of a controlling interest, to asset sales between competitor companies leading to the acquisition of a controlling interest, and to share purchases from third parties leading to the acquisition of a controlling interest in a competitor company.[93] The need and the opportunity for the Commission to pursue such reasoning was

---

[87]   The Advocate General appears to use arguments based on the notion of a market for corporate control.

[88]   Other criticisms of the Court's analysis may be found in Fine, *The Philip Morris judgment: does article 85 now apply to mergers* [1987] 8 ECLR 333, 340-341.

[89]   Supra note 77.

[90]   OJ 1975 L38/14, [1975] 1 CMLR D68; see 3.2.1.

[91]   See 5.1.2 *et seq.*

[92]   See 2.1 *et seq.*

[93]   In this last case certain conceptual difficulties remained to be overcome, such as whether the acquisition of shares from an individual amounts to an agreement between undertakings (but see *Nungesser*), and whether the 'network effect' of several such purchases could be taken cumulatively in order to demonstrate an effect of preventing, restricting or distorting competition (cf. 23/67 *Brasserie de Haecht* v *Wilkin (No 1)* [1967] ECR 407, [1968] CMLR 26.

removed by the adoption of the new Regulation, which avoids the conceptual problems and which expressly excludes the application of article 85 to mergers in these categories.[94] A further situation to be considered is the acquisition of an interest in a competitor by purchase of shares from a third party by virtue of stock market transactions (rather than by full takeover bid). In such a case it is almost certain that the interest acquired would only be a minority interest.[95] On the assumption that conceptual problems in respect of the application of article 85 can be overcome, it seems that the Court's judgment embraces cases of this kind. Such a transaction might create a structure likely to result in commercial cooperation between the competitors, which would fall within the terms of the statement of principle in *BAT & RJ Reynolds* v *Commission*.[96] Moreover, such a case would seem to fall outside the scope of the new Regulation.[97]

There can be little doubt but that the Court's decision in *BAT & RJ Reynolds* v *Commission* was an important catalyst in the evolution of Community controls over mergers. It led immediately to a number of informal investigations which were settled after negotiation with the Commission.[98] It was also almost certainly an important element in the adoption of the new Merger Regulation, serving to concentrate the minds of the Member States in the Council after some 15 years of fruitless negotiation. It seems that a purpose-built Regulation, with strict limits on the powers it conferred, was preferable to the prospect of the more extensive jurisdiction under article 85 in the hands of an interventionist Commission. Despite the fact that much of the Court's analysis is now obsolete because of the new Regulation,[99] there may be scope for the residual application of some of its reasoning, which will be examined in detail below.[100]

1.1.4 Merger control under articles 92 to 94 of the Treaty of Rome

Articles 92 to 94 of the Treaty of Rome provide measures which enable the Commission to control and monitor the award by Member States of

---

94 Art.22; see 2.1.2 *et seq* and 7.1 below.
95 Because most legal systems limit the extent to which such dealing may take place without giving way to a formal takeover bid; see City Code Rule 9, which makes it mandatory to make a full offer upon acquisition of 30% of voting rights, or, where 30% is already held, upon acquisition of a further 2% within any 12 month period.
96 [1988] 4 CMLR 24.
97 A minority interest would probably not give 'control'; see 2.1.5 *et seq.*
98 Cf. *Irish Distillers* (1988) 21 Bull. of EC 7-8/34; *Carnaud/Sofreb* (1988) 21 Bull. of EC 1/24; *Hudson's Bay & Annings*, Press release, 15.12.1988; (1988) 21 Bull. of EC 12/62; [1989] 4 CMLR 353; OJ 1989 C1002, [1989] 4 CMLR 746: *Metaleurop SA* Notice under art.19(3) of Regulation 17, inviting comment in the light of an intention to grant negative clearance. *GEC-Siemens/Plessey* (1989) 22 Bull of EC 9/26.
99 See generally Chapters 2 and 3. It is noteworthy that shortly before adoption of Regulation 4064/89 the Commission dropped an investigation into the *Coats/Tootal* merger which it had been conducting under article 85, on the ground that the proposed merger fell below the threshold of Community dimension set by the Regulation.
100 See 7.3.2 *et seq.*

state aids. State aids comprise an undefined and potentially limitless range
of measures that serve to confer an economic and commercial advantage
upon the recipient in circumstances where competition is distorted and trade
between Member States is affected.[101] The following are typical examples
of state aids: loans at a low rate of interest; the writing-off of accumulated
debt; an equity investment in a company that is in financial difficulties;
the granting of subsidies to meet operating losses; a reduction in public
charges, for example, social security payments. A state aid which has not
been notified to the Commission and approved before its award is illegal.[102]
The Commission is empowered to require a Member State to recover an
illegal state aid from the recipient undertaking.[103]

The Commission has recently intervened upon the basis of its powers
under articles 92 to 94 of the Treaty of Rome in a number of Member
State sales of (former) nationalised industries (most notably in the UK).[104]
While the intent of such interventions has been to control the award of
state aids, the practical consequences for the parties concerned has often
been a form of merger control. The significant role played by the
Commission's exercise of such control in the case of privatisations reflects
the important part that state aids, in particular the writing-off of accumulated
debt, play in such transactions. As a result, parties find themselves in a
position where, even assuming regulatory clearance on competition grounds,
the merger cannot or will not proceed unless the state aids element has
also been cleared by the Commission.

1.1.4.1 Sales at an undervalue

Governments will always be exposed to an allegation that they have sold
at an undervalue where they cannot demonstrate that they have sold (or
privatised) their former state-owned entity by a process of competitive
tendering. Neither Austin Rover nor Alfa Romeo was sold by competitive
tender. In both cases, the selling governments were subjected to an allegation
that they had sold at an undervalue. In both cases the governments successfully
resisted the claim.

1.1.4.2 Writing-off accumulated debt

The desire of governments to write-off or cancel accumulated debt can be
linked to the necessity of putting a former nationalised entity into a
'marketable' condition prior to its sale. Central to this aim is the limitation

---

[101] Art.92(1) and see, inter alia, 173/73 *Commission* v *Italy* [1974] ECR 709 and 61/79 *Denkavit*
[1980] ECR 1205.
[102] Art.93(3). The Commission can be expected to reply to a notification within a period of
two months.
[103] 70/72 *Commission* v *Germany* [1973] ECR 813, 52/84 *Commission* v *Belgium* [1986] ECR
89.
[104] *Alfa Romeo* OJ L349/9 30 December 1989, *Austin Rover* 18 RCP 179, *Renault* 18 RCP
175, *Short Brothers* 19 RCP 158, *Brel* 19 RCP 169.

imposed by Part VIII of the Companies Act 1985, which provides that a company cannot pay a dividend (i.e. profits cannot be distributed) unless, in essence, its historically accumulated profits exceed its historically accumulated losses. It can perhaps readily be understood that unless the historic indebtedness of former state-owned companies were eliminated (or at least substantially reduced) there would be no prospect of their paying dividends to their new private sector shareholders. Accordingly, without a debt write-off, they would be very unattractive investment propositions.

The Commission has shown itself willing to countenance debt write-offs where they are linked to a restructuring of a company's operations in order to enable it to cope with the harsher competitive environment of the private sector.[105] Such 'rescue' or 'restructuring' aid, as it has become known, will only remain valid to the extent that the company concerned adheres to the terms of its restructuring plan and necessarily incurs the cost involved (and provided for) in reducing capacity, staff and overheads.[106] The Commission will continue to monitor the extent to which companies comply with their restructuring schemes.[107]

1.1.4.3 Strategy in purchasing publicly owned companies

It is perhaps ironic that, in a merger context, an acquiring company has an express interest in ensuring that the Commission (where appropriate) exercises its powers under articles 92 to 94. This is because, as stated above, aid that has been paid to a company which has not been authorised is illegal and must be returned to the Member State government by the recipient undertaking.[108] As a recent Court of Justice judgment has confirmed,[109] undertakings receiving state aid (and, it follows, purchasers of such companies) have a clear interest in ensuring that such aid has been cleared by the Commission under articles 92 to 94 and that, accordingly, it is not repayable. As a matter of practice, this will not necessarily be easy for purchasers since traditionally, as Lord Young's frequent trips to Brussels during the course of the Austin Rover sale demonstrated, the clearance of state aid has been dealt with exclusively between Member State governments and the Commission. That, it is suggested, is no longer a tenable position for purchasers where state aid issues are in point; they must now satisfy themselves that the proper procedures have been followed and that there is no risk of a repayment of the aid being required.

---

[105] See *Renault, Austin Rover, Short Brothers* and *Brel*, supra note 104.
[106] Renault was required to pay back only FF6 billion of the initial state aid of FF12 billion it had received in recognition of the fact that it had incurred some FF6 billion restructuring expenditure.
[107] Renault was subject to this. Austin Rover, Short Brothers and Brel still are.
[108] Supra note 103.
[109] Case 5/89 *Commission v Germany*, unreported judgment of 20/9/90 at point 14.

1.1.5 Informal controls

The significance of the measure of merger control exercised by the Commission in recent years lies not in the volume of formal decisions reached on that basis, but in the unspoken threat of an activist Commission upsetting the apple cart in the middle of sensitive and delicately balanced negotiations, or in the middle of a full public takeover bid, by announcing its intention to conduct an investigation of the proposed merger under the terms of one of the above articles. The disruption caused by such an investigation, which involves diversion of management time, possibly adverse publicity, some risk of confidential business information becoming public and so reaching the ears of competitors, and cold feet among previously willing participants, not to say considerable cost, can prove fatal. For this reason, the scope of the Commission's powers was far greater at an informal level than an analysis of the jurisprudence of the Court of Justice would appear to indicate. For as long as the precise scope of articles 85 and 86 EEC in this field remained in doubt (because not clarified by an appeal to the Court), the fear of Commission intervention was in a great many cases sufficient to bring parties into negotiations with the Commission in order to have its assurance that the proposed merger was compatible with Community competition law. These negotiations frequently resulted in the Commission obtaining undertakings from the companies in return for its informal clearance of the proposed merger.[110]

It is understandable that the Commission, legitimately wishing to enable merger control negotiations with companies to be quickly achieved in order to protect the companies' commercial interests, should be willing to accept undertakings of this kind in order to be able to dispose of the matter. Nevertheless, the procedure makes the law much less certain, since the application of article 85 to mergers rests primarily on undertakings negotiated in private between the parties and the Commission. Such an informal basis of control presented considerable uncertainty for those taking part in merger transactions. It may well be that the more formal procedures to be introduced under the new Regulation will be a welcome relief from such uncertainty.

1.2 THE COMMERCIAL CONTEXT

To the casual reader of the business pages of broadsheet newspapers the impression of the late 1980s[111] was one of unprecedented levels of merger

---

[110] E.g., In *BAT & RJ Reynolds* v *Commission* the Commission's decision to reject the complaint, and the Court's approval of that decision depended to a considerable extent upon the undertakings required of the parties, and especially Philip Morris.

[111] The impression is confirmed by the EC Commission's own survey, *The Development of Concentration: Mergers, acquisitions and joint ventures*, based on data gathered from the specialist press on operations involving at least one of the 1,000 largest firms in the Community, ranked according to financial data. The survey is published as part of the Annual Reports on Competition Policy. Evidence from the survey is presented below.

activity. This phenomenon was not purely European; in North America and the Far East there had also been a surge in merger activity as firms became increasingly interested in achieving growth by merger, acquisition or joint venture. In part the increase in activity derived from the perception that the share value of companies was frequently well below the asset value, with the consequence that there were bargains to be had. Other motives such as expansion, rationalisation and strengthening market position were not exclusively European in origin, but moves to complete the internal market gave a heightened attraction to merger for those, whether established in a Member State or in a third country, seeking to trade in Europe. The need for some form of control was assumed by the policy makers behind the Single European Act.[112] That merger activity would increase because of the completion of the internal market was a central element in the reasoning in the Preamble to some drafts of the Council Regulation on Control of Concentrations between undertakings,[113] through which the Community authorities sought to achieve the formal powers of merger control they believed were required to regulate the anti-competitive effects of concentrations which have a genuine Community dimension. Whether in fact this level of activity will be sustained is less clear, not least because of continuing cultural and technical barriers to mergers and acquisitions, and because of uncertainty over the future of commercial activity in former Comecon countries.

1.2.1 Levels of merger activity

Between 1984 and 1987, national, Community and international mergers (including acquisitions of both majority and minority holdings, but not joint ventures) in the industrial sector effectively doubled in number.[114] In the services sector the pattern was broadly similar. The increase in total activity over the three year period was nearly 50%.[115] The most spectacular increase in acquisition activity occurred amongst firms with a combined aggregate turnover below 500 million ECU,[116] which appears to confirm the view that

[112] The Cecchini Report (*The European Challenge*, Paolo Cecchini, 1988) welcomes the opportunity which '1992' brings for companies 'to scale . . . up for European, and global, competition' (p.xix), but Lord Cockfield's enthusiasm for the opportunities for growth and economies of scale is linked with an emphasis upon 'healthier competition', and the Report calls for a 'cohesive regulatory environment' to facilitate 'the more integrated forms of cross-frontier links' (pp. 31–2).

[113] E.g., OJ 1989 No. C 22, 28.1.1989, p.14; see especially recitals (2), (3), and (5).

[114] Source: 17th Annual Report on Competition Policy (1987), *The Development of Concentration*, pp. 227–241. In the period immediately following the survey period there was some fall-off of overall activity, but sustained growth at the level of large concentrations. By the end of 1990 merger and acquisition activity had declined significantly, while joint ventures were increasingly prevalent.

[115] Source: 15th Annual Report: 480
16th Annual Report: 561
17th Annual Report: 708.

[116] At the time of writing, 1 ECU = £0.737881; US$1.19205 (OJ 1990 C78/1).

the approach of 1992 will encourage growth by merger for companies not big enough at their present size to take advantage of the opportunities of the enlarged market. Such mergers will not fall within the scope of the Regulation.[117] Of concern to the Commission, however, is the 100% increase during the survey period of merger activity involving firms with an aggregate turnover over 1,000 million ECU. The conclusion to the survey states:

> 'The increase in mergers involving firms of the largest size category . . . suggests risk for competition, the seriousness of which is accentuated by the continuing existence of fragmented European markets.'

Nevertheless, not all such mergers will immediately fall within the scope of the Regulation, and in addition the Regulation recognises that some mergers are more appropriately dealt with by national authorities. The lion's share of all activity remains at national level,[118] with the United Kingdom leading all Member States. However, the greatest percentage rise in acquisition activity is in relation to 'Community mergers' (acquisitions of other Community firms). Here again there is support for the view that the Community dimension is becoming progressively more significant as 1992 approaches. The survey does not in fact break down 'Community mergers' by aggregate turnover of the firms involved, but it seems that the Commission itself takes the view that a significant number of the largest aggregate turnover acquisitions have a Community dimension and carry the risk of increased concentration in the common market.[119] By contrast, the significant rise in relation to joint ventures is among international transactions. The Commission regards the motive for such transactions as a desire to improve marketing, with American and Japanese firms in particular anxious to find Community partners in order spread risks or by-pass trade policy measures.[120] It takes the view that such transactions may not be desirable from the point of view of competition policy.

1.2.2   Fortress Europe and Trojan horses

In recent years the Commission and the Court of Justice have given greater attention than previously to placing the Community competitive structure in the wider context of world markets. The impending completion of the

---

[117] Art.1(2)(a) has a threshold figure for application of an aggregate worldwide turnover of all the undertakings concerned of 5,000 million ECU. The figure was set at this relatively high level at the insistence of some of the larger members, including the UK; it is to be reviewed before the end of the fourth year following that of the adoption of the Regulation (art.1(3)).

[118] For example, in 1986/7 of 415 mergers (including acquisitions of majority holdings) 290 were classified as 'national'.

[119] 17th Annual Report, pp. 229, 232.

[120] Ibid, p. 237.

internal market has increased still further the need to consider the wider economic context in which firms must operate. For some products it is highly artificial to examine in isolation the competitive structure within the Communities, when the reality is that the market is world-wide and can only support a relatively small number of multinational companies. On the other hand, it is also the case that the effect of Community policy is sometimes to create the impression in the mind of firms in third countries that Europe is immune from world trade. They have in turn sought to penetrate that immunity.

Outside the Communities, the expression 'Fortress Europe' was used in the late 1980s to sum up fears that EC trade policy was to restrict the benefits of the single market to firms established within the Communities, and to exclude others from participation. This effect can be seen in the case of agriculture, where Community prices are much higher than world prices, and where producers in third countries believe that the Community keeps out their goods by means of crippling tariffs while also dumping Community surpluses on the world market. The fear arose that, by 1993, a similar ring fence will have been established around industrial goods, capital and services. American and Japanese firms in particular are attracted by the new trading opportunities which they believe the single market will bring, but are also anxious that they are excluded from a share of the benefits. Their reaction has been to plan to infiltrate the European defences from within, becoming established in the Communities by acquisition of existing European companies, or by entering into joint ventures with such firms.

In the first two months of 1989, American investment in European firms represented the largest source of cross-border acquisitions in Europe, and it has been predicted that this marks no more than the first trickle of what is likely to become a flood.[121] The Commission believes that the recent high level of joint venture activity involving international firms (equal to national and Community activity combined) is attributable to the desire of such firms to by-pass trade policy measures.[122] Japanese companies are more likely to proceed by way of friendly takeovers, rather than either joint ventures (for which it is thought that the necessary mutual adjustment of management styles might not be possible) or hostile takeovers.[123] As a consequence, the Communities will have to have regard to the world beyond its boundaries if it is to maintain effective merger control.

---

[121] 1992 Mergers & Acquisitions Monthly, March 1989. More recent experience, especially in the light of economic difficulties in European countries and the East European 'distraction', suggests that such predictions may be exaggerated.

[122] 17th Annual Report on Competition Policy, pp.235, 237.

[123] *Financial Times*, Thursday 11 May 1989: quoting Mr Don Pinchbeck, UK general manager of Epson.

1.3   A NEW ERA OF MERGER CONTROL

Soon after publication of its Memorandum on the Concentration of Enterprises in the Common Market, which concluded that article 85 EEC could not be applied to full mergers,[124] and the Court's decision in respect of article 86 EEC in *Continental Can*,[125] the Commission proposed that the Council should adopt a purpose-built regulation to provide proper means of merger control.[126] The original draft remained unadopted for several years, but then enjoyed a period of heightened topicality in the 1980s during which time it went through several further drafts.[127] The recent activity reflects the fact that successive Commissioners with responsibility for competition[128] made completion of the legislative process for the new regulation a high priority, and the fact that a number of Member States accepted that view during their Presidency of the Council. This higher ranking on the political agenda, while essential for the allocation of sufficient time to remove remaining difficulties, reflected more generally the inclusion of takeover activity within the drive to complete the internal market by 1992. Current efforts to establish a statutory-based takeover code (the draft Thirteenth Company Law Directive) and to remove artificial barriers to takeover activity (addressed primarily by means of amendments to the Second Company Law Directive and the draft Fifth Company Law Directive) can be seen as a continuation of a process of which the adoption of Regulation 4064/89 in December 1989 was the first step.

Difficulties in the early years of negotiations centred upon the problem of conflicts between Community merger policy and national interests in respect of issues such as industrial or social policy, on the need to exempt certain kinds of undertaking from the scope of the regulation (such as public enterprises and financial holding companies), and on the requirement of compulsory prior notification. On each of these issues the Member States were divided, and the Commission was faced with the task of renegotiating the terms of the draft regulation and persuading the Member States to withdraw their objections. In recent years the difficulties centred upon the demarcation between Community and national sovereignty over merger cases; the larger Member States wishing to retain sovereignty while the smaller wished Community control to fill the vacuum in their own legislation in this regard, and on the criteria to be used in assessing mergers, with the United Kingdom in particular being anxious to confine control to competition

---

[124] EEC Competition Series Study No. 3 (Brussels 1966); see 1.4.2.
[125] 6/72 [1973] ECR 215, [1973] CMLR 199; see 1.1.2.3.
[126] OJ 1973 C92/1.
[127] See OJ 1982 C36/3; OJ 1984 C51/8; OJ 1986 C324/5; OJ 1988 C130/4; OJ 1989 C22/14.
[128] Mr Peter Sutherland and Sir Leon Brittan.

criteria while France, for example, wanted to introduce criteria of industrial policy into the evaluation process.

Compromise on these issues finally led to the adoption of the new Regulation in December 1989, the best part of 17 years from the time of its first proposal. The fact that compromises were necessary means that there is every possibility that the text of the Regulation will present considerable difficulties of interpretation as the Commission and Court confront the language which the draftsman found to steer a middle course between the various competing interests. Nevertheless, it is also clear that the deficiencies of articles 85 and 86 as instruments of merger control,[129] coupled with the desire to achieve a form of Community merger control as a part of the legislative programme leading to the completion of the single market, make the achievement of any form of control after so many years of difficult negotiation very welcome.

With the adoption of Regulation 4064/89 much of the Commission's pioneering work in adapting the existing law to its desire for an instrument of merger control will become redundant. Even so, there can be little doubt that enactment will not mark the end of disputes over Community merger control: it will mark the beginning of a further set of disputes over sovereignty in such issues, especially when the Commission seeks to lower (as it is expected to do at the end of 1994) the threshold at which Community dimension is established and thus to widen, at the expense of national jurisdictions, the scope of its merger control powers.

---

[129] See 1.4.2.2 and 5.3.3 *et seq.*

TWO
The scope of Regulation 4064/89

On 21 December 1989 the Council formally adopted the text of the new Merger Regulation, which gives the Commission an express jurisdiction for merger control and which enables the Commission to abandon its efforts to dragoon articles 85 and 86 EEC into such service despite their apparent unsuitability. Regulation 4064/89 is intended to provide against those concentrations which may significantly impede effective competition in the common market or in a substantial part of it.[1] It is based both on article 87 EEC, which provides for the making of Council Regulations to implement the provisions of articles 85 and 86, and on article 235 EEC, which grants the Council a residual power to take appropriate measures where action proves necessary in order to attain one of the Community's objectives and the Treaty (of Rome) has not provided the necessary powers. It is to be the only form of control applicable to those mergers which fall within its scope, so that the definition of such mergers is a critical element in the Regulation.

2.1 DEFINITION OF CONCENTRATION

Article 3(1) of Regulation 4064/89 provides:

'A concentration shall be deemed to arise where:

(a) two or more previously independent undertakings merge, or
(b) one or more persons already controlling at least one undertaking, or
— one or more undertakings
acquire, whether by purchase of securities or assets, by contract or by any other means, direct or indirect control of the whole or parts of one or more other undertakings.'

Thus the Regulation is principally concerned with mergers and takeovers.

[1] Preamble, recital 5.

Although an attempt is made in the text that follows to catalogue common forms of transaction which fall within the respective terms of part (a) or (b) of article 3(1), it would be a mistake to regard the examples given as an exhaustive list of transactions falling within the scope of the Regulation. The definition in article 3(1) has been left deliberately broad and non-specific in order to be sure to embrace all forms of concentration within one or other head.

2.1.1   Article 3(1)(a): mergers

The word 'merger' is nowhere defined in the Regulation, and it is not an expression which has previously had any significant meaning attributed to it.[2] Where it has appeared it has been used generically to denote a number of forms of concentration, and has often then been qualified by more specific definitions of the particular form of transaction addressed.[3] Article3(1)(a) uses the term merger in contradistinction with the acquisition of control over an undertaking, which is provided for under article 3(1)(b). The most obvious significance of the term merger in this context is that it implies the formation of a single enterprise from undertakings which were previously separate and distinct; and that the formation was a voluntary act by both (or all) sides.[4]

2.1.2   Article 3(1)(b): acquisition of control

Article 3(1)(b) defines concentrations so as to include acquisitions, by whatever means, of control over the whole or parts of other undertakings. In the UK, acquisitions are the most significant part of merger activity. In other countries, corporate acquisitions, in particular hostile takeovers, remain infrequent.[5] Apart from the issue of control itself, which is separately defined,[6] this provision addresses the nature of acquirers, target undertakings, and the transactions by which the acquisition is effected.

---

[2] For example, although it occurs once in the Court's judgment in *BAT & RJ Reynolds v Commission* ([1988] 2 CMLR 24), it was not used as a term of art.

[3] E.g., Dir 78/855 OJ 1978 L295/36 ('merger by acquisition' and 'merger by the formation of a new company'): Draft 13th Company Law Directive OJ 1989 C64/8 ('legal or assets mergers' and 'shares mergers').

[4] That a merger must be a voluntary act is both generally implicit in the nature of the transaction and supported by the wording in article 4(2) of the Regulation which provides that a merger '. . . shall be notified jointly by the parties to the merger . . .'.

[5] See the Coopers & Lybrand report, HMSO, ISBN 0011515; the Department of Trade and Industry report of January 1990; and the Booz-Allen report to DG XV of December 1989.

[6] See Art. 3(3).

2.1.2.1 Common control by individuals
A concentration will arise, according to the wording in the first limb of article 3(1)(b), where:

'one or more persons already controlling at least one undertaking . . . acquire . . . control of the whole or parts of one or more other undertakings'.

The above language will catch undertakings that become subject to the 'common control' of one or more individuals. In such circumstances, the 'concentration' will take place between the two undertakings that fall under common control and not between the individual (acquiring control) and the target undertaking. The Regulation does not define the term undertaking. However, the Commission notice on cooperative and concentrative joint ventures[7] indicates that it is to be '. . . understood as an organized assembly of human and material resources, intended to pursue a defined economic purpose on a long-term basis'. In simple terms, the notion of undertaking can be equated in the context of the Regulation with a 'business'.[8] An individual may own or control a business but he may not be one in his own right. It follows that an individual *per se* cannot effect a concentration with an undertaking. At the risk of descending into semantics, this would appear to explain the requirement in the opening words of article 3(1)(b) that, for an individual to bring about a concentration, he must not only acquire a controlling interest in another undertaking, but must already have a controlling interest in one or more existing undertakings. Without an existing control in an undertaking, there would be no undertaking with which a concentration might take place. The concept of common control under article 3(1)(b) is illustrated in the example below.

Example 1

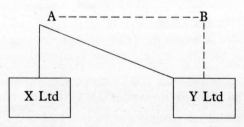

concentration between X Ltd and Y Ltd under the common control of A

---

7   OJ 1990 C203/10: see Appendix III.
8   However, note that this differs from the meaning ordinarily attributed to 'undertaking' in the context of articles 85 and 86 EEC, see further 5.1.2.1.

A (who is an individual and not a legal entity) controls X Ltd at the time of acquiring a controlling interest in Y Ltd from B (which could be a company or an individual). As a result of the transaction X and Y fall under the common ownership or control of A although they are in all other respects unrelated. Clearly, as A is not a corporate entity, they cannot form members of the same corporate group.

2.1.2.2 Common control by companies

It is unlikely that the use of the word 'persons' in the first limb of article 3(1)(b) quoted in paragraph 2.1.2.1 above was intended to cover legal entities such as companies. Although a target undertaking could, as a result of an acquisition, join other undertakings under the existing control of one or more corporate entities, it is submitted that an analysis upon the basis of 'common control' would be pointless since the acquisition of control would in any event be caught by the second limb of article 3(1)(b). This provides that a concentration will arise where '. . . one or more undertakings . . . acquire . . . control of the whole or parts of one or more other undertakings'. In any subsequent legal and economic analysis of the concentration, the acquirer's control by other undertakings would inevitably be taken into account.[9] The point is illustrated in the example below.

Example 2

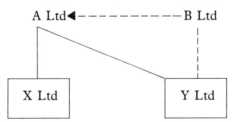

concentration between A Ltd, X Ltd and Y Ltd under the control of A Ltd

A Ltd, already possessing a controlling interest in X Ltd, acquires from B Ltd its controlling interest in Y Ltd. X and Y will fall under the common ownership of A. The requirement (set out in the first limb of article 3(1)(b)) that A must already own a controlling interest in an existing undertaking is redundant in this context. A, as an undertaking in its own right, is capable of effecting a concentration (between undertakings) simply by acquiring a controlling interest in Y Ltd, another undertaking. The transaction falls squarely within the second limb of article 3(1)(b).

---

⁹   See section 3 of Form CO. Form CO is set out as Annex 1 to Regulation 2367/90 (see Appendix II).

2.1.2.3 Joint control

Both the first and second limbs of article 3(1)(b) contemplate the acquisition of joint control. Under the first limb this would apply to individuals. Under the second, it would apply to legal entities, most obviously companies. In practice, for an acquisition of joint control to fall subject to the Regulation, it will, subject to one particular exception considered immediately below, be necessary for the parties concerned to have entered into a 'concentrative joint venture'.[10] The term 'joint control' is not defined in the Regulation[11] but is the subject of guidance in the Commission's notice on concentrative and cooperative joint ventures.[12] The notice makes clear that joint control cannot exist where one party 'can decide alone on the joint venture's commercial activities' but that it exists where '. . . the parent companies[13] must agree on decisions concerning the joint venture's activities, either because of the rights acquired in the joint venture or because of contracts or other means establishing the joint control'.[14] There is little doubt that the following joint venture structure (illustrated in Example 3 below), and analogous permutations, will give rise to joint control.

Example 3

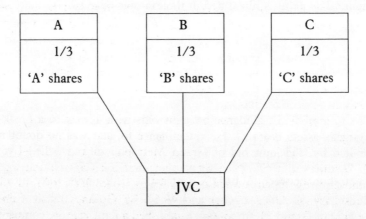

joint control of JVC by A, B and C: no shareholder alone can control any
decision in relation to JVC

---

[10] See 5.1.2.2. *et seq.*
[11] The concept of joint control is expressly referred to at article 5(5) of the Regulation with regard to the calculation of the turnover of jointly controlled undertakings — see further 2.2.4.4. below.
[12] See Appendix III.
[13] It is submitted that joint control could be exercised by individuals in such circumstances.
[14] See paragraphs (11) – (14) of the notice, see Appendix III.

The ordinary share capital of a joint venture company (JVC) is divided into A, B and C shares. Each of the A, B and C shareholders has an entitlement to appoint a nominated director to the board of the JVC. It is agreed between the A, B and C shareholders (for example in a shareholders' agreement or in the articles of association) that certain key decisions concerning the activities and constitution of the JVC will not be taken unless each of the A, B and C shareholders have given their prior approval.

As a matter of practice, the difficulty of joint ventures lies not so much in the identification of joint control (which is almost invariably expressly provided for in negotiated shareholders' agreements and articles of association) as in the assessment of whether the relationships between the joint venturers and the JVC are 'cooperative or concentrative'.[15]

2.1.2.4 Joint control upon a short term basis with a view to a break-up of the target's assets

In point 5 of its notice on concentrative and cooperative operations,[16] the Commission gives guidance on its approach to the 'joint acquisition of an undertaking with a view to its division'. The hallmark of such a transaction is that the joint venture set up to effect the purchase of the target undertaking is limited in duration; i.e., upon completion of the acquisition, the assets of the target will be divided between the joint venturers, and the joint venture, having served its objective of a joint bid, will be disbanded. The Commission states in its notice that, where a joint bid is made by undertakings but the ensuing break-up of assets is deferred to some future point in time, the arrangements must be considered as a joint venture.[17] In such circumstances, it will be necessary to consider whether the joint venture is concentrative or cooperative.[18]

The Commission's guidance on joint bids with a view to a break-up of the target's assets bears a close resemblance to, and was no doubt in part prompted by, the joint bid of Grand Metropolitan and Allied-Lyons for Irish Distillers in 1988. Pursuant to that joint bid Cantrell and Cochrane (a joint venture company owned as to 50.4% by Hiram Walker Allied Vintners (a subsidiary of Allied-Lyons) and 49.6% by Guinness) and Gilbeys (a subsidiary of Grand Metropolitan) established a joint venture company (GC & C Brands) in order to bid for Irish Distillers (see Example 4 below).

---

[15] See 5.1 *et seq.*
[16] See Appendix III.
[17] Appendix III, paragraph 48.
[18] Ibid.

Example 4

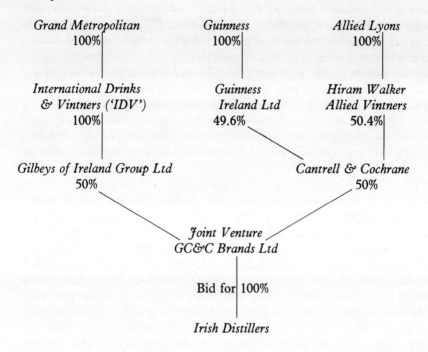

It was the parties' intention, if the bid proved successful, to divide-up the spirits brands of Irish Distillers between them but to leave the production of spirits with Irish Distillers. Irish Distillers complained to the Commission. The Commission intervened in the bid, issuing a statement of objections with a view to the award of interim measures. As a result of the Commission's intervention, the parties abandoned their joint bid.[19]

2.1.3 Summary of principal transactions falling within the definition of 'concentration' in article 3 of the Regulation

The following is a non-exhaustive summary of transactions that under UK law are likely to fall within article 3(1) of the Regulation. The examples concentrate upon a variety of legal structures that are commonly met in practice. It should, however, be borne in mind that the test of a concentration turns upon the acquisition of direct or indirect control and that this is a concept that is not bound by legal structure but entirely dependent upon the legal, economic and commercial effects.

[19] See further 8.2.1.

2.1.3.1 Mergers under article 3(1)(a)

There is perhaps only one UK transaction that clearly fits the Regulation's description of a merger, namely a scheme under s. 110, Insolvency Act 1986, or ss. 425 and 427 of the Companies Act 1985, pursuant to which the assets and liabilities of a company ('company B') are transferred to another company ('company A') in return for the issue to B's shareholders of shares in company A, following which company B is wound up or dissolved. In such a case, the entire business or undertaking of B is transferred to A in circumstances where only one legal entity (company A) remains at the end of the transaction. It is submitted that upon a strict interpretation, no transaction that leaves two or more legal entities remaining after completion of the concentration will fall within article 3(1)(a).

There is an important practical requirement that underlies the need to assess whether a concentration amounts to a merger within article 3(1)(a) or an acquisition within article 3(1)(b). Article 4(2) of the Regulation provides that in the case of a merger, the compulsory prior notification upon Form CO[20] must be made jointly by the parties to the merger whereas in all other cases, the notification must be effected by the person or undertaking acquiring control. In those cases where a joint notification is required it must be expected that the Commission will be more demanding in terms of the completeness of the information that is to be provided under Form CO. To put it another way, it will clearly not be possible for a party to argue that he could not obtain certain information with regard to the party with whom he was proposing to merge.[21]

2.1.3.2 Acquisition under Article 3(1)(b)

The following transactions will fall within article 3(1)(b) of the Regulation.[22] As a result they will require prior notification to the Commission only by the acquiring individual or undertaking. It should be noted that in the case of joint acquisitions, the notification must be made jointly '. . . by those acquiring joint control'.[23]

(a) Company A acquires the entire issued share capital of company B (by means of a hostile bid) — B becomes a subsidiary of A.

---

[20] Form CO is to be found at Annex 1 to Regulation 2367/90, see Appendix II.

[21] Parties should be aware that the procedural timetable will not begin to run until all necessary information has been provided, see article 4(2) of Regulation 2367/90 (Appendix II) and see further 4.1.1.1.

[22] It should be noted that the Commission is more concerned with the substance of arrangements than with their legal form. At paragraph 41 in its notice on cooperative and concentrative joint ventures the Commission states that '. . . Article 3(1) of the Regulation refers not only to legal, but also to economic concentration'. The examples given refer to two companies. It must, however, be appreciated that more than two parties might be involved; for example, in (b), a new company A might bid for two existing companies B so as to bring them all together.

[23] Art. 4(2).

(b)   Company A acquires the entire issued share capital of company B by a bid which is not hostile (e.g., it is recommended by the Board of company B), by agreement with each shareholder, or by a scheme of arrangement under s. 425 of the Companies Act 1985 whereby company B's shares are cancelled and new shares issued to company A (or simply transferred to company A) in consideration of company A paying cash or issuing shares or giving other consideration to former shareholders in company B. B continues to exist and as a result of the transaction becomes a subsidiary of A. It is to be emphasised that this is not a 'merger' and therefore by the terms of article 4(2) of the Regulation, only company A need make the notification on Form CO.

(c)   Company A acquires a controlling interest in the share capital of company B (i.e. less than the entire issued share capital but enough to satisfy the test of 'decisive influence'[24]), whether by means of a hostile bid, a recommended bid, agreement with shareholders, market purchases, or merely by a new share issue by company B to company A.

(d)   Companies A and B each take a shareholding in the other. The Commission's guidance note on cooperative and concentrative joint ventures[25] indicates that 'reciprocal shareholdings' will amount to a concentration where they give rise to a 'single economic entity'. A single economic entity is described as a grouping of undertakings that is both subject to permanent single economic management and '. . . amalgamated into a genuine economic unit, characterised internally by profit and loss compensation between the various undertakings'.[26]

(e)   Companies A, B and C establish (by acquisition or subscription for shares) a joint venture company that qualifies as a concentrative joint venture under the terms of the Commission's notice on cooperative and concentrative joint ventures.[27] Companies A, B and C jointly control the joint venture company.

(f)   Companies A, B and C establish (as in (e) above) a joint venture company with a view to the joint acquisition of company D and, immediately subsequent to such acquisition, the division amongst them of its assets. Note that where the division of assets does not follow 'immediately after the

---

[24] Art. 3(3); see further 2.1.5 *et seq.*
[25] See Appendix III, paragraph 41.
[26] See the Commission press release of 7/11/90 in respect of the cross shareholding arrangements entered into between Volvo and Renault (IP (90) 895).
[27] See Appendix III.

acquisition', the arrangements will be considered as a joint venture and must be subjected to the concentrative/cooperative test under (e) above.[28]

(g) Company A, currently a shareholder in a joint venture company with B and C, acquires C's interest in the joint venture company. As a result, company A moves from being a shareholder that exercises control jointly (with B and C) to a party that has sole control of the joint venture company. The acquisition of C's interest amounts to an acquisition of 'control' and therefore a concentration for the purposes of the Regulation.[29]

(h) Company A acquires the whole or a part of the assets and liabilities of company B (whether by agreement or by a scheme of arrangement under ss. 425 and 427 of the Companies Act 1985), in circumstances where company B is not dissolved, but will remain in existence after the disposal of its assets, either as a shell company or because it has retained a part of its assets. It should be noted that, according to the Commission's notice on concentrative and cooperative operations, the Regulation will only apply in the case of an acquisition of assets that '. . . results in the acquirer gaining control of all or of part of one or more undertakings'.[30] It will be recalled that the Commission describes an undertaking in the same notice as '. . . an organized assembly of human and material resources, intended to pursue a defined economic purpose on a long-term basis.'[31] The effect of these provisions in practice is to mark a distinction between the acquisition of an identifiable business (a term that can loosely be equated with the word undertaking) and the acquisition of a simple collection of assets (however great their value). In other words, the Regulation is unlikely to apply if company A acquires from company B ten heavy lifting cranes unless there can be associated with such acquisition an identifiable and discrete business possessing a related turnover.[32] The Commission in its guidance note on concentrative and cooperative joint ventures makes clear that a unilateral acquisition of assets

---

[28] See 2.1.2.4 above and Appendix III at paragraph 48. Case No IV/M024 *Mitsubishi/UCAR* was the first concentrative joint venture to be considered by the Commission under the Regulation. It obtained clearance on 4/01/91 (OJ 1991 C5/7). Two other cases are pending: Case No IV/M021, a joint venture between Banque Nationale de Paris and Dresdner Bank AG; and Case No IV/M058, the acquisition by Nestlé SA and Baxter International Inc of joint control of Salvia-Werk GmbH.

[29] There is a parallel here between a change in the level of control that a party may obtain for the purposes of the Fair Trading Act 1973. A change, for example, from the ability to exert material influence to *de facto* control' is capable of constituting a 'qualifying merger' for the purposes of that legislation. For an early example of an application of this principle see Case No IB/M023 *ICI/Tioxide*, in which ICI acquired the Cookson Group's 50% equity interest in Tioxide Group plc, thereby increasing its equity stake from 50% to 100%, and moving from joint control to sole control (Commission press release of 3/12/90 (IP (90) 971)).

[30] See Appendix III, paragraph 46.

[31] See Appendix III, paragraph 8.

[32] Article 5(2) of the Regulation provides that where part of an undertaking is acquired, '. . . only the turnover relating to the parts which are the subject of the transaction shall be taken into account . . .'.

will (subject to the requirement that they constitute an undertaking) generally fall within the Regulation whereas a reciprocal exchange of assets will as a rule be cooperative in character and therefore fall outside its terms.[33]

2.1.4 The acquisition of '. . . the whole or parts of one or more undertakings'

The target of an acquisition within the scope of the Regulation may be 'the whole or parts of one or more other undertakings'. This provision should present little difficulty. Clearly, there must be some business activity newly brought within the control of the acquiring company but there is no significance in whether that activity represents an entire undertaking or some severable part of it. The point has been made above[34] that, in the case of an acquisition of assets, the assets must constitute an identifiable business (or undertaking) as opposed to a mere collection of tangible (or intangible) assets. The provision allows for the aggregation of acquisitions that in combination confer control over an undertaking.[35]

2.1.5 The acquisition of control

Article 3(1) provides that the acquisition of direct or indirect control will fall within its terms whether it is achieved by means of an acquisition of '. . . securities or assets, by contract or by any other means . . .'. Clearly, acquisitions of securities (in most cases shares) and assets will be the most typical means of obtaining control. As a matter of practice, it will be rare that a party obtains control in the absence of an acquisition of property in the form of either securities or assets. In the case of securities, the broad terms of the wording will catch all those contractual arrangements (whether they be in shareholders' agreements or in a company's articles of association or in some other collateral agreement) that confer a measure of control upon an undertaking that is disproportionate to the number and value of the securities when taken as a proportion of the undertaking's total securities. In other words, as a result of contractual or 'behind the scenes arrangements', the securities in question confer a measure of control that one would not ordinarily expect given their number, type and face value.

There are in practice a great many ways of achieving such imbalances. Two frequent examples comprise the use of preferred shares that in identified circumstances acquire additional controlling powers[36] and the use of 'minority protection rights'. Minority protection rights as a rule rely upon a contractual

---

[33] See Appendix III, paragraph 47.
[34] See 2.1.3.2.
[35] See further 2.1.5 below.
[36] For example the shareholders may acquire the right to vote on identified strategic matters where the company has failed to pay a dividend.

agreement to the effect that a range of defined key decisions cannot be taken unless the minority shareholder has given his prior approval.[37] Typically such arrangements lead to the sharing of control between the joint venturers[38] as opposed to a single joint venturer obtaining outright or sole control. The words 'any other means' must be construed as a catch-all phrase that will embrace any basis of influence that does not rely upon title to the assets that confer control or a contractual arrangement. The words emphasise that the definition of a concentration, and more particularly the acquisition of direct or indirect control, rely not upon the legal structure adopted but upon the 'effects' of a given transaction.

Where control is acquired as a result of a series of transactions then the final measure that (in combination with all previous measures) confers control will trigger a concentration for the purposes of the Regulation. The wording of article 3(3) expressly covers situations where control is obtained as a result of an accumulation of factors with the words '. . . control shall be constituted by rights, contracts or any other means which, either separately or jointly and having regard to the considerations of fact or law involved, confer the possibility of exercising decisive influence on an undertaking . . .'. In addition, article 5(2) of the Regulation which concerns the turnover to be attributed to the acquisition of a part of an undertaking provides that where parties enter into a series of transactions relating to the acquisition of part of a business within a two year period, then the transactions shall be aggregated and '... treated as one and the same concentration arising on the date of the last transaction'.[39]

2.1.5.1 The definition of control

Control is defined by article 3(3) of the Regulation as being constituted by 'rights, contracts or any other means which, either separately or jointly and having regard to the considerations of fact or law involved, confer the possibility of exercising decisive influence on an undertaking'. Two particular instances of when this test would be fulfilled are then cited:

'(a) ownership or the right to use all or part of the assets of an undertaking;
(b) rights or contracts which confer decisive influence on the composition, voting or decisions of the organs of an undertaking.'

The importance of these instances is that they eschew any legalistic formula for the identification of control, and enable the Commission to enter upon a full economic analysis of a transaction in order to determine whether control

---

[37] The minority shareholder typically exercises his rights of protection at the level of the board through the appointment of a nominated director.

[38] See 2.1.2.3 above.

[39] The provision is primarily an anti-avoidance measure designed to prevent parties artificially splitting-up a transaction in order to fall below the turnover thresholds.

is at stake. The crucial element will be 'the possibility of exercising decisive influence'. In some cases the existence of control will be immediately demonstrable by virtue, for example, of ownership, in which case no further investigation will be necessary. This might be regarded as *per se* control. In other cases the existence of control will only be demonstrable after full economic analysis. For example, where the interest in question is a minority shareholding in another undertaking, it may still be possible to show that control can be exercised through that minority shareholding if in fact no other shareholder or group of shareholders can combine to oppose the wishes of the holder of that interest.[40] In practice even a very low percentage share of the votes may give rise to control.[41]

2.1.5.2   Direct and indirect control

The notion of 'direct' and 'indirect' control is amplified by the text in article 3(4) of the Regulation which provides that:

'Control is acquired by persons or undertakings which:

(a)   are holders of the rights or entitled to rights under the contracts concerned, or

(b)   while not being holders of such rights or entitled to rights under such contracts, have the power to exercise the rights deriving therefrom.'

Article 3(4)(a) addresses direct control and requires little comment. Article 3(4)(b) addresses those situations where title to the assets or contract conferring control is divorced from the ability to exercise and enjoy the benefits of such rights. The most common example of this is likely to arise where company A acquires a controlling interest in company B which has one or more subsidiaries. In such a case company A will have direct control of company B and indirect control of company B's subsidiaries. While not being a 'holder of the rights' to the shares in company B's subsidiaries, company A will nevertheless be able to exercise influence over such rights as a result of its control of company B. A further example of what might imprecisely be termed a split between the legal and beneficial interest is to be found in the case of securities where party A is placed in the register

---

[40]   Cf. *BAT & RJ Reynolds* v *Commission* 142 & 156/84 [1988] 4 CMLR 24 at [37] – [39]; see 1.1.3.4.

[41]   E.g., in the UK, P & O's acquisition of just 16.1% of European Ferries resulted in a reference to the Monopolies and Mergers Commission: (1986) Cm 31; note that under the Fair Trading Act 1973 three levels of control apply (material influence, *de facto* control and *de jure* control). The requirement of decisive influence under the Regulation is likely in practice to equate with the test of *de facto* control under the Fair Trading Act 1973. P & O with 16.1% of European Ferries was considered to be capable of exercising material influence, the lowest of the three tests of control under the Fair Trading Act 1973.

of shareholders of a company but is at all times subject to an obligation to vote and otherwise deal with the securities in accordance with party B's instructions. The relationship between party A (often referred to as the nominee) and party B (the beneficiary) will typically be addressed in a declaration of trust pursuant to which the nominee will, *inter alia*, undertake to pass all dividends and other income arising from the securities to the beneficiary (B) and otherwise vote and deal with them in accordance with B's instructions.

The language of article 3(4)(b) will mean that where an acquirer of control (whether by securities, assets or contract) is itself the subject of control, for example, where it is a wholly owned subsidiary of a holding company, then such holding company will be considered to have obtained indirect control of the target undertaking within the terms of article 3(4)(b). In filling in Form CO, the acquirer will be bound to mention the existence of its parent (and indeed any other controlling parties).[42] Such parties, their activities and their influence will inevitably fall subject to the Commission's overall analysis of the effects of the concentration under article 2 of the Regulation.

Beyond the relatively common legal structures of nominee shareholdings and parent/subsidiary relationships, it is clear that the language of article 3(4)(b) is sufficiently broad to include a potentially limitless range of variations to the manner in which one party exercises influence over another. Again, the emphasis of the Regulation upon 'effects' rather than legal structures comes across clearly.

2.1.6 Concentrative and cooperative joint ventures

Regulation 4064/89 applies to concentrations, and does not apply to the mere coordination of competitive behaviour, which remains the province of article 85 EEC.[43] It is therefore important to be able to identify the degree of integration between undertakings effected by an agreement, in order to determine to which form of control by the Community authorities the agreement will be subject. The distinction is established by article 3(2) of the Regulation. According to the first paragraph of article 3(2), all operations, including joint ventures, which have as their 'object or effect the co-ordination of the competitive behaviour of undertakings which remain independent' fall outside the scope of the Regulation, and so must be subject

---

[42] See Appendix II.
[43] Recital 23 to the Regulation reads: 'Whereas it is . . . necessary to exclude from the scope of this Regulation those operations which have as their object or effect the coordination of the competitive behaviour of independent undertakings, since such operations fall to be examined under the appropriate provisions of Regulations implementing Article 85 or Article 86 of the Treaty.'

to control, if any, under article 85 EEC or under national law. In contrast and by virtue of the second paragraph of article 3(2):

> 'The creation of a joint venture performing on a lasting basis all the functions of an autonomous economic entity, which does not give rise to coordination of the competitive behaviour of the parties amongst themselves or between them and the joint venture, shall constitute a concentration within the meaning of paragraph 1(b).'

The distinction between a concentrative and cooperative joint venture is the subject of a detailed Commission guidance notice.[44] As a matter of practice, it will be necessary to consider all joint ventures in the light of the positive and negative conditions set out in the notice[45] in order to determine whether they are 'concentrative' (and therefore subject to the Regulation) or 'cooperative' (and therefore outside the Regulation but potentially subject to article 85 EEC and national regulatory control). The issue of concentrative and cooperative joint ventures is addressed in Chapter 5 below.

2.1.7 Ancillary restrictions

Where a transaction resulting in a concentration also includes measures which have the object or effect of coordinating competitive behaviour, control of such measures will not be taken out of Regulation 4064/89 if the measures are ancillary to the implementation of the concentration. To qualify as ancillary restrictions the measures must satisfy the following conditions:

(a)   They must be subordinate in importance to the main object of the concentration.

(b)   They must be necessary; that is, implementation of the concentration without them cannot be achieved, or can only be achieved under '. . . more uncertain conditions, at substantially higher cost, over an appreciably longer period or with considerably less probability of success . . .'.[46]

2.1.7.1   Restrictions excluded from the principle
The Commission's guidelines on ancillary restrictions[47] identify a number of types of measure which will not qualify as ancillary restrictions for the purpose of Regulation 4064/89:

(a)   restrictions to the detriment of third parties (in so far as these are

---

[44] See Appendix III.
[45] See Appendix III, paragraphs (16)–(36).
[46] Commission Notice on Ancillary Restrictions (OJ 1990 C203/5) at paragraph 5 of Part II; see Appendix IV.
[47] Supra note 46.

created by the transaction they must be assessed along with the substance of the concentration; in so far as these are separable from the concentration, articles 85 and 86 EEC will apply);

(b) substantial restrictions wholly different in nature from those which result from the concentration itself (to which articles 85 and 86 EEC will continue to apply);

(c) contractual arrangements that form constituent elements of the technical steps necessary to effect the concentration (to which the full article 2 evaluation will apply since they form part of the substance of the concentration);

(d) where a concentration is implemented in stages, the contractual arrangements relating to the stages prior to the acquisition of control (before control is acquired articles 85 and 86 EEC will apply);

(e) additional restrictions agreed at the same time as the concentration but which have no direct link with it (to which articles 85 and 86 EEC will apply).

2.1.7.2 General principles

Restrictions which may fall within the ancillary restrictions rule under Regulation 4064/89 must be assessed by the Commission to determine whether they are acceptable, and article 8(2) of the Regulation provides for that assessment. Where such restrictions satisfy the test of being directly related to the implementation of the concentration, paragraph 6 of the Commission's notice makes it clear that the principal test of compatibility will be the doctrine of proportionality. Account must be taken of the nature, duration and subject-matter of the restriction, and the geographic field of its application. The essential test will be whether the restriction proposed is reasonably required in relation to the concentration in question. This assessment will require an analysis similar to that carried out in English law under the restraint of trade doctrine.[48] It must be possible to identify an interest which, in the light of the transaction leading to the concentration in question, needs to be protected. So, in the case of the sale of a company, the Commission's guideline identifies the need to guarantee the full value of the assets transferred, including intangible assets such as goodwill and know-how. Such a guarantee can be achieved by allowing the acquirer 'to benefit from some protection from competitive acts of the vendor in order to gain the loyalty of customers and to assimilate and exploit the know-how.' A non-competition clause intended to afford such protection is considered reasonable only if it does not extend beyond products and services within the scope of the transaction in question, or beyond the geographic area in which the vendor had previously operated, and was not of too long

---

[48] Cf. *Chitty on Contract* (26th ed, 1989), Vol I, paras 1190–1241.

a duration.[49] Reasonable duration is essentially a matter of interpretation which can only be determined in the light of the product and market in question. Although the point is not expressly made by the guideline, it must be assumed that what is reasonable must be assessed both in the light of the interests of the parties and in the light of the public interest. In other words, while it may suit the parties for a lengthy restriction to be imposed, the public interest in the maintenance of effective competition requires that only the minimum protection necessary to achieve the goal of the restriction should be permitted.

2.1.7.3 Application of the principles to common transactions

The Commission's guideline indicates that it is anticipated that the law and practice relating to ancillary restrictions will develop with experience in individual cases. It must certainly be recognised that the compatibility of such restraints with the common market will depend very largely upon the particular facts, and the presentation of the need for and reasonableness of restrictions will require careful attention. Nevertheless, it is recognised that there already exists a body of past experience relating to transactions resulting in concentration, and the guideline sets out a list of restrictions commonly encountered and the Commission's likely attitude to them. This information is summarised in tabular form below.

---

[49] The guideline suggests, as a rule of thumb, 5 years where the sale includes both goodwill and know-how, and 2 years where only goodwill is involved.

COMMON ANCILLARY RESTRICTIONS

Type of transaction	Restrictive clause	Interest protected	Limitations	Permitted duration
A Sale of an undertaking (the 'target')	1 non-competition by vendor with the target	Protecting value of assets transferred	Restricted to: (i) product/services which form economic activity of firm concerned	Goodwill and know-how: 5 years
			(ii) geographic area in which vendor had established those products/ services	Goodwill alone: 2 years
	2 licences of intellectual property, rights (incl. know-how)	Ensuring continuing exploitation of assets transferred	May be restricted to: (i) scope of activities of undertaking transferred (ii) may not normally impose territorial limitations on manufacture	No limit; may extend to the life of patent, or normal economic life of know-how etc.
	3 purchase and supply agreements between vendor and target	Transitional provision ensuring continuity of purchase and supply, where target and vendor previously integrated in single undertaking	Save exceptionally, may not be exclusive	Period necessary for replacement of relationship of dependency by autonomy in market
B Joint acquisition, with a view to division among acquirers	1 agreement not to make competing offers for same target company	Avoiding conflict of interest between individual bid and group bid	Must not extend to permitting coordination of future competitive behaviour of acquirers	Until completion (or failure) of joint acquisition and subsequent division
	2 restrictions relating to the division of the undertaking/ assets jointly acquired	Providing for orderly division of assets so acquired	Must not extend to permitting coordination of future competitive behaviour of acquirers	Period necessary to effect such orderly division
C Concentrative joint ventures	1 non-competition clauses between parents and JV	see (A) above	see (A) above	see (A) above
	2 intellectual property licences etc. to JV	see (A) above	see (A) above	see (A) above
	3 purchase and supply agreements between parents and JV	see (A) above	see (A) above	see (A) above

2.1.7.4   Practical significance of the distinction

It is important to emphasise that the question of whether or not a restriction is ancillary is not a mere academic exercise but rather a process that has important practical consequences. First, it can be expected to influence, in the context of a joint venture, the question of whether the arrangements as a whole are adjudged concentrative or cooperative. Ancillary restrictions which are subordinate and directly related and necessary for the implementation of the concentrative element of a transaction will be less likely to evidence cooperation than cooperative arrangements that fall outside the definition. Secondly, the analysis will determine whether the cooperative elements of a concentration are to be severed from the concentrative elements and considered under articles 85 and 86 EEC (assuming they are severable) or whether the parties can avoid such 'parallel proceedings' by having both the cooperative and concentrative elements considered together under the Regulation. Only ancillary restrictions will benefit from such 'one stop' regulatory control.

Parties will be keen to avoid the use of parallel proceedings in which the concentrative element of a transaction is considered under the Regulation while the cooperative element falls subject to articles 85 and 86 EEC. In such cases the parties would be obliged to submit Form CO in respect of the concentration and Form A/B in respect of the cooperative elements. Although clearly this represents a doubling of administrative effort, perhaps of more concern to the parties is the fact that while the consideration of the concentration will remain subject to the relatively tight and punctilious timetables of the Regulation, the cooperative elements (which could be of vital economic and commercial importance to the transaction as a whole) will be subject to the much slower and less certain timetable of articles 85 and 86. It remains to be seen whether, as a matter of practice, the Commission will ensure that the consideration of cooperative arrangements by DG/IV under article 85 coincides with the consideration by the Merger Task Force of the concentrative elements of a given transaction. It would clearly be regrettable if a concentration were cleared within say four months but the parties had then to wait a further nine to eighteen months to discover if the long-term supply agreement (which was central to the transaction but not an ancillary restriction) was acceptable or not.

It is the above types of practical consideration that cause parties to seek at an early stage confirmation of the question of whether a given ancillary arrangement will amount to an 'ancillary restriction' or not. As with the question of whether a joint venture is cooperative or concentrative, the Commission is the sole arbiter of such matters and the pragmatic advice must be that, where assistance is required, it can and should be sought informally at an early stage.[50] As with requests for informal guidance ᴄ the cooperative/concentrative test in the context of joint ventures[51], the recommended approach is by a letter containing a reasoned submission and a request for guidance. Confidentiality of the contents of the letter should be sought.

2.1.8 Exceptions

The definitions of concentration in article 3 of the Regulation are subject to three exceptions, all of which are based upon the fact that there are times when control must be held by an undertaking or an office holder for legitimate purposes which although, falling technically within the definition of concentration as broadly provided in article 3, may nevertheless be excluded from the Regulation provided the control is not exercised in a manner inconsistent with those purposes or is exercised for conventional commercial reasons.

The first exception is for credit or other financial institutions or insurance companies which as part of their business deal in securities, either on their own account or on behalf of others.[52] The essence of this dealing is that they do not acquire the securities in order to exercise long-term control of the commercial strategies of the undertakings in which they have an interest, but merely as a function of the trading in securities by institutional investors making their money work. The exception applies where the securities are held on a temporary basis (i.e. no longer than one year from the date of acquisition[53]) with a view to them being resold, provided the voting rights are not exercised in order to influence the competitive behaviour of the undertakings in question but only (if at all) to prepare for the sale of the undertaking, the securities therein or the assets thereof, or some part of any of these.

The second exception applies in the case of the acquisition of control by whatever means by an office holder under the law of a Member State for purposes relating to liquidation, insolvency and analogous proceedings.[54]

The third exception[55] is for certain financial holding companies,[56] provided

---

[50] Again recital 8 of Regulation 2367/90 supports current experience that the Merger Task Force will cooperate readily in such approaches.

[51] See further 5.1.3.

[52] Art. 3(5)(a).

[53] The period may be extended on application to the Commission where the holder of the securities can show that resale was not reasonably possible within the period of one year: art. 3(5)(a).

[54] Regulation 4064/89, art. 3(5)(b).

[55] Regulation 4064/89, art. 3(5)(c).

[56] As defined by art. 5(3) or Dir. 78/660 (OJ 1978 L222/11) [amended by Dir. 84/569 (OJ 1984 L3145/28)]: 'whose sole object is to acquire holdings in other undertakings and manage the holdings to turn them to profit, without involving themselves directly or indirectly in the management of those undertakings.'

that the voting rights in respect of such holdings[57] are exercised only to maintain the full value of the investments and not to determine directly or indirectly the competitive conduct of the undertakings in question. While the policy behind differentiating between a legitimate interest of such companies in protecting their investments and anti-competitive behaviour may be readily understood, it is possible to foresee that policing the distinction may not be an easy task for the Commission and Court of Justice. It may be assumed that the general principles of Community law will apply to this question, so that measures taken to protect investments must be proportional, while anti-competitive behaviour can never be proportional.

2.2 THE COMMUNITY DIMENSION

The boundary between the respective jurisdictions of Community and national authorities in respect of those transactions falling within the scope of the Regulation in terms of the definition of concentration in article 3[58] is marked by the concept of Community dimension. Article 1 provides:

'(1) Without prejudice to article 22[59] this Regulation shall apply to all concentrations with a Community dimension . . .'.

In turn, article 21(2) provides:

'No Member State shall apply its national legislation on competition to any concentration that has a Community dimension.'

Community dimension is principally to be determined by a consideration of aggregate worldwide and Community-wide turnover, with an exception applying to undertakings where turnover is mainly achieved in a single Member State.

2.2.1 The turnover criteria

Article 1(2) provides:

'For the purposes of this Regulation, a concentration has a Community dimension where

(a)   the combined aggregate worldwide turnover of all the undertakings concerned is more than ECU 5,000 million, and

---

[57] Especially in relation to the appointment of members of the management and supervisory bodies: art. 3(5)(c).
[58] See 2.1 generally.
[59] See 7.2.3.2.

(b)   the aggregate Community-wide turnover of each of at least two of the undertakings concerned is more than ECU 250 million . . .'.[60]

The detailed rules for the calculation of turnover are considered below.[61]

For the time being, and particularly at the instance of the United Kingdom, the thresholds of Community dimension have been set relatively high, and the intention is that they should be reviewed before the end of 1993 by the Council acting by a qualified majority on a proposal from the Commission.[62] To set the Community dimension turnovers at a lower level necessarily involves an incursion into the sovereignty of Member States as far as their own systems of merger control are concerned, given the all but exclusive application of the Regulation where the Community dimension criteria are satisfied. It also involves an increased workload for the Commission. It should be borne in mind that simply to leave the turnover thresholds as they stand over a long period will have similar effects, since the usual levels of corporate growth and inflation will cause the number of undertakings falling within the scope of the Regulation to increase slowly but steadily.

The dual and distinct cumulative tests of aggregate worldwide and aggregate Community-wide turnover reflect two basic concerns which dominated the later stages of debate before the adoption of the Regulation. The first was that only major mergers should fall within the scope of the Regulation in the first instance. The requirement of article 1(2)(a) that the combined aggregate worldwide turnover of all the undertakings concerned be in excess of ECU 5,000 million is intended to ensure that only very large corporate groupings resulting from merger activity will be caught by its provisions. The second was that control should only be exercised where there was a threat to competition in the common market. It appears that the requirement in article 1(2)(b) that at least two of the undertakings each have an aggregate Community-wide turnover greater than ECU 250 million is intended to mark the cut-off point below which it can be assumed that no significant anti-competitive effect would be felt as a result of the merger. Whether the Regulation will be entirely successful in excluding from its scope relatively minor transactions which have no impact on competition remains to be seen.

2.2.2   The single Member State exception[63]

There is a proviso to the definition of Community dimension by reference to aggregate Community-wide turnover of each of at least two undertakings concerned in article 1(2)(b) as follows:

---

[60]   1 ECU = £0.695814 OJ 1990 C203/1 13 August 1990.
[61]   See 2.2.2.3 and 2.2.2.4.
[62]   Art.1(3).
[63]   See Guidance Note IV (Application of the two-thirds rule) to Form CO: Appendix II below.

'. . . unless each of the undertakings concerned achieves more than two-thirds of its aggregate Community-wide turnover within one and the same Member State.'

The intention of the proviso is clear: it attempts to displace the *prima facie* finding of Community dimension where the Community-wide turnover is in practice predominantly achieved within a single Member State. The unstated policy is that in such a case the matter is more properly dealt with by the national merger authorities of the Member State in which the preponderance of the turnover is achieved.

Where only two undertakings are concerned, the proviso presents no difficulty in its application; where both undertakings each achieve an aggregate Community-wide turnover greater than ECU 250 million, it is two-thirds of the actual amount which must be considered for the purposes of the proviso, and not merely two-thirds of the threshold figure.

Where more than two undertakings are concerned, the proviso is ambiguous as to its precise scope, because it is not clear whether the criterion of two-thirds of aggregate Community-wide turnover within the same Member State applies to each and every participant in the concentration, or only to those participants with a turnover which is greater than ECU 250 million. For example, assume a concentrative joint venture between A, B and C, where: (i) the parties' aggregate worldwide turnover is in excess of ECU 5,000 million; (ii) A's aggregate Community-wide turnover is ECU 500 million (of which 80% is in the UK); (iii) B's aggregate Community-wide turnover is also ECU 500 million (of which 80% is in the UK); and (iv) C's aggregate Community-wide turnover is only ECU 150 million (of which only 20% is in the UK). Whether the proviso would then operate to exclude application of the Regulation would depend upon whether 'each of the undertakings' referred to in the proviso as achieving more than two-thirds of the relevant turnover in a single Member State means each participating undertaking or is directly linked to article 1(2)(b) and means only those participating undertakings which have an aggregate Community-wide turnover greater than ECU 250 million. The latter reading, under which, in the example above, the Regulation would not apply and the matter would be left to the UK authorities, would seem to be preferable, since the anti-competitive effect in the common market of C's participation is very slight given its low aggregate turnover within that market. Until clarification of this point is forthcoming from the Commission or the Court of Justice, it is recommended that parties seek informal guidance from the Commission.[64]

---

[64]   Cf. Recital 8 of Regulation 2367/90.

2.2.3 The calculation of turnover: basic principles

This section considers the calculation of turnover in the case of concentrations involving the whole of each participating undertaking where the undertaking concerned is not a credit or other financial institution or an insurance undertaking and where the undertakings concerned do not jointly have powers of control.[65] Aggregate turnovers must be assessed in relation to each undertaking concerned, and extend to the whole corporate group as defined in article 5(4). The definition is essentially the same as that used in, for example, the Notice on Agreements of Minor Importance.[66] It includes not only the undertaking concerned,[67] but also any subsidiary[68] and parent[69] thereof, any sister undertaking[70] (defined as an undertaking over which the parent has similar rights and powers to those it has over the undertaking concerned) and any undertaking over which any two or more of (a) the undertaking concerned, (b) the parent, (c) any subsidiary and (d) any sister undertaking jointly have powers or rights amounting to control.[71] All the interlocking relationships described by article 5(4) for the purposes of identifying the respective turnovers which must be aggregated depend upon definitions of control specified in article 5(4)(b), namely:

(a) ownership of more than half the capital or business assets;
(b) power to exercise more than half the voting rights;
(c) power to appoint more than half the members of the supervisory board, the administrative board or bodies legally representing the undertakings; or
(d) the right to manage the undertakings' affairs.

The purpose of this test is to differentiate between the legal niceties of corporate identity, which may be complex and fragmented, and the functional reality, which is that the whole corporate group should be treated as a single autonomous economic unit where such interlocking relationships of control exist.

Two early cases indicate that the analysis of such interlocking relationships may play a central role in the calculation of the turnover thresholds and, it follows, in the determination of whether or not the Regulation will apply to a given concentration. In the merger between Wiggins Teape Appleton

---

[65] For the excepted categories, see 2.2.4.
[66] OJ 1986 C231/2.
[67] Art.5(4)(a).
[68] Art.5(4)(b); this definition is closely mirrored by the new definition of 'subsidiary undertaking' adopted by Part I of the Companies Act 1989.
[69] Art.5(4)(c).
[70] Art.5(4)(d).
[71] Art.5(4)(e).

plc and Arjamari-Prioux SA[72], the Commission found that Groupe Saint Louis (the largest shareholder in Arjamari, with 40% of the voting equity) did not have control of Arjamari within the meaning of article 5(4)(b) of the Regulation. As a result, the Commission ruled that it was not necessary to consider the turnover of Groupe Saint Louis, or its parent Pechelbronn, in the calculation of the total aggregate turnover of all the undertakings concerned in the concentration; the resulting aggregate turnover, of ECU 3.687 billion, therefore fell below the threshold criteria of ECU 5 billion.[73] In the merger between British Satellite Broadcasting plc and Sky, the Commission is reported to have decided that, again upon the basis of the control provisions set out in article 5(4), it would not be appropriate to take account of the respective turnover of the principal shareholders in the holding company of British Satellite Broadcasting (including companies such as Pearson, Granada, Reed and Chargeurs of France). As a result the concentration was found to fall below the thresholds set out in the Regulation.[74]

Taking into account all such connected undertakings and the undertaking concerned, aggregate turnover comprises the amount for the previous financial year (not including any sales rebates, VAT or other taxes directly related to turnover) derived from the sale of products or the provision of services within the undertakings' ordinary activities.[75] It should be noted that sales of products and the provision of services to connected undertakings as defined in article 5(4) must not be taken into account in calculating aggregate turnover,[76] since they are purely internal transactions and do not represent actual turnover.

The Regulation requires assessment of worldwide aggregate turnover and aggregate turnover for particular geographical areas (either the Community or an individual Member State). Where aggregate turnover is to be assessed in respect of a particular geographical area, the test remains the same as for the worldwide aggregate, but applies only in respect of sales of products or provision of services to undertakings or consumers in the geographical area in question.[77] Form CO is accompanied by four Guidance Notes intended to assist in the calculation of turnover for the purposes of the Regulation.[78] It can be expected that the Merger Task Force will be willing to provide advice on an informal basis where there is a difficulty over the process of calculation.

---

[72] Commission press release of 11/12/90 (IP (90) 1003).
[73] See 2.2.1.
[74] It would appear that the BSB/Sky merger was not notified to the Commission, but that the Merger Task Force initiated its own investigation.
[75] Art.5(1).
[76] Ibid.
[77] Art.5(1), 2nd para.
[78] See Reg. 2367/90 Annex I, OJ 1990 L219/5; see Appendix II at 19.

2.2.4   The calculation of turnover: special rules

This section considers the calculation of turnover in the case of concentrations involving the acquisition of only part or parts of another undertaking, concentrations involving credit or other financial institutions or insurance undertakings, and concentrations involving undertakings which jointly have rights and powers of control.

2.2.4.1   Sale of part or parts of an undertaking

Where the concentration in question arises out of the sale of only part or parts of one or more undertakings, the aggregate turnover of the seller for the purposes of the Regulation is only the turnover (otherwise as defined above) achieved by the part or parts to be sold.[79] For example, where a group consists of a parent company and a number of subsidiaries and the controlling parent company sells one subsidiary to another undertaking, then as regards the vendor only the aggregate turnover of the subsidiary sold is to be taken into account. As far as the buyer is concerned the whole of its undertaking must, of course, be considered. In summary, aggregate turnover is to be determined by reference to the constituent parts of the new grouping (or concentration) which will result from the proposed transaction. It should be noted, however, that article 5(2) may not be used as a means of avoiding control under the Regulation by splitting acquisitions into smaller units each of which falls below the turnover criteria. The Regulation seeks to block such attempts by treating two or more partial acquisitions between the same persons or undertakings within a two-year period as a single concentration arising on the date of the most recent transaction.[80] A part of an undertaking, although nowhere defined, must be assumed to be either a subsidiary or a discrete business, and not merely assets, since it must have a turnover attributed to it.

Where a joint venture company upon its formation acquires part of the undertaking of one or more joint venturers, such transaction(s) will not constitute an 'acquisition of parts' for the purposes of article 5(2) of the Regulation. To regard the transaction from the perspective of the joint venture company (i.e. one or more purchases of parts of an undertaking) will, in the context of a joint venture, distort the true legal and economic effects of the arrangements. For the purposes of the Regulation, the transaction must be seen from the perspective of the joint venturers. One or more of them will transfer a part of their undertaking to the joint venture company, almost certainly in return for an equity share. The process involved is not an isolated sale and purchase but the creation of a joint venture which will, *inter alia*, involve an on-going relationship between the vendor and purchaser

---

[79]   Art.5(2).
[80]   Art.5(2), 2nd para.

of the relevant parts of the undertaking concerned. As a result, the concentrative/cooperative test set out in article 3(2) of the Regulation must be applied and not article 5(2).[81]

The point can perhaps be best illustrated by way of example. A, B and C have each transferred that part of their respective group undertakings that was involved in boat-building to a joint venture company ('JVC') in return for a share of the equity in JVC. The parties, by this process, are entering into a concentrative joint venture, ceasing from the point of transfer to engage in boat building individually and not being involved actually or potentially on neighbouring markets. The JVC will have substantial autonomy and independence in its policy and strategy as a commercial boat builder but will be subject to the joint control upon a long-term basis of A, B and C. The following figure illustrates the position.

Example 5

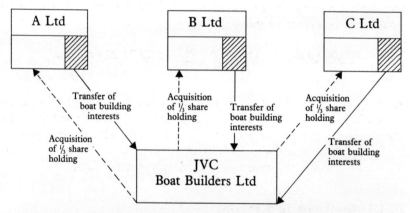

Transfer of part of an undertaking, in relation to joint ventures

In such a case, the provisions of the Regulation in respect of the transfer of part of an undertaking will not apply. The transaction must be considered from the perspective of the collaboration of A, B and C in a joint venture and not from the perspective of a joint venture company making one or more discrete partial acquisitions.

2.2.4.2 Credit and other financial institutions

Where an alleged concentration involves credit and/or other financial institutions, the existence of Community dimension is not tested by reference to aggregate turnover, but by reference to a proportion of the institutions's

---

[81] See the Commission's Notice on concentrative and cooperative operations: OJ 1990 C203/10: Appendix III.

total assets.[82] The reason is that, for such undertakings, transactions and dealings in securities and ownership of other undertakings are normal activities, which are carried out on a broad basis and without reference to any particular market or type of goods, with the result that turnover is a much less relevant indicator of economic strength than the value of its assets. In article 1(2)(a) the words 'combined aggregate worldwide turnover of all the undertakings concerned' is replaced by 'one-tenth of their total assets'.[83] This one-tenth of the parties' total assets must exceed ECU 5,000. In article (2)(b) the words 'aggregate Community-wide turnover' are replaced by 'one-tenth of total assets multiplied by the ratio between loans and advances to credit institutions and customers in transactions with Community residents and the total sum of those loans and advances'.[84] Thus, assets in the Community are assumed to bear the same relation to total assets as transactions in the Community bear to total transactions.

An example may help to clarify the formula. Assume total assets of ECU 6,000 million, loan transactions with Community residents of ECU 100 million and total worldwide loan transactions of ECU 300 million. The formula would then be expressed thus:

$$\frac{(6,000,000,000)}{10} \times \frac{(100,000,000)}{300,000,000} = \text{ECU 200 million}$$

As a result, the undertaking would fall below the requisite Community threshold in article 1(2)(b) of ECU 250 million. Turnover within a single Member State is replaced with the same formula, with the exception that for the words 'transactions with Community residents' one must substitute the words 'transactions with residents of that Member State'.[85]

2.2.4.3 Insurance undertakings[86]

Where an alleged concentration involves insurance undertakings, the word 'turnover' is replaced in the various parts of article 1 by the words 'the value of gross premiums written which shall comprise all amounts received and receivable in respect of insurance contracts issued by or on behalf of the insurance undertakings, including also outgoing reinsurance premiums, and after deduction of taxes and parafiscal contributions or levies charged by reference to the amounts of individual premiums or the total volume of premiums'.[87] This formula must also be used in respect of Community residents and residents of a single Member State.

---

[82]　See Form CO, Guidance Note I; Appendix II at 19.
[83]　Art.5(3)(a), 1st para.
[84]　Ibid, 2nd para.
[85]　Ibid, 3rd para.
[86]　See Form CO, Guidance Note II; see Appendix II at 20.
[87]　Art.5(3)(b).

2.2.4.4   Joint rights and powers of control[88]

Where a concentration involves undertakings which jointly have rights and powers of control over another undertaking (as referred to in article 5(5) and as addressed in more detail in the Commission's notice on concentrative and cooperative operations,)[89] no account is to be taken in assessing the turnover of the jointly controlled undertaking of sales of products or provisions of services between the jointly controlled undertaking and each of the participating parent undertakings or any undertaking connected with them.[90] On the other hand, account must be taken of transactions between the jointly controlled undertaking and any third undertakings; such turnover is to be apportioned equally amongst the undertakings concerned, irrespective of their equity holdings or any contractual arrangements as to the allocation of profits and losses.[91]

2.3   CONCENTRATIONS NOT HAVING A COMMUNITY DIMENSION

The aim of Regulation 4064/89 is to provide a single source of Community law in respect of concentrations, and to subject concentrations within its scope to its exclusive control.[92] However, by way of exception to this general principle, the Regulation provides for its application at the request of a Member State to concentrations not having a Community dimension.

2.3.1   Exclusive application of the Regulation

Article 22(1) provides that: 'This Regulation alone shall apply to concentrations as defined in Article 3.' This provision is not without difficulty, since article 3 does not contain any reference to Community dimension; the resulting implication that concentrations within the meaning of article 3 but not having a Community dimension within the meaning of article 1 could not be subject to any form of merger control, including control by national competition authorities, would make nonsense of the Community dimension provisions, and would be contrary to the announced legislative intent of leaving all but the largest mergers to be dealt with by national merger authorities. It would also be inconsistent with article 21(2), which provides that 'no Member State shall apply its national legislation on competition to any concentration that has a Community dimension.' In fact, while the provisions of article 22(2)–(6) take effect without reference to the

---

[88]   See Form CO, Guidance Note III; see Appendix II at 21.
[89]   OJ 1990 C203/10; see Appendix III.
[90]   Art.5(5)(a).
[91]   Art.5(5)(b).
[92]   Preamble, Recital 7.

question of Community dimension as defined in article 1,[93] it is almost certain that article 22(1) must be read subject to article 1. This approach to article 22(1) awaits a definitive ruling from the Court of Justice, but the only sensible reading is to interpret it as stating that concentrations as defined in article 3 will only be subject to Community control under the terms of this Regulation, and will not be subject to control under Regulation 17.

2.3.2 Application at the request of a Member State

Article 22(3)-(6) introduces a temporary procedure under which a Member State may request the Commission to deal with a concentration under the terms of Regulation 4064/89 even though it does not have a Community dimension. This procedure is intended to assist those Member States which would have preferred the thresholds of Community dimension to be set at a lower level so that control by the Commission would in a greater number of cases have obviated the need for national control. The Member State must make its request within one month of the date on which the concentration was made known to it, or on which it was effected, whichever is the sooner.[94] A Member State will automatically receive copies of all prior notifications of concentrations to the Commission under article 4 of the Regulation within three workings days.[95] Where an undertaking has not notified the Commission because it is confident that the Community dimension criteria are not satisfied,[96] the Member State may still raise the matter under this procedure by a request made as soon as it hears about it, which may be after the concentration has been effected. Given that Member States must apply to the Commission within a month of the date that the concentration was put into effect or the date that it became aware of the concentration, *whichever first occurs*, there is clearly a danger that Member States will miss their opportunity to make a request for Commission intervention under articles 22(3)-(6) of the Regulation unless they remain alert to merger activity in their jurisdiction. The ability of Member States to intervene 'after the event' will potentially cause considerable uncertainty for the participants to a concentration. In practice therefore, where national merger authorities do not exist or where national merger rules do not apply, it may be advisable to consult the 'competent authority' in the Member State in question, to determine whether it would be likely to make such a request in respect

---

[93] The effect of article 22(2) is to provide that other Regulations implementing the general competition policy of the Treaty of Rome (viz, Reg. 17 (general); Reg. 1017/68 (road, rail and inland waterways); Reg. 4056/86 (maritime transport); and Reg. 3975/87 (air transport)) shall not apply to concentrations as defined in article 3, and this rule clearly applies to all concentrations, whether or not they have a Community dimension. The effect of article 22(3)-(6) is considered below: 2.3.2.

[94] Art.22(4), 2nd and 3rd sentences.

[95] Art.19(1).

[96] See art.4(1): see 3.1 below.

of a planned concentration. Where national merger authorities do exist it is more likely that such requests will not be made and the matter dealt with by those national authorities; nevertheless, it will still be advisable to consult with the competent national authority.

Where, upon such a request, the Commission finds that the criteria of article 2[97] would be satisfied in respect of the territory of the Member State concerned (i.e. that the concentration would give rise to or strengthen a dominant position as a result of which effective competition in such Member State would be significantly impeded), the Commission is able to exercise the remedies normally available to it under article 8 of the Regulation. This right is subject, however, to the proviso that the concentration affects trade between Member States,[98] and the measures are 'strictly necessary to maintain or restore effective competition within the territory' of the relevant Member State.[99] The requirement of affecting trade between Member States, if given the effect established in articles 85 and 86 EEC,[100] would result in this control by the Commission under Regulation 4064/89, being less effective than national legislation on merger control, which need have no such criterion for its application.

The procedure in relation to the application of the Regulation at the request of a Member State is the same as the procedure relating to the application of the Regulation in the case of concentrations having a Community dimension, with the omission[101] of the article 7 provisions on the suspension of concentrations.[102] Even this omission might be argued to conflict with the express wording of article 7, which provides that the article applies 'to ensure the full effectiveness of *any decision* taken later pursuant to article 8(3) and (4)'.[103] Under article 22(3) the Commission has power to take decisions under articles 8(3) and (4) at the request of a Member State. The difficulty with this argument is that article 7(2), which governs the continuation of the automatic suspensions provided for in article 7(1), uses the phrase 'concentration as defined in Article 1' (i.e. those having a Community dimension). Concentrations which are the subject of the Commission's special powers under article 22(3)–(6) by definition lack such Community dimension.

The procedure for the application of the Regulation to a concentration not having a Community dimension, at the request of a Member State, is temporary in that it will 'continue to apply until the thresholds referred to in article 1(2) have been reviewed'.[104] The Regulation does not make

---

[97]   See further 3.5.1.
[98]   Art.22(3).
[99]   Art.22(5).
[100] See 1.1.2.1 and 1.1.3.1.
[101] Art.22(4), 1st sentence.
[102] See further 3.3.
[103] Art.7(2), emphasis added.
[104] Art.22(6); i.e., before the end of 1993: see art.1(3).

clear whether it remains open to the Council to continue this procedu even after that review, especially in the case, not contemplated by the Commission but no doubt within the contemplation of some Member States, that the thresholds are not revised downwards. The assumption must be that the Council may so provide, but it is unlikely that the Commission will make such a proposal to it.

2.4 DEROGATIONS FROM EXCLUSIVE APPLICATION

The general rule stated in article 21(2) of Regulation 4064/89 that Member States may not apply national competition legislation to mergers having a Community dimension is subject to three derogations.

2.4.1 Referral to Member State authorities: article 9

Under article 9 of Regulation 4064/89 the Commission may, in certain circumstances, refer a merger which has a Community dimension to the competent authorities of a Member State with a view to the application of the State's national law. To enable this procedure to take place, article 21(2), 2nd paragraph, provides a derogation from exclusive application of the Regulation both in respect of necessary enquiries which the Member State may have to make to determine whether to apply to the Commission for a referral of the concentration in question, and in respect of the decision it is empowered to make upon such a referral. This procedure is considered in more detail below.[105]

2.4.2 Protection of Member States' legitimate interests

Article 21(3) of Regulation 4064/89 provides:

'Notwithstanding paragraphs 1 and 2,[106] Member States may take appropriate measures to protect legitimate interests other than those taken into consideration by this Regulation and compatible with the general principles and other provisions of Community law.'

The Commission is empowered to scrutinise mergers only from the standpoint of an adverse effect on competition.[107] It is conceivable that merger control might take into account other interests apart from competition, as is the case in some Member States. Article 21(3) is intended to allow Member States to assert certain national interests not taken into account by the

---

[105] See 3.4.
[106] See 2.4.1 and 2.2 above.
[107] Art.2.

Regulation. Nevertheless, there is considerable uncertainty over which interests may be so protected and over the precise steps open to a Member State in respect of any such legitimate interests.

Some national interests are expressly provided for, namely, public security, plurality of the media and prudential rules.[108] Public security is an expression familiar from, for example, articles 36 and 48 EEC, and will almost certainly be interpreted accordingly. The Court of Justice is unlikely to be willing to countenance the protection of national economic interests under this heading.[109] Plurality of the media is intended to allow Member States to prevent domination of broadcasting and publishing by single undertakings. Prudential rules are those rules applied by national regulatory authorities to undertakings involved in financial services, insurance or banking. Member States will be able to pursue those regulatory interests despite the otherwise exclusive application of the Regulation. The Regulation also provides for other unexpressed national public interests to be protected, but in this case such protection can only be achieved after the Commission has come to a favourable decision on the compatibility of the interests which a Member State wishes to assert with the general principles and other provisions of Community law.[110] The interests in question must be communicated by the Member State to the Commission, which must come to a decision within one month of such communication. The requirement of a decision makes the Commission's ruling subject to review by the Court of Justice under article 173 EEC.

Present policy in the United Kingdom is that merger control should primarily be exercised on grounds relating to competition, so that it is unlikely that the UK Government will seek to establish recognition for other public interests.[111] Other Member States may seek recognition for interests arising out of, for example, industrial or social policy. It remains to be seen whether these will be accepted by the Commission. It is clear from the requirement that they be compatible with the other provisions of Community law, including the general principles, that any such public interest may not amount to a discrimination on grounds of nationality or to a measure of equivalent effect.

Article 21(3) states merely that a Member State 'may take appropriate measures to protect legitimate interests', without defining in any way what would be an appropriate measure. The expression appears clearly to include the imposition of further conditions in respect of an approval as far as

---

[108] Art.21(3), 2nd para.
[109] See 72/83 *Campus Oil Ltd* v *Minister for Industry and Energy* [1983] ECR 2727, [1984] 3 CMLR 544.
[110] Art.21(3), 3rd para.
[111] See the 'Tebbit Statement' made in a Commons Written Answer (Hansard 5 July 1984, v.63[213]), and reiterated in the DTI Pamphlet *Mergers Policy*, 1988, HMSO. Some non-competition issues are referred, eg, Elders IXL/Allied-Lyons (1988).

implementation in the particular Member State is concerned. It may also be possible to prevent a merger in respect of the particular Member State's territory, even though the Commission has approved it. The Commission has expressly acknowledged that such a measure would be permitted under the powers given to Member States in article 21(3), by way of derogation from the general principle that Member States may not apply their own law to concentrations which have a Community dimension.[112] In either case, to extend further conditions or prohibition beyond the territory of the Member State in question would presumably be contrary to the general principle of proportionality. The more difficult case would be where the Commission had issued a prohibition of the merger, but the Member State claimed that its legitimate interests could only be protected by authorisation of the merger. The Commission takes the view that a Member State would not be empowered under article 21(3) to reach such a decision,[113] although the Regulation itself makes no such express provision. The Commission's stance may be based on the argument that there is a general principle of Community law of the primacy of Community law which prevents a Member State from deciding any matter inconsistently with a Commission prohibition, while allowing Member States to take a stricter view than that taken by a Commission authorisation. This reasoning would be similar to that employed in *Wilhelm* v *Bundeskartellamt*,[114] and is examined in more detail below.[115]

2.4.3 National banking and investment service regulation

Article 21(2) of Regulation 4064/89 prohibits Member States from applying their legislation on competition to concentrations within the meaning of article 3. On the other hand, under the Second Banking Directive[116] and the Draft Directive on Investment Services,[117] the Member States are required to control acquisitions in the sectors concerned. Such legislation falls within the exception for prudential rules provided for in article 21(3), and Member States inevitably have legislation which furthers such policies.[118] The Directives require Member States to establish machinery of control, which in the United Kingdom will be exercised for banks by the Bank of England under the Banking Act 1987 and for investment services by the self-regulating organisations set up under the Financial Services Act 1986. As a consequence,

---

[112] Statements in the Minutes of Council, [1990] 4 CMLR 314.
[113] Ibid.
[114] 14/68 [1969] ECR 1, [1969] CMLR 100.
[115] See 8.33 *et seq.*
[116] OJ 1989 L386/32
[117] COM (89) 629 final; OJ 1990 C42/7.
[118] E.g., in the UK under the Banking Act 1979 (now the Banking Act 1987), passed partially in response to the Second Banking Directive; or under possible changes to the Financial Services Act 1986 made in response to the Draft Investment Services Directive when eventually adopted.

there is a *prima facie* conflict between the provisions of the Regulation and of the Directives, which appear to interfere with the 'one-stop shopping' principle of merger and acquisition control.

The simple resolution of this conflict is no doubt to explain that control of acquisitions under the Directives is to be focused exclusively on the regulation of the proper carrying out of the banking and investment services in question, to ensure that those who engage in such activities are proper persons to do so. Such issues no doubt require local knowledge and close cooperation between the regulatory agency, the commercial community and the subject of the regulatory control. These conditions are best met by control by a Member State authority, applying harmonised, Community-wide standards. Such control should not, however, consider broader questions of competition policy, which under Community law is now regarded as principally the concern of the Commission, and which may only be exercised by national authorities once it has been established that there is no Community dimension to the transaction in question.

On this basis it is possible to show that there is overlap but not conflict between the two sets of provisions, each having a sphere of activity upon which to focus. In practice, however, it may not be easy to make the simple conceptual distinction outlined above, and it is easy to imagine issues of competition and regulatory issues becoming inextricably entwined. In such a case, it might be argued that the effect of article 21(2) of Regulation 4064/89, which is of course directly applicable in Member States, should take precedence.

2.5 ENTRY INTO FORCE

The Regulation came into force on 21 September 1990,[119] and does not apply to mergers which were agreed upon or announced, or where control was acquired, before that date.[120] Equally, it does not apply to mergers against which proceedings have been initiated before that date by Member State competition authorities.[121] It appears that in practice the Commission may have adopted the Regulation's policy at an informal level in advance of the date of its coming into force. It discontinued investigations under existing EC competition law on the basis that the Community dimension criteria were not satisfied because both undertakings achieved more than two-thirds of their Community turnover in a single Member State.[122]

---

[119] Art. 25(1).
[120] Art. 25(2).
[121] Art. 25(2).
[122] Cf. Coats/Tootal; Siemens/Nixdorf.

THREE
Substantive appraisal under Regulation 4064/89

For merger control to be both effective and yet meet the needs of the business community, it is essential that three principles be embraced. The appraisal of concentrations which have a Community dimension, introduced by Regulation 4064/89, is founded on these principles.

The first is the principle of prior control. It is essential that so far as possible merger control prevents the potential merger from taking place, rather than attempting to repair the harm at some later point. One justification for the principle is simply the medical cliché: prevention is better than cure. Once a market has been distorted by the creation within it of a dominant force, it may never be possible to return it to the natural development it would otherwise have enjoyed. A further justification is that the process of merging is expensive: unscrambling a completed merger is even more so. If firms are to be subject to this form of regulatory control it should be administered in such a way as to impose the least possible cost.

The second principle is of predictability. As with any branch of commercial law, there is a need for clear and certain rules which a firm and its legal advisers may consider in advance of a proposed transaction and upon which advice may be given with confidence. This notion is usually expressed in Community law as the general principle of legal certainty.[1] While the protection of the competitive structure may be paramount, the efficient management of firms requires that firms be able to consider with some degree of certainty the likelihood of whether a merger would be permitted to proceed, without needing to have recourse to a formal evaluation process.

The final principle is speed. Mergers and acquisitions are commercially sensitive transactions in which large amounts of money may be at stake, and which depend to some extent upon sensitive market conditions. Where there is to be prior control it is essential that it be exercised sufficiently quickly for the crucial commercial moment not to be missed.

[1] Cf. 43/75 *Defrenne* v *Sabena (No. 2)* [1976] ECR 455, [1976] 2 CMLR 98.

3.1 PRIOR NOTIFICATION

Article 4(1) of Regulation 4064/89 provides:

'Concentrations with a Community dimension defined in this Regulation shall be notified to the Commission not more than one week after the conclusion of the agreement, or the announcement of the public bid, or the acquisition of a controlling interest. That week shall begin when the first of those events occurs.'

Under article 23 the Commission is given powers to adopt implementing legislation in respect of certain aspects of the Regulation, including article 4, addressing the 'form, content and other details of notifications'. The implementing legislation is Commission Regulation 2367/90.[2] Annex I to the Regulation contains the new Form CO, which is to be used for prior notification of concentrations. The form is altogether more complex and demanding than Form AB, which is used for article 85 notifications and applications for negative clearance. The form is less complex than originally envisaged, but it is still very demanding. Moreover, according to article 10(1) and (4) of Regulation 4064/89,[3] the Commission must be supplied with 'complete information', otherwise it need not adhere to the strict timetable for appraisals. Consequently, completion of Form CO and provision of all the necessary information will require early consideration when a merger or acquisition is being planned. The details of Form CO are considered more closely in Chapter 4.

In the case of mergers[4] and joint acquisitions of control by more than one undertaking,[5] the undertakings participating in the merger or the joint acquisition of control must, under the terms of article 4(2) of Regulation 4064/89, jointly notify the concentration to the Commission. Where, within the terms of article 3(1)(b), control is acquired by a single person who already controls an undertaking,[6] or by a single undertaking,[7] article 4(2) requires that the concentration be notified by that single person or undertaking. This differentiation in respect of who must notify the Commission may be the only significant consequence of the distinction drawn by article 3(1) of Regulation 4064/89 between mergers and single and joint acquisitions of control.[8] In cases of doubt the Commission has to date proved willing to

---

2   OJ 1990 L219/5; see Appendix II.
3   See also arts. 3, 4 and 9 of Reg. 2367/90.
4   As defined in art.3(1)(a): see 2.1.1 and 2.1.3.1.
5   See 2.1.2.2 and 2.1.3.2 (e) and (f).
6   See 2.1.2.1.
7   See 2.1.3.2.
8   See 2.2.1 and 2.1.2.

advise upon an informal basis prior to notification whether joint or individual notification is required.

3.1.1 Time of notification

Prior notification of a concentration with a Community dimension must be made not more than one week after the conclusion of the agreement, the announcement of the public bid, or the acquisition of a controlling interest, whichever is the first to occur. Each of these triggering events is considered briefly below.

Conclusion of the agreement In the context of a private acquisition of shares or assets, the expression conclusion of the agreement raises the question of whether an agreement can be said to be concluded when it is signed and exchanged by the parties upon the basis that it will become complete at some later point in time only if certain specified conditions are satisfied. Where there is such a delay between exchange and completion, title to the shares or assets will only pass to the acquirer on completion. As a matter of construction, it is suggested that 'conclusion' must be read to mean signature and exchange and not completion. As a matter of practicality, it is perhaps unlikely that parties to a private acquisition which *prima facie* fell within the terms of the Regulation would be prepared to complete the transaction before obtaining a formal reaction from the Commission as to the transaction's compatibility with Regulation 4064/89. It can be seen that, where an agreement is concluded upon a conditional basis, a controlling interest will not be acquired until completion. In contrast, where an agreement is signed on an unconditional basis and exchange and completion occur simultaneously, the conclusion of the agreement and the acquisition of a controlling interest will coincide.

Announcement of the public bid On a narrow interpretation, these words will not apply to the announcement of a private share or asset acquisition. In practice, the point is unlikely to give rise to difficulty since a private transaction is rarely (if ever) announced prior to the signature and exchange of agreements. In the context of public offers (whether hostile or agreed), the announcement of the bid will, as a result of both stock exchange and City Code requirements, invariably precede either the conclusion of the agreement or the acquisition of a controlling interest. In practice, the announcement will be made the same day as the offer document is 'posted' to shareholders. It follows that the offer is not capable of acceptance, and control is not capable of acquisition, until a later point in time. Under a scheme of arrangement, the public announcement will again precede the acquisition of control.

Acquisition of a controlling interest On the assumption that parties will invariably record their agreements in writing, it will be rare that this triggering event occurs in isolation. It is most likely to occur in those cases where an agreement is exchanged on an unconditional basis, i.e. where the conclusion of the agreement and the acquisition of control coincide. In practice, it must be doubted whether parties to a private transaction which *prima facie* falls subject to Regulation 4064/89 would be prepared to proceed immediately to completion. The alternative and more prudent course would be to sign and exchange the agreement subject to a condition, *inter alia*, that completion would take place only if the parties obtained a satisfactory ruling in respect of the transaction from the Commission (in exercise of its powers under Regulation 4064/89). Such a condition would invariably be included in the making of a public bid.

Given that the prior notification of a concentration with a Community dimension is mandatory,[9] that the implementation of a concentration without prior clearance may lead to a subsequent forced divestiture[10] and the imposition of fines,[11] it can readily be seen that it is important to identify accurately which of the triggering events is likely to apply and to plan accordingly.

3.1.2 Commission's duty to publish information

Article 4(3) of the Regulation provides that where the Commission finds that the notified concentration falls within the scope of the Regulation it must publish certain information in relation to the proposed merger, namely, the fact of notification, the names of the parties, the nature of the concentration and the economic sectors involved.[12] The publication of this information must take account of the legitimate interest of the undertakings concerned in the protection of their business secrets.[13]

The purpose behind this provision is to afford interested third parties an opportunity to submit their views in respect of the concentration in accordance with the provisions of article 18(4) of the Regulation. Early experience of the Commission's practices in this area indicates that:

---

9   Regulation 4064/89, art. 4(1).
10 Regulation 4064/89, art. 8(4).
11 Regulation 4064/89, art. 14(1)(a) and (2)(c).
12 Art.4(3); information is published in the Official Journal. Cf. Reg.17. art.19(3); the purpose
    is to allow third parties with a legitimate interest an opportunity to make their views known,
    as provided for by article 18(4) of Regulation 4064/89.
13 Art.4(3). See also 53/85 *AKZO* v *Commission* [1986] ECR 1965, [1987] 1 CMLR 231 (see
    further 4.2.4); in practice the issue seems moot, since the Notices published to date reveal
    almost no information at all.

(a)   it will publish the details in respect of the receipt of a notification (as required by article 4(3) above) within a few days of its submission;

(b)   it will often reserve its position as to the 'completeness' of the notification;

(c)   it will reserve its position as to the applicability of the Regulation (stating merely that it 'could' apply); and

(d)   it will allow interested third parties a period of 10 days (commencing with the date of publication of the notification in the Official Journal) in which to submit their comments by fax or by post.

The result, it would appear, is the emergence of a practice which is different from that provided for in article 4(3), namely the publication of notifications and the request for third party comments *before* a decision has been taken as to the applicability of the Regulation (and often as to the completeness of the notification). It is noteworthy that no time-limit is provided for the publication of a notice in accordance with article 4(3). It is suggested that the time-limit of one month (which applies to article 6 decisions) must apply, although the point would appear academic in view of the Commission's handling of its article 4(3) powers.

3.2   EVALUATION OF THE NOTIFICATION

Once a concentration has been notified, article 6(1) requires the Commission to conduct a preliminary examination to discover whether a full investigation of the proposed merger is required on grounds of potential incompatibility with the common market. The Commission is required to make its determination in the form of a decision. It must be assumed that this requirement is a deliberate move by the Council to prevent the Commission continuing under the new Regulation the previous practice of conducting merger control through a combination of informal procedure, negotiation and comfort letters. The result of this previous practice was often an absence of legal certainty for the parties, because without a formal decision of the Commission there was no possibility of appeal to the Court of Justice, and any clearance received was without binding force should the subsequent merger be challenged on grounds of EC competition law either by a complaint to the Commission or in the national courts.[14] By making the three possible outcomes of the preliminary investigation subject to a decision by the Commission the Regulation will increase legal certainty. It may do so, however, at the cost of some speed and flexibility of response on the

---

[14]   See the perfume cases: 253/78 *Procureur de la République* v *Giry and Guerlain* [1980] ECR 2327, [1981] 2 CMLR 99; 99/79 *Lancome* v *Etos* [1980] ECR 2511, [1981] 2 CMLR 164; 37/79 *Marty* v *Lauder* [1980] ECR 2481, [1981] 2 CMLR 143; 31/80 *L'Oréal* v *De Nieuwe AMCK* [1980] ECR 3775, [1981] 2 CMLR 235.

Commission's part. Moreover, it is not beyond doubt that such decisions will prove inviolable in national court proceedings.[15]

3.2.1 Concentration outside the scope of the Regulation

Where the Commission finds that the notified concentration does not fall within the scope of the Regulation it must record its finding 'by means of a decision'.[16] The result of such a finding appears to depend upon the ground on which it rests. If the proposed transaction falls within the definition of concentration in article 3,[17] so that the ground for the Regulation not applying is some aspect of the test of Community dimension as set out in article 1 (i.e. the turnover thresholds), then it appears that the effect of article 22(1) is that it will not be subject to EC competition law at all, at least in the Commission, but may be subject to national control.[18] If, on the other hand, the proposed transaction does not fall within the definition of concentration in article 3 then, whatever the relevant turnover figures for the undertakings concerned, it may be subject to both Community control under the ordinary competition rules (i.e. articles 85 and 86 EEC) and national merger control.[19]

3.2.2 No *prima facie* incompatibility with the common market

Where upon preliminary examination the Commission finds that the criteria for falling within the scope of the Regulation are satisfied but that there are no serious doubts about the compatibility of the concentration with the common market, then it may decide not to proceed against the merger and instead declare it compatible with the common market.[20] Again, as a result of article 22(1), the Commission would not seek to apply the ordinary competition rules to such a merger. Equally, since in this case the Commission's clearance is in respect of a concentration with a Community dimension, article 21(2) would prevent a Member State's merger control authorities challenging the merger under national law. However, a Member State might seek to protect its legitimate interests by exercising the powers

---

[15] See 7.2.3.2, 7.2.4.2 and 8.1.1.1 - 8.1.1.3.
[16] Art.6(1)(a); the Commission has to date published a short notice in the Official Journal C series under the title: 'Inapplicability of the regulation to a notified operation', stating briefly why the Regulation was found not to apply.
[17] See 2.1 *et seq.*
[18] See further 2.3.1 and 7.2 *et seq.*
[19] See 7.2.1 and 7.2.2 (Summary: 7.2.4.4); under article 5 of Regulation 2367/90, where it is determined that the notified concentration falls outside the scope of Regulation 4064/89, the Commission may, at the request of the parties, treat the notification as an application or notification for the purposes of anti-trust control under articles 85 and 86 EEC.
[20] Art.6(1)(b); the Commission has to date published a short notice in the Official Journal C series under the title: 'Non-opposition to a notified concentration'.

granted in article 21(3)[21] and such protection may result in the prohibition of the merger within that Member State.

3.2.3 *Prima facie* incompatibility with the common market

Where upon preliminary examination the Commission finds that the criteria for falling within the scope of the Regulation are satisfied and that there are serious doubts about the compatibility of the concentration with the common market, then it must decide to open proceedings against the merger.[22] As a result, the Commission may choose to continue the suspension of the concentration under article 7(2),[23] to enable it to undertake a detailed appraisal in the light of the criteria stated in article 2.[24]

3.2.4 Time limits for decisions and the default presumption

By virtue of article 10(1), the decisions provided for in article 6(1) must be taken within one month of the day following the receipt of a complete notification. Notification is regarded as incomplete when it fails to supply all the information required by the Commission under the notification procedure. Where a Member State requests the referral of a concentration to its own competent authorities with a view to application of its national law under the procedure provided for in article 9, the time limit for the Commission's decision is extended to six weeks.[25] Decisions made within these time limits are to be communicated to the undertakings concerned and to the competent authorities of the Member States without delay.[26] Given the complexity of the form, and the difficulty firms may encounter in supplying some of the information required, it is likely that the Commission will on occasion (perhaps frequently) judge itself released from the above fixed appraisal periods, on the basis that the notification is incomplete. It should be noted that the Commission can exert considerable influence over the timetable because it will be the sole arbiter of when a notification is complete or incomplete.

It remains to be seen whether the Commission will exercise this influence with the restraint and conscience that representatives of its Merger Task Force have informally indicated. The practice to date suggests that it will regard the rejection of a notification upon grounds of its incompleteness

[21] See 2.4.2 - 2.4.3.
[22] Art.6(1)(c); at the time of writing the Commission had initiated only one formal proceeding: Case IV/M042 *Alcatel/Telettra*.
[23] See 3.3.
[24] See 3.5 et seq.
[25] Art.10(1), 2nd para.
[26] Art.6(2).

as a very serious step, and that there are informal mechanisms available which ought to enable parties to avoid such drastic and potentially punitive measures. These informal mechanisms include:

(a) the willingness of the Commission to see parties at an early stage to discuss, *inter alia*, the information which will be required under Form CO;

(b) the ability of parties to submit Form CO to the Commission in draft form in order that its completeness can be established prior to formal submission and the commencement of the procedural timetable;

(c) the opportunity for parties (in practice as part of the informal procedure under (b) above) to agree in advance the exercise by the Commission of its discretion to waive the provision of certain information under Form CO. In the case of concentrations which raise few (if any) competition concerns this may lead to the agreed submission of a substantially shortened or abridged Form CO.

Where the Commission has failed to take a decision in respect of the article 6 preliminary examination procedure within the time limits laid down by article 10(1) then 'the concentration shall be deemed declared compatible with the common market, without prejudice to article 9'.[27] The expression 'shall be deemed declared compatible', as opposed to the more natural 'shall be deemed compatible', is a little cumbersome, but it does not appear to be significant except in so far as it may be intended to provide greater legal certainty by equating this presumption with a full decision rather than merely with a comfort letter. The point is of no great importance since by virtue of article 21(2), which prevents Member States applying national legislation to concentrations which have a Community dimension, there should be no question of a conflict with national law.

3.3 SUSPENSION OF THE MERGER

In order to preserve the competitive status quo pending the Commission's preliminary examination under article 6, and to allow the Commission time to make its preliminary findings, article 7(1) provides that concentrations may not be put into effect either before notification or for a period of three weeks following notification. Although the Regulation is silent on this point, it may be assumed that this article will follow article 10 in that the period will commence on the day following receipt of a complete notification.

If, after the preliminary examination, the Commission is of the opinion that any decision it may take against a proposed merger, either to prohibit

---

[27]   Art.10(6).

it or to order divestiture,[28] might be prejudiced by actions of the undertakings involved, it may decide to continue the suspension of a concentration in whole or in part until it takes a final decision.[29] Alternatively, it may take other interim measures intended to achieve such protection. The Commission's decision to this effect must be made 'following a preliminary examination of the notification within the period provided for in paragraph 1',[30] namely three weeks. Rather surprisingly, this period is shorter than the time limit set by article 10(1) for preliminary examinations under article 6(1), which is one month. There is no apparent reason for this discrepancy, the result of which is to place the Commission under even greater time constraint in conducting preliminary examinations. The difficulty can however be overcome. Where the Commission has not reached its provisional conclusion in respect of a notified concentration as it nears the end of the three week period but where there is every likelihood of deciding to open proceedings against it under article 6(1)(c), it appears to be possible to extend the suspension until a final decision is adopted, since only the decision to extend the suspension must be taken within three weeks. The Regulation does not require that any decision made under article 6 be made at the same time as a decision under article 7(2), although the Regulation appears to contemplate these decisions usually being made simultaneously.

Failure to comply with the automatic suspension of a concentration under article 7(1), or with a suspension continued by the Commission under article 7(2), may, where the failure is intentional or negligent, make the undertakings concerned liable to a fine not exceeding 10% of their aggregate turnover.[31] However, the Regulation makes clear the intention that such fines shall be the only penalty consequent upon failure to comply with a suspension: article 7(5) states that the validity of a transaction entered into in order to implement a concentration with a Community dimension is to be determined by the rules set out in the Regulation[32] even if it was entered into in contravention of a suspension. Even then, transactions in securities[33] made in contravention of a suspension are not themselves invalid unless the buyer and seller knew or ought to have known that the transaction was carried out in contravention of a suspension.[34] The rule is no doubt intended to overcome the difficulty which potentially arises under article 85(2) EEC in relation to share transactions caught by article 85(1) and thus said to be 'void'; most

---

[28] Art.8(3) and (4).
[29] Art.7(2).
[30] Art.7(2).
[31] Art.14(2)(b).
[32] I.e. arts. 6(1)(b), 8(2) and (3), and 10(6).
[33] Being 'securities including those convertible into other securities admitted to trading on a market which is regulated and supervised by authorities recognized by public bodies, operates regularly and is accessible directly or indirectly to the public': art.7(5), 2nd para.
[34] Art.7(5), 2nd para.

commentators take the view that this should not prevent property passing, even if the full rights deriving from ownership cannot be exercised.[35]

The difficulty is raised at least in part by article 222 EEC which provides that the Treaty of Rome is not to prejudice the rules in Member States governing the system of property ownership. Since Regulation 4064/89 is made under articles 87 and 235 of the Treaty, the same restriction will apply. Nevertheless, where both the buyer and the seller are or ought to be aware of the contravention of a suspension, then the transaction may be invalid under the terms of article 8(3), as provided for by article 7(5), second paragraph. Such invalidity might ultimately result in forced divestiture under article 8(4). It is likely that the Commission will be unwilling to accept that a buyer (seeking to obtain control and invariably professionally advised), or an institutional seller, was not in a position reasonably to have known about a suspension; non-professional sellers would thus seem likely to be the main (if not only) beneficiaries of this rule.

Under article 7(3), the suspension of a concentration by virtue of article 7(1) and (2) is said not to prevent the implementation of a public bid which has been properly notified to the Commission prior to its announcement, provided the acquirer does not exercise the voting rights in question. However, although this provision allows the process of the takeover bid to continue, it does not operate to approve concentrations which are otherwise incompatible with the common market. As a consequence, such a bid might ultimately have to be unscrambled,[36] so that it is unlikely that this approach will appeal to many undertakings, given the cost of such an activity. In the United Kingdom the concession would appear to be of only limited value, since by virtue of amendments to the City Code on Takeovers and Mergers made by the Takeover Panel in September 1990, offers must be made subject to the term that they lapse upon the Commission deciding to commence proceedings.[37] In addition, in the course of the Commission's appraisal of the concentration, the offeror will not be entitled to effect further acquisitions of the target's shares.[38]

Paragraphs 1 (automatic suspension), 2 (extended suspension) and 3 (non-exercise of voting rights) may be the subject of a derogation granted by the Commission, in order to prevent serious damage to one of the undertakings concerned or to a third party.[39] In the case of a derogation from the rule against the exercise of voting rights acquired through the continued implementation of a public bid, the exercise of such rights must be for

---

[35] See 7.3.3.3.
[36] See art.8(4): see 4.6.3.
[37] See the appendix to the Panel's statement dated 21 September 1990 (1990/18). Note that the amendments to the City Code are '. . . subject to review once the Panel has had an opportunity to assess the practical impact of the Regulation.' (Statement of 21/9/90).
[38] Ibid.
[39] Art.7(4).

the purpose of maintaining the full value of the investments in question.[40] Derogations may themselves be made subject to conditions, and may be applied for at any time.[41] It is likely that this will remain a very limited exception to the main rule. In the UK, its application in the context of a public bid will be subject to the requirements of the City Code described above.

3.4 REFERRAL TO MEMBER STATE AUTHORITIES

Pursuant to article 9(1) a Member State (and the Commission) is entitled to decide that a notified concentration be considered by the requesting Member State under its national merger control (as opposed to by the Commission under the Regulation) where the concentration in question is likely to impede significantly effective competition on a distinct market in the Member State in question. The procedure, along with the turnover thresholds in article 1 (another instance of political compromise), will be reviewed before the end of 1993. Since the request comes from a Member State, parties seeking to allege that a distinct national market may be affected should note that representations would need to be addressed to the national regulatory authority (in the UK the relevant body is the Office of Fair Trading and not the Department of Trade and Industry). In the United Kingdom, powers of investigation and enforcement are conferred on the Office of Fair Trading by the EEC Merger Control (Distinct Market Investigations) Regulations 1990 (SI 1990 No. 1715). A similar approach would be required in the event that one or more parties were of the view that a concentration threatened a legitimate national interest.[42]

3.4.1 Nature of the procedure

While the article 22(3)-(6) procedure is intended to allow Commission jurisdiction over concentrations lacking a Community dimension at the request of a Member State,[43] this procedure provides for the reverse: Member State authorities may be granted jurisdiction despite the fact that there is a Community dimension. Nevertheless, it should be noted that the Commission retains a discretion as to whether to accede to such requests, and it is very unlikely that it will cede its jurisdiction in cases with a Community dimension unless it feels that any anti-competitive impact is likely to be restricted to a distinct market within the single Member State making the request (that is in cases where no other EC markets are likely to be affected). To that extent, article 9 may be regarded as a long-stop

[40] Art.7(3).
[41] Art.7(4).
[42] See 2.4.2.
[43] See 2.3.2.

provision intended to return to Member State jurisdiction those cases which (by chance) qualify as being of Community dimension even though their economic impact is essentially of concern solely to a single Member State. The provision was included at the insistence of Germany (and is sometimes referred to as the 'German clause'), which wished to retain some residual jurisdiction even over major mergers, but it remains to be seen whether the Commission will be willing to grant this in many cases.

3.4.2 The Commission's decision

Under article 19(1) the Commission must transfer copies of notifications to the competent authorities of the Member States within three working days. Article 9(2) then provides:

'Within three weeks of the date of receipt of the copy of the notification a Member State may inform the Commission which shall inform the undertakings concerned that a concentration threatens to create or to strengthen a dominant position as a result of which effective competition would be significantly impeded on a market, within that Member State, which presents all the characteristics of a distinct market, be it a substantial part of the common market or not.'

Informing the Commission in this way is to be treated as a request for the matter to be referred to the authorities in the Member State in question. The basic criterion of impact on the alleged distinct market is the same, in relative terms, as is applied in full Commission investigations of concentrations which have a Community dimension under article 2. Under the article 9 procedure, the Commission's decision whether to refer, therefore, centres upon two issues:

(a)   whether there is a distinct market; and
(b)   whether the matter is better dealt with at national or supra-national level.[44]

On this basis the Commission must decide whether to refer the matter to the national regulatory body, or to deal with it itself.

3.4.2.1   Distinct market
The notion of distinct market must encompass elements of both relevant products and geographical market, although the Regulation only addresses the latter. The notion of 'products or services in question'[45] will be determined

---

[44]   Art.9(3).
[45]   Art.9(3).

according to the now familiar criteria developed in the context of the general competition law of the Treaty of Rome, relying on forms of the test of cross-elasticity of demand and of supply, usually phrased as 'reasonable substitutability'.[46] Article 9(7) of Regulation 4064/89 defines the geographical reference market as the area in which, in respect of the relevant products or services, 'the conditions of competition are sufficiently homogeneous and which can be distinguished from neighbouring areas because, in particular, conditions of competition are appreciably different in those areas'. Expressly listed for consideration in making this assessment are, in addition to the characteristics of the products or services in question, barriers to entry, consumer preferences, significant price differentials, and appreciable differences in the undertaking's market share between neighbouring areas.[47]

3.4.2.2 The Commission's discretion

Once a distinct market has been identified, upon which effective competition is being threatened, the Commission must exercise its discretion under article 9(3) as to whether to refer the case to the competent authorities of the relevant Member State. The choice available to the Commission appears to rule out the possibility of it dealing with the matter at a Community level *and* allowing the Member State to deal with the matter as far as the local difficulties are concerned. If that is the case, then it seems likely (as stated above) that the Commission will only refer cases to Member State authorities when satisfied that the proposed concentration has no Community-wide implications. Concomitantly, the Commission may also be unwilling to refer a case where it believes that the treatment of the case by the Member State authorities might itself have Community-wide repercussions. Until the Commission has had the opportunity to consider a number of such requests for referral it will be difficult to advise with any degree of confidence about the likely outcome of the exercise of this discretion, although it is thought that the Commission will take a restrictive view of its power to make such referrals.

The decision to refer may be taken within the preliminary period of six weeks laid down for the preliminary examination of notifications under article 10(1)[48] or within three months of notification if the Commission has commenced proceedings against the merger, provided it has not actually taken steps towards making any order against it under article 8.[49] Failure to decide either to take steps against a notified merger or to refer it to a Member State, having been so requested, will result in the Commission being deemed to have decided to refer the case to the Member State

---

[46] See 1.4.2.1.
[47] Art.9(7): information upon which the assessment is made is gathered by means of Form CO - see 4.1.1.2.
[48] Art.9(4)(a).
[49] Art.9(4)(b).

concerned.[50] This presumption will operate only if the Member State has reminded the Commission of its request for a referral.[51]

3.4.3 Member State powers

Under article 9(8) the Member State may, in dealing with a case referred to it by the Commission, take only those measures necessary to safeguard or restore effective competition on the market concerned.[52] This limitation on the power of competent authorities in Member States, whatever powers they enjoy under national merger control legislation, reflects the principal criterion of control exercised by the Commission in general under the Regulation,[53] and almost exactly mirrors the limitation placed on the Commission when dealing with a merger not having a Community dimension at the request of a Member State under article 22(3).[54] Member States may not request referral of a concentration on grounds of its effect on a distinct market in order to apply something other than strict competition policy criteria to it: in particular, the Commission is unlikely to look favourably on a request for referral intended as a means of championing some aspect of national industrial policy.

The competent authorities in the Member State concerned must make any determination under these powers within four months from the date of the Commission's referral of the case to them.[55]

3.4.4 Right of appeal

By virtue of article 9(9), Member States have an expressly stated right of appeal against adverse Commission decisions under the article 9 procedure. The right includes a general entitlement to apply to the Court of Justice for interim measures under article 186 EEC. Under the article 9 procedure there are three principal decisions which the Commission must take and which are capable of giving rise to an appeal by a Member State:

(a) a decision that no distinct market exists;

(b) a decision that a distinct market exists but that competition on that market is not threatened; or

(c) a decision that competition on a distinct market is threatened but that the Commission will not refer the matter to the Member State in question.

---

[50] Art.9(5).
[51] Ibid.
[52] Art.9(8).
[53] Cf. art.2.
[54] Cf. art.22(5).
[55] Art.9(6).

It is submitted that article 9(4), which provides that the decision whether or not to refer (i.e. (c) above) must be taken within certain specified periods[56] will apply equally to the taking of decisions under (a) and (b) above, although the Regulation does not expressly provide for this.

3.4.5 Procedural safeguards

The second sentence of article 19(2) provides that, for the purposes of the article 9 procedure, the Member State has an on-going entitlement to participate in the Commission's formal procedure. Thus, the Commission must obtain information from the competent authority of the Member State and allow the competent authority the opportunity to make known its views at every stage of the procedure up to the adoption of a decision under article 9(3). Finally, it must also allow the Member State access to the file.

3.5 SUBSTANTIVE APPRAISAL[57]

It would appear that the Council is concerned that the Commission should not adopt the approach of informal control of mergers under the new Regulation which characterised its previous practice in respect of mergers under articles 85 and 86 EEC, and by which it has coped with the great volume of notified agreements under its general jurisdiction under article 85. To this end, the Regulation provides that, once proceedings have been commenced pursuant to article 6(1)(c) as a result of the preliminary examination procedure, they must be concluded by means of a decision as provided for in article 8. This provision appears to rule out the possibility of a 'comfort letter' approach to merger control under the Regulation, since the preliminary examination procedure also requires that the Commission proceed by making decisions rather than by informal measures.[58]

3.5.1 Compatibility with the common market

Article 2(1) of Regulation 4064/89 provides:

'Concentrations within the scope of this Regulation shall be appraised in accordance with the following provisions with a view to establishing whether or not they are compatible with the common market.'

---

[56] See 3.4.2 above.
[57] This heading relates to appraisal for compatibility under art.2(1)–(3); the analysis in this section assumes that a preliminary decision to initiate proceedings under art.6(1)(c) has already been made.
[58] Cf. art.6(1)(b); see 3.2 above.

This provision must be read in the light of article 6(1)(b),[59] which permits the Commission to decide not to carry out a full investigation of a notified concentration if it is satisfied that there are no serious doubts as to its compatibility with the common market. Article 2(1) then lists factors to be taken into account in making this assessment, and these factors are considered below.[60] Before that, it is necessary to consider the principal criterion of incompatibility, and the Commission's powers in respect of its findings on that matter.

3.5.1.1 The test of incompatibility
Article 2(3) provides:

'A concentration which creates or strengthens a dominant position as a result of which effective competition would be significantly impeded in the common market or in a substantial part of it shall be declared incompatible with the common market.'

This provision provokes a number of comments. First, it is clear that the test of incompatibility is based on a single criterion of effect on competition, and this is borne out by the factors to be taken into account listed in article 2(1). Whether in practice the Commission will be able to sustain this single-minded approach in the real world of commercial decision-making, lobbying and pressure from Member State governments remains to be seen.

Second, article 2(3) is clearly similar to the basic provision of article 86 EEC, with the important distinction that it allows for Commission intervention not only in the case of illegal exploitation of an existing dominant position, but also in the case of the creation for the first time of a dominant position. There are, however, other significant differences, which make the drawing of parallels with the application of article 86 EEC potentially misleading. Under article 86 a distortion of competition[61] would attract Commission intervention only if it amounted to an abuse of the dominant position; under Regulation 4064/89 it seems that to impede competition significantly will result in intervention whether that effect results from abusive behaviour or simply from the size of the concentration relative to the rest of the market. As a result, under the Regulation, the option of good behaviour, which would avoid Commission intervention under article 86, will not avail if the prohibited effect (the impeding of effective competition) is in fact present or likely to result. Furthermore, it may be that the notion of dominant position cannot be given precisely the same meaning as it has under article 86. Article 86 deals with existing dominant positions, and uses a definition

---

[59]   See 3.2.2 above.
[60]   See 3.5.2 *et seq.*
[61]   Defined in art.86 EEC as 'an effect on trade between Member States'.

of relevant product market coupled with tests of relative market share and barriers to entry for other firms.[62] Although all such tests involve an element of economic speculation, the fact that what is to be assessed is whether a dominant position already exists makes the exercise finite and dependent upon concrete data. Under Regulation 4064/89 the assessment must be whether the future consequence of particular transactions will be to create or to strengthen a dominant position. In this case there may be little concrete data and the exercise is far from finite. In the circumstances, it may not be possible to insist on as high a standard of proof from the Commission simply because it has to operate in the realm of prediction.

Third, it should be noted that the reference to 'dominant position' may prove to be a restriction on the scope of Regulation 4064/89 as an instrument of merger control, because the Commission and Court of Justice would appear to be constrained by that formulation to considering the effect on competition in respect of a particular market for goods or services. In particular, it would appear to rule out control of 'conglomerate mergers' (which result in the combining of firms which do not compete in the same product markets) because what is at stake in such cases is not the pooling of market share and turnover in respect of products competing on the same market but simply the acquisition of corporate assets and power.[63]

Fourth, the test of significantly impeding effective competition is new to Community legislation on competition law, although it closely follows the test approved by the Court of Justice in respect of article 86 EEC in the *Michelin* case.[64] The Court there defined dominant position in the following terms:

'. . . a position of economic strength enjoyed by an undertaking which enables it to hinder the maintenance of effective competition on the relevant market by allowing it to behave to an appreciable extent independently of its competitors and customers and ultimately of consumers.'

Since the appraisal rules of the Regulation apply only where the concentration has a Community dimension,[65] it is understandable that it does not impose the further qualification found in article 86 EEC of 'affecting trade between Member States'. Significantly, impeding effective competition must be taken as the functional equivalent of the requirement in article 85 EEC of 'preventing restricting or distorting competition'. It should be noted that the Regulation, by use of the phrase '*significantly* impeding effective

---

[62] See 1.1.2.2.
[63] Whether such mergers are harmful at all is questioned by some commentators; cf. Whish 697–8. Consequently, the restriction may be of no significance.
[64] 322/81 [1983] ECR 3461.
[65] But see the exception in art.22(3) for concentrations not having a Community dimension referred to the Commission by Member States.

competition' (emphasis added) makes express provision for the *de minimis* rule introduced by the case law of the Court of Justice in respect of article 85.[66]

Finally, the requirement that the anti-competitive effect be felt in the common market or a substantial part of it raises the question of the geographic extent of the adverse effect. Under article 86 EEC it must be an area in which, for the product or services in question, conditions of competition are the same for all concerned.[67] A narrower definition of the area in question may be allowed where circumstances justify it; for example, the area in which the adverse effect on competition is felt. Whether the area qualifies as 'substantial' depends upon the geographic area and the nature of the product.[68]

3.5.1.2 The consequences of incompatibility

Where the Commission finds that a concentration fulfils the criterion of significantly impeding effective competition in the common market laid down by article 2(3), it must issue a decision declaring the concentration incompatible with the common market.[69] It may also impose fines[70] for the implementation of a concentration in defiance of such a declaration. Where a concentration has already been implemented the Commission has apparently wide powers to order necessary measures of divestiture.[71] In most circumstances decisions taken under article 8(3) in respect of incompatibility under article 2(3) must be made within four months of the date on which the proceedings against the concentration were commenced,[72] which in turn must be within one month of notification.[73] As a consequence, a full appraisal of a proposed merger under Regulation 4064/89 should take no more than five months at the very most, subject to the Commission's willingness to regard the notification as complete and not to require further information.[74] The time limit set by article 10(3) may be extended when, for reasons attributable to one of the undertakings involved, the Commission has had to request information or order an investigation.[75]

---

[66] See 5/69 *Volk* v *Vervaecke* [1969] ECR 295, [1969] CMLR 273, which established the principle that the art.85 EEC prohibition only applies where there is an *appreciable* effect on competition. See also 22/71 *Béguelin Import* v *GL Import & Export* [1971] ECR 949, 960.

[67] 27/76 *United Brands* v *Commission* [1978] ECR 207, [1978] 1 CMLR 429 paras [44]-[55].

[68] See *Suiker Unie* [1975] ECR 1663, 1977, in which both Belgium and Luxembourg, and Southern Germany, were found to be substantial.

[69] Art.8(3).

[70] Art.14(2)(c); see 4.6.1 *et seq*.

[71] Art.8(4).

[72] Art.10(3).

[73] Art.10(1); see 4.4 and Table 4-1.

[74] Ibid.

[75] Art.10(4); a further exception to this time limit is provided by art.8(6): see 4.4.

3.5.1.3 The consequences of compatibility

If a concentration is found not to create or strengthen a dominant position, so that there is no significant impediment to effective competition in the common market, it must be declared compatible with the common market.[76] Such a declaration must be in the form of a decision.[77] It is open to the parties to modify the proposed merger if they believe that it may be made compatible with the common market by so doing.[78] Commission officials may indicate that that is the case, and may be willing to enter into negotiations with undertakings in order to assist them in complying with the Regulation. Nevertheless, it must be noted that the time limits for decisions under article 8 are short and strict,[79] and there is no provision for extension of the time limits to allow further negotiation and modification. Consequently, it will not be possible to carry out lengthy negotiations, such as occurred in *BAT & RJ Reynolds* v *Commission*[80] (when negotiations were conducted over a period of more than two years), without the Commission being obliged to come to what would almost certainly have been an adverse decision. This difficulty may be overcome by entering into informal negotiations with the Commission in advance of notification in order to anticipate and forestall any problems which may arise, provided Commission officials are available for such discussions. Recital 8 of the Preamble to Regulation 2367/90 indicates that the Commission intends its officials to be available for pre-notification discussions. The alternative of abandoning a proposed merger and then re-launching it in a new structure designed to achieve compatibility would run into difficulty with domestic regulations on the frequency of takeover bids,[81] and is not a practical consideration.

3.5.1.4 Conditions and obligations

In issuing a declaration that a proposed merger is compatible with the common market the Commission may impose 'conditions and obligations' on the undertakings concerned in order to ensure that they comply with any deals made with the Commission in respect of modifications required to achieve compatibility.[82] The power to impose conditions and obligations is similar to the Commission's power to impose them in the case of the grant of exemptions under article 85(3) EEC,[83] but it seems unlikely that similar

---

[76] Art.2(2).
[77] Art.8(1) and (2); and see note 20 above.
[78] Art.8(2), 1st para.
[79] Art.10(2): decisions under art.8(2) must be taken as soon as it appears that serious doubts about compatibility have been removed, particularly as a result of modifications made by the undertakings concerned, and at the latest within not more than four months of the date on which proceedings were commenced.
[80] [1988] 4 CMLR 24; see 1.1.3.4.
[81] Cf. City Takeover Code Rule 35.1; see further 8.2 and 4.4.
[82] Art.8(2), 2nd para.
[83] Under art.8(1) of Regulation 17; see Kerse 174 - 177.

obligations or conditions will be imposed under the two procedures. In the case of article 85(3) exemptions, which are temporary and must be renewed from time to time, conditions are not often imposed. However, there is commonly an obligation to supply necessary information to the Commission so that it can continue to monitor the effects on competition of an exempted agreement. In the case of mergers, the determination of compatibility must be a once-and-for-all assessment, so that ordinarily there would be no reason to impose an obligation to supply further information at a later date. On the other hand, it is common practice in merger control proceedings for the authorities to make approval of a proposed merger conditional upon certain courses of action, such as selling a part of the merged group, and it may be anticipated that this kind of condition will be imposed under the Regulation. In imposing conditions, it is likely that the Commission will insist upon permanent structural changes, rather than accepting undertakings as to future conduct which require further monitoring. It may, indeed, withhold approval unless evidence of a legally binding change in structure can be produced.

3.5.1.5 Revocation of decisions declaring compatibility

Under article 8(5) of the Regulation, a decision declaring the concentration compatible with the common market may be revoked by the Commission where:

(a)   the information upon which the decision was based was incorrect and that fact was attributable to one of the undertakings concerned; or

(b) the decision was obtained by deceit; or

(c)   the undertakings concerned commit a breach of an obligation attached to the decision.

Breach of condition is not included as a ground of revocation but, in the case of article 8(3) of Regulation 17 (which provides for the revocation of exemptions under article 85 EEC), Kerse explains[84] that revocation is unnecessary as failure to comply with the conditions automatically invalidates the exemption. It must be assumed that the same reasoning would apply to breach of condition in respect of a declaration of compatibility. Of course, such a revocation might raise problems for the Commission in terms of declaring the merger incompatible with the common market within four months of commencing proceedings: this problem is met by waiving the article 10(3) time-limit of four months for declarations of incompatibility in the case of a revocation under article 8(5).[85] There is a serious omission in the Regulation in this respect, however, since there is no express waiver

[84]   op.cit. at 175.
[85]   Art.8(6).

of the article 10(3) time-limit in the case of a breach of condition. Article 8(6) overrides the time-limit only in the case of a breach of obligation under article 8(5). Nevertheless, it must be assumed that the intention was that where such a breach occurred the merger should not be allowed to proceed. Since in the absence of a negative decision within the time-limit there is a presumption of compatibility,[86] the absence of a waiver of the article 10(3) time-limit in the case of breach of condition would, on a strict interpretation, result in the merger being presumed compatible even though the express declaration of compatibility had become invalid. Such an interpretation is clearly in conflict with the spirit of the legislation, and it is very likely that the Commission and Court of Justice will by a purposive interpretation of the provisions of the Regulation avoid this difficulty.

3.5.1.6 Presumed compatibility

Article 10(6) provides that in the event of the Commission's failure to comply with any of the time limits for decision in respect of any issue relating to a concentration which falls within the scope of Regulation 4064/89,[87] the concentration shall be deemed declared compatible with the common market. This provision may reflect concern felt in some quarters about the Commission's ability to handle the volume of extra work, thought to be about 40 or 50 cases a year, which even under the current relatively high thresholds are likely to be generated by the Regulation, and about the time taken currently to process article 85 EEC cases. In practice, however, in recent years the Commission has dealt expeditiously with cases raised under the informal scrutiny procedures which had been established. Article 10(6) may therefore be no more than a formalised comfort letter procedure. Where it becomes apparent after proceedings have been commenced that there is unlikely to be an anti-competitive effect, the Commission may simply abandon the proceedings in order to concentrate on those in which an adverse decision is contemplated, in the knowledge that at the end of four months the merger will be presumed compatible with the common market. Such a practice may not be satisfactory for the undertakings concerned, but may become inevitable by reason of the workload of the Merger Task Force.

In respect of an earlier draft of the Regulation containing a provision not unlike article 10(6), Hornsby has argued that it would be open to national courts to override such a 'deemed' finding of compatibility where there is a stricter national rule applicable to the merger.[88] Under the final version of Regulation 4064/89 there should be no scope for such conflicts because of article 21(2), which prevents Member States applying their own law to

---

[86] See below 3.5.1.6; contrast Regulation 17, art.8(3) and art. 85(3) EEC, where the presumption upon lapse of an exemption is of incompatibility.
[87] I.e. art.6(1)(b), art.6(1)(c), art.8(2) and art.8(3).
[88] (1988) 13 ELRev 295 at 304.

mergers having a Community dimension. The point is pursued further in Chapter 7.

3.5.2 Factors to be taken into account in the appraisal of a concentration

The second paragraph of article 2(1) lists a series of factors to be taken into account in the appraisal of whether a merger is compatible with the common market. Many of them are familiar from experience under articles 85 and 86 EEC and/or are self-explanatory, but all are listed below. These factors must be considered in the light of the principal test of incompatibility in article 2(2), which is the likelihood of significantly impeding effective competition. Nevertheless, some of them appear to leave open the possibility of consideration of other policy interests apart from competition, and it will be important to monitor the Commission's performance in the early years of application of the Regulation to determine whether it is in fact amenable to arguments based on, for example, industrial policy.

3.5.2.1 Preservation and development of effective competition
This first factor to be taken into consideration expresses the main philosophy of the Regulation. It was particularly the UK government's concern that control under the Regulation should be limited to effects on competition. Nevertheless, there is ample scope for the Commission's discretion in the appreciation of the facts in any given case in determining what is the desirable level of 'effective competition'. Moreover, while it is mainstream competition policy to *preserve* competition, there may be more than a little industrial policy in the notion of the *development of effective* competition. This factor would appear to justify the Commission finding a merger compatible with the common market where it resulted in the creation of a new large-scale undertaking able to compete effectively with other large undertakings already operating on the market in question, just as the Commission has in the past granted article 85(3) exemptions on such grounds.[89] Consequently, it may be impossible to maintain the strict limitation to competition criteria which the Regulation was said to have incorporated; indeed, such differentiation may be meaningless.

3.5.2.2 Competition from within or without the Community
The Commission must also take into account the structure of all the markets concerned, and the actual or potential competition from undertakings located either within or without the Community. This factor groups together a number of points which the Court of Justice has in the past found to be

---

[89] Cf. *Transocean Marine Paint* JO 1967 163/10, [1967] CMLR D9; OJ 1974 L19/18, [1974] 1 CMLR D11; OJ 1980 L39/73, [1980] 1 CMLR 694.

relevant to the application of articles 85 and 86 EEC. In the first place it makes express what is implicit in the use in article 2 of the concept of dominant position, which it has long been recognised cannot be identified except in respect of a particular market:[90] hence the need to consider the structure of all the markets concerned.[91] Further, it introduces, through the consideration of actual or potential competition, the notion of cross-elasticity of supply, or production substitutability,[92] into the identification of all potential competitors on a given market. The Commission's failure to take this element into account was criticised in the Court's ruling on dominant position in the *Continental Can* case.[93] Finally, it introduces a requirement of considering not only competition from within the Community but also competition from world markets. The Commission has been criticised in the past for failing to take such competition into account, and the need to do so was expressly laid down by the Court in *BAT & RJ Reynolds v Commission*.[94]

3.5.2.3 Market position and economic power

The next four factors are mainly concerned with the identification of a dominant position. The first, most obviously, is market position and economic power. These considerations are likely to be assessed by reference to both absolute and relative market share. Where the absolute market share is particularly high that may in itself be an indication of a dominant position; where there is a substantial market share which is not so high as to lead to the automatic presumption of a dominant position, it may be possible to demonstrate the existence of such a position on the market by considering the relative market share of competitors. Where an undertaking's share of the relevant market although not predominant is nevertheless considerably greater than that of competitors then there may well be a dominant position. Thus, even quite a low absolute market share may take on far greater significance if the firm is the only sizeable undertaking in the market.

This factor was taken into account by the Commission and the Court in the *United Brands* case.[95] The absolute market share lay somewhere between 40% and 45%, and was clearly not sufficient alone to justify a finding of dominant position. However, there was really only one other competitor of any size on the relevant market, which was itself several times smaller than United Brands. This fact, coupled with other elements, was held to indicate that there was a dominant position.

90 6 & 7/73 *Commercial Solvents v Commission* [1974] ECR 223, [1974] 1 CMLR 309.
91 See 1.1.2.1 for a general account.
92 Ibid.
93 6/72 [1973] ECR 215, [1973] CMLR 199.
94 142 & 156/84 [1988] 4 CMLR 24 at para 40.
95 27/76 [1978] ECR 207.

In all but extreme cases the competition authorities are unwilling to regard the fact of high market share alone, without regard to the conditions of competition and especially the market shares of other firms, as an indicator of dominance. This is because it is in the nature of markets to evolve, and for firms to respond to and drive that evolution, so that market share changes as new entrants join the market or existing competitors take the benefits of their relative efficiency. On the other hand, where the absolute market share has been held for a period of time without significant loss, there may be an indication that conditions are not attractive for new entrants. At that point it may be acceptable to base a finding of dominance on market share alone.

In *Hoffman-La Roche*[96] Advocate General Reischl suggested a formula for dealing with the issue of absolute market share which ranked market shares in descending order of size and proposed corresponding presumptions to be made in the case of each rank. Thus a market share of 90% or more would lead to an almost irrebuttable presumption of a dominant position. A market share of the order of 75% would be a strong indication of dominance, but would require some corroborative evidence before such a finding could be made. Below that figure, the lower the absolute market share the greater the evidence required of other factors contributing to the existence of a dominant position, until at a share of 50% or below the burden of proving dominant position would not be in any way displaced by the market share shown, and would have to be borne instead by showing a combination of factors, including relative market share, to demonstrate a dominant position. Such an approach may also commend itself to the Commission in merger cases, although it should be remembered that, at least where the threat to effective competition results from the creation of a dominant position, it will not be possible to take into account the length of time a significant market share has been held. As a general principle, the Court is likely to adopt a test of economic power based on the test it uses in respect of article 86 EEC.[97]

3.5.2.4 Access to supplies and markets

Where the allegedly dominant firm enjoys a high degree of vertical integration in the relevant market the Court may regard that as contributing to the existence of a dominant position.[98] The value of such integration is the control it gives over the means of distribution or supply, whether it is achieved by wholly owning a significant part of the relevant link in the chain or by operating a series of exclusive distribution or supply contracts. In the *United Brands* case,[99] the Court was of the opinion that the fact that United

---

[96] 85/76 [1979] ECR 461, [1979] 3 CMLR 211.
[97] *Michelin* [1983] ECR 3461; see 3.5.1 above.
[98] *United Brands* at [70] - [81]; *Hoffman-La Roche* at [48].
[99] [1978] ECR 207 at [72] - [77].

Brands grew most of the bananas it needed, and in addition had a network of independent suppliers operating to its own recommended standards, was a significant element in the establishment of a dominant position. The reasoning must be that a new entrant seeking to compete with United Brands on the identified market would have had to achieve a similar security of supply, and that to do so would raise the cost of competing effectively[100] to a point at which new entrants would be discouraged. Information directly relating to this issue is gathered in Form CO.[101]

3.5.2.5 Barriers to entry[102]

Access to supplies and markets as an indicator of dominant position is probably just a particular example of a series of factors which contribute to dominance known collectively as barriers to entry. In essence, the thesis is that new competition is less likely to arise if the cost of entry is particularly high.[103] No undertaking can be said to be in a dominant position unless it can be shown that if it does act independently of its competitors, customers and consumers there is no reasonably foreseeable possibility of competition from a source as yet not present in the market. In other words, an allegedly dominant position is no such thing where inefficient behaviour would provide the incentive for new entrants to the market to attempt to take away some of the market share. For this reason, where a substantial market share exists at the same time as significant barriers to entry of new firms, there is a considerably increased likelihood of there being a dominant position.

Barriers to entry may be either legal or economic. A legal barrier to entry would be the possession by the allegedly dominant firm of the necessary intellectual property rights for a particular process, or the enjoyment of an exclusive or near-exclusive governmental licence.[104] It is sometimes argued that the only economic barrier to entry is the minimum efficient scale necessary to operate competitively on the market in question.[105] Where the minimum efficient scale for the relevant product market is relatively high then an established firm with a substantial market share is likely to be in a dominant position because new entrants are likely to be dissuaded by the level of turnover which must be achieved in order to attain profitability and hence to be competitive. On the other hand, where the minimum efficient scale is low then firms with substantial market shares are unlikely to be dominant because any inefficiency (i.e. acting independently of competitors, customers or consumers) would be an invitation to new entrants to supplant them

---

[100] Sometimes called the 'minimum efficient scale'; see note 103 below.
[101] See parts 5(6), 6.5, 6.7, 6.8, 6.10.
[102] See Form CO, part 6.4.
[103] See Baden Fuller, *Article 86 EEC: Economic analysis of the existence of a dominant position* (1979) 4 ELRev 423; the notion of 'barriers to entry' is no more than an application of the principle of cross-elasticity of supply.
[104] E.g. *Tele-Marketing* 311/84 [1986] 2 CMLR 558.
[105] *Supra* note 103.

in the market. Many of the factors referred to by the Court as contributing to proof of dominant position in respect of article 86 EEC are no more than ingredients which drive up the minimum efficient scale. In some of the later cases under article 86 there is evidence that the Court acknowledges this argument, for there are specific references to the significance of barriers to entry in assessing dominant position.[106] It should be noted that the list below is far from exhaustive: it identifies factors which have been found to make life difficult to new entrants by increasing the minimum efficient scale, in the hope that it may provide a general principle which will assist in the identification of other such barriers to entry.

Access to technology. Where one company has easy access to all existing technology, and will have greater or more likely access to future technology, then this will contribute to the existence of a dominant position.[107] Access to technology contributes to a high cost of entry for new entrants to the market, although access to future technology is an obstacle which may be overcome if some position on the market can be established in the first place. It would still drive up the minimum efficient scale if competition on the particular market required investment in research and development for future technology.

Access to finance. Where an industry is capital intensive, access to finance may be an important contribution to the establishment of a dominant position.[108] It is not so much the fact that the allegedly dominant firm has access to capital which is important, but that access to finance is essential for new entrants. It may therefore act as a barrier to entry.

Advertising. The Court has held that if the allegedly dominant firm's market share is maintained by advertising and promotional techniques at a level which competitors would find difficult to match, then that is an indicator of dominant position.[109] If the market in question is responsive to advertising and promotional activities, then any new entrant would have to attempt to match the level of such activity carried out by the allegedly dominant firm in order to be able to penetrate the market and attract market share away from that firm. That would raise the cost of entry, and would presumably increase the minimum efficient scale since the cost of such activity would only be acceptable if spread over a relatively high turnover.

---

[106] 27/76 *United Brands* v *Commission* [1978] ECR 207 at [122]; 322/81 *Michelin* v *Commission* [1983] ECR 3461 at [55] - [60].
[107] See *Hoffman-La Roche* at [48]; *United Brands* at [82] - [84].
[108] *Continental Can* at [30]; *Hoffman-La Roche* per A-G Reischl .
[109] *United Brands* at [91] - [94].

3.5.2.6 Supply and demand trends

The Commission must also take into account supply and demand trends for the relevant goods and services. The intention here appears to be to ensure that in assessing the likely impact of a merger on effective competition in a particular market the Commission does not rely on a static analysis of the market in question, but rather assesses the merger in the light of the way in which the market may reasonably be predicted to develop. In the *Michelin* case,[110] the Court of Justice stressed that it is not sufficient to limit examination to the 'objective characteristics only of the relevant products' but that rather it was essential to consider 'competitive conditions and the structure of supply and demand in the market'. This element of the Regulation clearly reflects those considerations.

3.5.2.7 Interests of intermediate and ultimate consumers

There is no direct equivalent of this consideration in the competition rules of the Treaty of Rome, although in determining whether an exemption may be granted under article 85(3) the Commission must be satisfied that the agreement allows a fair share of the resulting benefit to consumers. In that context, because direct evidence of benefit to consumers is not easily obtained, the Commission has often to rely on a presumption that consumers will obtain a fair share of the benefit. It is willing to make that presumption provided there remains effective competition in the relevant market. In the context of merger control it may also be difficult to identify the interests of intermediate and ultimate consumers, except at a fairly general level. Thus, it is probably safe to predict that consumers are interested in fair prices, a reasonable choice of suppliers, efficient suppliers and security of supply. The priority between these concerns will change from market to market. In practice, these interests will most commonly best be met by ensuring effective competition on the market in question. If that is the case, then this consideration will rarely add anything to the general test of compatibility with the common market in article 2.

3.5.2.8 Development of technical and economic progress

The final factor to be taken into account looks a little out of place in the list. Amid criteria largely drawn from the Court's jurisprudence on article 86 EEC it is a refugee from the exemption criteria for article 85(3) EEC, which are not solely based on narrow grounds of protecting competition but rather have always been interpreted as allowing reference to criteria of economic and industrial policy. It does not fit with a view that only criteria relating to competition are to be applied in assessing compatibility with the common market. The development of technical and economic progress is not principally a criterion of competition, but of industrial or

---

[110] 322/81 [1983] ECR 3461.

economic policy. The difficulty of relating this factor to other factors in the list is enhanced by the proviso in article 2(1), which says that these elements may be taken into account 'provided that it is to consumers' advantage and does not form an obstacle to competition'. Even assuming that the latter means an 'appreciable obstacle to competition', it is not clear why this factor had to be included at all. The premise of article 2 is that a merger should be allowed to proceed unless it will result in a dominant position giving rise to a significant impediment to effective competition in the common market. Thus it will be allowed to proceed, even in the absence of positive benefits, provided there is no disadvantage in terms of effective competition. The only reason for considering positive benefits in an authorisation process is if they may outweigh disadvantages in some form of cost benefit analysis, as occurs under article 85(3) EEC. The wording of the proviso, and of the rest of article 2, appears to rule out an analysis of that kind. Technical or economic progress are not allowed to operate as an obstacle to competition: consequently, where a merger offers technical or economic progress that fact is to be welcomed, but if the proviso will be satisfied then the merger would have been compatible with the common market even without these elements. It remains to be seen whether the Commission will adhere to the logic of this position, or will, as some Member States wanted in the drafting of Regulation 4064/89, allow itself to enter into a cost benefit analysis when assessing compatibility with the common market in the case of mergers which may be slightly anti-competitive but which offer compensating technical or economic advantages.[111]

3.5.3 Ancillary restrictions

Under article 8(2), second sentence, of Regulation 4064/89 a declaration that a concentration is compatible with the common market applies also to restrictions which are directly related and necessary to the implementation of the concentration. The identification of ancillary restrictions which fall to be evaluated in this way is addressed in Chapter 2.[112] The Commission has issued a Notice containing guidelines to the evaluation of ancillary restrictions, which includes practical examples of common ancillary restrictions.[113]

---

[111] For an example of how such an analysis might work see the *GEC/Weir* joint venture discussed at 5.3–5.3.4 generally.

[112] See 2.1.7 – 2.1.7.4.

[113] Notice 90/C 203/05; OJ 1990 C203/5; see Appendix IV.

FOUR

Procedure

The procedure governing the control of concentrations by the Commission is laid down in part by Regulation 4064/89 and in part by Regulation 2367/90. It follows closely the procedure for articles 85 and 86 EEC laid down by Regulation 17 and Regulation 99/63,[1] and it may be anticipated that the general principles of procedural law established by the Court of Justice in respect of those provisions will also be held to apply in the case of concentrations.

4.1   INITIATING PROCEEDINGS

The majority of proceedings will be commenced by notification by the undertaking or undertakings concerned under article 4(1) of Regulation 4064/89. The Commission is given powers under article 23 to adopt implementing provisions setting out the form, content and other details of such notifications,[2] and those implementing provisions are to be found in articles 1-5 of Regulation 2367/90. It is also anticipated that some proceedings will be commenced in default of notification, and this is obviously essential to ensure appraisal of mergers where the undertakings concerned seek to avoid control under Regulation 4064/89 by failing to notify, and where the Commission wishes to question the assessment by the undertakings concerned that they need not notify because the merger does not have a Community dimension.

4.1.1   Notification

Notification to the Commission by the undertaking or undertakings involved is a crucial step in the clearance process for concentrations. The notification is intended to provide the Commission with the information it requires to make an assessment of the compatibility of the proposed merger with the

---

[1]   For an account of the procedure in relation to arts.85 & 86 EEC, see Kerse, *EEC Antitrust Procedure*.

[2]   See further 4.3.1.

common market. A 'complete' notification marks the start of the timetable for the clearance procedure, while for as long as the notification remains incomplete the timetable is not implemented. Consequently, it is very much in the interest of those seeking clearance to comply exactly with the notification requirements, to ensure that the process is not unnecessarily prolonged. Nevertheless, Form CO, which must be used to notify the proposed concentration, is complex and requires information to be provided about which firms may have no clear record. Planning for the completion of Form CO will necessarily be an important element in preparing for a takeover or merger.

4.1.1.1 Submission of notification[3]

Article 2(1) of Regulation 2367/90 requires that notifications be submitted in the manner prescribed by Form CO.[4] The Form consists of an introductory section, explaining how to go about notifying, followed by seven sections listing in considerable detail the information required. Article 3(1) of Regulation 2367/90 requires that the information be correct and complete; where the Commission takes the view that it is not complete 'in a material respect', it must inform the notifying party without delay, and set a time limit for the supply of complete information (article 4(2)). Parties must also inform the Commission of material changes in facts stated in the notification.[5] It is, however, open to the Commission to determine that missing, inaccurate or misleading information – although technically causing the notification to be incomplete by virtue of article 3(3) – is not in fact material to the proceedings, and in such a case article 4(3) of Regulation 2367/90 permits the Commission to dispense with the need to supply the information in question. The introduction to Form CO explains that the Commission will be willing to overlook the incompleteness of a notification where the notifying party gives good reasons for failing to supply the information required, and may accept a partial answer on the basis of such information as is available, again provided reasons are given. It must be assumed that in the case of hostile takeovers the would-be acquirer may not have access to full information about the target company, and the Commission will be willing to accept a more limited notification in that respect. As stated above (at 3.2.4) the Merger Task Force has shown itself willing to meet the parties concerned at an early stage and discuss informally with them the completeness of the Form and the exercise of the right to dispense with the provision of certain information. This important cooperation extends to the consideration in draft of Form CO before it is officially filed and in certain circumstances the use of an abridged Form CO.

---

[3] For details of the number of copies and permissible languages, see art.2.
[4] Form CO is set out in Annex I to Reg. 2367/90.
[5] Art.3(2) of Reg.2367/90.

In the case of mergers and joint acquisitions of control, article 4(2) of Regulation 4064/89 requires that notification be made jointly;[6] article 1(3) of Regulation 2367/90 requires that in such cases the notification be submitted by a joint representative authorised to transmit and receive documents on behalf of all parties concerned. Whenever a notification is submitted by a representative, either a joint representative or a representative of a single acquiring undertaking or person, it must be accompanied by written proof of the representative's authorisation to act.[7] Where a joint notifier is anxious that the provision of information may result in the disclosure of business secrets to which it is not intended that other joint notifiers should have access, such information may be submitted under separate cover.

4.1.1.2 Information to be provided
Form CO requests information under the following headings:

(a) party information;

(b) details of the concentration (nature of the transaction, economic sectors concerned, relevant turnover statistics etc.);

(c) ownership and control (details of all undertakings belonging to the same group, and details of acquisitions and mergers by the group in recent years);

(d) personal and financial links (details of significant minority holdings, i.e. those of 10% or more, in undertakings active on affected markets, and lists of directors and cross-directorships);

(e) information on affected markets (product markets, geographic markets, markets in which the concentration[8] will have a share of 10% or more);

(f) market conditions (barriers to entry, competitive environment, world market context);

(g) general (interests of intermediate and ultimate consumers, development of technical progress).

Full details of the information required in complying with Form CO may be obtained by consulting Appendix II; the above outline is intended to highlight the complexity and volume of information required. The complexity is heightened by the fact that some of the information is not capable of simple quantification or identification, especially that relating to product markets and market share. In such cases, all that a notifying party can do is submit an estimate which must be justified by accompanying reasons.

---

6 See 3.1.
7 Art. 4(2) of Reg. 2367/90.
8 The concentration may be horizontal (i.e. where parties are engaged in business activities in the same product market) or vertical (i.e. where parties are engaged in business activities in product markets upstream or downstream of one another).

The drafting of such justifications will be difficult and time-consuming, and may well require an input from economic as well as legal advisers.

4.1.1.3 Transmission and receipt of documents and effective date of notification

Article 10(1) of Regulation 4064/89 makes it clear that the timetable for clearance proceedings begins on the day following receipt by the Commission of a complete notification. Article 4(1) of Regulation 2367/90 provides that notification is effective on the day when it is received by the Commission, subject to the Commission's finding that the purported notification is incomplete, which would delay commencement of the timetable. In general, documents may be transmitted by delivery by hand, registered letter, fax and telex,[9] although notifications must either be delivered by hand or sent by registered letter.[10] In each case receipt is deemed to occur on the date of sending, since fax and telex are presumed to have been received by the addressee on the day of sending under article 16(3), and article 18(1) provides that it is sufficient to comply with the time period for notification if the notification was dispatched by registered letter before the expiry of that period.

4.1.2 Proceedings brought in default of notification

Despite the fact that Regulation 4064/89 is designed to operate on the basis of prior notification, and the fact that it will almost always be in the parties' own interests to notify in order to obtain prior clearance (or at least to be spared the need to undo the concentration which would result), there will inevitably be some concentrations within the scope of the Regulation which are not notified. Article 8(4) allows for the Commission to impose measures of divestiture where a concentration has already been implemented, and article 14(1)(a) enables the Commission to impose a fine for failure to notify a concentration. In some circumstances the Commission's own staff, by their monitoring of the specialist press and broadcast media, will become aware of mergers which have taken place and so will commence an investigation. In others the Commission's interest may have been stimulated by a complaint from a third party. In either case, in the absence of a formal Statement of Objections as is provided for in the case of article 85 or 86 EEC proceedings by Regulation 99/63, it will be essential for the Commission to communicate to the undertakings concerned the nature and detail of the allegations against them. Such communication will be required because article 18(3) of Regulation 4064/89 provides for the rights of defence to be fully respected in proceedings taken under it, and in particular for

---

[9]   Art.16(1)(2) of Regulation 2367/90.
[10] Arts.16(2) and 18(1).

all decisions to be based only on objections on which the parties have been able to submit their observations. In the case of Regulation 99/63, complainants[11] in respect of breaches of articles 85 and 86 EEC are granted specific rights to be informed if the Commission decides that there are insufficient grounds on which to commence proceedings. No such right exists under either Regulation 4064/89 or Regulation 2367/90.

In respect of the Treaty of Rome competition rules the Court of Justice has ruled that the Commission must investigate complaints.[12] This ruling is founded in part upon the express provision in Regulation 17 for complaint by 'natural or legal persons who claim a legitimate interest'.[13] Again, there is no such provision in Regulation 4064/89, and it remains to be seen whether complaints in respect of mergers will be as carefully considered as complaints have been in respect of articles 85 and 86 EEC. It should be remembered that the Court's important decision with regard to the application of article 85 to mergers in *BAT & RJ Reynolds* v *Commission*[14] resulted from the complainants' challenge to the Commission's decision not to prevent the merger in question.

4.1.3 Statement of objections

Under article 6(2) of Regulation 4064/89 the Commission must notify the undertakings concerned of its decision to commence proceedings against a concentration within the scope of the Regulation which raises serious doubts about its compatibility with the common market. In proceedings under articles 85 and 86 EEC it is an essential part of the right of defence of an undertaking that a Statement of Objections be communicated to it.[15] It might be expected that a similar procedural requirement be introduced in respect of the merger control process. Article 18(3) of Regulation 4064/89 states that the Commission may only base any decision it may make on objections on which the parties have been able to submit their observations, and article 12(2) of Regulation 2367/90 states that the Commission shall inform the parties concerned in writing of its objections, fixing a time-limit within which the parties may respond. This requirement is stipulated within the context of

---

[11] In respect of arts. 85 & 86 EEC, a complainant may be a Member State or a natural or legal person claiming a legitimate interest. Legitimate interest will clearly exist on the part of a party to a merger, and it will be legitimate for the target of a hostile takeover bid to attempt to organise legal resistance by complaint to the Commission. Legitimate interest will also be demonstrated by a party who has suffered or who is likely in the future to suffer loss as a result of an alleged infringement. In *BAT & RJ Reynolds* v *Commission* [1988] 4 CMLR 24, the appellants were complainants who feared that they would suffer from the anti-competitive effect of a proposed merger between two other firms.

[12] 210/81 *Demo-Studio Schmidt* v *Commission* [1983] ECR 3045, [1984] 1 CMLR 63; 298/83 *CICCE* v *Commission* [1985] ECR 1105, [1986] 1 CMLR 486.

[13] Regulation 17, art.3(2).

[14] [1988] 4 CMLR 24; see 1.1.3.4.

[15] Reg.99/63, art.2.

procedure relating to the making of an adverse finding under article 8, which assumes that communication of objections is a necessary concomitant of a decision under article 6(1)(c) of Regulation 4064/89 to initiate substantive proceedings.

4.2 COMMISSION INVESTIGATIONS

The Commission's powers to conduct merger control proceedings are supported by very important powers to establish the relevant facts by means of both requests for information and powers of investigation at an undertaking's place of business. Failure to cooperate with the Commission in the exercise of these powers may incur a penalty. Any information so obtained is entitled to a degree of confidentiality, and certain information qualifies for legal professional privilege. The Commission's fact-finding powers under Regulation 4064/89 closely follow the rules governing such powers in respect of article 85 and 86 EEC proceedings. Although there may be some grounds for differentiation arising out of the functional differences between those provisions and the merger Regulation, it is most likely that the Court of Justice will regard its jurisprudence in respect of those powers as providing a foundation for the interpretation of the corresponding provisions in the new Regulation. These powers in relation to Commission fact-finding are supplemented by a power to request the competent authorities of Member States to conduct investigations on the Commission's behalf.[16] This power has rarely been exercised under Regulation 17,[17] and it remains to be seen whether it will be any more significant under the new merger Regulation.

4.2.1 Requests for information

Under article 11(1) of Regulation 4064/89, the Commission is empowered to obtain necessary information from the governments and competent authorities of Member States and from undertakings. An equivalent power exists under article 11(1) of Regulation 17.

Information gathering by the Commission is carried out in close liaison with the authorities in the Member States. In the UK, the designated competent authority is the Secretary of State,[18] although in practice these functions are carried out by the Office of Fair Trading. Article 11 creates a two-tier process: the first stage is a simple request inviting voluntary compliance; in default of compliance the Commission may take a formal decision under article 11(5) requiring the supply of information. Further

---

[16] Regulation 4064/89, art.12; Regulation 17, art.13.
[17] Goyder at pp. 428-9.
[18] There is apparently no formal legislative designation of a competent authority in the UK: see Kerse at 5.04.

default may make the undertaking liable to a penalty under article 14 of Regulation 4064/89.

The process is commenced by the Commission addressing a request for information in writing to the undertaking concerned, and sending a copy of the request to the competent authority in the Member State where the undertaking has its seat.[19] An undertaking requested to supply information in this way may be the subject of a merger clearance proceeding, or may be a third party from which the Commission seeks background information. The request must state its legal basis, the purpose of the request and the penalties for supplying incorrect information.[20] By requiring the Commission to state the purpose of its request it is thought that the Regulations prevent the Commission from making speculative requests ('fishing expeditions') without having a reasonable ground upon which to require the supply of information. Nevertheless, the obligation to supply necessary information[21] is only vaguely defined, and the Commission need not specify precisely what it expects, and indeed appears to expect undertakings to supply all information relevant to its stated purpose. On the other hand, the Commission must draft its request with some care, since a decision under article 11(5) can only be made in terms corresponding to the original request with which the undertaking failed to comply. The request for information must also state a time limit for response, since article 11(5) only permits a decision to be taken where the undertaking fails to comply 'within the time limit fixed by the Commission'. Most firms choose the route of voluntary compliance, although it is important to steer a careful path between an insufficient disclosure (and the risk of sanctions) and the disclosure of too much information (especially given the access which competitors may have to the information[22]).

Failure to comply with the request for information will result in a decision requiring the information to be supplied. A copy of the decision must be sent to the competent authority in the relevant Member State,[23] and the decision must specify both the information required and a further time limit for compliance. Thereafter the Commission may take a second decision imposing a penalty for non-compliance and periodic penalty payments to enforce compliance.[24]

4.2.2 Powers of investigation

By article 13 of Regulation 4064/89 the Commission is empowered to carry out necessary investigations into undertakings, by which the Regulation means

[19] Regulation 4064/89, art.11(2).
[20] Regulation 4064/89, art.11(3).
[21] Regulation 4064/89, art.11(1).
[22] Subject to the confidentiality doctrine: see 4.2.4.
[23] Regulation 4064/89, art.11(6).
[24] Regulation 4064/89, art.14(1)(c) and art.15(1)(a).

a power to visit the undertaking's place of business in order to pursue its enquiries. An equivalent power exists for articles 85 and 86 EEC under article 14 of Regulation 17. There are some minor amendments from the earlier Regulation intended either to formalise what has in fact become practice or to increase procedural safeguards. So, in paragraph 1(b) the Commission's power to take copies of extracts from books or business records, which in the absence of cooperation from the officers of the undertaking being investigated used to result in Commission officials having to take written notes, is augmented by a power to demand copies. In paragraphs (2) and (4) the obligation to inform the competent authorities of Member States is strengthened by the addition of the requirement that such information be communicated in writing. In paragraph (4) such information must now be provided 'in good time', and the obligation to consult the Member State in question becomes the more finite requirement that it be given the opportunity to be heard.

Perhaps most surprising is that article 13 does not make provision for the powers of investigation to extend to persons who already control at least one undertaking[25] in the way that article 11 does. The reasons for this omission are not clear. It may be thought that investigation of the undertaking controlled will be sufficient, in that any documents relating to the control of that undertaking which may be in the possession of such a person may in any case be required to be produced. Certainly, it seems generally to be accepted that there is no ancillary power attached to the powers of investigation to enter the private homes of directors to seek papers which it is suspected may be kept there.[26]

4.2.2.1 The powers conferred

The purpose of such investigations has been described by the Court of Justice as being to establish the actual existence and scope of a given factual situation.[27] This statement, coupled with the reference to necessary investigations[28] must be taken to exclude speculative investigations without any reasonable ground to believe that relevant evidence will be found. The precise powers conferred are as follows:

(a) to examine the books and other business records;
(b) to take copies of or extracts from the books and business records;
(c) to ask for oral explanations on the spot;
(d) to enter any premises, land or means of transport of undertakings.[29]

---

[25] Cf. art.3(1)(b).
[26] Cf. Kerse at 107.
[27] 136/79 *National Panasonic* v *Commission* [1980] ECR 2033, 2058.
[28] Regulation 17, art.14(1); Regulation 4064/89, art.13(1).
[29] Regulation 17, art.14(1); in Regulation 4064/89 art.13(1) the powers are identical but for a power to 'demand' copies or extracts.

These powers do not include a power of forced entry, although in some circumstances refusal to cooperate will result in a periodic penalty to enforce compliance.[30] It is a matter of some uncertainty whether the power to ask for oral explanations is restricted to matters arising out of the examination of books and records, or whether the power is not so restricted. In *National Panasonic v Commission*[31] A-G Warner suggested that only the more restricted power exists, but the Court appears to have been more circumspect in limiting the power of the Commission to ask for explanations at large. In either case, it is clear that undertakings must exercise great care when asked for oral explanations on the spot: for the sake of consistency, ease of maintaining a record and simple caution it is advisable to restrict the giving of oral explanations to as few employees as possible and even to channel all such explanations through a single person. Where possible it is advisable to arrange for the undertaking's independent legal adviser to be present.

Investigations may take place under either authorisation[32] or formal decision.[33] It is not a two-tier process, in that the Commission may choose to proceed by way of decision from the beginning, without going through the authorisation process. Where proceeding by decision it is not necessary to allow the undertaking the prior right to be heard. This is essential if surprise, which is sometimes a necessary attribute of such investigations, is to be maintained. The Commission is likely to proceed by way of decision if it believes that it may encounter difficulties in carrying out the essentially voluntary form of investigation under authorisation. In recent years, in the context of articles 85 and 86 EEC, the Commission has made much greater use of the decision procedure, although in fact few firms refuse to comply with investigations under authorisation, not least because of the danger of any adverse inference which may be drawn from such refusal. In either case officials of the competent authority of the Member State[34] may be in attendance to assist the Commission's officials.[35] Although surprise investigations[36] have always caught the headlines, in practice the majority of investigations are preceded by telephone notice to the undertaking concerned.

4.2.2.2 Investigation under authorisation

Where the investigation is to be carried out under authorisation the requisite authority (the mandate) must indicate the subject-matter and purpose of

---

[30] Regulation 17, arts.14(3) and 16(1)(d); Regulation 4064/89 arts.13(3) and 15(1)(b).
[31] Supra note 27.
[32] Regulation 4064/89, art.13(2).
[33] Regulation 4064/89, art.13(3).
[34] In the UK, in practice, officials of the Office of Fair Trading.
[35] Regulation 4064/89, art.13(5).
[36] So-called 'dawn-raids' although they take place during ordinary business hours in order to be sure to gain access to key personnel.

the investigation.[37] The competent authority in the relevant Member State must be informed of the proposed investigation in good time beforehand. Investigation of this kind is voluntary, and the undertaking is entitled to refuse to cooperate. However, such a refusal would be very likely to be answered by a compulsory investigation under decision. The amount of time won by a refusal might be very little, since such a decision can be taken almost overnight. The mandate must also indicate the penalties for failure to produce books or records in complete form. It goes without saying that it is not permissible to respond to a proposed investigation by voluntary but selective cooperation.

4.2.2.3   Investigation under decision

Where the investigation is to take place under decision the Commission official must present a copy of the decision stating the subject-matter, purpose, and starting date of the investigation. It must also state the penalties for failure to comply, and that the decision is subject to review by the Court of Justice.[38] The value of such review should not be exaggerated, however, since it is unlikely that it could occur before the investigation would take place, nor is it likely that an interim measure suspending the investigation would be available. A decision may only be taken after prior consultation with the competent authority of the relevant Member State, which requires that the competent authority be informed in writing and in good time, and that it be heard.[39] Where an undertaking refuses to comply with the decision ordering an investigation, the Member State concerned is required to assist the Commission's officials to make their investigation.[40] In the UK, the anticipated procedure, as required by Regulation 17, is for an *ex parte* injunction to be obtained by the Treasury Solicitor requiring the undertaking to submit to the investigation.

4.2.2.4   Rights of undertakings subject to investigation

An undertaking subject to an investigation enjoys a number of rights in respect thereof. It is entitled to have its lawyer present, although the summoning of a lawyer will not be allowed to delay the investigation unduly, especially if there is a danger that evidence will be destroyed in the meantime.[41] It is entitled to receive a copy of the inspector's minute, recording any on-the-spot oral explanations, and to have a signed inventory of any copies

---

[37]   Regulation 4064/89, art.13(2).
[38]   Regulation 4064/89, art.13(3).
[39]   Regulation 4064/89, art.13(4).
[40]   Regulation 4064/89, art.13(6) - measures are to be adopted by Member States in this regard by September 1991.
[41]   *National Panasonic v Commission*, supra note 27.

or exhibits taken.[42] In the *Hoechst* case[43] the Court, in upholding the right of Commission officials to gain access to premises to conduct an investigation, said that the Commission must respect the procedural guarantees provided for the purpose of access to undertakings' premises under national law. This decision was expressly linked to the existence of fundamental rights which are an integral part of the general principles of Community law, including those deriving from the European Convention of Human Rights. In practice there is a difficult balance to be drawn between the rights of those subject to investigation and the need for the Commission to be able to conduct an effective investigation in the course of anti-trust proceedings.

4.2.3 Penalties for non-compliance

Article 14(1) of Regulation 4064/89 provides for the imposition of fines[44] of between ECU 1,000 and 50,000 in the event of the following instances of non-compliance:

(a) supply of incorrect or misleading information in a notification pursuant to article 4 of Regulation 4064/89;

(b) supply of incorrect[45] information in response to a request under article 11;

(c) failure to supply information within the time limit laid down by a decision requiring it under article 11(5);

(d) production of books or other business records in incomplete form during an investigation under article 14;

(e) refusal to submit to an investigation ordered by decision made under article 14(3).

Under article 15(1) of Regulation 4064/89 the Commission is empowered to impose[46] periodic penalty payments of up to ECU 25,000 per day, calculated from the date set by the decision imposing such penalties, in order to compel compliance in the following circumstances:

(a) failure to supply complete and correct information in response to a decision requiring such supply taken under article 11;

(b) failure to submit to an investigation ordered by decision taken under article 13.

---

[42] As provided in the explanatory note to an authorisation or decision, provided by Commission officials to an undertaking upon arrival for an investigation.

[43] 46/87 and 227/88 *Hoechst AG* v *Commission* Decision of 21 September 1989.

[44] Subject to the Advisory Committee procedure under art.19(3)-(7).

[45] Information is likely to be 'incorrect' if it is false or so incomplete as to be misleading: cf. *Telos* OJ 1982 L58/19, [1982] 1 CMLR 267.

[46] Subject to the Advisory Committee procedure under art.19(3)-(7).

In the case of both article 14 and article 15, fines and penalties must be imposed by decision, and the undertaking must be allowed the opportunity to be heard in advance of the decision being taken.[47] It should be noted that in the case of both fines and periodic penalties the maximum amounts set by the Regulation are significantly higher than those set by Regulation 17.[48]

4.2.4 Confidentiality and legal professional privilege

The provisions of Regulation 4064/89 relating to publication of decisions[49] and to professional secrecy[50] do not differ materially from the equivalent provisions of Regulation 17.[51] It seems most likely that the associated case law of the Court of Justice, and the judicially created doctrine of legal professional privilege, will apply equally to merger control proceedings.

Information obtained by the Commission may only be used for the purpose for which the request or investigation was made,[52] and the Commission is required to maintain confidentiality in respect of information covered by the obligation of professional secrecy, especially business secrets.[53] The obligation of professional secrecy, although never properly defined, is clearly wider in scope than business secrets alone, which are entitled to a greater degree of protection than other elements of professional secrecy. So, the general obligation of professional secrecy is made expressly subject to the parties' right to a hearing[54] and the obligation to publish Commission decisions.[55] However, the provisions relating to hearings and publication are themselves subject to 'the legitimate interest of undertakings in the protection of their business secrets'.[56] It would seem, therefore, that other aspects of confidentiality (those falling within the more general and less sensitive ambit of professional secrecy) may have a lower priority than have business secrets.

---

[47] Regulation 4064/89, art.18(1).
[48] Under Regulation 17, fines were set at between ECU 100 and 5,000, and periodic penalties at between ECU 100 and 1,000.
[49] Art.20.
[50] Art.17.
[51] Arts. 21 and 20, respectively.
[52] Regulation 4064/89, art.17(1).
[53] Regulation 4064/89, art.17(2); see also 53/85 AKZO v Commission [1986] ECR 1965, [1987] 1 CMLR 231.
[54] Regulation 4064/89, art.18.
[55] Regulation 4064/89, art.20.
[56] Regulation 4064/89, arts.18(3) and 20(2). In fact, as far as hearings are concerned, the limit on the disclosure of business secrets applies only to the publication of invitations to comment on a proposed negative clearance; but, all disclosure of business secrets is clearly forbidden by the Court's decision in AKZO (supra note 53).

The potential conflict between the confidentiality principle, especially in respect of business secrets, and the undertaking's right to a fair hearing,[57] has in large measure been resolved by the Court's ruling that information which cannot be disclosed to a defendant company cannot be relied upon in proceedings.[58] The Commission's obligation to maintain confidentiality, if breached, may give rise to a liability on its part towards the injured party under article 215 of the Treaty.[59] In practice, an undertaking should take careful steps to assist the Commission in maintaining confidentiality, by clearly marking all documents which do contain sensitive material, and preferably by presenting all such material in a separate file. If some disclosure will be necessary, it may be worth preparing, for the Commission's use, a précis to accompany relevant documents which discloses necessary information but omits that which is sensitive. In so doing, an undertaking may find it helpful to distinguish between the highly sensitive category of business secrets (which the Commission cannot disclose without informing the undertaking[60]) and the more general and less sensitive category of professional secrets, in respect of which the Commission would appear to enjoy an element of discretion as to disclosure, being in effect obliged to perform a balancing exercise between a party's entitlement to confidentiality and the Commission's obligations as to publication and the interests of other parties.

Although neither Regulation 4064/89, nor Regulation 17 before it, makes any provision for legal professional privilege, the Court has laid down such a doctrine in *AM&S v Commission*.[61] As a consequence, documents passing between an undertaking and its independent lawyer[62] need not be disclosed to the Commission in the course of an investigation or a request for information, provided such documents relate to a procedure commenced by the Commission against the undertaking. Documents will clearly relate to such a procedure if they concern the client's rights of defence and were drawn up after the initiation of proceedings; they may also qualify even if written before proceedings were commenced if they anticipate such a possibility and advise accordingly. For example, a document would be entitled to legal professional privilege if it had been drafted to advise on the

---

[57] The problem is acute in the light of the access to the Commission's file allowed to undertakings. This practice, which is provided for expressly by art.18(3) of Regulation 4064/89, is not actually required by Regulation 17. In practice, however, the Commission has allowed undertakings fairly full access (save for business secrets, internal memoranda, and information which it agrees to keep confidential) to its own file, in order to allow the undertaking to know what case it has to answer.

[58] 85/76 *Hoffman-La Roche v Commission* [1979] ECR 461, [1979] 3 CMLR 211 at para 14.

[59] Cf. 145/83 *Adams v Commission* [1985] ECR 3539, [1986] 1 CMLR 506.

[60] 53/85 *AKZO v Commission* [1987] 1 CMLR 231; the Commission must, after adopting a decision to disclose such information, allow time for the decision to be reviewed by the Court of Justice: see para 29.

[61] 155/79 [1982] ECR 1575, [1982] 2 CMLR 264.

[62] Who must be qualified to practise in one of the Member States.

compatibility of a particular practice with Community competition law.[63]
It should be noted that this doctrine of legal professional privilege does
not apply to communications with an undertaking's in-house lawyers.

4.3   JURISDICTION

The Commission's jurisdiction under Regulation 4064/89 is established on
the basis of Community dimension, without reference to the territorial seat
of the undertakings concerned.[64] As a consequence, a merger which does
not principally concern European undertakings or markets may nevertheless
fall within the scope of the Regulation. So, for example, an acquisition by
a US-based multinational of another firm based outside the Community
might fall within the scope of the Regulation if both carry out significant
levels of business on European markets. As such, the acquisition would need
to be notified, and failure to comply either with this requirement or with
any final decision would make the undertakings liable to fines. In the recent
Wood Pulp case[65] the Court of Justice upheld the Commission's jurisdiction
in respect of articles 85 and 86 EEC over undertakings established outside
the Community but implementing their agreement with effect within it.
It seems likely that a similar decision would be reached in respect of the
exercise of jurisdiction over third country undertakings under the express
provisions of article 1 of Regulation 4064/89. As a result, such companies
might well find that they were subject to merger control by more than one
authority, despite the supposed one-stop shopping principle of the new
Regulation, because merger law in other parts of the world would apply
to them. This potential conflict of jurisdictions led Sir Leon Brittan, Vice-
President of the Commission and Competition Commissioner, to call for
a treaty on merger jurisdiction between the United States and the European
Community.[66]

4.4   TIME-LIMITS

The Commission's powers under the new Regulation must be exercised within
very strict time-limits, and failure to comply with these will result in the
proposed merger being deemed to be declared compatible with the common
market.[67] On the other hand, the Commission has some control over the
timetable by virtue of the provision in article 10(1) to the effect that the

---

[63]   As was the case in *AM&S* v *Commission*, the document having been written some 6 years
       before the proceedings in question.
[64]   Art.1: see further 2.2 *et seq*.
[65]   89/85 etc *Ahlstrom Osakeyhtio and others* v *Commission* [1988] 4 CMLR 901.
[66]   Speech to EC Chamber of Commerce in New York, 26 March 1990: [1990] 4 CMLR
       324.
[67]   Art.10(6); see 3.5.1.6.

period for preliminary evaluation of the notified transaction under article 6 shall not begin until the Commission has received complete information. Since nearly every aspect of the timetable is dependent upon the preliminary evaluation, the Commission - which is sole judge of whether information is complete or not - is able to determine the point at which the clock starts to run. Form CO requests highly detailed answers to a large number of complex questions[68] and firms are likely to find it a very demanding task to supply the complete information required, and so start the clock. Against this possibility, representatives of the Commission's Merger Task Force have indicated informally[69] that the Commission will regard the outright rejection of a notification upon the ground that it is incomplete as a very serious matter, and as a measure only to be taken in exceptional circumstances. As an added insurance against rejection, it has been suggested (again informally) by members of the Merger Task Force that notifying parties might submit their notifications in draft form in order to obtain advance notice of problem areas. Clearly, only time will indicate how the Commission's apparent control of the procedural timetable will evolve in practice. The above informal observations lend support, for the moment, to the view that they will exercise potentially far-reaching powers with some caution and restraint.

Once the timetable is running, the seemingly strict regime may be delayed by a number of exceptions provided for under Regulation 4064/89. Under article 10(4), the period of four months for the taking of a decision against a concentration (set by article 10(3)) may be suspended if the Commission has to act by decision to obtain information or to order an investigation. This exception applies only where the need for such a decision is due to 'circumstances for which one of the undertakings involved in the concentration is responsible'.[70] Such suspensions of the timetable are likely to prove rare. Experience under articles 85 and 86 EEC is that the Commission has not had to resort to decisions to carry out necessary fact-finding very often, and in the case of mergers and acquisitions most firms will recognise that it is in their interest to assist the Commission in order to be able to obtain a final decision in the shortest possible time.

A further exception to the strict timetable exists under article 8(5) and (6), which is the provision allowing the Commission to revoke a clearance given under article 8(2) where there has been a supply of incorrect information, deceit or breach of an obligation. In such circumstances, the revocation and accompanying decision made under article 8(3) declaring the concentration incompatible with the common market may be made outside

---

[68] See 4.1.1.2.
[69] DTI Seminar on EC Merger Control, September 1990.
[70] Art.10(4).

the time-limit of four months set by article 10(3). Here again, such exceptions are likely to be rare.

The relevant time-limits, which have already been considered in the context of the powers to which they relate are summarised in the Table opposite.

Table of Commission Powers and Time-Limits

	Commission power	Time-limit
1	Preliminary examination of the notification leading to clearance on grounds of not being within the scope of the Regulation or because there is no serious doubt as to compatibility with the common market: article 6(1)(a) & (b)	One month beginning on the day following receipt of notification, or receipt of complete information (if later): article 10(1).
2	Preliminary evaluation leading to initiation of proceedings and communication of statement of objections: article 6(1)(c)	One month beginning on the day following receipt of notification, or receipt of complete information (if later): article 10(1).
3	Preliminary examination where a Member State has requested referral: article 9(2) & (3)	Six weeks: article 10(1).
4	Period of automatic suspension of the concentration	Any time before notification, or receipt of complete information (if later), and for three weeks thereafter: article 7(1).
5	Commission decision to adopt interim measures continuing the suspension of the concentration: article 7(2)	Within a period of three weeks beginning on the day following receipt of notification, or receipt of complete information (if later). The period coincides with the period of automatic suspension after notification referred to in point 4 above and stipulated by article 7(1): article 7(2).

Commission power

6   Issue of statement of objections prior to Commission decision to:

–continue suspension of a concentration: article 7(2)
–permit derogation from article 7(1)–(3): article 7(4)
–declare a concentration compatible with the common market (including the imposition of conditions and obligations): article 8(2)
–declare a concentration incompatible with the common market: article 8(3)
–order divestiture in the case of a concentration which has already been implemented: article 8(4)
–revoke a prior decision declaring a concentration compatible with the common market: article 8(5)
–impose a fine: article 14
–impose a periodic penalty payment: article 15

Time-limit

Communication of a statement of objections must be accompanied by a time-limit fixed by the Commission within which a party may inform the Commission of its views: Regulation 2367/90 article 12(2).

In fixing the time-limit the Commission must have regard to the time taken in preparing statements and to the urgency of the case: Regulation 2367/90 article 17(1).

This 'response time' is a constituent element of the general principle of Community law of the right to a fair hearing, recognised in 85/76 *Hoffman-La Roche AG* v *Commission* and re-affirmed in 100–103/80 *Musique Diffusion Française (Pioneer)*.

The appropriateness of the time-limit set is one ingredient in the discretion - ultimately to be exercised by the Court of Justice - in determining what is 'fair'. It should be noted that in respect of articles 85 and 86 EEC Regulation 99/63 set a minimum time-limit of two weeks (and in practice longer is normally allowed), while no such minimum is set in respect of Regulation 4064/89. The commercial need for speedy decisions in merger and acquisition cases should mean that the time-limits set are short.

	Commission power	Time-limit
7	Final decision declaring the merger compatible with the common market: articles 2(2) and 8(2)	Consequently, statements of objections must be communicated no later than is necessary to allow a fair hearing prior to the time when the decision is finally made.
8	Final decision declaring the merger incompatible with the common market: articles 2(3) and 8(3)	As soon as serious doubts have been removed, and not later than four months from the date on which the proceeding was initiated: article 10(2). Not later than four months from the date on which the proceeding was initiated: article 10(3).
9	Final decision where Commission has had to request information or make an investigation for reasons for which an undertaking is responsible	Article 10(2) and (3) time-limit suspended to allow these procedures to be completed: article 10(4).
10	Decision to refer the matter to the competent authority of a Member State because competition is threatened on a distinct market therein	Either within 6 weeks of receipt of notification (article 9(4)(a)) or within 3 months of notification if the Commission has initiated article 6(1)(c) proceedings but not taken preparatory steps to making an order under article 8: article 9(4)(b).

Where the Court of Justice annuls the whole or part of a decision of the Commission in respect of fines or periodic penalties in the exercise of its powers under article 16 of the Regulation, the time-limits for decisions laid down by article 10 are revived, and run from the date of the Court's judgment.[71] Under article 23 the Commission has the power to adopt implementing provisions concerning time-limits pursuant to article 10. These ancillary provisions are contained in Regulation 2367/90.[72] They govern the beginning of time-limits (article 6), the end of time-limits (article 7), the definition and effect of 'working days' (articles 6(3) and 7(4)) and public holidays (articles 8 and 19), and the suspension of time-limits pending request for information or investigation under Commission decision (article 9). These provisions contain essential technical rules, but are self-explanatory and require no detailed comment here.

Strict adherence to the time-limits under Regulation 4064/89 would contribute to reducing the potential for conflict between the Regulation and the UK City Code on Takeovers and Mergers. It has been feared that the Commission's frequently lengthy procedures in competition cases would prove incompatible with the strict limits under the Takeover Code. Under the Code 'Except with the consent of the Panel, an offer . . . may not become or be declared unconditional as to acceptances after midnight on the 60th day' after posting.[73] Since, according to the strict timetable, the Commission must ordinarily have determined within 5 weeks of the announcement of the offer whether or not to carry out a full appraisal or to refer the merger to the competent authority of a Member State,[74] it ought to be possible to know within the Code's timetable whether any investigation under Community law is to take place..[75] In theory, there is a risk that the potential for delay in the timetable because the notification was incomplete will cause the actual time, before it is known whether proceedings are to be initiated under Community law, to exceed the period permitted under the City Code. The amendments to the City Code effected as a result of the inception of the merger Regulation seek to take account of this point by permitting the Panel to use its discretion in allowing an amendment to the offer timetable

[71] Art.10(5).
[72] Cf. art. 11 of Regulation 99/63 in respect of arts. 85 and 86 EEC.
[73] Rule 31.6(a).
[74] I.e. notification must take place not later than one week from the announcement (which in practice will coincide with posting of offers: see 3.1.1) of a public bid (art.4(1)), and the Commission's preliminary examination must be completed within one month of notification (art.10(1)), or at most six weeks if a Member State issues a request under article 9 (art.10(1), 2nd para): the maximum possible total is 7 weeks. These limits may be extended only if the undertaking(s) responsible for notification fail to supply complete information.
[75] Where there is to be such an investigation the participating undertakings should have provided for the offer to lapse pending approval: see further 8.2 et seq.

where there is a significant delay in, *inter alia*, the initiation of Commission proceedings.[76]

4.5 DUE PROCESS

Although Commission proceedings are administrative rather than an adversarial trial,[77] so that the Commission is both prosecutor and decision-maker, an undertaking subject to investigation is entitled to certain rights of defence. For example, the Commission must not go into proceedings with a closed mind.[78] These rights effectively divide into two important categories: the right to know the case to be answered and the right to be heard.

4.5.1 The right to a hearing[79]

Where the Commission proposes to make a decision involving a suspension of a concentration (article 7(2) & (4)), a clearance subject to the imposition of conditions and obligations (article 8(2)), an adverse finding against a concentration (article 8(3)-(5)), a fine (article 14) or a periodic penalty (article 15), article 18 of Regulation 4064/89 requires it to allow the person or undertaking concerned the opportunity of being heard on the matters to which the Commission has taken objection.[80] The 'matters to which the Commission has taken objection' are those raised in the Statement of Objections.[81] This mandatory right to a hearing in respect of the Commission's stated objections applies only to the right to submit written replies to, or observations on, the Commission's objections. Such replies may consist of factual information, the undertaking's own interpretation of admitted facts, or legal or economic arguments.

4.5.1.1 Who may be heard
The 'person or undertaking concerned' is any person or undertaking in respect of which the Commission proposes to take its decision, and thus to which it would be addressed. Article 18(1) provides for the fact that the Regulation addresses individuals as well as undertakings[82] by including persons within the ambit of the 'right to be heard'.[83] Moreover, it makes clear that the

---

[76] See amended Note 4 on Rule 31.6 of the City Code as introduced on 21 September 1990 by the Takeover Panel (1990/18).
[77] 56 & 58/64 *Consten & Grundig* v *Commission* [1966] ECR 299, [1966] CMLR 418.
[78] 86/82 *Hasselblad* v *Commission* [1984] ECR 883 per A-G Slynn at 914.
[79] Note: the notion of 'hearing' includes both oral and, more importantly, written proceedings.
[80] Regulation 4064/89, art.18 .
[81] See below: 4.5.2.
[82] Cf. art.3(1)(b).
[83] In fact, the right to make one's views known; cf. Reg.17, art.19(1).

right to be heard applies to every stage of the procedure up to the consultation of the Advisory Committee.

Third parties not subject to investigation in the proceedings may also be heard. Under article 18(4) of Regulation 4064/89, entitlement is subject to the discretion of the Commission unless the party can show a legitimate interest, when there is a right to be heard. Article 18(4) identifies members of the administrative or management organs of the undertakings concerned, and recognises workers' representatives, as having such a legitimate interest. This provision is consistent with developments under Community law anticipated by the Social Charter, but such recognition of Community social policy may mean that there will be some inconsistency with the supposed single-minded focus of the Regulation on competition-based criteria. It is likely that a complainant would also be considered to have a legitimate interest and thus the right to be heard.[84]

4.5.1.2 Nature of the hearing
Article 18(1) makes clear what has always in fact been the case that the so-called right to a hearing is in practice the right to make one's views known *in writing* to the Commission. Regulation 4064/89, like Regulation 17, contains no provision for oral hearings. In the case of the main Treaty of Rome competition rules, oral hearings are provided for under Regulation 99/63.[85] Under article 23 of Regulation 4064/89 the Commission has the power to adopt implementing provisions concerning hearings pursuant to article 18, and these rules may now be found in Commission Regulation 2367/90.

Under article 13 of Regulation 2367/90, an oral hearing must be granted if requested by a party upon which the Commission proposes to impose a fine or a periodic penalty, or which demonstrates a sufficient interest.[86] The drafting of this provision is a little surprising, since it appears to imply that the addressee of a decision is only entitled as of right to an oral hearing in certain circumstances: in the light of experience in relation to articles 85 and 86 EEC under Regulation 99/63 it seems inconceivable that such an undertaking would be considered not to have a sufficient interest.

Third parties may also be permitted to attend and be heard at an oral hearing under article 15(2) of Regulation 2367/90, although even where they can bring themselves within the qualification of demonstrating sufficient interest there does not appear to be a mandatory right to it.[87] The right to an oral hearing upon showing sufficient interest is restricted to 'parties

---

[84]   See 1.1.3.4; *BAT & RJ Reynolds* v *Commission* [1988] 4 CMLR 24.
[85]   Art.7.
[86]   Regulation 99/63, art.7(1).
[87]   Contrast Reg.99/63, art.7(1).

concerned'.[88] Consequently, third parties may only be permitted an oral hearing at the discretion of the Commission.

The oral hearing is the responsibility of the Hearings Officer, who is independent of other DG IV officials. In the case of article 85 and 86 EEC proceedings, his terms of reference have been published,[89] and these are likely to remain the same for proceedings in respect of concentrations. He summons parties to be heard on an appointed day,[90] presides at the hearing, supervises the preparation of a record of the hearing, and is responsible for protecting the interests of undertakings subject to investigation. Hearings are held in private,[91] and parties may be summoned to appear alone or in the presence of others who are to be heard. The decision in this regard is likely to depend upon whether business secrets may be revealed at the hearing, since otherwise the Commission adheres to the principle of hearing all parties at the same time.[92] Undertakings appearing at an oral hearing must be represented by an authorised agent from among their permanent staff, but may be assisted by a lawyer.[93] Persons other than undertakings may either appear in person or be represented by a legal representative. In addition to making a presentation at the hearing, the undertaking may be asked questions by Commission officials, officials from the competent authorities of Member States who may be present and by the Hearings Officer. The undertaking may also be invited to make a closing statement.

4.5.1.3 Derogation from the right to a hearing

Article 18(2) provides a temporary derogation from the right to a hearing in the case of Commission decisions under article 7(2) or (4), which provides for the continuation of suspensions of mergers and for exemptions from such suspensions. Decisions under both these rules may have to be made very quickly if the purpose behind the decision, which will be to protect the interests of one of the parties or the competitive structure from irreparable harm pending the Commission's decision, is not to be frustrated by the delay in making it. Where the Commission takes such a decision without allowing persons or undertakings concerned an opportunity to make their views known beforehand, it must give them that opportunity as soon as possible after taking the decision. Until such time as that opportunity has been granted the decision must be regarded as provisional, although that does not seem to detract in any way from its effectiveness.

---

88 Art.13(1).
89 Thirteenth report on Competition Policy (1984) pp. 273–4.
90 Regulation 2367/90, art.13(2).
91 Ibid, art.14(4).
92 Ibid.
93 Ibid, art.14(2) and (3).

4.5.2 Natural justice

Article 18(3) introduces the requirement that the Commission must only base its decisions on objections on which the parties have been able to submit their observations. The right to know the case to be answered is met under Regulation 4064/89 by the Statement of Objections, which is the Commission's notification to the undertakings concerned under article 6(2) that after preliminary examination the merger falls within the scope of the Regulation and that in terms of article 6(1)(c) there are serious doubts as to its compatibility with the common market. The due process requirement of the right to know the case to be answered is also met by the Commission allowing access to the file. Article 18(3) provides:

> 'The rights of the defence shall be fully respected in the proceedings. Access to the file shall be open at least to the parties directly involved, subject to the legitimate interests of undertakings in the protection of their business secrets.'

These are new legislative provisions. In relation to articles 85 and 86 EEC the practice developed, after the Court of Justice had laid down minimum requirements of disclosure to the parties,[94] of allowing access to the Commission's file.[95] It is clearly intended to ensure that the established practice should be carried over to this new area of jurisdiction in competition matters.

4.6 ENFORCEMENT

Where the Commission finds that a proposed concentration, or a concentration which has been implemented without Commission clearance, is incompatible with the common market, in addition to making a declaration to that effect under article 8(3) it may enforce its decision by means of fines, periodic penalty payments or an order for divestiture. Although the framework of rules in respect of fines and periodic penalty payments is essentially the same as exists under Regulation 17 for infringements of articles 85 and 86 EEC, the new Regulation introduces both separate specific offences and new financial amounts.

4.6.1 Fines

The imposition of fines is provided for by article 14 of Regulation 4064/89,

---

94 See especially 85/76 *Hoffman-La Roche* v *Commission* [1979] ECR 461, [1979] 3 CMLR 211 at [11]; 43 & 63/82 *VBVB and VBBB* v *Commission (Dutch Books)* [1984] ECR 19, [1985] 1 CMLR 27.
95 For a statement of this practice, see 12th Report on Competition Policy at para 35.

which provides that fines may be imposed upon persons who control undertakings involved in concentrations[96] as well as upon undertakings and associations of undertakings.[97] The article distinguishes between procedural infringements,[98] such as the supply of incorrect information, and substantive infringements, such as the implementation of a concentration in defiance of a finding of incompatibility. In the case of the procedural measures, article 14 adds a new infringement of 'failure to notify a concentration in accordance with article 4'.[99] This is a noticeable departure from the law relating to restrictive agreements, under which there is no obligation to notify the Commission of an agreement, although there are disadvantages in not notifying when an agreement is found to infringe article 85. For these procedural infringements, the fine for behaviour which is either intentional or negligent may be set between ECU 1,000 and 50,000. These amounts are noticeably higher than those which apply in the case of similar infringements under Regulation 17.[100]

4.6.1.1 Substantive infringements

All the substantive infringements under article 14(2) are specifically referable to the terms of the merger Regulation. They are:

(a)   failure to comply with an obligation imposed by the Commission under either article 7(4) (derogation from suspension of a concentration) or article 8(2) (declaration of compatibility with the common market);[101]

(b)   implementation of a concentration contrary to either the automatic suspension under article 7(1) or an extended suspension under article 7(2);[102]

(c)   implementation of a concentration contrary to a declaration of incompatibility with the common market under article 8(3);[103]

(d)   failure to comply with an order to take measures of divestiture made under article 8(4).[104]

It is probably the case that these powers will rarely be significant in respect of the control of mergers and acquisitions, where the emphasis is on rapid settlement of issues before the transaction takes effect, and so before there is any substantial infringement. Nevertheless, there remains the possibility of fines being imposed[105], especially where undertakings proceed with merger

---

[96]   See art.3(1)(b).
[97]   Art.14(1).
[98]   The principal penalties for procedural infringements are considered at 4.2.3.
[99]   Art.14(1)(a).
[100]   Cf. Regulation 17, art.15(1): ECU 100 to 5,000.
[101]   Art.14(2)(a).
[102]   Art.14(2)(b).
[103]   Art.14(2)(c).
[104]   Ibid.
[105]   In which case, before any final decision is taken, the Advisory Committee on Concentrations must be consulted: Regulation 4064/89, art.19(3).

plans in defiance of Commission opposition or without cooperating with the Commission's declared wish to examine the proposed merger and to attempt to regulate it so that it is not anti-competitive in effect.

4.6.1.2 Assessment of the fine to be imposed

Fines imposed are declared not to be of a criminal law nature.[106] For those obliged to pay, this non-criminal nature may be their least concern: it is thought that the declaration was included in order to avoid constitutional arguments over Member State surrender of sovereignty over criminal law matters.[107] The Commission's powers to impose fines in respect of infringements of articles 85 and 86 EEC were subjected to a comprehensive review by the Court of Justice in the *Pioneer* case,[108] in which the Commission radically revised upwards the level of fines imposed. The purpose of imposing fines was said to be to secure the implementation of competition policy, by suppressing illegal activities, preventing their recurrence and deterring others from engaging in similar activity.[109] This basic philosophy is likely to underlie the imposition of fines under Regulation 4064/89.

In the case of substantive infringements, the fine must be set after taking account of the nature and gravity of the infringement,[110] and must not in any case exceed 10% of the aggregate turnover of the undertaking concerned.[111] Although this rule is articulated in a slightly different form, the level of fine is in fact the same as is provided for under article 15(2) of Regulation 17 for substantive infringements of articles 85 and 86.

In assessing the gravity of the infringement the Commission may take into account a number of factors. Probably most significant is the nature and effect of the infringement. In respect of articles 85 and 86 EEC the Commission has been severe on practices which tend to fragment the single market, and especially those which interfere with exports, and on those which operate to fix prices. In the case of concentrations, the matter of greatest concern, in addition to ancillary effects of the concentration falling within the above descriptions, will be the elimination of competitors. In *BAT & RJ Reynolds* v *Commission*,[112] although in the final result the Commission and the Court of Justice decided in favour of the proposed transaction, the great concern was the elimination of a major competitor and the consequent adverse effect on competition in the market.

A second factor to be taken into account is the behaviour of the parties. Fines may only be imposed if the parties have behaved intentionally or

---

[106] Art.14(4).
[107] Kerse, 7.02, with reference to Regulation 17, art.15(4).
[108] 100/80 *Musique Diffusion Française* v *Commission* [1983] ECR 1825, [1983] 3 CMLR 221.
[109] E.g., *ECS/AKZO* OJ 1985 L374/1, [1986] 3 CMLR 273, in which a fine of 10,000,000 ECU was set with such a purpose in mind.
[110] Art.14(3).
[111] Art.14(2).
[112] [1988] 4 CMLR 24; see 1.1.3.4.

negligently,[113] and, in principle at least, a differentiation may be made in the level of fine according to the type of behaviour in question. However, in the case of article 85 and 86 EEC infringements, the Commission often describes the conduct as 'intentional, or at least negligent', and since it need not account precisely for the manner in which the fine was assessed it is not always easy to establish the precise effect of behaviour on that assessment. It is clear that intention and negligence may be established despite an absence of knowledge of Community competition law where the parties knew or ought to have realised the anti-competitive effect of their behaviour.[114] The parties' behaviour may also have the effect of mitigating the fines to be imposed, especially where they have cooperated with the Commission in establishing mechanisms whereby future infringements can be avoided.[115]

Finally, the Commission should take account of the market share and turnover of the undertakings concerned. The turnover to be considered is the total turnover for the undertaking worldwide, and not merely the turnover for related products in the market in question. This definition is necessary in order to achieve the aim of fining all undertakings in a proportionately equivalent manner for similar infringements. Nevertheless, where the infringement relates to products which are only a small proportion of the total turnover, this factor may be taken to reflect on the gravity of the infringement, and so to allow fines to be fixed at a lower level.[116]

Where an infringement of either article 85(1) or article 86 may also have been the subject of national anti-trust proceedings in a Member State, the Commission must, in assessing the fine to be imposed, take account of any fine which may have been imposed in respect of the same acts in those national proceedings.[117] It remains an open question whether a similar rule applies to national proceedings in a non-member state.

4.6.1.3 Payment and enforcement

The Commission's decision to impose a fine should state a date by which the fine should have been paid. In *AEG-Telefunken* v *Commission*,[118] a case under Regulation 17, the Court of Justice rejected the parties' claim that the Commission was not entitled to charge interest on unpaid fines. Liability for interest is an important incentive for enforcement, and the Commission's practice is now to require payment no later than three months from the date of the decision and to order payment of interest from that date onwards. Other enforcement procedures must be carried out in accordance with 'the

---

[113] Regulation 4064/89, art.14(2).
[114] 19/77 *Miller* v *Commission* [1978] ECR 131; [1978] 2 CMLR 334; *Nederlandsche Michelin* 1981 OJ L353/33, [1982] 1 CMLR 643 at point [56].
[115] *Wood Pulp* OJ 1985 L85/1, [1985] 3 CMLR 474.
[116] *Pioneer*; supra note 108 at 1909.
[117] 14/68 *Wilhelm* v *Bundeskartellamt* [1969] ECR 1, [1969] CMLR 100.
[118] 107/82 [1983] ECR 3151, [1984] 3 CMLR 325.

rules of civil procedure in force in the State in the territory of which it is carried out'.[119] In the UK a fine can be enforced as if it were a judgment of the High Court by registration of the decision in that court[120] in accordance with the European Communities (Enforcement of Community Judgments) Order 1972.[121]

4.6.2 Periodic penalty payments

The distinction between procedural and substantive infringements is maintained by article 15 which provides for periodic penalty payments against persons, undertakings and associations of undertakings. The purpose of these penalties is to enforce compliance with an order made by the Commission. For the procedural infringements[122] the daily rate is set at a maximum of ECU 25,000.[123] For the substantive infringements[124] the daily rate is set at a maximum of ECU 100,000.[125] These amounts are noticeably higher than the daily rates set by Regulation 17.[126] In either case, as under Regulation 17, the Commission may set the total amount payable at a lower figure than that which would arise from a simple multiplication of the daily rate by the number of days' delay in complying with the order in question.[127]

4.6.3 Divestiture

Under article 8(4) the Commission may 'require the undertakings or assets brought together to be separated or the cessation of joint control or any other action that may be appropriate in order to restore conditions of effective competition'. The effect of such a decision would not simply be to reverse the original transaction or transactions by which the concentration had been achieved, but rather to oblige the controlling firm to dispose of the interests acquired. Such a decision by the Commission would have very serious consequences for undertakings which had implemented a significant degree of integration. The cost of unscrambling a merger, and the wasted expenditure which would have gone into the initial integration, would be very high, and would themselves amount to a considerable penalty for 'jumping the

---

[119] Art.192 EEC.
[120] Or, in Scotland, the Court of Session.
[121] SI 1972 No. 1590.
[122] Failure to supply complete and correct information (art.11), and failure to submit to an investigation (art.13).
[123] Art.15(1).
[124] Failure to comply with an obligation imposed by the Commission under either article 7(4) (derogation from suspension of a concentration) or article 8(2) (declaration of compatibility with the common market), and failure to comply with an order to take measures of divestiture made under article 8(4).
[125] Art.15(2).
[126] Reg.17, art.16(1) sets them at ECU 50–1,000 per day.
[127] Art.15(3).

gun' and going ahead with a merger without waiting for Commission approval and perhaps without notifying it to the Commission. For this reason, undertakings must be very careful in planning merger activity so as to comply with the obligation to notify[128] and any temporary suspension of the merger.[129]

4.7 RELATIONS WITH MEMBER STATES[130]

Regulation 4064/89 calls for a series of complex inter-relationships between the Community authorities and the competent authorities of the Member States. Three procedures have already been considered:

(a) under article 22 (3)–(5), whereby the Commission may, at the request of a Member State, rule on a proposed concentration even if it does not have a Community dimension;[131]

(b) under article 9, whereby the Commission may, at the request of a Member State, refer a proposed concentration which does have a Community dimension to the Member State authorities if it threatens competition on a distinct market in that Member State;[132]

(c) under article 21(3), whereby Member States may take appropriate measures to protect legitimate interests other than those of competition.[133]

This section will consider the liaison between the Commission and Member State authorities under the Advisory Committee procedure. The possibility of conflict between national law and Community law in respect of Regulation 4064/89 is considered in Chapter 8.[134]

Article 19(3) provides for the creation of an Advisory Committee on concentrations, which must be consulted before decisions under article 8 and under articles 14 and 15 are taken. It must also be consulted before measures are adopted under article 23. It need not be consulted before a decision is taken to refer a matter to the competent authorities of a Member State under article 9. This omission is a little surprising, since it might be thought that the other Member States might be concerned to express an opinion on whether such a reference should be made, especially since such references run counter to the general premise of Regulation 4064/89, which is that where a proposed concentration has a Community dimension it should be assessed on behalf of all Member States by the Community authorities. The Advisory Committee consists of one or two representatives

---

[128] See 3.1 *et seq.*
[129] See 3.3.
[130] See also 7.2.4.4.
[131] See 2.3.2.
[132] See 3.4.
[133] See 2.4.2.
[134] See 8.3 *et seq.*

of each member State, at least one of whom must be competent in competition matters.[135] Meetings are held at the invitation of and are chaired by the Commission, and in normal circumstances the Commission must allow 14 days' notice.[136] Members of the Committee are supplied with key documents and a preliminary draft of the Commission's decision.[137]

Regulation 4064/89 attempts to increase the significance of the role of the Committee by comparison with its sister Advisory Committee on Restrictive Practices and Monopolies created under article 10 of Regulation 17. So, the Committee is required to deliver an opinion on the Commission's draft decision, and if necessary may put the matter to a vote.[138] This opinion must be in writing.[139] Article 19(6) also provides as follows:

'The Commission shall take the utmost account of the opinion delivered by the Committee. It shall inform the Committee of the manner in which its opinion has been taken into account.'

These requirements appear to reflect the view that consultation of the Advisory Committee established under Regulation 17 has at times been somewhat perfunctory, and that the Commission has not had to account for its occasional decisions to go ahead with its original conclusions despite the opposition of the Committee.[140] The Advisory Committee on concentrations is given new powers to recommend that the Commission publish the Committee's opinion, taking into account the protection of business secrets and the interests of the undertakings concerned.[141] This marks a clear change from previous policy, under which the Committee's report was not to be made public.[142] Whether these modifications will strengthen the role of the Advisory Committee in merger appraisals remains to be seen.

4.8 SUPERVISION BY THE COURT OF JUSTICE[143]

Article 164 of the Treaty of Rome confers upon the Court of Justice the obligation to ensure, in the interpretation and application of the Treaty, that the law is observed. In respect of competition policy the relevant elements

---

[135] Art.19(4).
[136] Art.19(5): the period of notice may exceptionally be shortened in order to avoid serious harm to any of the undertakings concerned.
[137] Ibid.
[138] Art.19(6).
[139] Ibid.
[140] See Goyder 41–2.
[141] Art.19(7).
[142] Reg.17, art.10(6).
[143] Regulation 4064/89, art.16.

of the Court's competence are its jurisdiction over fines, over the legality of acts of the Commission, and over the Commission's failure to act.

4.8.1 Jurisdiction over fines: article 172 EEC

Article 172 EEC provides that the Court of Justice may have, by Regulations made under the Treaty, unlimited jurisdiction in regard to the penalties provided for in such Regulations. Article 16 of Regulation 4064/89 provides:

'The Court of Justice shall have unlimited jurisdiction within the meaning of article 172 of the Treaty to review decisions whereby the Commission has fixed a fine or periodic penalty payments; it may cancel, reduce or increase the fine or periodic penalty payments imposed.'

It is not entirely clear what is meant by 'unlimited jurisdiction', and in particular whether the absence of limit applies to every aspect of the decision or (more probably) only to those aspects relevant to the fine or penalty. In practice, jurisdiction in other respects under article 173 is sufficiently flexible for undertakings not to have sought to develop a broad jurisdiction under article 172.

4.8.2 Annulment proceedings: article 173 EEC

Article 173 EEC gives the Court of Justice jurisdiction to review acts of the Commission, on stated grounds, in proceedings instituted by the Council or a Member State, or, where a decision has been addressed to a natural or legal person or is of direct and individual concern to such a person, in proceedings instituted by natural or legal persons.[144] So, for example, in *BAT & RJ Reynolds v Commission*[145] the proceedings were brought by complainants who had received a letter from the Commission rejecting their complaint.

Acts which are reviewable were defined in *IBM v Commission*[146] as comprising 'any measure the legal effects of which are binding on, and capable of affecting the interests of, the applicant by bringing about a distinct change in his legal position', and which are the final stage in a particular administrative procedure. Clearly this definition includes decisions,[147] but the language of article 173 suggests that certain acts other than decisions also fall within the scope of review under the article. In respect of articles 85 and 86 EEC

---

[144] The apparent restriction of jurisdiction in the case of legal or natural persons to decisions (rather than the more general acts) does not appear to be strictly adhered to.
[145] [1988] 4 CMLR 24; see 1.1.3.4.
[146] 60/81 [1981] ECR 2639, [1981] 3 CMLR 635.
[147] Almost all matters under Regulation 4064/89 must be disposed of by decision.

these have been held to include letters rejecting complaints,[148] but not comfort letters,[149] or Statements of Objections.

Four grounds of review are cited in Article 173:

(a) lack of competence;
(b) infringement of an essential procedural requirement;
(c) infringement of the Treaty or any rule of law relating to its application;
(d) misuse of powers.

Although it is important to frame an application for review within one or more of these headings, in practice there is considerable overlap between them, and they combine to produce grounds of review not unlike those found in respect of judicial review in English law or, for that matter, in French *droit administratif*.

Lack of competence provides a ground of review where the Commission acts in circumstances not within the scope of the powers given to it by the Treaty or secondary legislation. In competition cases it has been invoked by undertakings seeking to challenge the Commission's extra-territorial jurisdiction.

Infringement of an essential procedural requirement may be invoked in respect of either an express procedural provision of the Treaty or secondary legislation, or of a procedural requirement embodied in a general principle of law. A good example is the right to be heard.[150] In most cases the right to a hearing is expressly provided for by article 19 of Regulation 17. However, the Court of Justice has held that the right exists as a general principle of law even in the absence of express provision in the relevant legislation. In *Transocean Marine Paint Association* v *Commission*,[151] the applicant argued that a condition imposed in the course of the grant of an exemption under article 85(3) was invalid because it had not been given the opportunity to express its view about the proposed imposition of the condition. The Court annulled that part of the Commission's decision on the basis that it infringed a procedural requirement. The Court will only annul a decision on procedural grounds of this kind if it can be shown that the decision might have been affected by the procedural irregularity.[152]

Infringement of the treaty, or any rule of law relating to its application, is the most important ground of review, almost to the extent of being a

---

[148] 210/81 *Demo-Studio Schmidt* v *Commission* [1983] ECR 3045, [1984] 1 CMLR 63; 142 & 156/84 *BAT & RJ Reynolds* v *Commission* [1988] 4 CMLR 24. But must not such a letter stem from a decision for the purposes of *locus standi* under article 173(2).

[149] See the *perfume* cases. The point is not without difficulty because not expressly addressed; but, they are not decisions, which causes difficulty as far as the standing of legal and natural persons is concerned, and they are not binding.

[150] See 4.5.1 *et seq.*

[151] 17/74 [1974] ECR 1063, [1974] 2 CMLR 459.

[152] 209/78 *Van Landewyck* v *Commission* [1980] ECR 3125, [1981] 3 CMLR 193 at para 47.

'catch-all' ground. Under this head it is possible to raise substantive issues of law or fact, as well as issues of both competence and procedure. Two grounds are of particular significance. Article 190 of the Treaty of Rome requires that decisions 'state the reasons on which they are based'. Such a rule is essential to enable judicial review of the decision, but in practice the Court will find it to have been satisfied provided the decision recites the main issues of fact and legal principles applied.[153] It has not used this rule as a means of examining the merits of a case by requiring that the reasons given be legally and logically satisfactory in substance. Where, however, a decision takes the interpretation of the law beyond the previously accepted position, the Court will require the Commission to provide fuller reasoning for its decision.[154] Secondly, and seemingly more significantly, under this head the Court requires the Commission to sustain the burden of proof by bringing evidence sufficient to support its case. It may be recalled that it was on this ground that the decision in *Continental Can*[155] was overturned: the Commission's finding of a dominant position was based on an identification of the relevant market which the Court found was not sustainable on the evidence provided. In practice, it is on this ground that the Court may be persuaded to take a different view of the facts from that taken by the Commission.

Misuse of powers has not yet proved to be a significant ground of review in competition cases.

4.8.3   Failure to act: article 175 EEC

Under article 175 of the Treaty of Rome, the Commission may be required to act where, provided it is under a specific duty to act under the Treaty, it has failed so to do. This obligation does not arise until the applicant, which may be a Member State, another Community institution or in some circumstances a legal or natural person, has called for action by the Commission which in turn has failed to define its position within a period of two months from the request.[156] A definition of position which is in terms of a refusal to act does not constitute an infringement under article 175, but it may be subject to review under article 173, provided it is a reviewable act.[157] Individuals, whether legal or natural persons, have standing under the article provided their complaint is that the Commission has failed to address to them an act, not being a recommendation or an opinion, which they are entitled to receive. So, an individual third-party complainant about

---

[153] 41/69 *ACF Chemifarma* v *Commission* [1970] ECR 661, 690.
[154] 73/74 *Groupement des Fabricants de Papiers Peints de Belgique* v *Commission* [1975] ECR 1491, [1976] 1 CMLR 589.
[155] 6/72 [1973] ECR 215, [1973] CMLR 199.
[156] Art.175(1) and (2).
[157] See 4.8.2.

a concentration could not use this procedure to require the Commission to take a decision on the matter, since the final decision would not be addressed to the complainant but to the parties.[158] However, it seems likely that such a third party would be entitled to a formal Commission decision rejecting his complaint; such a decision would be an 'act' capable of review by the Court of Justice.[159] A party under investigation would not need to oblige the Commission to act by using this procedure, because under article 10(6) of Regulation 4064/89 the Commission's failure to act within the prescribed time-limits results in the concentration being deemed to be declared compatible with the common market.

4.8.4   Procedure[160]

Appeals against Commission decisions in competition matters are heard by the new Court of First Instance, with a right of appeal on points of law to the Court of Justice.[161] The proceedings are largely of a written nature, followed by a brief oral hearing which ends with the conclusions of the Advocate General. The proceedings are technically of the nature of a review rather than an appeal, so that opportunities to introduce new evidence or new arguments are limited. It should be noted that, by article 37 of the Court's Statute, Member States, other Community institutions and individuals able to show a legitimate interest are permitted to intervene in Court proceedings to support one or other of the parties. As far as costs are concerned, the Court's general rule is that costs follow the outcome of the case,[162] so that where either the Commission or the applicant is completely successful in the Court it will be awarded its costs against the other. Commission costs are in any case low, since it is not entitled to recover the costs of its in-house lawyers. Where the outcome is split between the parties each will bear its own costs.

Review proceedings must be brought within a short limitation period. In proceedings under article 173 they must be commenced within two months of notification or publication of the decision.[163] For the addressee of a decision,

---

[158] 125/78 *GEMA* v *Commission* [1979] ECR 3173, [1980] 2 CMLR 177.

[159] See 210/81 *Demo-Studio Schmidt* v *Commission* [1983] ECR 3045, [1984] 1 CMLR 63; 142 & 156/84 *BAT & RJ Reynolds* v *Commission* [1988] 4 CMLR 24; and see Kerse 2.34–2.37.

[160] Art.188 EEC, Rules of Procedure OJ 1982 C39/1; see Usher, *European Court Practice*: Sweet & Maxwell, 1983; Lasok, *The European Court of Justice: Practice and Procedure*: Butterworths, 1984.

[161] Art.168A EEC, inserted in the Treaty by the Single European Act; and Council Decision OJ 1988 L319/1. Actions brought by Member States, or on reference from national courts under article 177 EEC are within the exclusive jurisdiction of the full Court of Justice.

[162] It is essential to include a request for costs in the pleadings.

[163] Art.173(3); since the Court has stated that it is preferable that notification to the parties should always precede publication (e.g., in *United Brands*) it seems that the former will be the critical date.

time starts to run on the day following notification, but for third parties seeking to challenge the decision, time runs from the fifteenth day following publication.[164] Under article 175 proceedings must be commenced within two months of the expiry of the period of two months within which the Commission was obliged to have defined its position.[165] There is no specific limitation period prescribed in respect of article 172 proceedings in relation to fines and penalties. In practice such proceedings are almost always brought in conjunction with proceedings under article 173, and in any case the safest procedure is always to comply with the article 173 limitation period of two months.

Under article 186 of the Treaty of Rome the Court has power, where proceedings have already been instituted before it, to 'prescribe any necessary interim measures'. This power is by way of exception from the general rule under article 185 EEC by which Court proceedings do not have a suspensory effect on the Commission's decision. In the case of fines, it is not normally necessary to apply for interim relief pending the outcome of the Court's review, because the Commission's practice is of its own volition to suspend enforcement until after the Court has ruled on the matter. The Court may require some guarantee that payment will be made should the application for review prove unsuccessful.[166] In the case of Commission orders, the Court may be willing to suspend their effect pending the appeal where there is a serious question as to the correctness of the Commission's decision, where the matter is urgent because of a risk of serious and irreparable damage to the applicant, and where there is no risk of prejudice to the final outcome of the case by taking interim measures of the kind requested.[167]

4.6 RELATIONS WITH THIRD COUNTRIES

It has been a matter of some concern in recent years among some Member States that the Community was more tolerant of inward investment, particularly by way of acquisition of undertakings established within the Community by undertakings from outside, than some non-member countries were towards EC undertakings wishing to acquire firms in those third countries. Regulation 4064/89 provides a mechanism through which the Commission may co-ordinate efforts to achieve reciprocal treatment of proposed mergers.[168] Member States are required to inform the Commission of 'any general difficulties with concentrations . . . in a non-member country'.[169] By the end of September 1991, and periodically thereafter, the

---

[164] Rules of Procedure, art.81.
[165] Art.175(2).
[166] E.g., 107/82R *AEG* v *Commission* [1982] ECR 1549.
[167] 60 & 190/81R *IBM* v *Commission* [1981] ECR 1857, [1981] 3 CMLR 93.
[168] Art.24.
[169] Art.24(1).

Commission must report to the Council on the treatment of undertakings in respect of concentrations in non-member countries, and may make recommendations.[170] In particular, where the Commission believes that Community undertakings do not receive comparable treatment in a non-member country to that accorded to undertakings from that country under Community law, it may seek from the Council an appropriate mandate for negotiation with a view to obtaining such comparable treatment.[171]

The matters covered by these provisions are delicate and often raise counter-accusations in relation to world trade. It should not be thought that the provision of this power on the part of the Commission will lead to an early solution to the problems of reciprocity and discrimination in the treatment of international mergers and acquisitions.[172] The Community's ability to achieve such goals will depend much more on its economic power vis-a-vis the countries in question than it does on the legal mechanisms available to it.

[170] Art.24(2).
[171] Art.24(3).
[172] But note that Sir Leon Brittan has called for a treaty with the USA to avoid clashes of interest: supra note 66.

FIVE

Control of joint ventures in the Economic Community

Joint ventures have a special place in the field of EC merger control. In the first place, they fall into a grey area between concentrations and cartels, so that identifying the applicable controlling provisions of Community competition law (if any) is a complex preliminary task.[1] In the second place, joint ventures come in so many different shapes and sizes that they present a microcosm of all elements, positive and negative, of competition policy. As a result, whether they fall within the scope of Regulation 4064/89 or of article 85 EEC, they raise significant issues in relation both to potential adverse effect upon competition, and potential compensating benefits. From the joint venture cases already decided by the Commission we may discern something of the Commission's attitude to the issue of concentration. One particular factor to have emerged is that joint ventures require individual consideration, with the result that it has as yet proved impossible to achieve a block exemption for joint ventures in general, although it is possible that a joint venture might fall into the block exemption for research and development agreements[2] or that for specialisation agreements.[3]

5.1 SCOPE OF CONTROL

A joint venture is a form of integration of economic activity by previously independent undertakings, by which the participants create a jointly controlled enterprise to which they both make an input of resources in some form (capital, personnel, know-how, goodwill etc) and to which they also allocate a particular function, which either was previously the responsibility of a participant, or would have been had the participant been involved in

---

[1] See 5.1 below.
[2] Reg 418/85 OJ 1985 L53/5; see 5.3.5.
[3] Reg 417/85 OJ 1985 L53/1.

that field.[4] This definition is inevitably vague, because the precise form which a joint venture might take varies. Put another way, the expression joint venture is of no particular legal significance: it describes a commercial or economic arrangement. The legal consequences depend upon which of several possible legal forms the participants adopt for their joint economic activity. In particular, it is important to be able to identify exactly what degree of integration between undertakings will be effected by an agreement in order to determine to which form of control by the Community authorities the agreement will be subject. This is because control under Regulation 4064/89 applies to joint ventures which create for an indefinite period an autonomous economic entity, while article 85 EEC applies to joint ventures which do no more than coordinate the competitive behaviour of independent undertakings.[5] It is necessary, therefore, to distinguish between those joint ventures which are akin to a merger (*concentrative* joint ventures) and those which are akin to a cartel agreement (*cooperative* joint ventures).

The distinction has been significant since long before the adoption of the new Regulation; previously it determined whether or not control could be exercised at all. The result of the Commission's 1966 Memorandum on Concentrations was that concentrative joint ventures were regarded as outside the scope of anti-trust control under article 85 EEC, which applied only to cooperative joint ventures. After the decision in *BAT & RJ Reynolds* v *Commission*,[6] the significance of the distinction became less clear cut, because the Court appeared to indicate in that case that certain kinds of merger, going beyond the cartel form of joint venture, were subject to article 85.[7] With the advent of Regulation 4064/89[8] the distinction has again become significant, although the impact will be different: the distinction will now determine whether an agreement falls exclusively within the terms of the Regulation or falls to be dealt with under the general rule contained in article 85.[9] The distinction may, in addition, offer advantages to the participants apart from the different tests of compatibility with the common market which Regulation 4064/89 and article 85 EEC apply. A transaction falling within the scope of Regulation 4064/89 is to a degree immune from

---

4   See Brodley (1982) 95 Harvard LR 1523, cited in Bellamy & Child at 193: 'An integration of operations between two or more separate firms in which the following conditions are present: (i) the enterprise is under the joint control of the parent firms, which are not under related control; (ii) each parent makes a substantial contribution to the enterprise; (iii) the enterprise exists as a business entity separate from its parents; (iv) the enterprise creates significant new enterprise capability in terms of new productive capacity, new technology, a new product or entry into a new market.'
5   Art.3(2).
6   [1988] 4 CMLR 24; see 1.1.3.4.
7   See 1.1.3.4.
8   See generally Chapters 2 - 4.
9   See Reg 4064/89, art.3(2).

examination by national authorities, whereas article 85 carries no such immunity; indeed it is directly applicable by national courts.[10]

5.1.1 Legislation and guidelines

The test which distinguishes between the application of the new Regulation and that of article 85 EEC is introduced by article 3(2) of Regulation 4064/89.[11] It proposes a somewhat simplistic division between those operations, including the creation of joint ventures, which have as their object or effect the coordination of competitive behaviour of undertakings, and operations which do not give rise to coordination of competitive behaviour, but which are intended to create on a lasting basis all the functions of an autonomous economic entity. However, the Preamble to Regulation 4064/89 recognises that such a clear division cannot be maintained, and accepts in Recital 25 that a concentrative joint venture may nevertheless be supported by necessary ancillary restrictions (which might at first sight appear to have the effect of coordinating competitive behaviour) without losing its concentrative characteristics and so without being removed from the scope of the Regulation.[12] It must also be recognised that some concentrations are accompanied by restrictive agreements which are not merely ancillary, but which quite independently of the concentrative element have an adverse impact on the competitive structure. This more complex definition of the line to be drawn between concentrative and cooperative operations, including joint ventures, is the subject of a Commission Notice which attempts to chart the precise nature of the distinction.[13] This guideline is supported by a further Notice on restrictions ancillary to concentrations,[14] and the legal regime applicable to any particular joint venture can only be determined after careful consideration of both.

The basic rule is that where a transaction consists of both concentrative and cooperative elements, and the latter are not merely ancillary restrictions, then unless these different elements can be separated out the application of Regulation 4064/89 must give way to the application of article 85 EEC. The extent to which this residual rule will apply remains to be seen, not least in the light of the Court of Justice's interpretation of the notion of ancillary restrictions and its development of a doctrine of severance.[15] In

---

[10] See further 8.1.1.1.
[11] See 2.1.7.
[12] See 2.1.8 *et seq.*
[13] Notice No.90/C 203/06 OJ 1990 C203/10; for a checklist outlining the Commission's guideline in general terms see 2.1.4, for the notice see Appendix III.
[14] Notice No.90/C 203/05; see Appendix IV.
[15] Such a doctrine is admitted in 56/65 *Société Technique Minière* [1966] ECR 235, 250 and in 319/82 *Soc. de Vente de Ciments et Bétons* v *Kerpen & Kerpen* [1983] ECR 4173, 4184, and was applied by the English Courts in *Chemidus Wavin* v *TERI* [1978] 3 CMLR 514 CA.

practice it is rare for joint ventures to be set up without some restrictive covenants intended to manage the relationship between the participating controlling parties themselves and between them and the joint venture. If the Court takes a very strict view of ancillary restrictions, or rarely finds the competition coordinating elements of joint venture transactions to be sufficiently independent of the concentrative elements to be severable, then very few joint ventures will satisfy the criteria for control under Regulation 4064/89.

5.1.1.1 Joint ventures as defined by the Commission's Notice

According to the Commission, in terms of Regulation 4064/89 a joint venture consists of an undertaking which is jointly controlled by other undertakings. Any joint economic activity falling short of this basic definition is not even potentially within the scope of the Regulation. The requirement of the joint venture's existence as an undertaking is apparently intended to indicate the existence of 'an organized assembly of human and material resources, intended to pursue a defined economic purpose on a long-term basis'.[16] It appears to require at least some functional commercial identity, without requiring separate legal identity and without implying complete autonomy from the parent undertakings. Indeed, such autonomy would be inconsistent with the notion of joint control.

The use of the expression 'undertaking' in relation to the joint venture is potentially confusing, because it seems to be crucially different from the usual meaning of undertaking in articles 85 and 86 EEC. In that context, undertaking has been interpreted as meaning an individual, a company or a group of companies which carry out autonomous economic activity so that, for example, there can be no agreement between undertakings for the purposes of article 85 EEC where the agreement is in fact between a parent and subsidiary within the same group, since only one undertaking (the group comprising parent and subsidiary) is involved.[17] In the context of Regulation 4064/89, the requirement that a joint venture must be an undertaking is perhaps best understood in the rather looser sense that it must amount, in terms of its activities, to a business.

Control of the joint venture is not defined in any particular way, but it is anticipated that it will be achieved in most cases by either ownership of or the right to use assets, influence over the composition or voting of the managing or supervisory bodies, voting rights in those bodies, or contracts relating to the conduct of the joint venture's business. What matters is that this control be exercised jointly; that is, it must be necessary for the parent companies to agree on decisions which affect the joint venture's activities.

[16] Notice 90/C 203/06; see Appendic III, para.8.
[17] 15/74 *Centrafarm* v *Sterling Drug* [[1974] ECR 1147, 1167; 170/83 *Hydrotherm* v *Compact* [1984] ECR 2999, 3016.

Where the participants have equal shares in the joint venture this requirement is met automatically, since neither is able to exert unilateral control and both will be obliged to act together in order to overcome their mutual powers of blocking any vote. In such a case no express provision for joint control is needed.

Where shares in the joint venture are not equal and, in the case of three or more participants, the parent companies with minority holdings cannot combine to outvote the majority parent so as to determine the joint venture's behaviour, joint control can only be established by some express arrangement, which may be provided for contractually (for example, in a shareholders' agreement) or in the constitution of the joint venture (for example, in the articles of association). As a matter of practice, joint control is almost invariably expressly provided for in the context of joint ventures through the use of shareholders' agreements and specially adapted articles of association.[18]

Where there are a number of parent companies, none of which has a dominant share in the joint venture, it may still be possible to identify the existence of joint control if a group of those parent companies are collectively able to establish a majority in any vote. However, the Notice stresses that the mere fact of reaching a decision by majority vote does not of itself indicate joint control. Control implies some lasting direction over the joint venture, which requires that the majority group be shown to have a deliberate common policy towards the joint venture, rather than occasional *ad hoc* convergences of interest. It may be difficult to find evidence to establish the existence of such a common policy, although the Notice appears to anticipate that it may be inferred from factual circumstances and especially a convergence of economic interests. Evidence of actual practice in voting, coupled with identification of a clear economic motive for such action, might lead to the presumption of joint control. Consequently, companies seeking to avoid the allegation of joint control will not be safe merely because no legal arrangement can be shown, if the circumstantial evidence supports such an inference.

5.1.1.2 Concentration as defined by the Commission's Notice
The Commission's Notice states that the Commission regards the existence of a concentrative joint venture as established where the participants create an enterprise which performs on a lasting basis all the functions of an autonomous economic entity without also causing a coordination of competitive behaviour.

The notion of economic autonomy is not without difficulty when viewed in the light of the requirement of joint control by the participants of the joint venture, as is noted above. The Commission clearly envisages that control over the joint venture (i.e. the possibility of exercising decisive influence on it) may exist without impeding its economic autonomy. Control

[18] See 2.1.5.

appears to be intended to relate to strategic questions relating to the joint venture, such as ownership, alteration of the objects of the joint venture, changes in its capitalisation, or deployment of profits, while economic autonomy appears to be intended to relate to the conduct and development of everyday business. The principal characteristic of economic autonomy is thus said to be that the joint venture must act as an independent supplier and buyer on the market, and must not be wholly or substantially dependent on its parent companies for sales or supplies. The joint venture must be in a position to determine its own commercial policy, and especially its competitive behaviour, in the light of what it perceives to be its own best economic interests and without reference to the commercial and competitive stance of the parent companies. This will largely depend on whether the joint venture has been endowed with sufficient human, financial and technological resources for it reasonably to be anticipated that within a reasonable period of time the joint venture will become commercially self-sufficient.

Once the test of enduring economic autonomy has been satisfied, the joint venture will be regarded as concentrative providing there are no cooperative effects[19] other than permitted ancillary restrictions.[20]

5.1.1.3 Permitted restrictions ancillary to concentration[21]

A potentially concentrative joint venture will not be taken out of control under Regulation 4064/89 simply because it also includes measures which have the object or effect of coordinating competitive behaviour, if the measures are ancillary to the implementation of the concentration. To qualify as ancillary restrictions the measures must be subordinate in importance to the main object of the concentration and they must be necessary to the implementation of the concentration. The guidelines identify some typical restrictions which are to be treated as ancillary to various forms of concentration.

In the case of a concentrative joint venture, these include non-competition clauses intended to protect the goodwill of the business transferred,[22] intellectual property licensing designed to equip the transferee to make full use of the assets transferred, and transitional purchase and supply agreements. Restrictions which are identified as ancillary to the main concentrative purpose of the transaction within the meaning of recital 25 of the Preamble to Regulation 4064/89 are permitted only if the Commission is satisfied that they are acceptable, and article 8(2) of the Regulation provides for that assessment. The principal criterion will be the requirement of proportionality, so that ancillary restrictions will only be approved if they are no more

---

[19] See 5.1.1.4.
[20] See 5.1.1.3.
[21] See 2.1.7 generally; and see Notice 90/C 203/05; OJ 1990 C203/5, Appendix IV.
[22] The Commission has previously approved such terms: cf. *Carbon Gas Technologie* OJ 1983 L376/17 [1984] 2 CMLR 275; *Amersham/Buchler* OJ 1982 L314/34 [1983] 1 CMLR 619.

restrictive than is necessary to achieve the protection sought. For example, a non-competition clause imposed upon parent companies to the benefit of the joint venture will only be approved if it is no wider in geographical and material scope nor longer in duration than is required to protect the goodwill transferred. On the other hand, the withdrawal of the parent companies from the intended market of the joint venture is accepted to be integral to the establishment of the joint venture,[23] so that, provided the scope of the non-competition clause is not too widely drawn, it would be valid even if indefinite in duration. In general, restrictions will be regarded as legitimate ancillary elements in a concentrative joint venture where they are intended to smooth the path to economic autonomy. Normally such restrictions will be short-lived, but where the interest in question demands it, as might be the case with a non-competition clause (as above) or an intellectual property licence, they may be quite substantial in duration.

5.1.1.4 Unpermitted cooperation as defined by the Commission's Notice

The Commission's guidelines identify a number of transactions and restrictive clauses which are respectively neither concentrative joint ventures nor ancillary restrictions for the purposes of Regulation 4064/89, and consequently amount to unpermitted cooperation. Restrictions which may arise in the context of the creation of an intended concentrative joint venture, but which do not qualify as ancillary restrictions, are considered in detail in Chapter 2.[24] This section considers those transactions which may have constituent parts which make them appear to be concentrative in nature, but which run an unacceptably high risk of permitting coordination of competitive behaviour and so are treated as cooperative for the purposes of anti-trust control.

A first difficulty which must be confronted is to distinguish between the community of interest which inevitably exists between the parent companies of the joint venture, which is the foundation of their collective decision to create the joint venture, and coordination of competitive behaviour. The essential is that this community of interest must not translate into community of future action to the detriment of the competition which might otherwise be expected between the participants. Paragraph 20 of the Notice on concentrative and cooperative operations[25] states the basic principle in the following terms:

'The JV is not to be regarded as concentrative if as a result of the agreement to set up the JV or as a result of its existence or activities it is reasonably

---

[23] Ibid.
[24] See 2.1.8.1.
[25] Supra note 13.

foreseeable that the competitive behaviour of a parent or of the JV on the relevant market will be influenced. Conversely, there will normally be no foreseeable coordination when all the parent companies withdraw entirely and permanently from the JV's market and do not operate on markets neighbouring those of the JV's.'

Two types of problem in particular may lead to a presumption that coordination will take place: overlapping management structures and activity in the same or proximate markets.

The problem of overlapping management structures relates back to the difficulty considered earlier[26] of the conflict between the notion of joint control (which implies the power to exercise decisive influence over the joint venture) and the requirement of autonomous economic activity. Control implies the right to participate in strategic decision-making in relation to the joint venture, but the Commission makes it clear that the lower the profile of the parents in such decision-making the less likely it is that unpermitted cooperation will occur.

Economic autonomy requires that the joint venture's competitive behaviour is not likely to be influenced by the commercial policies of the parent companies. In general, the Commission assumes that where the areas of activity of the parents and the joint venture are closely related, then such influence is reasonably foreseeable; whereas if the respective areas of activity are not closely related, the likelihood of such influence is deemed to be small. The application of these general principles will vary according to the particular facts of individual cases, and it is not possible, especially in the absence for the time being of Commission decisions, to make categorical statements about how this policy will work out in practice. The Commission's analysis will depend upon the familiar process of identification of relevant product and geographic markets, which is particularly developed in relation to article 86 EEC.[27] Where the joint venture and the parent company or companies operate in the same product markets or geographic markets, the Commission believes that cooperation can be presumed, so that such activity would negative the conclusion that the joint venture is concentrative. A similar presumption, with the same negative conclusion in respect of the concentrative nature of the joint venture, would arise where the parent companies and the joint venture operate in proximate markets; that is, in markets which are upstream, or downstream, of or neighbouring the markets of the other.[28] Conversely, where the joint venture takes over the parents'

26   See 5.1.2.2.
27   See 1.1.2.1.
28   CSV OJ 1978 L242/15 [1979] 1 CMLR 11 and Amersham/Buchler OJ 1982 L314/34 [1983]
     1 CMLR 619 (downstream markets); Optical Fibres OJ 1986 L236/30 (JVs with common
     parent operating in neighbouring geographic markets). See also Elopak/Metal Box-Odin
     OJ 1990 L209/15.

existing activities, and the parents move out of those markets permanently, and also where the joint venture undertakes new activities in an area which the parents are consequently very unlikely to enter, no such presumption of cooperation would arise, and the transaction would almost certainly be regarded as concentrative.

5.1.2 Early experience of the application of the legislation and guidelines

Experience to date has demonstrated that in a number of cases it will be impossible for an adviser to judge determinatively whether a joint venture is concentrative or cooperative. The pragmatic advice here must be to take advantage of the Merger Task Force's willingness[29] to offer informal guidance upon the question. In such cases it is helpful to prepare a brief outline of the transaction and the parties and to submit this, together with a copy of the latest report and accounts of the parties and a request for confidentiality, to the Merger Task Force. The outline should in addition contain an assessment of how the Commission's notice on concentrative and cooperative operations applies to the arrangements.[30] The outline, although unlikely to provide all the information that the Task Force will require, will as a minimum serve as a basis for discussion. The response of the Commission, as with a comfort letter,[31] will not have the force of law but, in the absence a change of facts or circumstances, will almost certainly prove morally binding and the Commission will be unlikely to reverse its earlier view of the matter. The Commission's response will not bind third parties, nor will it affect its obligation to act, upon receipt of a third party complaint.

Some care needs to be exercised in submitting even a short-form outline of a joint venture as a basis for discussion when it comes to presenting arguments as to whether the arrangements are concentrative or cooperative. In particular where parties are anxious to obtain a ruling that arrangements are cooperative, there is a danger that they will over-emphasise the manner and extent to which the joint venture will or may be expected to lead to the coordination of competitive behaviour. This is likely to lead to difficulty when the same parties later find themselves making a notification for negative

---

[29] This perceived willingness is based not only on practical experience but also the provisions of recital 8 to Regulation 2367/90 which provides as follows: 'Whereas the Commission will give the parties concerned, if they so request, an opportunity before notification to discuss the intended concentration informally and in strict confidence; whereas in addition it will, after notification, maintain close contact with the parties concerned to the extent necessary to discuss with them any practical or legal problems which it discovers on a first examination of the case and if possible to remove such problems by mutual agreement'.

[30] Notice No.90/C 203/06; see Appendix III.

[31] A comfort letter is an informal means by which the Commission frequently closes its file on a case, but is without legal force: see 253/78 *Procurer de la République* v *Giry and Guerlain* [1980] ECR 2327.

clearance or exemption under article 85. Here, they will be at pains to emphasise that the arrangements restrict competition between them only to a minimal or indispensable extent. As a generality, it may be said that a typical article 85 notification will go full circle and argue (to the extent credible and supportable) that the restrictions on competition are limited to the specifics of the joint venture itself and that, outside such joint efforts, the parties will compete as normal. There is a certain irony in the observation that parties supporting applications for the exemption of joint ventures under article 85(3) will generally find themselves raising arguments along the lines that the arrangements are in truth 'concentrative'!

Parties to a joint venture have a clear requirement to be certain that they have correctly analysed the concentrative/cooperative question. Pursuant to the terms of the Regulation, concentrations with a Community dimension:

(a) *must* be notified to the Commission within a week of the first to occur of the conclusion of the agreement, the announcement of the public bid or the acquisition of a controlling interest;[32]

(b) are subject to forced divestiture (and other measures) where they are implemented prior to notification;[33] and

(c) will give rise to a liability to fines for the parties concerned (of between ECU 1,000 and ECU 50,000 each) where they are implemented prior to notification.[34]

Pursuant to Article 5 of Regulation 2367/90,[35] it is possible for parties to a concentration with a Community dimension to request that the Commission accept a notification of the concentration on Form CO as an application for negative clearance or exemption under article 85. Article 5 states that in the instance of a 'conversion' of a Form CO, the Commission may require additional information.

It may appear that the ability to convert a Form CO into an Article 85 notification, in one stroke, answers the dilemma of assessing whether a joint venture is concentrative or cooperative. The pragmatist might advise: 'assume it is concentrative but if you are wrong "convert" under article 5 of Regulation 2367/90'. For a number of essentially practical reasons this is unlikely to be an attractive proposition and parties will almost certainly continue to rely upon the type of informal guidance referred to above. The principal difficulties of relying upon the right to convert are as follows:

(a) Form CO is demanding in terms of the scope and sophistication of information that parties are required to provide. In a majority of joint

[32] Art.4(1).
[33] Art.8(4).
[34] Art.14.
[35] OJ 1990 L219/5; see Appendix II.

ventures, it will clearly not be open to the notifying parties to reduce this burden by asserting that they could not obtain certain information in respect of the target undertaking; the joint venture vehicle being as a rule clearly within their sphere of knowledge.[36]

(b) The complexity of Form CO raises clear cost implications for the parties in terms of professional fees and management time.

(c) The complexity of Form CO imposes material timing difficulties upon the parties. In practice, it will almost certainly not be possible to prepare the document within a week of the triggering event.[37] Thus considerable preparatory work will be necessary if the deadline is to be met.

(d) Under the Regulation, the parties are in effect bound to meet the notification timetable since in default they risk the imposition of fines.[38]

(e) Form CO, particularly in terms of its legal and economic reasoning, addresses quite different questions from those relevant to an application for negative clearance or exemption under Article 85. In summary, Form CO will address the creation or strengthening of a dominant position whereas Form AB will address the inapplicability of articles 85 or 86 to given arrangements or, accepting a *prima facie* application of article 85(1), the reasons why the arrangements should be exempted under article 85(3).[39] It can perhaps readily be seen that a conversion of Form CO to a notification under article 85 is likely to prejudice materially the presentation of the applicant's case. As a matter of practice, the applicant(s) would wish to recast materially the manner in which the facts and arguments were presented quite irrespective of whether the Commission seeks additional information pursuant to its entitlement under article 5 of Regulation 2367/90.

A consideration of the cooperative/concentrative issue will generally place considerable emphasis upon any collateral agreements or restrictions between the joint venturers and the joint venture company or between the joint venturers *inter se*. In particular, the existence of licensing, supply and distribution arrangements, when coupled with an assessment of the parties' presence on the relevant product markets,[40] is likely to prove central to a determination of the issue of whether, on balance, the arrangements will have as their object or effect the coordination of the parties' competitive behaviour or, in contrast, the establishment of an autonomous economic entity (i.e. a concentrative joint venture). Where such arrangements are regarded as ancillary restrictions,[41] they are probably less likely to tip the

---

[36] See Part A (the Introduction) of Form CO which sets out the Commission's policy in respect of claims that information can not or need not be provided.

[37] Art.4(1).

[38] Art.14.

[39] See generally the complementary note to Form A/B.

[40] See generally the Commission's Notice on concentrative and cooperative operations, Appendix III.

[41] See 2.1.8 and 5.1.2.3.

balance in favour of a finding of cooperation, since by definition they will be adjudged directly related, necessary and subservient to the attainment of the concentration.

A great many of the questions that a consideration of the concentrative/cooperative test in the context of a joint venture will give rise to can perhaps be better understood in the context of an example:

> A, B and C establish a joint venture to mine and sell iron ore. Pursuant to the joint venture A and B transfer either the shares or the assets of their existing iron ore mining operations to a joint venture company. As a result, they cease to have an interest in the mining of iron ore and, in addition, have no interest in related markets. C has no equivalent business interests to assign to the joint venture company by way of contribution but instead injects capital by means of a cash subscription for shares. The result is a joint venture company owned as to 1/3 A, 1/3 B and 1/3 C. The joint venture company is jointly controlled by A, B and C. Pursuant to a shareholders' agreement, C operates a foundry and requires supplies of iron ore for smelting. Pursuant to the terms of the joint venture arrangements between the parties, the joint venture company enters into a long-term exclusive purchasing agreement with C, pursuant to which C agrees to obtain its supplies of iron ore from the joint venture company for a period of fifteen years.

(a) The joint venture must first be considered in the light of the Commission's guidance Notice on cooperative and concentrative joint ventures. Had C, like A and B, placed all its mining operations into the joint venture and had C, like A and B, not had any interest in a related market, the arrangements would almost certainly be concentrative and not cooperative. However, the presence of C upon a market that is downstream of the joint venture company and the existence of the long-term exclusive purchasing agreement at once raise elements that may make the arrangements cooperative and not concentrative. First, there is a danger that the joint venture company will be regarded as being substantially dependent on its parents (in this case only one of its parents: C) for the maintenance and development of its business.[42] As such, it runs the risk of failing the first (positive) condition of a concentrative joint venture, namely that it must perform '. . . on a lasting basis all the functions of an autonomous economic entity.' Second there is a danger that the presence of the joint venture company and C on neighbouring markets (the joint venture company as a supplier of raw materials being upstream of C) will lead to a failing of the negative condition for the existence of a concentrative joint venture, namely the 'absence of coordination of competitive behaviour'. In both cases, the extent

---

[42] Appendix III paragraph (16).

to which the joint venture company is dependent upon C for the success of its on-going business and the extent to which it modifies its competitive behaviour to suit C's requirements is likely to prove decisive.

(b)   The long-term exclusive purchasing agreement must be considered in the light of the Commission's Notice on ancillary restrictions, in particular section B of Part III.[43] The Commission recognises in its Notice that, where a business is sold outside a group, it may be necessary during a transitional period to preserve the former group relationship between the vendor and the undertaking sold. The requirement for a transitional period may stem from the fact that the business in question needs a continuing source of supplies (for example of raw materials) or outlets for sales (for example of its finished products) or because the vendor's group is dependent upon the activities of the business sold. In either circumstance, the intention is that any transitional period during which the group relationship is preserved be temporary, in fact no longer than is necessary to enable the undertaking sold or the vendor group to switch from a position of dependence to one of independence. In the present example, the joint venture company was not formerly a part of C's group and accordingly the grounds (described above) for considering the long term exclusive purchasing agreement as a necessary temporary preservation of a former group relationship are absent. It follows that the long-term purchasing obligation between C and the joint venture company will almost certainly not amount to an ancillary restriction.

(c)   The long-term supply agreement will exert a strong influence upon the question of whether the joint venture as a whole is to be regarded as cooperative or concentrative. It is possible however that the joint venture may be regarded as concentrative but that the arrangement (not qualifying as an ancillary restriction) will be judged separately under article 85. This would be an example of a cooperative element of an essentially concentrative transaction being severed and considered separately.[44]

5.1.3   Case law

Commission decisions under Regulation 4064/89 are subject to review by the Court of Justice, by virtue of article 21, and the Notices, on concentrative and cooperative operations and on restrictions ancillary to concentrations, are both expressed to be without prejudice to the interpretation which may be given by the Court of Justice. Perhaps unfortunately, there is little Court of Justice authority on the distinction between concentrative and cooperative joint ventures prior to Regulation 4064/89, although obviously the decision in *BAT & RJ Reynolds* v *Commission*[45] sheds some light on the Court's

---

43   OJ 90/C 203/5; see Appendix IV.
44   See recital 23 of Regulation 4064/89.
45   142 & 156/84 [1988] 4 CMLR 24; see 1.1.3.4.

view. On the other hand, the Commission has confronted the question previously, and it may be possible to derive some guidance from its decisions. The leading case is *SHV/Chevron Oil*.[46] The participants in the joint venture, respectively a Dutch and a US company, each had distribution networks for petroleum products. To some extent they were in competition with each other, although SHV's principal interest was in distributing petroleum products (and not in production or refining) while Chevron Oil's business extended across all aspects of such products, and it distributed some products not handled by SHV (e.g., asphalt). The companies agreed to combine their distribution activities. They achieved this by setting up a joint holding company and a number of jointly owned subsidiaries, which were to sell their products in a number of EEC countries where previously the participants had maintained separate distribution networks. They transferred to the subsidiaries for a period of at least 50 years all such networks, including equipment and other assets previously belonging to the participants. As a result both companies ceased independent activity as distributors of petroleum products. The Commission decided that the agreement was more than a temporary coordination of the competitive behaviour of the undertakings involved: it caused an effectively permanent change in the two undertakings which should be classed as a concentration of the form commonly known as a 'partial merger'. Although there was some residual competition between the participants in respect of unrelated products, it was unlikely to be affected by the agreement. As a consequence, the agreement was said to fall outside the scope of article 85, and the Commission duly issued a negative clearance.[47] Such a joint venture would now fall within the scope of the new Regulation.

De Laval/Stork[48] provides an example of a joint venture which also involved a degree of pooling of resources and activities, but which the Commission eventually determined fell on the other side of the dividing line, so that it fell within the control of article 85. The participants were respectively American and European producers of engineering equipment. Their agreement pooled research, production and marketing for the EEC market of steam turbines, compressors and pumps for a period of five years. De Laval continued to sell such equipment in the USA, and Stork retained some EEC activity in other products. The agreement provided for direct sales on the European market by the participants in certain conditions. The agreement was found not to be a concentration, and so fell within article

---

[46] OJ 1975 L38/14, [1975] 1 CMLR D68.

[47] See also *Zip Fasteners* (Seventh Report on Competition Policy, 1977, 29–32): the crucial factor in the decision is reported as being the fact that the participants had effectively made it impossible for themselves to re-enter the market as competitors of the joint venture they had established.

[48] OJ 1977 L215/11 [1977] 2 CMLR D669. See also *Elopak/Metal Box-Odin* OJ 1990 L209/15.

85. There are two significant elements to the Commission's analysis. In particular, the joint venture was far from permanent; it envisaged coordination of activity over the relatively short period of five years. Moreover, the participants did not simply become holding companies as far as the relevant field of activity was concerned; they remained autonomous undertakings capable of economic activity in their own right in this area.

The decision of the Court of Justice in *BAT & RJ Reynolds* v *Commission* is considered in detail in Chapter 1.[49] It must suffice here merely to recall that the Court's narrower description of the issue in that case, which in the light of the adoption of Regulation 4064/89 may be the one more likely to provide a rule to be subsequently followed by the Court, was that it concerned the acquisition of a minority shareholding in a competing company which remained independent. The Court found that such a transaction did fall to be considered under article 85 EEC in order to review whether it gave rise to opportunities for influencing commercial conduct or to structures which were likely to be used for cooperation. In terms of the definition of concentrative and cooperative operations offered by the Commission in its Notice, this decision appears to treat the transaction as falling into the category of potentially concentrative operations with cooperative overtones so inextricably mixed in that it must be considered under the residual scope of article 85 EEC. Similarly, the Notice on ancillary restrictions[50] defines 'contractual arrangements relating to stages before the establishment of control' as subject to article 85 EEC.

While it must be stressed that there can be no hard and fast rules determining the exact point of distinction between concentrations of the partial merger kind and simple joint ventures falling within article 85, because each case has individual facts which must be assessed in the relevant economic context,[51] it is possible on the strength of the above cases to identify some general principles. The crucial test of whether the agreement falls within article 85 as opposed to Regulation 4064/89 is whether the pooling of resources and the allocation of functions to the joint venture is a temporary or permanent development. If it is only temporary it seems likely that article 85 will be held to apply, whatever the other terms of the agreement. If it is a permanent transfer of resources and functions then the presumption will be that it is a partial merger and so falls outside article 85, but the Commission will examine two further factors.

In the first place, the Commission will want to know the extent to which the participating undertakings have retained a capacity to compete in the same field as the joint venture. The permanence of the transfer will be corroborated by the fact that the participants are no longer in a position

---

[49] See 1.1.3.4.
[50] See Appendix IV para.4.
[51] See 5.3.3.

to compete in the same field. On the other hand, where the participants have retained such capacity there is likely to be a presumption that, even in the absence of express clauses, the participants and the joint venture will in practice be unwilling to compete with each other, to the detriment of the competitive structure of the market.[52] Secondly, the Commission will wish to be satisfied that the partial merger does not cause the participants to modify their competitive stance vis-a-vis one another in respect of business not falling within the scope of the joint venture. Where the closer relationship brought about by participation in the joint venture results in a reduction of competition in unrelated fields then, although the partial merger itself may be beyond the control of article 85, the agreement by which it came about would be subject to such control. It is noticeable, for example, that in the *SHV/Chevron* case[53] the Commission was at pains to point out, in holding that the joint venture did not fall within article 85, that the agreement was unlikely to have any effect on competition between the participants in respect of those aspects of the business which had not been confided to the joint venture.

5.1.4   The legal framework

In the light of the above analysis it is possible to attempt to map the scope in relation to joint ventures of Regulation 4064/89 and article 85 EEC respectively.[54] It must still be made clear that the exact boundaries of the categories below cannot be precisely defined except by reference to the particular facts of a case and any future interpretations of article 3(2) of Regulation 4064/89 by the Court of Justice.

Scope of legal control over joint ventures

Category of joint venture	*Applicable law*
1 JV created to take over existing activity of parent companies, which move out of those markets: the only competitive restrictions can be classed as ancillary to the main purpose.	Regulation 4064/89 applies: competitive restrictions fall to be assessed under article 8(2).

---

[52]   Cf. *GEC/Weir* OJ 1977 L327/26, [1978] 1 CMLR D42.
[53]   Supra note 46.
[54]   Control under Regulation 4064/89 is discussed in Chapter 3; control under article 85 EEC is briefly considered in 5.3 *et seq.*

2	JV created to enter new markets not previously occupied by the parent companies, and it is not reasonably foreseeable that the parents will also enter those markets: the only competitive restrictions can be classed as ancillary to the main purpose.	Regulation 4064/89 applies: competitive restrictions fall to be assessed under article 8(2).
3	JV of category 1 or 2 above, but parent companies and/or JV accept restrictions which cannot be classed as ancillary, but which may be regarded as severable from the concentrative element (e.g., a long-term exclusive supply agreement).	Regulation 4064/89 applies to the concentrative element. Article 85 EEC applies to the severable, non-ancillary element.
4	JV of category 1 or 2 above, but parent companies and/or JV accept restrictions which cannot be classed as ancillary, and which may not be regarded as severable from the concentrative element (e.g., interlocking directorships regarded by the parties as essential to their JV).	Article 85 EEC applies to all aspects of the JV.
5	JV created to take over existing activity of parent companies, but the parent companies do not move out of those markets: the only express competitive restrictions can be classed as ancillary to the main purpose.	Article 85 EEC applies unless the presumption of cooperation can be rebutted.
6	JV created to enter new markets not previously occupied by the parent companies, but it is reasonably foreseeable that the parents will also enter those markets; or the parent companies operate on proximate markets; the only express competitive restrictions can be classed as ancillary to the main purpose.	Article 85 EEC applies unless the presumption of cooperation can be rebutted.
7	Short-term JV expressly intended to enable cooperation between parent companies (e.g., joint R & D).	Article 85 EEC applies (but there may be a block exemption).

5.2 COMMON TYPES OF JOINT VENTURE

Joint ventures come in too many different forms for it to be possible to pin them down to simple categories. Indeed, many joint ventures spill across the borders of the broad types listed below. Nevertheless, it may be useful to describe the common characteristics of the more commonly encountered joint ventures. It should be noted, however, that these joint ventures are being considered because they have the potential at least to be concentrative. This Chapter does not consider joint ventures which are only ever cooperative in nature, such as specialisation agreements.[55]

5.2.1 Production joint ventures

This name is given to joint ventures where, whatever other joint elements there may be in the pooled activities transferred to the new undertaking by the participants, the central activity is actual production. As a broad generalisation it may be suggested that joint ventures in this form are the most likely to fall into the category of partial mergers and so be subject to Regulation 4064/89, although many such joint ventures will not reach that level of integration and will remain subject to article 85.[56]

The motives for such ventures vary. The Commission has noted that they may often have beneficial effects by contributing to cross-border integration, facilitating high-risk investments,[57] technological innovation[58] and transfer,[59] and development of new markets, as well as enabling small and medium-size firms to become more competitive and eliminating overcapacity.[60] On the other hand, the result of this form of integration of business activity is usually to leave one undertaking operating on the relevant market where previously there were two, with a potentially adverse effect on the competitive structure.[61] As a consequence, there are good reasons for ensuring that all such joint ventures are subject to scrutiny to ensure that they do not in fact have such adverse effects.

5.2.2 Joint selling

A joint selling arrangement exists where producers who are independent of each other and supposedly competing choose to cooperate in selling their

---

55   There is a block exemption for such agreements: Reg. 417/85 OJ 1985 L53/1.
56   There is a possibility of their taking advantage of the block exemption for specialisation agreements: see note 55.
57   *GEC/Weir* OJ 1977 L327/26 [1978] 1 CMLR D42; *KEWA* OJ 1976 L51/15 [1976] 2 CMLR D15.
58   *Carbon Gas Technologie* OJ 1983 L376/17 [1984] 2 CMLR 275.
59   *Olivetti/Canon* OJ 1988 L52/51.
60   15th Report on Competition Policy (1986), para 26.
61   *Carbon Gas Technologie* (above note 58); *Amersham/Buchler* OJ 1982 L314/34 [1983] 1 CMLR 619.

products through some form of separate, jointly controlled operation. A common form of such cooperation would be the establishment of a jointly owned subsidiary charged with the sales activity of all the participants. Such an arrangement is an express coordination of commercial behaviour, and would result in the joint venture operating in markets downstream from the parent companies. Consequently, Regulation 4064/89 would not normally apply, and the joint venture would be subject to article 85 EEC. Since such cooperation would eliminate competition in sales between the participants, which would normally be one of the key aspects of competition on any given market, the *prima facie* case for prohibition under article 85(1) is very strong,[62] although there are circumstances where an exemption under article 85(3) might be justified.[63]

5.2.3 Joint purchasing

Joint purchasing may be in one of two forms. As the mirror image of joint selling, it may consist of an agreement by two or more undertakings to buy all or a certain percentage of their requirement of a certain product or products through a particular channel, possibly a jointly owned subsidiary established for the purpose. Where the undertakings accept an obligation to purchase all requirements through the joint venture they eliminate the potential for competition between them in respect of the terms upon which they acquire the products in question and reduce the number of available outlets for third party suppliers, and so article 85(1) will inevitably apply. Even where the percentage which they are committed to acquire through the joint venture is lower than 100% the agreement will fall foul of article 85(1), but the countervailing advantages brought by security of supply and possibly lower prices derived from the economies of scale in purchasing by the joint venture may give grounds for an exemption under article 85(3).[64] The other form of joint purchasing is simply an agreement as to the prices which the participants will pay when buying certain products. As such it is simply a form of reverse price-fixing, and will inevitably have an adverse effect on competition. In either case, the essence of the operation is the coordination of competitive behaviour, and so Regulation 4064/89 cannot apply.

---

[62] *CSV* OJ 1978 L242/15 [1979] 1 CMLR 11.
[63] *Vacuum Interrupters* OJ 1977 L48/32 [1977] 1 CMLR D67; *Amersham/Buchler* (note 61); *GEC/Weir* (note 57); *Rockwell/IVECO* OJ1983 L224/19 [1983] 3 CMLR 709: in each case the restrictions were regarded as necessary to ensure full benefit from the approved joint production.
[64] Cf. *National Sulphuric Acid Association* OJ 1980 L260/24, [1980] 3 CMLR 429.

5.2.4 Joint research and development

'Joint R & D' exists where independent and supposedly competing undertakings suspend that competition in the area of research and development. Such agreements again inevitably involve the coordination of competitive behaviour, and so fall within article 85(1) rather than Regulation 4064/89.[65] R & D offers a particular opportunity for competition between undertakings, which may be able to gain considerable advantages over one another by virtue of technical breakthroughs achieved as a result of such activity. Where participants in a joint venture opt to forego these competitive advantages by sharing the results of R & D with firms who are otherwise competitors there will inevitably be some adverse impact on competition.[66] Nevertheless, the Commission always recognised that such agreements are among the most likely to bring compensating benefits, and therefore granted a considerable number of individual exemptions[67] and has now established a block exemption.[68]

The particular advantages of joint R & D are that it may allow the cost of very expensive research to be shared, and economies of scale to be achieved in the operation of necessary laboratories etc; high-risk activities may be undertaken which individual firms might be unwilling to attempt alone; cross-border cooperation may contribute to integration of the single market, not least by allowing technology transfer which enables European industries to compete with firms on the world market. The block exemption seeks to encourage these advantages while ensuring that the restriction on competition does not spill over into other areas of the participants' activity, reducing competition in the sales of finished products.[69]

5.3 THE APPLICATION OF ARTICLE 85 EEC TO COOPERATIVE JOINT VENTURES[70]

In many respects the application of article 85(1) to cooperative joint ventures of the types outlined above raises questions which arise in relation to the

[65] In *Eurogypsum* JO 1968 L57/9 [1968] CMLR D1 even article 85(1) EEC was held not to apply in the case of the pre-industrial stage of an industry research association.
[66] *Henkel/Colgate* JO 1972 L14/14.
[67] E.g., *BP/Kellog* OJ 1985 L369/6 [1986] 2 CMLR 619; *Carbon Gas Technologie* OJ 1983 L376/17 [1984] 2 CMLR 275; *Beecham/Parke Davis* OJ 1979 L70/11 [1979] 2 CMLR 157.
[68] Regulation 418/85 OJ 1985 L53/5. In *BBC/Brown Boveri* OJ 1988 L301/68 the agreement was to last too long to come within the terms of the block exemption, but was granted individual exemption.
[69] See 5.3.5 below.
[70] The following section offers only a very general outline treatment, and the reader should consult more specialist works on articles 85 and 86 EEC and on joint ventures in particular; e.g., Bellamy & Child Chapters 4 & 5, Fine, *Mergers and Joint Ventures in Europe* (Kluwer, 1989). The section does not consider specialisation agreements, for which there is a block exemption: supra note 55.

general application of article 85. Issues of whether both participants are undertakings, whether there is an agreement, whether there is an effect on trade between Member States and whether the effect on competition is so insignificant as to fall below the threshold at which the Commission will impose the prohibition of article 85(1) are all issues of general application which do not raise specific problems in relation to joint ventures.

The distinctive question, therefore, over the application of article 85(1) to cooperative joint ventures is the determination of whether they have the object or effect of preventing, restricting or distorting competition. In *Consten & Grundig v Commission*[71] the Court of Justice established a fairly low threshold at which the criteria would be satisfied by holding that where competition would develop in a manner which was different from what might have been expected in the absence of the agreement then competition would have been distorted. Since cooperative ventures inevitably involve parties adopting business strategies which are at variance with what they had done previously, usually involving some limitation on previous competition or the potential for it, it is not difficult to see that all such joint ventures may be regarded as satisfying this criterion. Consequently, the only question would seem to be whether the effect was so insignificant as to fall within the *de minimis* rule. The critical test, therefore, is of whether the joint venture has the object or effect of so affecting competition.

5.3.1 The *per se* approach

Since the purpose of joint ventures is usually to carry through some positive plan, and not simply to restrict competition, the scope for the application of the *per se* rule is slight. This approach has been used where the inevitable and immediate effect of the agreement will be either to fix prices or to partition the single market.[72] It will be rare that this can be said of a joint venture, although there is a small number of cases which at least come close to such an analysis.[73] More normally it will be possible to identify an advantageous purpose underlying the joint venture, so that a full economic assessment is necessary.[74]

---

[71] 56 & 58/64 [1966] ECR 299.
[72] E.g., 41/69 *ACF Chemifarma v Commission* [1970] ECR 661; 48/69 etc *ICI v Commission* [1972] ECR 619; 209/78 etc *Van Landewyck v Commission* [1980] ECR 3125; 123/83 *BNIC v Clair* [1985] ECR 391; 40/73 etc *Suiker Unie v Commission* [1975] ECR 1663.
[73] E.g., *Belgian Industrial Timber* 5th Report on Competition Policy (1976) para 36: joint buying under which maximum prices were fixed; Commission announced intention to investigate the agreement, whereupon the joint venture was abandoned.
[74] E.g., 61/80 *Cooperative Stremsel-en-Kleurselfabriek* [1981] ECR 851, [1982] 1 CMLR 240; joint buying group had effect of partitioning market; analysis allowed to show that agreement did produce improvements in production and distribution; no exemption granted because degree of restriction outweighed gains achieved.

5.3.2 Clearance under the article 85(1) EEC rule of reason

The scope for clearance under the article 85(1) rule of reason (on the ground that the main thrust of the agreement is not anti-competitive and only certain necessary, ancillary terms have an anti-competitive effect[75]) is slight. Indeed, where such conditions existed the joint venture might be treated as concentrative, and the restrictions as merely ancillary, thus falling under Regulation 4064/89. Cooperative joint ventures inherently involve in their principal purpose elements of combination and coordination which are potentially anti-competitive. Those cases where the agreement, though containing restrictive terms, was found not to infringe article 85(1), had as their principle purpose straightforward commercial transactions, such as franchising, new product licensing and the sale of a business.[76] Such transactions were not of themselves restrictive of competition, although one can well see that the commercial value of the transaction might be questionable unless some ancillary restraint were imposed. Since joint ventures appear to be inherently restrictive of competition,[77] this type of analysis seems unlikely to apply. The only possible opening for such an approach lies in the relatively early decision on the rule of reason in *Metro v Commission (No 1)*.[78]

In this case the Commission's finding, confirmed by the Court, was that the restrictive elements in the agreement did not fall within article 85(1), since they were 'objectively justified' as a means of ensuring the proper distribution of the goods. The agreement appears to have had an inherently restrictive purpose, as opposed to being merely a commercial transaction for which certain restrictions were necessary but ancillary, since the purpose was from the outset only to appoint certain selected retailers as outlets for the goods in question. If, despite this inherently anti-competitive element in the agreement, the rule of reason approach may still apply, allowing a balancing of the gains to be made under an agreement against the anti-competitive elements, then there may be some scope for the same approach to apply in the case of joint ventures. This would result in making it unnecessary to notify such agreements and permitting greater scope to national courts for finding such agreements to be valid. Many joint ventures offer the same balance of inherent gains and restrictions as were found in the *Metro* case. The best example is joint R & D, where this approach would

---

[75] Infra note 76.
[76] *Pronuptia de Paris* v *Schillgalis*.161/84 [1986] ECR 353, [1986] 1 CMLR 414. See also: 26/76 *Metro* v *Commission (No 1)* [1977] ECR 1875, [1978] 2 CMLR 1; 258/78 *Nungesser* v *Commission* [1982] ECR 2015, [1983] 1 CMLR 278; 42/84 *Remia* v *Commission* [1987] 1 CMLR 1.
[77] Cf. the Commission's comments in *GEC/Weir* OJ 1977 L327/26 [1978] 1 CMLR D42.
[78] 26/76 [1977] ECR 1875, [1978] 2 CMLR 1. There is evidence of such reasoning in *Elopack/ Metal Box-Odin* OJ L209/15.

probably be otiose in view of the block exemption.[79] Nevertheless, the approach might apply equally well to production joint ventures where there is no block exemption. Some evidence of the Commission's willingness to take such an approach can be found in the *Mitchell Cotts/Sofiltra* decision.[80]

5.3.3   Economic analysis of anti-competitive effect

The majority of joint venture cases are likely to fall within the economic analysis of effect approach, first espoused in the *Société Technique Minière* case.[81] The Commission has provided a list of the criteria it may use in making this assessment:[82]

> '*Input of the joint venture*: Does the investment expenditure involved substantially exceed the financial capacity of each partner? Does each partner have the necessary technical know-how and sources of supply of input products?
> *Production of the joint venture*: Is each partner familiar with the process technology? Does each partner itself produce inputs for or products derived from the joint venture's product and does it have access to the necessary production facilities?
> *Sales by the joint venture*: Is the actual or potential demand such that it would make it feasible for each of the partners to manufacture the product on its own? Does each have access to the necessary distribution channels for the joint venture's product?
> *Risk factor*: Could each partner bear the technical and financial risks associated with the production operations of the joint venture alone?'

These criteria amount to a relatively straightforward question, which the Commission may put in two ways. At its most simple the test is: are the parties actual or potential competitors in the field in question? Actual competition should be relatively easy to detect: potential competition, especially in respect of a new product or process, is less easy to discern, and the detailed criteria listed above represent an attempt to formulate guidelines to the existence of potential competition. At this level the question becomes: should these parties really be 'going it alone' as far as this particular business venture is concerned, given their technical, financial and commercial resources? The evidence suggests that in most cases the Commission is satisfied that at least the potential for competition exists between the

---

[79]   Regulation 418/85 OJ 1985 L53/5.
[80]   OJ 1987 L41/31, [1988] 4 CMLR 111.
[81]   56/65 [1966] ECR 235, [1966] CMLR 357.
[82]   13th Report on Competition Policy, para 55.

participants in joint ventures,[83] although occasionally the outcome may be
influenced by a finding that the extent of competition (actual or potential)
between participants is very small.[84] Where barriers to entry are high, as
may well be the case with new technology, one might expect the Commission
to take a more lenient view of the capacity of individual undertakings to
go it alone.

Once it is established that the participants are actual or potential
competitors, it is necessary to determine the effect of the joint venture on
competition between them, both in respect of the field in question and in
other fields not within the joint venture but in which the participants also
compete. As far as the former is concerned, the Commission clearly takes
the view, not without good reason, that, where participating undertakings
have put effort and resources into a joint venture charged with given tasks
in a particular field, those participants will inevitably modify their competitive
stance vis-à-vis one another and the joint venture in that field, even in the
absence of formal requirements in their agreement that they should so do.[85]
For the latter, the Commission will be vigilant over arrangements such as
interlocking shareholdings, cross-directorships or shared management
between the participants and the joint venture which might result in the
coordination of competitive strategy in other areas.[86] Finally, the Commission
will examine the extent to which the joint venture may affect the position
of third parties on the market. Here it is difficult to make general predictions
about the Commission's attitude, although at least some common effects
on third parties may be noted. Many joint ventures are established as suppliers
of requirements to the participants and others: this may result in the
participants ceasing purchasing from other suppliers,[87] and in those who
previously purchased from the participants being faced with a reduction
in the number of suppliers.[88] In almost all cases, the fact that the participants
enter into a joint venture with each other will result in the same advantage
being denied other firms on the market who might otherwise have wished
to seek that form of cooperation.

5.3.4   The application of article 85(3) to cooperative joint ventures

Exemption under article 85(3) EEC may be granted where the agreement
contributes to improvements in production or distribution or to technical

---

[83] E.g., *Vacuum Interrupters* OJ 1977 L48/32 [1977] 1 CMLR D67; cf. *Vacuum Interrupters
      (No 2)* OJ 1980 L383/1 [1981] 2 CMLR 217: new participant; *KEWA* OJ 1976 L51/
      15 [1976] 2 CMLR D15; *Rockwell/IVECO* OJ 1983 L224/19 [1983] 3 CMLR 709; *BP/
      Kellog* OJ 1985 L369/6 [1986] 2 CMLR 619.
[84] This may have contributed to the decision in *Mitchell Cotts/Sofiltra*, supra note 80.
[85] Cf. *GEC/Weir* OJ 1977 L327/26 [1978] 1 CMLR D42.
[86] Ibid; and see *Bayer/Gist-Brocades* OJ 1976 L30/13, [1976] 1 CMLR D98.
[87] E.g., *WANO Schwarzpulver* OJ 1978 L322/26, [1979] 1 CMLR 403.
[88] E.g., *GEC/Weir* supra note 85.

or economic progress, provided a fair share of the benefit is passed to consumers, there are no unnecessary restrictions on competition and the agreement does not allow the possibility of eliminating competition in a substantial part of the market in question. The first step must therefore be to identify the qualifying benefits which result from the joint venture agreement. In most cases this presents little difficulty.

In joint selling and joint purchasing agreements there may be improvements in distribution resulting from the joint venture.[89] Research and development are generally recognised as bringing, respectively, technical and economic progress and improvements in production and distribution, to such an extent that such agreements benefit from a block exemption.[90] It is less easy to generalise about the benefits to be derived from production joint ventures, but that is not to say that such benefits do not exist.[91] Even in the relatively rare cases where the Commission has not looked favourably upon the agreement and has refused to grant an individual exemption the reason has usually been because the benefits are insufficient to outweigh the adverse effect, rather than because there were no benefits at all.[92]

In most cases, therefore, the crucial question will be whether, after formation of the joint venture, competition in the market in question will be so impaired that the effect cannot be counterbalanced by the gains resulting from the agreement. Thus, the Commission will be much less likely to grant an exemption to a joint venture in which the participants are some of the few major manufacturers on the market than it will to a joint venture which will allow small or medium-sized firms to achieve the necessary market presence to compete with the larger undertakings already there. Even large firms may be able to persuade the Commission to grant an exemption if their agreement will in fact improve the competitive structure by adding to the number of undertakings actually competing on the market. This may be the case if firms can show that each would not have carried out the particular venture without the participation of the other firm.[93] Even then, the Commission will wish to be satisfied that there are no indispensable restrictions on competition, and to that end may require the agreement to be modified before giving approval, and may impose conditions.

In assessing the indispensability of restrictions, the Commission's first aim will be to ensure that the same benefits could not have been achieved through a less restrictive arrangement. For example, in the

---

[89] But see *Floral* OJ 1980 L39/51 [1980] 2 CMLR 285 and *CSV* OJ 1978 L242/15 [1979] 1 CMLR 11.

[90] Reg.418/85 OJ 1985 L53/5.

[91] Cf. *Vacuum Interrupters* (supra note 83); *De Laval/Stork* (supra note 48); *GEC/Weir* (supra note 85); *Rockwell/IVECO* (supra note 83).

[92] Cf. *WANO/Schwarzpulver* (supra note 87); but see *Floral* OJ 1980 L39/51 [1980] 2 CMLR 285 (joint selling).

[93] E.g., *Vacuum Interrupters* (supra note 83); *GEC/Weir* (supra note 85); *KEWA* (supra note 83).

Bayer/Gist-Brocades case[94] the participants wished to establish a specialisation arrangement in the production of raw penicillin and a derivative product. In addition, they proposed a production joint venture involving joint ownership of the respective plants where the products were manufactured. The Commission took the view that the production joint venture would greatly increase the risk of further cooperation in sales, and was not indispensable to the major benefits in specialisation of production which the agreement offered. The specialisation element in the agreement was granted an exemption, but not the production joint venture.

Once the Commission accepts that a joint venture is an appropriate means of achieving the identified benefits, it will consider the individual restrictions to determine whether they are indispensable. In this, the Commission's policy has become relatively clear, as can be seen from the 'black' and 'white' lists of the block exemptions,[95] so that it is to some extent possible to generalise about unacceptable and acceptable restrictions. In particular, restrictions will be unacceptable which provide absolute territorial protection and thus serve to partition the market, or which encourage cooperation and coordination in relation to products not within the joint venture agreement, or which would continue to affect competition after the joint venture agreement has ended. Restrictions which will be accepted as indispensable include those preventing competition during the currency of the agreement between the participants in the field of the joint venture, and exclusive purchasing obligations on the participants towards a production joint venture. In joint research and development it will be regarded as indispensable for the participants to agree not to engage independently in R & D in the field in question, nor to engage in similar work with third parties, and, where the agreement extends to production, to purchase exclusively from the joint venture.

5.3.5   The joint R & D block exemption

Regulation 418/85[96] applies article 85(3) to categories of agreements relating to research and development, as defined in article 1.[97] The exemption applies, where the participants are competing manufacturers of relevant products, only to agreements where the participants' market share in relation to relevant products is no more than 20% of the market for such products in the common market or a substantial part thereof;[98] there is no qualifying criterion in

---

[94]   OJ 1976 L30/13 [1976] 1 CMLR D98.
[95]   Cf. Reg.418/85 arts. 6 and 5 respectively.
[96]   OJ 1985 L53/5.
[97]   I.e. joint research and development of products or processes, with or without joint exploitation of the results of that R & D, and whether exploitation is provided for in the same or a subsequent agreement. For a more detailed definition see art.1(2).
[98]   Art.3(2).

terms of aggregate turnover. Where the participants are not competing manufacturers in this sense the market share criterion does not apply. The exemption endures for the period of the specified programme, and, in the case of joint exploitation, for a period of five years from the time when the contract products are put onto the common market.[99] This period may be extended indefinitely for as long as the market share does not exceed 20%.[100] The Regulation provides a relatively complex classification of restrictions. Article 2 lists obligations which the agreement must contain, including:

(a) both research and development must be carried out within a specific programme;

(b) all participants must have access to results;

(c) each party must be free to exploit results independently;

(d) joint undertakings or third parties charged with manufacture of the contract goods must be required to supply them only to the participants.

Article 4 lists the approved restrictions which it is accepted are indispensable to such agreements,[101] including:

(a) a requirement that there be no independent R & D in the field in question, or any closely connected field;

(b) a similar requirement that there be no such R & D agreements with third parties;

(c) an obligation to procure contract products from the undertaking charged with manufacturing them;

(d) an obligation not to manufacture the contract products in territories reserved for other participants;

(e) a requirement that, for a period of five years, there be no active marketing in the territory of another participant;

(f) a requirement for communication of experience gained in exploitation, and non-exclusive licensing for related innovations or new applications.

Article 5 lists restrictions which are accepted as not unduly harmful to competition and commonly feature in such agreements,[102] including:

---

[99] Art.3(1).

[100] Art.3(3). There is a margin of error of 10% on the permitted market share for any period of up to 2 financial years (i.e. not >22%) without prejudice to the exemption: art. 3(4). Once the termination of the exemption is set in motion by an increase in market share, the exemption is to end after six months of the financial year following the financial year in which the market share was exceeded.

[101] Preamble, recital 6.

[102] Preamble, recital 11.

(a) an obligation to treat know-how received from another participant in confidence, even after the expiry of the programme, and to use it only for the purpose of the programme;

(b) an obligation to obtain and maintain in force intellectual property rights in respect of contract products;

(c) an obligation to supply other participants with minimum quantities and qualities of contract products.

There are indications[103] that the lists given are not be regarded as exhaustive. Finally, article 6 lists restrictions which must not be included (the so-called 'black' list),[104] including:

(a) a restriction on freedom to enter joint R & D agreements with third parties in unrelated fields;

(b) a restriction on the quantity of contract products which may be manufactured or on the number of operations to which the contract process may be applied;

(c) restrictions on any aspect of price setting;

(d) restrictions on marketing in another participant's territory after expiry of the five year period;

(e) restrictions on supplying dealers in their own territory who might market contract goods elsewhere, or similar restrictions on behaviour which might contribute to absolute territorial protection.

Where the agreement contains restrictions which do not fall within the 'black' list, but which are not specified within either articles 4 or 5, the opposition procedure applies, so that if the agreement is notified in accordance with Regulation 27 and not opposed by the Commission within six months thereof it is exempt.[105] On the other hand, the exemption may be withdrawn from any individual agreement if the Commission finds that it is incompatible with article 85(3).[106]

5.4 CONCLUSION

Joint ventures have already been described as having a special place in EC merger control. It seems likely that they will continue to do so. In part this is because companies regard them as an appropriate vehicle for moving into new markets as part of the process of European integration. Nowhere is this more true than in the efforts to develop trade with former Eastern bloc countries. The use of joint ventures for such purposes may be attributable

---

[103] Ibid, and art.5(1): '. . . any of the following obligations, *in particular*, . . .' (emphasis added).
[104] Preamble, recital 12.
[105] Art.7.
[106] Art.10.

to the lower cost of joint ventures by comparison with outright acquisitions in a time of recession, and perhaps a perception of lower risk associated with a lower level of initial commitment. In addition, where companies wish to move into new geographic markets, joint ventures with local partners offer the advantage of a management structure with local knowledge already in place. Whatever the reasons, it is clear that while the rush for acquisitions witnessed in the United Kingdom in the late 1980s has subsided dramatically, joint venture activity is increasingly prevalent. However, joint ventures are also likely to attract attention in the field of EC merger control because of the difficulties of pinning down an appropriate and consistent means of regulating them. The fact that they may take the form of either non-concentrative cooperation between companies which remain independent, or alternatively a concentration with a permanent change in the structure of the companies involved, makes the job of regulation much more difficult, because no single body of rules under Community law is sufficient to cope with their complexity. One of the most difficult tasks facing the Commission, both in the Merger Task Force and in the rest of DG IV where articles 85 and 86 EEC are handled, will be to establish a clear and fair practice in relation to joint ventures, so that businesses planning new enterprises may know where they stand. It is understood that the Commission intends to publish a further notice giving general guidance in relation to joint ventures, and it is clear that such advice will be welcomed by the business community.

SIX
Merger control in the
Coal and Steel Community

The European Coal and Steel Community was created by the Treaty of Paris of 1951, and came into being in July of the following year.[1] Although the Treaty of Paris contains merger control provisions, and may be regarded as a stepping stone on the way to the foundation of the full Economic Community under the Treaty of Rome, for which it was clearly in many respects a model, there are significant differences between the regimes instituted by the two Treaties which make reasoning by analogy from one to the other inappropriate. For the purposes of this work, the most important difference is the absence of specific merger control provisions in the Treaty of Rome. As a result, the exploration of the outer limits of controls on restrictive agreements and on abuse of dominant position, to discover whether they might be used as instruments of merger control, has not been necessary in the case of the Treaty of Paris. A second important distinction is the fact that for most of the period during which the Coal and Steel Community has been in existence, both of these sectors have suffered considerable difficulty caused by over-capacity and a lack of competitiveness by comparison with producers on the world market, which in each case had a significant role to play within the Community. For that reason there has been a much greater emphasis on rationalisation. No doubt this factor led to the third important distinction between the Coal and Steel Community and the Economic Community, which is that while the latter is in many respects an aggressively free market economy, with great emphasis placed on competition and the need to create the 'level playing field' in which such competition can prosper, the former has been subject to a more *dirigiste* implementation by the Commission.[2] Finally, in respect of the sectors falling within the scope of the Treaty, the Member States have transferred all authority, so that there should be no question of overlap of Community and national law. As a consequence, although the provision of merger control in the Treaty of Paris and its omission in the Treaty of Rome may be thought

[1] UK accession to ECSC came in 1973 at the same time as accession to the Economic Community.
[2] Formerly the High Authority: art.8 ECSC - see now art.9, Merger Treaty 1965.

unusual and perhaps significant, in fact, the two regimes are so different that there are few parallels to be drawn. Merger control under the Treaty of Paris is a well established and frequent activity, which presents relatively few difficulties.

6.1 THE SCOPE OF MERGER CONTROL UNDER THE TREATY OF PARIS

6.1.1 The Treaty in general

The Treaty applies to certain products falling within the general definition of 'coal' and 'steel', as specified in Annex I.[3] As well as applying to the Member States,[4] the Treaty applies to any 'undertaking' falling within the definition in article 80, which reads:

'For the purposes of this Treaty, "undertaking" means any undertaking engaged in production in the coal or steel industry within the territories referred to in the first paragraph of article 79, and also, for the purposes of articles 65 and 66 and of information required for their application and proceedings connected with them, any undertaking or agency regularly engaged in distribution other than sale to domestic consumers or small craft industries.'[5]

6.1.2 The scope of merger control

Merger control under the Treaty of Paris is provided for in article 66. Consequently, the more specific definition of 'undertaking' in article 80 applies in this case.[6] Article 66 is expressed as applying to 'action by any person or undertaking or group of persons or undertakings' which results in 'a concentration between undertakings at least one of which is covered by article 80, whether the transaction covers a single product or a number of different products'.[7] It would seem from these provisions that not all the undertakings involved need be established within the Community, and that, of the parties to the concentration, only one need be a 'coal and steel'

---

[3] Art.81. Annex I may be amended by unanimous decision of Council, and has been: see JO 1962 129/2810. Annex II makes provision for the application, subject to certain limitations, of the Treaty to ferrous scrap. Cf. Halsbury's Laws, 4th ed. (1986) Vol.51, 9.10-9.11.

[4] Cf. arts.79, 86, 88.

[5] In 20/61 *Klöckner-Werke AG and Hoesch AG v High Authority* [1962] ECR 325 at 341 the Court ascribes the definition 'undertaking' to a company within a group if it has its own legal personality; this approach contrasts with the enterprise entity analysis used in respect of article 85 EEC, under which legal personality is irrelevant if there is no economic independence.

[6] See 6.1.1.

[7] See 6.2 below.

undertaking within the meaning of article 80. Nevertheless, this element of the scope of merger control under the Treaty has been restricted by Decision 25/67, which exempts certain classes of merger from the requirement of authorisation, including mergers with non-coal/steel companies, except where the coal/steel consumption of the companies concerned exceeds a prescribed limit.[8] Furthermore, the reference to 'a number of different products' would appear to be otiose if such products must all fall within the article 81 definition, so that the conclusion must be that it is intended that article 66 should apply to mergers where some of the products concerned do not fall within the definition of 'coal and steel' in article 81. However, while such a merger may fall within the scope of article 66, the exclusion of national jurisdiction appears only to apply in the case of 'coal and steel' products, and national authorities may exercise their own merger jurisdiction in respect of products not falling within the scope of the ECSC Treaty.[9]

6.1.3   Mergers exempt from the authorisation process

Article 66(3) requires the Commission to make regulations, with the assent of the Council, which operate to exempt from the prior authorisation process categories of concentration which may be deemed to meet the requirements for authorisation by virtue of the size of the undertakings concerned and/ or the nature of the concentration to be effected. This requirement was implemented by Decision 25/67,[10] from which it is possible to identify seven separate categories of exemption. By virtue of article 9(2) of Decision 25/ 67, where the concentration satisfies the definition of more than one of the categories, exemption from the authorisation process will only be granted if it meets the requirements for exemption for each category within which it falls. The categories are as follows:

(a)   Under article 1 of Decision 25/67, concentrations between producer undertakings will be exempt if, in the case of most products,[11] total annual output does not exceed a specified tonnage, or, in the case of certain steel products,[12] total annual output does not exceed 30% of overall output of goods of this kind within the Community.

(b)   Under article 2 of Decision 25/67, concentrations between coal

---

8   JO 1967 154/11, as amended by Decision 2495/78 OJ 1978 L300/21. For further exemptions see 6.1.3.
9   See the treatment of the *GKN/Sachs* merger by the German competition authority ([1977] 1 CMLR D10 and [1978] 1 CMLR 66) and the comment by the Commission in the 6th Report on Competition Policy (1976), at 110-113.
10   Supra note 8.
11   I.e. coal, fuel manufactured from coal, coke, agglomerated ore, pre-reduced ore, pig iron and ferro-alloys, crude steel, alloy and non-alloy special steels, finished rolled steel products. Iron ore is not subject to a limit.
12   Specified in article 1(2).

producers and undertakings outside the article 80 definition will be exempt if the annual coal consumption of the undertakings concerned does not exceed a specified tonnage. The limits apply both to the aggregate consumption of all the undertakings and to the individual consumption of each undertaking falling outside the article 80 definition.

(c) Under article 3 (as amended) of Decision 25/67, concentrations between steel producers and undertakings outside the article 80 definition will be exempt if the annual steel production and consumption of the undertakings concerned does not exceed specified tonnages, or the undertakings outside the article 80 definition do not use steel as a raw material. The steel producers' production is subject to a limit, as is the aggregate consumption of all undertakings. Steel used in production and/or upkeep and renewal of installations of the undertakings involved is not taken into account for the purpose of the limit on consumption.

(d) Under article 4 (as amended) of Decision 25/67, concentrations between coal distributors, other than distributors to domestic consumers and small craft industries (which require no such exemption,[13]) will be exempt if their total annual volume of business, other than distribution to domestic consumers and small craft industries, does not exceed the limit specified.

(e) Under article 5 (as amended) of Decision 25/67, concentrations between steel distributors or between scrap distributors, other than distributors to domestic consumers and small craft industries (which require no such exemption), will be exempt if respectively the total annual steel turnover or the total annual volume of business does not exceed the limit specified. In the case of steel distributors, it is necessary both to consider the turnover of each individual distributor involved and, where more than one distributor is involved, to consider the extent of the increase in turnover resulting from the concentration, to which a limit also applies for the purposes of the exemption.

(f) Under article 6 of Decision 25/67, concentrations between producers of either coal or steel and undertakings which distribute only to domestic consumers or small craft industries are exempt.

(g) Under article 6 of Decision 25/67, concentrations between distributors which fall within the article 80 definition and undertakings which are outside that definition are exempt.

These exemptions are subject to the further general qualifying rule, under article 7 of Decision 25/67, that they will not apply in the case of 'group control'. Group control exists where undertakings, which are not themselves concentrated, but of which at least one falls within the article 80 definition, together exercise legal or *de facto* control over one or more undertakings which produce, distribute or process coal or steel as a raw material. Of

---

[13] Art.80 ECSC; see 6.1.1 above.

course, the result of this provision is simply to expose such undertakings to the requirement of authorisation: it does not of itself provide that a concentration of this kind is necessarily prohibited. Finally, in the case of concentrations entitled to exemption because falling within categories (a) - (e) above, article 10 (as amended) requires notification to the Commission where the turnovers, tonnages etc. for the undertakings concerned are equal to or greater than half of those specified for each category of exemption.

6.2 THE APPLICATION OF ARTICLE 66

Article 66(1) provides:

> 'Any transaction shall require the prior authorisation of the High Authority, subject to the provisions of paragraph 3[14] of this article, if it has in itself the direct or indirect effect of bringing about within the territories referred to in the first paragraph of article 79,[15] as a result of action by any person or undertaking[16] or group of persons or undertakings, a concentration between undertakings at least one of which is covered by article 80, whether the transaction concerns a single product or a number of different products,[17] and whether it is effected by merger, acquisition of shares or parts of the undertaking or assets, loan, contract or any other means of control. For the purposes of applying these provisions, the High Authority shall, by regulations made after consulting the Council, define what constitutes control of an undertaking.'

Subject to the exemptions of a general character provided for in article 66(3), therefore, it is necessary first to establish whether a given transaction amounts to a concentration for the purposes of the article[18] before determining whether the proposed transaction is entitled nevertheless to authorisation.[19] It should be noted that although article 66(1) provides for 'prior authorisation', article 66(5) allows authorisation to be granted retrospectively to a concentration which has already been brought into effect without application for prior authorisation, subject to payment of a fine.

6.2.1 The notion of control

Article 66 ECSC provides no express definition of 'concentration'. It does, however, refer to concentrations being effected by merger, acquisition of

---

[14] See 6.1.3 above.
[15] I.e. 'the European territories of the High Contracting Parties' with certain exceptions as listed in article 79 (e.g., the Faroe Islands, the UK's Sovereign Base Areas in Cyprus).
[16] See 6.1.1 above.
[17] See 6.1.2 above.
[18] See 6.2.1 below.
[19] See 6.2.2 below.

shares or parts of the undertaking or assets, loan, contract or any other means of control. Thus it appears that the intention was that rather than resort to a technical or formalistic definition of concentration, which might always be avoided by careful drafting, the existence of concentration should be determined by a functional test of control. In order to implement that intention, article 66 provides that 'the High Authority shall, by regulations made after consulting the Council, define what constitutes control of an undertaking.' This requirement is satisfied by Decision 24/54.[20] Article 1 lists the relevant elements of control:

(a) ownership of or the right to use some or all of the assets of an undertaking;

(b) rights or contracts through which the power to influence the composition, voting or decisions of the organs of an undertaking has been acquired;

(c) rights or contracts enabling a person, alone or in association with others, to manage the business of an undertaking;

(d) contracts with an undertaking governing the computation or appropriation of its profits;

(e) contracts with an undertaking in respect of the whole or an important part of its supplies or outlets, where such contracts cover time periods or quantities greater than are normal in the circumstances.

Article 1 also provides that these elements are to be assessed to determine the extent to which they make it possible to govern how an undertaking operates in respect of production, prices, investments, supplies, sales and appropriation of profits. Article 3(1) of Decision 24/54 describes the persons by whom such control is exercised, being those who either hold the rights or are entitled to the contract rights; or those who, while not holding or being so entitled, enjoy the power to exercise the rights deriving from them; or those who in a fiduciary capacity have an interest in an undertaking and have powers to exercise the rights attaching to that interest. However, by virtue of article 2, banks and financial institutions do not have control when they acquire shares in an undertaking at the time of its formation or an increase in its capital, when they do so with the intention of selling the shares on the market and do not exercise the voting rights in them.

It might seem that the effect of Decision 24/54 is to undermine the flexibility of the functional test based on the notion of control, by its excessive attention to detail. However, it seems that the Commission does not feel constrained by the definitions supplied, and is able to operate what are simply questions of fact within the framework laid down. Most important is that the Commission conducts a proper analysis of the structure of the undertaking

[20] JO 1954, 345.

and so is able to identify the existence of control in practice, whether or not the arrangement amounts to legal control. For example, in *Re GKN/ Miles Druce Merger*[21] GKN had acquired a 29.9% holding in the target company, which clearly did not amount to legal control. Nevertheless, the Commission was able to show that never more than 60% of the total voting rights were represented at an Extraordinary General Meeting, so that GKN enjoyed *de facto* majority voting rights, and so control. The case is a good example of the practical approach the Commission takes. In the reported cases the issue of control has rarely raised legal difficulties, and is usually disposed of in a single sentence as part of a preliminary explanation of the requirement of authorisation.

6.2.2   The authorisation process

Article 66(2) provides:

> 'The High Authority shall grant the authorisation referred to in the preceding paragraph if it finds that the proposed transaction will not give to the persons or undertakings concerned the power, in respect of the product or products within its jurisdiction:
>
> –   to determine prices, to control or restrict production or distribution or to hinder effective competition in a substantial part of the market for those products; or
>
> –   to evade the rules of competition instituted under this Treaty, in particular by establishing an artificially privileged position involving a substantial advantage in access to supplies or markets.
>
> In assessing whether this is so, the High Authority shall . . . take account of the size of like undertakings in the Community, to the extent it considers justified in order to avoid or correct disadvantages resulting from unequal competitive conditions.'

The application of article 66(2) depends very largely upon the particular facts of the given case. Although it appears to require specific attention to the particular adverse effects listed (i.e. determining prices, controlling or restricting production or distribution, hindering effective competition, evading the rules of competition), in practice many of the cases address all such issues without detailed explanation of how they arise.[22] Nevertheless, the decisions of the Commission reveal a number of general themes central

[21]   [1974] 2 CMLR D17, at paras [13]-[16].
[22]   For a good example of this blanket approach see *GKN/Sachs* [1977] 1 CMLR D19.

to the authorisation process, two of which are introduced by article 66(2) itself.

6.2.2.1 Negative criteria for authorisation

Authorisation does not depend upon the demonstration of positive benefits resulting from the proposed merger. The negative criteria for authorisation may all be summarised as embodying a requirement that the merger should not cause harm;[23] once that is demonstrated the merger is entitled to authorisation. In this respect, article 66 ECSC is similar to Regulation 4064/89. Under the Regulation, a declaration of compatibility with the common market must be made when it can be shown that the concentration will not result in competition in the common market being significantly impeded. So, in respect of the Treaty of Paris, in *Fa J Nold KG v Commission*[24] the applicant complained that the Commission's reasoning in granting authorisation to new conditions of sale imposed by a previously merged undertaking[25] was defective in that it would exclude the applicant from dealing directly with the undertaking in question and that in particular the conditions of sale did not bring any 'substantial improvement' in distribution. This latter argument was drawn from article 65 ECSC, and was said to apply by analogy to article 66 proceedings. The argument was rejected. Although it was possible to find some positive justification for authorising the new conditions of sale,[26] the principal reasoning was that under article 66 there was no requirement of substantial improvement for the grant of authorisation.

6.2.2.2 Relative size and market share

The second theme to emerge directly from article 66 is that, in assessing whether harm might be caused by a proposed merger, the Commission will pay particular attention to the relative size and relative market shares of competing undertakings. The point is made expressly in the following passage from *Geitling Ruhrkohlen Verkaufs GmbH v High Authority:*[27]

'In a market like the coal market . . ., which is characterised by the competition of large industrial units, the power of a marketing organisation to sell depends not so much upon the volume of products it controls as upon the relative volume controlled by rival organisations.'

This concern is well illustrated by two merger authorisations involving

---

[23] As opposed to the article 85 EEC requirement of positive benefit before an exemption may be granted. For the distinction, and an attempt to draw consequences from it, see Hornsby (1988) 13 ELRev 295, 300, 304.

[24] [1974] 2 CMLR 338.

[25] *Ruhrkohle AG*; submission to the authorisation process of new conditions of sale was a condition of the authorisation of the original merger.

[26] Infra note 31.

[27] 13/60 [1962] CMLR 113 at 163; see also *Re Röchling Eisenhandel* [1984] 4 CMLR 213.

the British Steel Corporation. In the first,[28] BSC proposed to acquire a controlling holding in a steel stockholder operating almost entirely within the United Kingdom. At the time BSC had very limited stockholding interests, while the target company obtained 70% of the steel it distributed from BSC. The combined stockholding interests after the merger would amount to about 7% of the UK market, which was deemed to be the relevant market because exports were negligible; on that market one stockholder accounted for about 20% of distribution, and there were many others including several of a size similar to that of the merged undertaking. The Commission granted authorisation on the ground that the new undertaking would not have 'a particularly important position within the UK stockholders' market, but together they will be brought more into balance with some of the largest UK stockholders.'[29] Four years later BSC sought authorisation for a further merger in the stockholding sector;[30] in this case BSC's national market share would increase from 8% to 11%. The Commission again rested the justification for authorisation on the existence of one stockholder with 18% of the market, and three or four others with up to 7%, as well as several hundred others, so that BSC's stockholding operations did not have power to hinder effective competition and did not enjoy an artificially privileged position.

6.2.2.3 Rationalisation

The need for rationalisation in both coal and steel sectors because of over-capacity has had a significant impact on merger authorisation decisions. In the first place, the Commission has sought to encourage this process of rationalisation, and secondly the continuing over-capacity has enabled the Commission to point to continuing competition as a justification for the authorisation given. In *Fa J Nold KG* v *Commission*[31] 'particular economic difficulties created by the recession of coal production' which created a need for rationalisation of coal distribution were held to justify authorisation of new conditions of sale which excluded certain dealers from trading directly with the merged undertaking.

6.2.2.4 International markets

A final theme to have preoccupied the Commission is the significance of the international market, of which the Community is only a part and from which it is not immune. Since imports to the Community from this international market are significant, and since the international market has also suffered from over-capacity, it has been the case that many proposed

---

[28] *Re BSC/Lye Trading Merger* [1975] 1 CMLR D38.
[29] Ibid, at para [11].
[30] *Re BSC Takeover* [1979] 3 CMLR 631.
[31] [1974] 2 CMLR 338; see also *Re Sacilor and Usinor* [1984] 3 CMLR 445, [1990] 4 CMLR 611; *Re Sheffield Forgemasters* [1983] 2 CMLR 219; *Ugine Aciers de Chatillon* [1989] 4 CMLR 540.

mergers, viewed in the light of competition emanating from the international market, could not be considered likely to have an adverse effect on competition. The influence of the international market is noted by the Commission in *Re Hoogovens/Hollandia Takeover*,[32] in a decision concerning the market for scrap steel. It said:

'The level of and movements in scrap prices are governed mainly by the interplay of supply and demand in the international scrap market. There is a tendency for scrap prices to react upon each other round the world. . . . Having regard to the importance of scrap exports from the USA, the lead in the movements tends to be set by the USA scrap price.'

As a consequence, the acquisition by the leading steel producer and scrap consumer of the leading scrap merchant on the Dutch market was held to be entitled to authorisation because the acquiring company still could not determine prices or hinder effective competition in the light of this world market. The way in which the influence of the international market is linked to the need for rationalisation as a justification for authorisation of a merger can be demonstrated by reference to the Commission's decision in *Re Sheffield Forgemasters*.[33] The concentration in question was a production joint venture in which the British Steel Corporation and Johnson & Firth Brown Ltd were participating. The purpose of the joint venture was to rationalise production of forgings and castings, and it had the effect of restricting production in as much as the participants undertook to withdraw from production which might compete with that of the joint venture. The resulting company would be the largest UK producer of such products, but it was no bigger than several other Community producers. Moreover, 25% of such products supplied in the UK were imported, and the Commission took the view that the existence of surplus capacity in the world market would ensure that competition would continue and that the figure for imported supplies would increase. Thus, the joint venture might be regarded as achieving the desirable goal of making UK industry more competitive by the process of rationalisation, while not reducing the level of competition on the UK market.

6.2.3   Authorisation subject to conditions

By article 66(2), sub-paragraph (3), the Commission may make its authorisation 'subject to any conditions which it considers appropriate for the purposes of this paragraph'. This power enables the Commission to maintain a fairly liberal policy towards authorisation, since the elements

---

[32] [1980] 2 CMLR 605 at para [16].
[33] [1983] 2 CMLR 219; see also *Monks Ferry* [1988] 4 CMLR 192.

of a proposed merger which give cause for concern may be made subject
to conditions which either allow the Commission to maintain supervision[34]
or require the undertakings to give up some element of the proposal or
of their existing business operation. An example of comprehensive terms
imposed as a condition of authorisation is provided by the Commission's
decision in *Re Thyssen/Rheinstahl Merger*.[35] The concentration involved a
takeover by one firm of a sizeable competitor, while the acquiring company
already had close links with another large competitor. Conditions were
imposed because the Commission felt that the existing links gave a potential
for the merger to permit a hindrance to competition; the effect of the
conditions was considerably to weaken the existing links. The conditions
were as follows:

(a)   reduce holding in existing joint venture to 25%, and cease management
co-operation agreement;
(b)   cease all shareholding in joint venture partner;
(c)   withdraw from two existing specialisation agreements;
(d)   cease all interlocking directorships, except in the case of the existing
joint venture;
(e)   do not acquire more than a 10% holding in a steel production/
processing/dealing company with an annual consumption over 50,000 tonnes
without prior authorisation.

6.3   PROCEDURE IN RESPECT OF ARTICLE 66

6.3.1   Commission investigations

The Commission's ability to conduct an investigation as part of the
authorisation process depends upon the availability of the necessary
information upon which the evaluation must be based. The Commission's
powers to obtain information depend upon whether the legal or natural person
by whom the information must be supplied is within the jurisdiction of
the ECSC Treaty, i.e. whether it falls within the definition of article 80.[36]

6.3.1.1   Obtaining information from article 80 undertakings
Article 47 ECSC gives the Commission a general power to 'obtain the
information it requires to carry out its tasks'. This provision is silent, however,
on the question of whether there is an obligation to supply information
in the absence of a request from the Commission. There is provision in
article 47(3) for the imposition of fines for evading obligations under 'decisions

---

[34]   E.g., by requiring regular communication of information, or by requiring further authorisation
       of any changes made: cf. *Nold* at note 31.
[35]   [1974] 2 CMLR D1.
[36]   See 6.1.1 above.

taken in pursuance of this Article' and for supplying false information. Such a 'decision' might be addressed to a specific undertaking, or might introduce regulations imposing a general duty to notify the Commission in prescribed circumstances; but no decision of general effect for undertakings within the article 80 definition has been brought into force.[37] Consequently, the supply of the information necessary to trigger a merger investigation appears to rest on a combination of Commission vigilance over activity within the coal and steel sectors and voluntary supply of relevant information.

The key element is the voluntary supply of relevant information. In the first place, the Court of Justice has held that the Commission's right to obtain necessary information translates into an obligation on undertakings to furnish such information voluntarily.[38] More importantly, in the case of merger control, article 66(5) provides a great incentive for voluntary supply of information. If the Commission finds that a merger has taken place without authorisation, but that it would have qualified for authorisation had it been sought, then it may approve the merger provided it imposes a fine.[39] It appears to be accepted that failure to supply the information may result from a genuine mistake as to the extent of the Commission's jurisdiction under the Treaty, since article 66(5), sub-paragraph (1), also provides that the amount of the fine shall not be less than half of the maximum provided for where it is 'clear that authorisation should have been applied for'.

6.3.1.2 Obtaining information from undertakings outside Treaty jurisdiction

Article 66(4) gives the Commission power to make regulations requiring communication of information to it by, and to make specific requests under such regulations for information from, natural or legal persons who have acquired or regrouped or are intending to acquire or regroup the rights or assets in question. This power is expressed to be 'without prejudice to the application of article 47 to undertakings within its jurisdiction', and is apparently intended to allow for the situation in which undertakings outside the article 80 definition, and so outside Commission jurisdiction over mergers, nevertheless engage directly or indirectly in merger activity with coal or steel undertakings.[40] Such regulations were introduced in Decision 26/54,[41] and apply to all legal or natural persons 'except persons engaged within the Community in the production of coal and steel or in the distribution of those products other than by way of sale to domestic consumers or small

---

37 For legal and natural persons not within the article 80 definition, see 6.3.1.2 below.
38 18/62 *Barge* v *High Authority* [1963] ECR 259 at 278, [1965] CMLR 330 at 342.
39 As 'provided for in the second subparagraph of paragraph 6': i.e. not exceeding 10% of the value of the assets acquired or regrouped.
40 See Preamble, recital 1, to Decision 26/54 (infra note 41).
41 JO 1954 350; OJ (Spec Ed) 1952–58 (Oct 1972: English language version).

craft industries'.[42] Article 1 of these regulations requires the supply of specified information in the event of engaging in prescribed transactions. In particular, persons subject to the regulations must notify the Commission of any acquisition of rights, or the power to exercise rights, in any undertaking falling within the article 80 definition by which they acquire more than 10% of the voting power where the total value of the rights held exceeds 100,000 units of account.[43] Under article 7 of the regulations the Commission may make a specific request for information by the Commission.

6.3.2 Interim measures

Article 66(5), sub-paragraph (3), provides:

'The High Authority may at any time, unless the third paragraph of article 39 is applied,[44] take or cause to be taken such interim measures of protection as it may consider necessary to safeguard the interests of competing undertakings and of third parties, and to forestall any step which might hinder the implementation of its decisions. Unless the Court decides otherwise, proceedings shall not have suspensory effect in respect of such interim measures.'

In exercising this power, the Commission must balance the interests of would-be acquirer undertakings, target undertakings and third parties. Its policy in respect of interim measures has been restrictive; measures will not be imposed unless they are urgently required to avoid irreversible damage.[45] Generally, the Commission prefers not to act by imposing interim measures where a party is willing to give voluntary undertakings which achieve the same effect. So, in *Miles Druce & Co Ltd* v *Commission*[46] the Court of Justice upheld the Commission's refusal to take interim measures on the application of a target company, where one ground for the refusal was an undertaking by the would-be acquirer not to exercise existing shareholder rights to call a sharholders' meeting, which made acceptance of the offer impossible. Where some interim protection is necessary, the policy is to take the minimum measures required to achieve it. In *Johnson & Firth Brown*

---

[42] Art.1: in the case of such persons the general rules under article 47 ECSC apply. See 6.3.1.1.
[43] This obligation to notify is subject to an exemption in some circumstances in the case of banks (art.4) and accredited stockbrokers (art.5). Notification must be made within 4 weeks of the date on which the person in question had knowledge of a qualifying transaction (art.6).
[44] Article 39 gives the Court power to impose interim measures, which take precedence over Commission interim measures.
[45] 3/75RI *Johnson & Firth Brown Ltd* v *Commission* [1975] 1 CMLR 638.
[46] 161/73R [1973] ECR 1049, [1974] 1 CMLR 224.

Ltd v *Commission*[47] the applicant was the target of a takeover bid by the British Steel Corporation, and sought interim protection of its position pending an appeal in relation to the Commission's authorisation of the takeover. The Court refused a stay of the authorisation because that would cause an at least equal risk to third parties affected by the merger, but it did provide limited protection by disallowing exercise of voting rights and staying the sale of two subsidiaries (which had been ordered as a condition of authorisation).[48]

6.3.3 Enforcement against mergers which cannot be authorised[49]

Where the conditions for authorisation of article 66(2) are not met, then under article 66(5), sub-paragraph (2), the Commission must, by reasoned decision, declare the concentration unlawful. The Commission's aim must then be to return the undertakings or assets in question to independent operation and restore normal conditions of competition. Subject to the parties being allowed the opportunity to submit their comments, therefore, the Commission must order the separation of undertakings which have merged without authorisation, or order the parties to cease joint control, or take such other measures as it considers appropriate to achieve that aim.

Once a merger has been ruled unlawful, and separation orders have been made, the Commission may not take further steps to enforce its decision without first allowing the undertakings concerned a reasonable period of time to comply with it.[50] Upon expiry of a reasonable period it may impose daily penalty payments.[51] The Commission also has further enforcement measures open to it, should the parties fail to fulfil their obligations.[52] These include suspension of the exercise of rights inherent in assets acquired unlawfully, the appointment by the appropriate national authorities of a receiver for such assets, the forced sale of such assets,[53] and the annulment of acts or decisions of the supervisory and managing bodies of undertakings over which control has been obtained irregularly, in so far as they relate to persons who have obtained the rights or assets in question through an unlawful transaction. The Commission may also make recommendations to

---

[47] Supra note 45.
[48] See also 170/73RII *Miles Druce & Co Ltd* v *Commission* [1974] ECR 281, [1974] 2 CMLR 217: stay of implementation of authorisation for 3 weeks.
[49] 'In the exercise of its powers the High Authority (Commission) shall take account of the rights of third parties which have been acquired in good faith.' Art.66(5), sub-para 7.
[50] Art.66(5), sub-para 4.
[51] Ibid; the daily payments must not exceed 0.1% of the value of the rights or assets in question.
[52] Art.66(5), sub-para 5.
[53] Subject to the protection of the legitimate interests of their owners.

national authorities to ensure that its orders are implemented under national law.[54]

In addition to ordering the separation of unlawfully merged companies, and taking such measures as are necessary to implement its decision, the Commission may impose fines on unlawful behaviour.[55]

6.3.4 Appellate proceedings

Where the Commission has ruled a merger to be unlawful, an interested person may under article 66(5), sub-paragraph (2), commence proceedings in the Court of Justice to challenge that decision. This right of challenge is founded on article 33[56], but there is an important derogation from the general right of challenge, which does not permit the Court to 'examine the evaluation of the situation, resulting from economic facts or circumstances, in the light of which the High Authority took its decisions'. Article 66(5) provides an exception to this embargo in the case of merger control:

> 'By way of derogation from Article 33, the Court shall have unlimited jurisdiction to assess whether the transaction effected is a concentration within the meaning of paragraph 1 and of regulations made in application thereof.'[57]

Proceedings may not be commenced against a Commission decision that a merger is unlawful until measures have been ordered for the separation of the undertakings or assets,[58] unless the Commission consents to the commencement of proceedings on the issue of unlawfulness alone. By way of derogation from the general rule in article 39, the commencement of proceedings under article 66(5) has suspensory effect.

Standing to commence proceedings is given to 'any person directly concerned'. This term would clearly include both would-be acquirer and target undertakings. In this case 'undertaking' should presumably be read in a sense wider than the article 80 definition, and so standing would not be exclusively available to 'coal and steel' undertakings, since the Commission

---

[54] Art.66(5), sub-para 6.

[55] Art.66(6): Fines range from 3% of the value of assets acquired or regrouped (in the case of evading obligations to supply information) to 15% of such value (in the case of engaging in transactions contrary to article 66).

[56] Which provides, *inter alia*, that proceedings must be instituted within 1 month of notification of the decision.

[57] This exception does not apply to challenges to authorisation decisions, which fall under the general rule in article 33, which restricts the Court's jurisdiction to examine economic evaluations save where it is alleged that the Commission has misused its powers or has manifestly failed to observe the provisions of the Treaty.

[58] Or other orders appropriate to return the undertakings to independent operation and to restore normal conditions of competition: art.66(5), sub-para 2.

has jurisdiction over undertakings of all kinds in circumstances which may at times be sufficient to constitute them as directly concerned.[59]

---

[59] There is a suggestion to this effect by A-G Reischl 74/81 *Rudolf Flender KG* v *Commission* [1982] ECR 395,409; [1983] 2 CMLR 265, 271.

SEVEN

The 'one-stop shopping' principle and articles 85 and 86 EEC

The purpose of this Chapter is to examine the relationship between Regulation 4064/89 and the principal competition policy provisions of the Treaty of Rome. It considers the aim of the Member States in the Council when adopting the Regulation of creating a simplified procedure and single authority for the control of proposed mergers and acquisitions. It then goes on to consider derogations from that aim and to identify the occasions on which article 85 EEC may still apply, and to examine some conceptual difficulties which may be encountered in applying it.

7.1 INTRODUCTION: THE 'ONE-STOP SHOPPING' PRINCIPLE

One of the principal benefits of the new merger Regulation, especially in the eyes of those Member States which already had national systems of merger control, was that it promised a division of jurisdiction between Community and national competition authorities which would make it possible for all proposed mergers to be subjected to a single clearance procedure effective for all purposes within the Community. This 'one-stop shopping' would be a considerable advance on the state of affairs existing before adoption of Regulation 4064/89, under which a merger involving European competitors established in different Member States might be subjected to three or more clearance procedures. Thus, the competition authorities in each of the relevant Member States might wish to rule on the merger, as might the EC Commission under articles 85 and 86 EEC.[1] The desire to avoid these multiple hurdles was a very significant factor in persuading some Member States to vote in favour of adoption of the Regulation after many years of resistance.[2]

Consideration of each proposed merger by a single competition authority involves the imposition of limits on existing competition jurisdictions. In

---

[1]   E.g., the *Nestlé/Rowntree* merger, which was considered by the Commission and by competition authorities in the UK and France.

[2]   Notably the UK: the point was stressed by Junior Trade Minister John Redwood at a press conference held to mark adoption of Regulation 4064/89 (*Independent*, 22 December 1989).

some circumstances Member State competition authorities will be constrained from exercising their jurisdiction over mergers which would once have fallen within the scope of their national legislation. Equally, the Commission will be constrained from exercising its jurisdiction under articles 85 and 86 EEC in the case of mergers falling within the scope of the new Regulation, and possibly in the case of all mergers.

The starting point for this scheme of distribution of jurisdiction in merger control cases is the precise ambit of Regulation 4064/89. It applies to *concentrations* which have a *Community dimension*. Concentration is defined in article 3 of Regulation 4064/89.[3] Community dimension is defined in article 1 of Regulation 4064/89 in terms of the aggregate worldwide turnover of the undertakings concerned and the relative Community-wide and single Member State turnovers.[4] The Regulation then purports to vest the Commission with exclusive jurisdiction over the application of its provisions to concentrations falling within its defined scope, and to prevent the application of other means of control to such transactions. It does this first by article 21(1), which restricts the exercise of powers under the new Regulation to the Commission:

'Subject to review by the Court of Justice, the Commission shall have sole jurisdiction to take the decisions provided for in this Regulation.'

This provision closely follows article 9(1) of Regulation 17, which restricts the exercise of the article 85(3) EEC exemption powers to the Commission. The result is that the provisions so restricted are without direct effect, and cannot be invoked in national courts. Next, in article 21(2), the Regulation prohibits the application of national law to mergers within its scope:

'No Member State shall apply its national legislation on competition to any concentration that has a Community dimension.'

This provision is the central tenet of the 'one-stop shopping' principle, although it will be seen below that it is subject to some important exceptions. It may be noted that it applies only to competition legislation, and not other regulatory measures. The necessary restriction of UK merger control is achieved technically by the EEC Merger Control (Consequential Provisions) Regulations 1990 (SI 1990 No. 1563). Finally, article 22 (1) and (2) of the Regulation purports to exclude the application of existing Community competition law to *all concentrations* whether or not they have a Community dimension. Some of the difficulties with this provision have already been considered.[5] Even assuming that it may be interpreted purposively as meaning

---

[3]   For detailed treatment, see 2.1 *et seq.*
[4]   For detailed treatment, see 2.2 *et seq.*
[5]   See 2.3.1.

that the Commission may not normally apply articles 85 and 86 EEC to concentrations of any kind, so that those which do not have a Community dimension and so fall outside the scope of Regulation 4064/89 need only be referred to national merger authorities, there remain questions about whether it is legally possible for the Regulation to achieve this purpose.[6]

Within this framework of rules governing the scope of Regulation 4064/89 it is possible to discern a simple division of competence which is based on the principle of 'one-stop shopping'. Unfortunately, that simple scheme is subject to a number of exceptions which cloud the apparent clarity of the principle.

7.2 POTENTIAL DEROGATIONS FROM THE 'ONE-STOP SHOPPING' PRINCIPLE

A number of derogations from the principal scope of Regulation 4064/89 have already been considered. These include:

(a) The possibility of a merger which has a Community dimension being referred by the Commission to a Member State at its request because of a threat to competition on a distinct market within that Member State (article 9 of Regulation 4064/89).[7]

(b) The possibility of a Member State taking appropriate measures against a merger which has a Community dimension to protect a legitimate national interest other than one of competition policy (article 21(3) of Regulation 4064/89);[8] an important example is the possibility of a Member State applying other (non-competition) regulatory legislation to the transaction, such as control over credit institutions and investment firms.[9]

(c) The possibility of the Commission taking jurisdiction at the request of a Member State to apply the Regulation's rules to a merger which does not have a Community dimension but which does threaten effective competition within the territory of the Member State concerned (article 22(3)–(5) of Regulation 4064/89).[10]

This section will consider other possible derogations from the principal division of jurisdiction attempted by Regulation 4064/89.

---

[6] See 7.2.4; it should be noted that the Commission appears to accept that the Regulation cannot entirely sweep away its powers under articles 85 and 86 EEC.

[7] Cf. 3.4. *et seq.*

[8] Cf 2.4.2.

[9] E.g., in the UK under the Banking Act 1979 (now the Banking Act 1987), passed partially in response to the Second Banking Directive; or under possible changes to the Financial Services Act 1986 made in response to the Draft Investment Services Directive when eventually adopted; cf 2.4.3.

[10] Cf. 2.3.2.

7.2.1   Commission application of article 86 EEC

The Commission's first venture into merger control was on the basis of article 86 EEC.[11] But for any constitutional arguments about the supremacy of Treaty law over mere regulations,[12] the continued application of article 86 to mergers would, according to article 22, rest on the merger not being a concentration within the meaning of article 3 of Regulation 4064/89. That would require that the previously dominant undertaking remained independent of the other undertaking concerned, and acquired an interest in it which did not give the dominant undertaking the possibility of exercising decisive influence over it within the terms of article 3(1) and (2). It is difficult to imagine circumstances in which the acquisition of such an interest could amount to an abuse of a dominant position. In *Continental Can*[13] the alleged abuse was said by the Commission to have been constituted by the effective elimination of competition by the acquisition; it is not clear that competition would be eliminated by the mere acquisition of an interest which gave no control. Indeed, in *BAT & RJ Reynolds v Commission*[14] the Court of Justice ruled that an abuse of dominant position could only arise when the interest acquired resulted in effective control of the undertaking or at least some influence on commercial policy. It is suggested that in these circumstances there is very little scope for the continued application of article 86 EEC by the Commission as an instrument of merger control. This conclusion would necessarily be different, however, if the constitutional arguments considered below prevail, in which case the law as first developed by the Court would still apply.

7.2.2   Commission application of article 85 EEC

Despite the 'one-stop shopping' principle, and without recourse for the moment to the constitutional arguments addressed below,[15] there are clearly situations in which transactions, which may loosely be regarded as mergers or acquisitions, fall outside the scope of Regulation 4064/89 and within the scope of the Commission's accepted jurisdiction under article 85 EEC. In the first place, joint ventures which have the effect of coordinating the 'competitive behaviour of undertakings which themselves remain independent' are expressly outside the scope of Regulation 4064/89.[16] Secondly, it appears from the decision in *BAT & RJ Reynolds v Commission*[17]

[11] See 1.1.2 *et seq.*
[12] See 7.2.4.
[13] 6/72 [1973] ECR 215, [1973] CMLR 199; see 1.1.2.3.
[14] 142 & 156/84 [1988] 4 CMLR 24 at para 65; see 1.1.3.4.
[15] See 7.2.4.
[16] Art.3(2), 1st para; see Chapter 5.
[17] 142 & 156/84 [1988] 4 CMLR 24; see 1.1.3.4.

that some acquisitions of an interest in another undertaking which do not result in decisive influence over the undertaking in question being obtained, and so do not fall within the scope of Regulation 4064/89, may nevertheless constitute infringements of article 85(1) EEC. In such cases the question of Community dimension would be irrelevant. The identification and regulation of restrictive agreements of this kind are discussed below.[18] Whether the Commission retains a power beyond these instances to apply article 85 to mergers depends upon the constitutional arguments considered below.

7.2.3   Articles 85 and 86 EEC in national courts

Articles 85(1) and 86 EEC have been found to be of direct effect,[19] and so they are in general applicable in national courts either as a defence to proceedings brought to enforce a contract or as the basis for an action for damages for loss caused by the infringement in question.[20] Since both article 85(1) and article 86 have been found to allow some control of merger activity, it follows that, at least before Regulation 4064/89 came into force, they might be relied upon in national courts in attempts to prevent the implementation of mergers. It must be stressed that both articles are cumbersome tools of merger control, particularly in English courts where there are limits on the effectiveness of both. Nevertheless, in the hands of a company seeking merely to use national proceedings as a spoiling tactic to frustrate attempts to win a takeover battle, they may be sufficient to the task, and cannot be ignored. The question which is then raised is whether the possibility of using articles 85 and 86 EEC as a spoiling tactic in national litigation remains now that Regulation 4064/89 has come into force.

7.2.3.1   Non-concentrations in national courts
In the first place, it is clear that, in so far as article 85(1) may be applied to certain transactions which do not amount to concentrations within the meaning of article 3 of Regulation 4064/89,[21] then a national court could so apply it, just as the Commission may continue to do so.

7.2.3.2   Concentrations in national courts
The continuing applicability in national courts of articles 85 and 86 to mergers which are concentrations within the meaning of article 3 appears to depend upon the meaning and effect of article 22(1) and (2) of the new Regulation. Article 22(2) of Regulation 4064/89 states that Regulation 17, *inter alia*, shall not apply to concentrations as defined in article 3. Since the purpose

---

[18]   See 7.3 *et seq.*
[19]   127/73 *BRT* v *SABAM* [1974] ECR 51, [1974] 2 CMLR 238.
[20]   See 8.1.1.1 and 8.1.1.2.
[21]   See 7.2.2 and 7.3 *et seq.*

of Regulation 17 is to implement the Treaty's competition policy in articles 85 and 86 EEC by providing the necessary procedural rules for Commission investigations and Court of Justice supervision, it appears that the intention of article 22(2) of the new Regulation is to prevent *the Commission* applying articles 85 and 86 to concentrations. Whether it is legally possible for it to do so is discussed below.[22] For present purposes, the question is whether article 22(2) also prevents *national courts* applying articles 85(1) and 86 to concentrations, which they would otherwise be entitled to do since they are of direct effect. In the case of article 85(1), in *Nouvelles Frontières*[23] the Court of Justice re-affirmed its view that, in the absence of necessary implementing legislation such as Regulation 17, article 85(1) loses its direct effect and so cannot be relied upon in ordinary national courts. The reference to 'ordinary courts' is to allow for the fact that, under article 88 EEC, articles 85 and 86 would be applicable by a 'competent authority' in a Member State, e.g., the Restrictive Practices Court. Consequently, the effect of article 22(2) of Regulation 4064/89 appears to be to rule out the application of article 85(1) to concentrations by national courts. The same does not appear to be true in the case of article 86. The Court of Justice recently held in *Ahmed Saeed*[24] that the argument by which article 85(1) was deprived of direct effect, which rested on the principle of legal certainty,[25] did not apply in the case of article 86. Consequently, it appears that article 86 remains of direct effect even in the absence of the legislation implementing Regulation 17, so that article 22(2) of Regulation 4064/89 does not prevent its application in national courts.

The question which then remains is whether article 22(1) has any wider effect than that ascribed above to article 22(2), so that even the application of article 86 is excluded. Article 22(1) says that Regulation 4064/89 'alone shall apply to concentrations as defined in article 3'. It has already been pointed out that this provision cannot be taken at face value, since it implies that, even where there is no Community dimension, no other legislation, whether originating in the Community or at national level, may be applied to concentrations.[26] The preferable interpretation would be that only Regulation 4064/89 will be applied by the Commission as a Community instrument of merger control, and that it will not seek to apply articles 85 and 86 EEC to concentrations which fall below the Community dimension thresholds.[27] As such it would simply contribute to the demarcation between Community and national jurisdiction in merger cases, which is an essential

---

22 See 7.2.4.
23 209-213/84 *Ministère Public* v *Asjès* [1986] ECR 1425, [1986] 3 CMLR 173, paras [52] – [56], [61] – [63].
24 66/86 *Ahmed Saeed Flugreisen* v *Zentrale zur Bekampfung Unlauteren Wettbewerbs* [1990] 4 CMLR 102 at paras [32] – [33].
25 *Nouvelles Frontières* (supra note 23) at para [61]; Goyder at p. 78.
26 See 2.3.1.
27 The legal validity of such a rule is considered below: 7.2.4.

element in the 'one-stop shopping' principle. It would not then prevent Member States applying those articles in national courts. This interpretation suffers, however, from the objection that the Commission itself does not appear to place this interpretation on article 22(1); or at least, in its statement recorded in the minutes of the EC Council it says that it wishes to reserve its legal position on the meaning of this provision and may take the view that it remains empowered to apply articles 85 and 86 to concentrations below the Community dimension threshold.[28]

Until the Court of Justice rules on the matter it is impossible to be certain how article 22(1) will be interpreted, and in interpreting the provision consistently with the purpose of the Regulation the Court may well conclude in favour of treating it as only restricting the jurisdiction of the Commission. Alternatively, the Court may conclude that in addition to preventing the application of articles 85 and 86 EEC to concentrations by the Commission, article 22(1) also prevents their application to concentrations by national courts. If such a meaning were to be preferred, whether the provision was effective to achieve that result would depend upon its legality.

7.2.4 Constitutional arguments against exclusive application of Regulation 4064/89

Regulation 4064/89 contains four important measures intended to preserve the principle of 'one-stop shopping' in Community merger control: article 21(1) and (2) and article 22(1) and (2). The article 21 provisions present no legal difficulties as a matter of Community 'constitutional' law. They depend for their effect upon the direct applicability of regulations and the supremacy of Community law. The article 22 provisions, however, raise difficult questions about their legality in the light of the provisions of the Treaty of Rome.

7.2.4.1 The legal effect of article 22(2) of Regulation 4064/89
It can be argued that, since the Court of Justice has held that both articles 85 and 86 EEC apply to concentrations, the application of those provisions to concentrations cannot subsequently be excluded except by an amendment of the Treaty. This argument rests in part on the somewhat technical reasoning that in the event of the non-applicability of Regulation 17, which implements the Treaty of Rome's competition provisions, article 89 EEC grants to the Commission residual powers to enforce those provisions. Treaty amendments require a special procedure, laid down in article 236 EEC.[29] It is clear that Regulation 4064/89 was not passed by using that procedure. Regulation 17, on the other hand, was made under the powers conferred by article

[28] See [1990] 4 CMLR 314, and article 22.
[29] See Hartley, 88 - 92.

87 EEC and so can be amended by a subsequent regulation made under the same powers without constitutional difficulty. Regulation 4064/89 was adopted under articles 87 and 235 EEC. Consequently, article 22(2) of Regulation 4064/89, which provides that Regulation 17 is not to apply to concentrations as defined in article 3, may be regarded as no more than a legitimate amendment not of the Treaty but of Regulation 17. This argument avoids the constitutional difficulty in respect of article 22(2), but results in the potential for the continuing application of articles 85 and 86 EEC by virtue of the residual powers of article 89 EEC.[30] It is also arguably inconsistent with the statement in recital 8 of the Preamble to Regulation 4064/89 that the Regulation is based principally upon article 235 EEC, which implies that its main concern is not articles 85 and 86 EEC but new substance.[31]

7.2.4.2 The legal effect of article 22(1) of Regulation 4064/89

In the case of article 22(1) the argument is more difficult. The problem raised above of not being able to avoid, except by a valid Treaty amendment, the residual applicability of articles 85 and 86 under the provisions of article 89 applies equally here. Additionally, however, it is not immediately apparent what meaning can be given to article 22(1) which does not conflict with these Treaty provisions. Article 22(1) appears to prohibit the application of any competition law (that is, presumably, Community-based competition law: a wider meaning would be inconsistent with article 21(2)) other than the Regulation itself to concentrations as defined in article 3. If that is the case, article 22(1) would be *ultra vires*.

A possible, but scarcely explicit, meaning is that articles 85 and 86 EEC must not be applied by national courts to any kind of concentration within the meaning of article 3. The new Regulation's basis in article 87 would then provide an argument in favour of the legality of the provisions in question. Article 87 enables the Council, acting on a proposal from the Commission, to adopt regulations to implement the Treaty's competition policy. The regulations called for are particularly intended, *inter alia*, 'to define, if need be, in the various branches of the economy, the scope of the provisions of articles 85 and 86',[32] and 'to determine the relationship between national laws and the provisions . . . adopted pursuant to this article'.[33] If article 22(1) is regarded as excluding the application of articles 85 and 86 by national courts, it may simply be a provision determining both the scope of articles 85 and 86 and the relationship between the remedies available under national law by virtue of the Treaty's competition rules and Regulation 4064/89. As such it would be valid under article 87 EEC, but it would leave open

---

[30] For a contrary view, see Fine, *EC merger control: an analysis of the new Regulation* (1990) 11 ECLR 47.
[31] Infra note 35.
[32] Art.87(2)(c) EEC.
[33] Art.87(2)(e) EEC.

the possibility of the residual application of articles 85 and 86 by the Commission under article 89.

A second possible meaning is that article 22(1) is no more than declaratory of the Council's view of the existing scope of articles 85 and 86, intended to establish that those provisions do not in fact apply to concentrations, and indeed have never done so. The advantage of such an interpretation is that it would not then amount to a regulation trying to achieve an amendment of the Treaty, but rather it would simply establish that the field of control of concentrations was untouched by articles 85 and 86, so that further legislation could be adopted in that field without conflict with the Treaty provisions. This interpretation is supported by the fact that Regulation 4064/89 is partially based in article 235 EEC.[34] Article 235 may only be used for measures in respect of matters for which the Treaty does not provide the necessary powers.[35] Reliance on article 235 appears to indicate that the Council takes the view that, at least in some respects, Regulation 4064/89 addresses matters which are not within the scope of articles 85 and 86 EEC.

For such an argument to prevail, however, it would require the Court of Justice to take a very restrictive view of its earlier judgments in the two key cases on the applicability to mergers of articles 85 and 86 EEC. In the first place, it might be argued that article 85 EEC has never been found to apply to concentrations as defined in article 3 of Regulation 4064/89. There is a narrow ruling in *BAT & RJ Reynolds v Commission*[36] which may be interpreted as saying that article 85 only applies to the acquisition of minority shareholdings, which would not amount to a concentration. Adopting the terminology of English law for a moment, that is the ratio of the decision, and any statements about the wider application of article 85 are clearly obiter dicta. In the case of article 86 the argument is similar: although the Court has indicated a willingness in the appropriate circumstances to endorse the application of article 86 to mergers, it has never actually done so, because the *Continental Can*[37] case failed at the hurdle of establishing a dominant position. These arguments must be acknowledged to be artificial, but they might appeal to a Court anxious to find a legal basis for the 'one-stop shopping' principle of demarcation which article 22(1) was clearly intended to implement.

7.2.4.3 The Commission's approach after Regulation 4064/89 comes into force

It must be recognised that there is at least the potential for article 22(1) to be found ineffective as a means of implementing a watertight 'one-stop

---

[34] See Preamble.
[35] See Hartley, 106 – 109.
[36] 142 & 156/84 [1988] 4 CMLR 24 at paras 30-31; see 1.1.3.4.
[37] 6/72 [1973] ECR 215, [1973] CMLR 199; see 1.1.2.3.

shopping' principle. The Commission has issued a statement clarifying its future policy on the application of articles 85 and 86 EEC to concentrations which fall below the Community dimension thresholds.[38] Its policy appears to be one of holding those provisions in reserve but rarely if ever using them in such cases. In view of the possibility of the Court of Justice finding that the Council's attempt in Regulation 4064/89 to exclude the application of articles 85 and 86 to concentrations was illegal, such a position on the Commission's part is inevitable. In the event of such a finding, a complainant would be able to ask the Commission to apply either article 85 or article 86 to a proposed concentration which fell below the Community dimension thresholds, and when it refused, the complainant could bring proceedings against the Commission in the Court of Justice under article 175 for failure to act. The Commission would be unable legitimately to refuse such a request from an interested party because of the illegality of article 22(1), and so it would be obliged to apply the relevant article to the concentration. It must be said that such an argument may never arise, because a company looking for a delaying or spoiling tactic in the course of a takeover bid is likely to find cheaper and more certain methods, such as applying to the national court for the application of articles 85 and 86 EEC. Should the argument ever be raised it seems that it would be a considerable embarrassment to the Community authorities. Although the Court of Justice would be an impartial and objective arbiter of the legality of the measures, it would also be likely to wish to maintain the policy of the new Regulation as much as possible, including the principle of 'one-stop shopping'. It would, therefore, be very likely to uphold arguments which supported the legality of the provisions in question.

It should not be thought that such a policy on the Commission's part is an indication of an intention to bring many, or any, such actions. It should be seen as no more than a recognition by the Commission that it may be under a duty under article 89 EEC to apply the Treaty competition provisions in such cases, and is perhaps an attempt to forestall any proceedings under article 175 EEC. The Commission indicated that it does not intend to take proceedings by virtue of its powers under article 89 EEC against concentrations which fall below a given level.[39] The Commission's proposal is for levels the same as those previously proposed as the thresholds for Community dimension, and which the Commission continues to hope will become the relevant thresholds before the end of 1993 under the review

---

[38] See [1990] 4 CMLR 314.
[39] The Commission's statement recorded in the Minutes of the EC Council (see [1990] 4 CMLR 314 and article 22) is in the following terms:
   '(The Commission) does not intend to take action in respect of concentrations with a worldwide turnover of less than ECU 2,000 million or below a minimum Community turnover level of ECU 100 million or which are not covered by the threshold of two-thirds provided for in the last part of the sentence in article 1(2), on the grounds that below such levels a concentration would not normally significantly affect trade between Member States.'

called for in article 1(3). The effect of such a policy would be to create, at least potentially, a transitional period during which articles 85 and 86 EEC could be applied to concentrations falling below the current Community dimension thresholds but above the Commission's proposed levels, and thereby to increase the pressure on reluctant Member States such as the United Kingdom to agree in due course to the lowering of those thresholds, in order to achieve the 'one-stop shopping' principle.

7.2.4.4 The fiction of one-stop shopping in practice

Whatever legal arguments there may be about the extent to which the Regulation achieves the aim claimed for it of establishing a one-stop shopping principle in respect of merger control in the Community, it is clear from the express terms of the Regulation (in particular article 19) that there will be substantial cooperation and consultation between national competition authorities and the Commission.[40] In practice, there is evidence that such cooperation may extend beyond the terms of the Regulation; for example, the Merger Task Force is said to have agreed that it will inform national authorities even of informal approaches, subject to the party in question having no objection to such communication. Equally, in the United Kingdom the Office of Fair Trading is said to favour being kept informed by UK parties of all submissions to the Merger Task Force.

Parties seeking to influence a national competition authority in the exercise of its powers under article 9(2) (distinct national market) or article 21(3) (legitimate national interest) should consider keeping the national competition authority informed of all dealings (formal and informal) with the Merger Task Force. The perceived advantages of this approach may be summarised as follows:

(a)   It will ensure that the national authority has before it the notifying party's version of its case, rather than a summary or distillation prepared by the Merger Task Force.

(b)   It will enable the national regulatory body to consider at an early stage the potential application of its powers under articles 9(2) or 21(3), and to consider the notifying party's case for the exercise of such powers.

(c)   It may enable the notifying party to seek informal guidance as to the possible use by a national regulatory authority of its powers under articles 9(2) and 21(3), and as to the substance of its case were national as opposed to Community considerations to apply;[41] and

(d)   To the extent that a concentration gives (or is likely to give) rise

---

[40]   See also 4.7.
[41]   At the moment, such informal procedures (known as 'confidential guidance') are a developed aspect of UK merger control under the Fair Trading Act 1973, but are as yet undeveloped under the merger Regulation.

to a jurisdictional dispute between the national regulatory body and the Commission, it has the probable advantage of bringing that debate to the fore at an early stage.

Where parties elect to keep both[42] sets of regulatory authorities informed simultaneously, it will generally be preferable to rely on identical documentation. Ignoring questions of time and expense, such an approach will ensure a consistent statement of the party's case.

7.2.4.5 Summary

Subject to the important qualification that many of the arguments are untested before the Court of Justice, and some require an interpretation which goes some way beyond the literal, it is now possible to attempt a summary of the legal effects on articles 85 and 86 EEC of the provisions of Regulation 4064/89 intended to implement the 'one-stop shopping' principle. The following Table summarises these provisions.

Potential application	*Effect of Regulation 4064/89*
1 Application by national courts of article 85(1) EEC to transactions not amounting to concentrations	Permitted: see 7.3 *et seq.* below, and see 1.1.3 *et seq.*
2 Application by national courts of article 85(1) EEC to concentrations within the meaning of article 3 of Regulation 4064/89	Not permitted: article 85(1) EEC is deprived of direct effect by article 22(2) of Regulation 4064/89; see 7.2.3.2
3 Application by national courts of article 86 EEC to concentrations within the meaning of article 3 of Regulation 4064/89	Probably not permitted, by virtue of the interpretation of article 22(1) of Regulation 4064/89 which treats it as a valid determination of the relationship between national law and EC law in respect of competition under article 87 EEC; see 7.2.3.2 and 7.2.4.2

---

[42] In some cases it may be necessary to consider two sets of national authorities as well as the Commission, but such cases are likely to be rare. In the UK powers of investigation and enforcement in respect of article 9 references are conferred on the Office of Fair Trading by the EEC Merger Control (Distinct Market Investigations) Regulations 1990 (SI 1990 No. 1715).

Potential application	Effect of Regulation 4064/89
4 Application of articles 85 and 86 EEC by Commission to concentrations below the Community dimension threshold	In view of the possible unconstitutionality of the widest interpretation of article 22(1) of Regulation 4064/89, still perhaps permitted, by virtue of the residual power under article 89 EEC; but Commission likely to exercise considerable restraint unless it loses patience with Member States over their reluctance to lower Community dimension thresholds — see 7.2.4.3
5 Application of articles 85 and 86 EEC by Commission to concentrations above the Community dimension threshold	Technically permitted perhaps, in view of the possible unconstitutionality of the widest interpretation of article 22(1) of Regulation 4064/89; but since the Regulation is partially based on article 87 EEC, which provides for the making of regulations to implement articles 85 and 86 EEC, it can be argued that Regulation 4064/89 achieves such implementation, thus excluding the residual application of articles 85 and 86 EEC under article 89 EEC.

In the case of the future application by the Commission of articles 85 and 86 EEC, it should be noted that although it is possible to mount a credible if not cogent argument that article 22(1) is effective to exclude such application, it is equally possible to argue that such exclusion is unconstitutional and therefore ineffective. For the time being, the Commission may have decided to err on the side of caution, and to prepare at least for the possibility that articles 85 and 86 remain applicable.

7.3 THE RESIDUAL SCOPE OF ARTICLE 85 EEC

The purpose of this section is to assess the scope of article 85 in the case of transactions which fall outside the scope of Regulation 4064/89, and which are neither concentrations within the meaning of article 3 of that Regulation nor joint ventures as described in Chapter 5.[43] It must be stressed that such cases are likely to be rare, and seeking them out is unlikely to be given a high priority by the Commission. This section does not consider the case of concentrations falling below the level of Community dimension. If the argument prevails that the Commission is under an obligation under article 89 EEC to continue to apply article 85 to concentrations within the meaning of article 3 of Regulation 4064/89, which do not have a Community dimension within the meaning of article 1, then the scope of proceedings on that basis would appear to be as described in Chapter 1 in reference to the Court's decision in *BAT & RJ Reynolds v Commission*.[44]

7.3.1 *BAT & RJ Reynolds v Commission*

The possible continued application of article 85 to transactions which do not amount to concentrations depends upon the precise scope of the Court of Justice's decision in the *BAT & RJ Reynolds v Commission* case.[45]

That judgment begins with a limiting statement about the ambit of the Court's decision, saying that it was concerned with the question 'whether and in what circumstances the acquisition of a minority shareholding in a competing company may constitute an infringement of Article 85 and 86 of the Treaty.'[46] The Court also drew attention to the fact that the acquisition was achieved by agreements entered into by companies which remained independent. As a result of these statements it is possible to limit the precedent value of the decision to those cases where only the acquisition of a minority interest in a competing company which has remained independent after the entry into force of the agreements is involved. The Court found that article 85(1) might apply to such a transaction, but on the facts found in favour of the Commission's decision to allow the transaction to proceed. The necessary prevention, restriction or distortion of competition would be caused in such a case:

'where the agreement provides for commercial co-operation between the companies or creates a structure likely to be used for such co-operation. That may also be the case where the agreement gives the investing company the possibility of reinforcing its position at a later stage and taking effective control of the other company.'[47]

---

[43] The general rules governing the application of article 85 to restrictive agreements are outlined at 1.1.3 *et seq.*
[44] 142 & 156/84 [1988] 4 CMLR 24; see 1.1.3.4 where the facts are fully set out.
[45] Ibid.
[46] Ibid, paras 30 – 31.
[47] Ibid, paras 38 – 39.

The Court also referred to the possibility of a restriction of competition arising where 'the investing company obtains legal or *de facto* control of the commercial conduct of the other company'[48], but of course in that case the transaction would amount to a concentration within the meaning of article 3 of Regulation 4064/89, and so would be beyond the ambit of the present discussion. As a result of this decision there appears to be some scope for the continuing application of article 85 to certain transactions which may loosely be described as mergers but which do not fall into the technical category of concentrations, and this much is envisaged by the Commission's Notice on concentrative and cooperative operations.[49]

7.3.2 The scope of *BAT & RJ Reynolds v Commission* after September 1990[50]

There can be little doubt that article 85 still applies to share transactions directly entered into between competitor companies for the acquisition by one undertaking of a minority shareholding in the other. That is the fact pattern considered in *BAT & RJ Reynolds v Commission*,[51] which was treated by the Commission as at least potentially within the scope of article 85(1) and which falls within the narrow construction of the Court's judgment. It may also be that the Court's judgment would extend to include the acquisition of an interest in a competitor by purchase of shares from a third party by virtue of stock market transactions (rather than by full takeover bid). In such a case it is almost certain that the interest acquired would be only a minority interest.[52] On the assumption that conceptual problems in respect of the application of article 85 can be overcome,[53] there is some potential for it to apply since such a transaction might create a structure likely to result in commercial cooperation between the competitors. Nevertheless, the number of cases in which a restriction would result would be likely to be few, and it may be that not many transactions in this category would be caught by the principle developed in *BAT & RJ Reynolds v Commission*.

It should also be considered whether article 85 will continue to apply

---

48   Ibid.
49   OJ 1990 C203/10, para. 1; see Chapter 5 generally.
50   Regulation 4064/89 came into force on 21 September 1990.
51   Supra note 44.
52   Most Member States limit the extent to which such dealing may take place without giving way to a formal takeover bid, so that for transactions of this kind it is quite likely that, in the majority of cases, the transition to full takeover bid will occur at or before the time a controlling interest is obtained. For example, in the UK, City Code Rule 9 makes it mandatory to make a full offer upon acquisition of 30% of the voting rights, or, where 30% is already held, upon acquisition of a further 2% within any 12-month period. As a result, it seems that few stock market share transactions would actually involve more than a minority interest.
53   See 7.3.3.

to consortium bids of the kind involved in the *Irish Distillers*[54] case, in which three companies combined to launch a bid for the Irish Distillers company. The Commission intervened on the ground, *inter alia*, that the participants should have been competing for control, rather than dividing it between them. There may also have been some fear that the arrangement might lead to other future coordination of competitive conduct by the joint venture participants. The Commission threatened to impose interim measures to prevent share acquisitions unless it was satisfied that the takeover did not infringe article 85. The Commission's intervention was not based on the agreements to buy shares from third parties, but on the agreement between the participants in the consortium bidding for the target company. Eventually, a settlement was reached under which only one company maintained the bid (which was ultimately unsuccessful). In most cases such agreements will result in concentrations because the aim will be to acquire control of one or more undertakings in order to share them or their assets between the parent companies, and so will fall to be determined under Regulation 4064/89, as recital 24 of the Preamble indicates.[55] However, if, in such circumstances, there is no Community dimension, the only possibility of control will be under article 85 EEC.[56] If there is no issue of concentration, because only a non-controlling interest is to be acquired, or because there is a cooperative purpose inherent in the scheme, then the only possibility of regulating any anti-competitive effects of the consortium agreement will be under article 85.

7.3.3 General difficulties in applying article 85 to mergers and acquisitions

If article 85 is to apply to mergers and acquisitions, other than those effected by direct agreement between competing companies (in so far as that remains possible since Regulation 4064/89 came into force), it will be essential to identify a conceptual framework for its application. Can article 85 EEC apply to the transfer of shares to the acquiring company from a third party shareholder in the target company who is not within the control of that company's directors and management?

7.3.3.1 The basic requirements of article 85(1) EEC

The prohibition in article 85(1) applies (for present purposes) to agreements between undertakings which have the object or effect of preventing, restricting

---

[54] 7-8 Bull, (1988) p. 34, and see 2.1.6.
[55] See also the Notice on concentrative and cooperative operations: OJ 1990 C203/10, para.2; see Appendix III.
[56] See 7.2.4.3.

or distorting competition.[57] The component of agreement should never be a problem, since all transactions inevitably involve agreements between the sellers and purchasers of the shares, whoever they may be. Greater difficulty may be encountered with the concept of 'undertaking' in article 85(1). A company or a financial institution would clearly fall within the term, and no further issue need be raised in that respect. The difficulty arises in the respect of individual shareholders who are not part of such an immediately recognisable 'undertaking' as far as their shareholding is concerned. The application of article 85(1) to any transaction entered into by such a person will depend upon whether an individual in those circumstances can be regarded as an undertaking. There are some indications to suggest that an individual may be regarded as an undertaking for these purposes. In the first place, there are examples of individuals being treated as undertakings in respect of other transactions. In *Nungesser v Commission*[58] the appellant was in fact an individual sole trader, who was licensee of certain plant breeders' rights, and who was treated as an undertaking for the purposes of article 85(1). In *Vaessen/Morris*[59] the Commission held that the position of being a controlling shareholder conferred the status of undertaking. Moreover, if the market in question is regarded as being the market for the control of the target company in question[60] (whatever motives the various players may have, including the desire to affect the market for that company's goods), any share-dealing in that company's shares at a time of a potential merger must be regarded as significant economic activity on that market. On this analysis an individual shareholder dealing in those shares would legitimately be regarded as an undertaking.

More difficult and more important is the issue of whether the agreement has the object or effect of preventing, restricting or distorting competition, which raises the issue of appreciable effect, or the *de minimis* rule. The Commission and Court will not normally declare prohibited an agreement which has no appreciable effect on competition, even if technically it may be regarded as preventing, restricting or distorting it. It could be argued that an individual shareholder selling shares, which themselves do not amount to a significant holding in the target company, cannot by his transaction have an appreciable effect on competition. In addressing that issue it is important to distinguish between share transactions which take place in an

[57] See generally 1.1.3.1. It is not proposed at this stage to consider other matters, most importantly the question of effect on trade between Member States. That omission must not be read as implying that it will not be significant in merger control cases, but it does not raise questions which require separate treatment in the context of merger control.
[58] 258/78 [1982] ECR 2015.
[59] OJ 1979 L19/32 [1979] 1 CMLR 511.
[60] This would appear to be borne out by the statement in *BAT & RJ Reynolds v Commission* to the effect that acquisition of a shareholding in a competitor constitutes conduct restricting competition where it results in acquisition of legal or *de facto* control of the commercial conduct of the other.

isolated or adventitious manner, and those which are part of a campaign to acquire shares, whether it be the acquisition of a minority holding through stock exchange dealing or a full takeover bid. In the case of the former, the circumstances would not appear to be exceptional, so that such share acquisition agreements, even if satisfying the other requirements of article 85(1), would not be prohibited. However, it is possible to argue that in the case of a campaign of acquisitions the circumstances would be exceptional, because it would in fact be wrong to examine each share transaction in isolation; rather, it must be examined in the light of the campaign which will, if successful, give rise to a whole network of agreements of a similar kind which taken together will have an appreciable effect on competition. Outside the field of share transactions there is good authority for such an approach.[61]

7.3.3.2 The property problem in regulating share transactions

Although a case can be made out in this way for saying that share transactions can be dealt with under the same rules as other agreements such as cartels, there is an additional ingredient in that the parties are dealing with property rights, or with rights akin to property rights, in the form of shares. Article 222 of the Treaty of Rome provides that its provisions shall in no way prejudice the rules in Member States governing the system of property ownership. The question then must be whether the application of article 85(1) to share transactions would amount to prejudice to the system of ownership of those shares. For present purposes it will be assumed that the application of article 85(1) will result either in a prohibition on transferring shares, or, where the transfer has been completed, in some limit on the use to which transferred shares may be put.

The problem of prejudice to the system of property ownership is raised in acute form by article 85(2) EEC. If article 85 is to apply to share transactions then the Commission and Court will have to find a means of saying that article 222 is not infringed. A solution to the problem may lie in an analogy with the treatment of industrial/intellectual property rights under the Treaty, under which a distinction is made between existence and exercise of such rights, thereby permitting Community law to prevent abuses of such rights which would have the effect of partitioning the market.[62] In the case of share transactions, the attributes of shares which might be said to be involved in their exercise and which might be thought to have an effect upon competition would be the exercise of the voting right inherent in the shares, since that is the means by which any influence over the target company would be exercised. The existence of the shares, on the other hand, would

---

[61] *Brasserie de Haecht* v *Wilkin (No 1)* 23/67 [1967] ECR 407, [1968] CMLR 26 — art.177 reference.

[62] Cf. 78/70 *Deutsche Grammophon Gesellschaft* v *Metro* [1971] ECR 487. For a full account of the existence/exercise dichotomy see Bellamy & Child, 319-321, 346-348, 355-356.

be preserved even if the voting right were temporarily in abeyance provided the value of the shares were not diminished. It might be thought that the value would inevitably be diminished if the purpose for which the shares were bought (i.e. to exercise control over the target company through the voting rights) could not be pursued. In practice, however, the value would be maintained provided the present owner (who is deprived of the voting rights) is able to resell the shares to others who would themselves be able to exercise the voting rights (unless they too fell within the scope of article 85(1)).[63] Thus, although the exercise of the voting rights in the shares would be prohibited in order to prevent the realisation of the anti-competitive effect, the existence of the property right in the shares would not be harmed because that property right could always be realised by resale of the shares.

7.3.3.3 Article 85(2) EEC and 'void' share transactions

Finally, a further difficulty facing the application of article 85(1) to mergers and acquisitions is the consequence, under article 85(2), of a finding that an agreement is prohibited: namely, that the agreement is void. While it is possible to fashion an argument which overcomes the difficulty of article 222 in respect of non-interference with property ownership, that argument assumes that the application of article 85(1) and (2) will result in the transfer of title to the shares (or assets) to the acquiring company. The difficulty is that article 85(2) may prevent that transfer ever taking place. Such a rule would not only jeopardize the existence/exercise solution to the property question, it might generate a host of related problems, for example for sub-purchasers of shares, which would become greater as the time between the original transaction and the ruling against it under article 85(1) increased.[64] The only solution would be to construe the word 'void' in article 85(2) as meaning something other than what it means in English contractual usage, in which the effect of a contract being void is to prevent property passing.[65] Although it is far from certain that that could be achieved, it is not beyond the bounds of possibility. In early decisions in relation to article 85(2) the Court appears to have taken the view that an agreement being automatically void should not affect property rights which have accrued or been transferred under it.[66] More recently the Court has taken the view that the consequences

---

[63] There would, of course, be a risk of loss in the case of a would-be acquiring company which was prevented from carrying through a takeover by operation of a rule such as this, since it is likely that it would have paid a premium for the acquisition of the shares which could not be recouped on resale. Such risks are always present, however, where takeovers are attempted which run the risk of falling within merger regulations of any kind.

[64] Cf. Korah, *The Philip Morris judgment: does article 85 now extend to mergers?* [1987] 8 ECLR 239, 252–3.

[65] E.g., *Cundy* v *Lindsay* (1878) 3 App Cas 459.

[66] Cf. 40/70 *Sirena* v *Eda* [1971] ECR 69, [1971] CMLR 260; 56 & 58/64 *Consten & Grundig* v *Commission* [1966] ECR 299, [1966] CMLR 418.

of nullity for those elements of the agreement which are not themselves restrictive of competition are a matter not for Community law but for national law to decide.[67] In English law there would be no good reason to assume that 'void' in article 85(2) means the same as it means for domestic contract law as far as the passing of property is concerned, not least because when article 85(2) was drafted it did not contemplate the common law meaning of the word but rather the civil law meaning of its equivalent in the languages of the original Member States, which did not know the English distinction between void and voidable agreements. Moreover, there is a precedent in English law for disregarding the strict meaning of the word 'void' in a statute in so far as its impact on the passing of property is concerned,[68] and in the light of the Court of Justice's early attitude it might be argued that it would be appropriate to do the same in this instance. In that event, title to shares would pass, and it would be open to the anti-trust authority to prevent the anti-competitive effect of the agreement by prohibiting the exercise of the voting rights inherent in the shares.

7.3.3.4 Conclusion

After the decision in *BAT and RJ Reynolds* v *Commission*[69] it became clear that article 85 EEC would apply to certain aspects of merger and acquisition activity. Although the scope of its application is reduced by Regulation 4064/89, the analysis in the early part of this Chapter, and in Chapter 5, makes clear that some residual scope for the application of article 85 remains. Such a conclusion raises the question of the supposed obstacles to the application of article 85 to transactions of this kind which, prior to the *BAT and RJ Reynolds* v *Commission* decision, were taken to rule out merger and acquisition control in this way. If this broader scope of article 85 survives Regulation 4064/89, then legal and conceptual means of overcoming those obstacles must be found. It is suggested that the analysis in the last section of this Chapter demonstrates that, although the reasoning is often complex, the legal foundation already exists in the case law of the Court of Justice to overcome what were previously conceived of as insurmountable conceptual hurdles.

---

[67] 10/86 *VAG France SA* v *Etablissements Magne SA* [1986] ECR 4071; see Kerse at p. 12.
[68] Under the (now repealed) Infants Relief Act 1874 minors' contracts were said to be 'absolutely void', but in *Stocks* v *Wilson* [1913] 2 KB 235 this was said not to prevent property passing under such an agreement. It is noticeable that in this case the unusual construction put on the word appears to derive from a policy decision that the unacceptable consequences of the more usual meaning were to be avoided.
[69] 142 & 156/84 [1988] 4 CMLR 24; see 1.1.3.4.

EIGHT
The interface of Community law and national law

Just as the Community legal system itself does not exist independently of the legal systems of the Member States, so merger control in the European Community does not exist in a vacuum. All Member States contribute through their own court structures to the legal system of the Community, and some individual Member States have systems of merger control which are intended to promote their individual industrial and competition policies. The absence of a clear institutional or functional demarcation between Community and national systems gives rise to a number of problems and conflicts in the implementation of the policy of merger control. Many of these are examples of the broader, familiar conflicts between national sovereignty and Community supremacy which are the inevitable consequence of membership of an international organisation with centralised powers. Nevertheless, the resolution of these conflicts will be crucial if a coherent strategy is to emerge, double jeopardy is to be avoided, and the business community is to be given clear directions as to which authorities are empowered to scrutinise their activities. On some issues it is now possible to give reasonably clear guidance, because they have been provided for by legislation or have been settled by clear rulings from the Court of Justice. In other cases, however, it is only possible to go back to first principles of Community law and, on the basis of the declared policy in relation to merger control, to predict how such conflicts are likely to be resolved as and when they arise.

Three quite distinct issues may arise:

(a)   the extent to which Community merger control legislation[1] may be invoked before national courts, and if so by whom, and under what limits;

(b)   the correlation between Community control of whether mergers should take place at all and national supervision of the processes involved;[2]

(c)   the risk of direct conflict between Community law and national law, and more seriously between a decision of the Community authorities and

---

[1]   I.e. arts. 85 and 86 EEC, art. 66 ECSC, in addition to Reg. 4064/89.
[2]   The Community takes the view that the appropriate form of Community action in this field is harmonisation rather than direct legislation; see 8.2.3.

a decision of the national authorities, over whether a particular merger should be allowed to proceed.

8.1 COMMUNITY LAW IN NATIONAL COURTS[3]

Although it is not explicit in the Treaty of Rome, it is an essential cornerstone of the Community legal order, emphasised by the Court of Justice from its inception,[4] that Community law is to be applied, implemented and enforced by an integrated legal system comprising both the European Court of Justice and the courts of the Member States. Such an arrangement is implicit in the provision that certain Community legislation is to be directly applicable in the Member States,[5] and in the Court of Justice's jurisdiction to give preliminary rulings concerning interpretation of the Treaty and the validity and interpretation of acts of the Institutions.[6] In certain circumstances Community law gives rise to rights enforceable by individuals against either the state or other individuals through the national courts of a Member State, in which case the Community law is described as 'directly effective'. These basic principles of Community law apply in the course of civil proceedings between private parties. There is also the technical possibility, under article 9(3) of Regulation 17, and article 88 EEC, of articles 85 and 86 EEC being applied by 'competent authorities' directly in competition scrutiny proceedings where the Commission has not itself initiated any procedure. In the United Kingdom this possibility is entirely academic.

8.1.1 The consequences of direct effect

Once a provision has been classed as being of direct effect it becomes an equivalent but superior rule to those of national law which may be used by one party against another in the course of litigation. However, the remedies which may be granted to vindicate these rights derived from Community law remain whatever remedies the national legal system of the particular Member State provides. Thus, the scope of Community law in national courts depends upon a complex amalgam of Community and national law.[7]

8.1.1.1 Direct effect and articles 85 and 86 EEC in English law
In general, the provision of remedies for breach of obligations arising under

---

3 This section assumes some knowledge of the Community legal system, and especially of the concepts of direct effect and supremacy of Community law. For a good general account, see Hartley, 181 – 281.
4 Cf. *Van Gend en Loos v Nedelandse Belastingadministratie* [1963] ECR 1, 1963 CMLR 105.
5 Art.189(2): 'A regulation shall have general application. It shall be binding in its entirety and directly applicable in all Member States.'
6 Art.177.
7 Cf. Green & Barav, (1986) 6 Ybk European Law 55, esp 114-119 and Steiner, (1987) 12 ELRev 102.

Community law in English law is complicated by the distinction between private law and public law rights. Nevertheless, that distinction need not concern us here, since parties to litigation in the English courts involving a proposed or executed merger will in almost every case be private parties asserting either contractual or tortious rights.[8]

Contractual rights are most likely to be at issue in the course of an action to enforce a contract, made in the course of a merger and intended to effect some aspect of the merger, which one party seeks to resist by arguing that the contract is unenforceable as a matter of English law because the merger is prohibited under Community law. Agreements which infringe article 85(1) are automatically void under article 85(2). In the case of agreements made after 1962, or agreements which would fall within the scope of article 85 on the accession of a new Member State and made after the date of accession, article 85(2) takes effect immediately.[9] Assuming that the evidential issues are resolved in favour of the party pleading infringement of article 85(1) in such a case, the contract would be unenforceable (subject to the severance doctrine).[10]

Tortious rights are most likely to be at issue where a third party seeks an injunction to prevent a merger taking place or seeks compensation for loss allegedly suffered as a result of the consummation of a prohibited merger. It is apparently accepted that articles 85 and 86, which have been ruled to be of direct effect by the Court of Justice,[11] give rise to tortious rights under the head of breach of statutory duty.[12] Consequently, English law provides the necessary processes for the assertion in the English courts of rights arising under Community competition law. Nevertheless, it should be recognised that the tort of breach of statutory duty is not without

---

[8] See *An Bord Bainne Co-operative Ltd* v *Milk Marketing Board* [1984] 1 CMLR 519, [1984] 2 CMLR 584. The exception might be the case of judicial review sought against UK competition authorities seeking to rule against (or perhaps in favour of) a merger which has already been the subject of a definitive ruling by Community authorities: see generally 8.3.3.

[9] In the context of merger control there are strong policy arguments against the application of article 85 to 'old' (i.e. in existence at the time when the Treaty came into force) and 'accession' (i.e. in existence at the time of accession to the Community of a new Member State and not previously within the scope of article 85) agreements. To question the validity of mergers after the lapse of any great length of time would be to threaten the legal certainty of the commercial transaction, and would be unacceptable. Equally, it would be extremely difficult to carry out a proper economic analysis.

[10] E.g., *Sirdar* v *Les Fils de Louis Mulliez* [1975] 1 CMLR 378: agreement not to sell certain goods in the UK void as contrary to article 85(1). For the consequences for share transactions, see 7.3.3.2 and 7.3.3.3.

[11] 127/73 *BRT* v *SABAM* [1974] ECR 51, [1974] 2 CMLR 238. The Court also ruled in this case that the opening of a procedure by the Commission did not prevent (under art.9(3), Reg.17) a national court applying article 85 or 86 *by virtue of its direct effect* as opposed to application for the purpose of direct competition scrutiny by the state authority.

[12] *Garden Cottage Foods Ltd* v *Milk Marketing Board.* [1984] AC 130.

complexity, and a plaintiff seeking to rely upon it must sustain a considerable burden of proof.[13]

8.1.1.2 Limits on the direct effect of article 85 EEC

The conclusion that there exist processes necessary for the assertion in English courts of rights arising under Community competition law is sterile without some indication of what those rights are. Until now the analysis has proceeded upon the relatively simple proposition that articles 85 and 86 are of direct effect, since it is in relation to these provisions that the English courts have established the governing principles. It is now necessary to examine in more detail the extent of that direct effect, and to consider the position in relation to other measures of control of mergers and acquisitions and analogous transactions.

The potential limits on the direct effect of articles 85 and 86 stem from express reservations about the power of national courts to apply all or part of those provisions. An important reservation arises out of the provisions of Regulation 4064/89 and its attempt to establish a principle of 'one-stop shopping' in respect of merger control. As far as concentrations as defined in article 3 of the Regulation are concerned, the effect of article 22(2) is to deprive article 85 EEC of any direct effect.[14] There is a further significant reservation relevant to transactions which do not amount to concentrations in the case of article 85(3), expressed in Regulation 17, article 9(1).[15] The effect of this provision is to remove all decisions under article 85(3) from the scope of the powers of national courts. In principle such a rule does not prevent national courts using article 85(1) in relation to challenges to mergers and acquisitions presented to them, but in practice it deprives article 85 of much of its necessary subtlety as an instrument of control. One of the potential advantages of article 85 over article 86 as an instrument of merger control is its express exemption procedure. A national court deprived of that policy tool and so unable to differentiate between prohibited and permissible mergers would be unable to apply article 85 except in the clearest cases of infringement, and would in all other cases have to suspend its own proceedings pending the outcome of a ruling by the Community authorities. In some cases that might be achieved by seeking a preliminary ruling from the Court of Justice under article 177, but since the Court does not rule upon the facts or the merits of individual cases that approach would not be sufficiently precise. The alternative would be an indefinite stay of the national proceedings until such time as the Commission had ruled on the

---

[13] See Buckley, (1984) 100 LQR 204.
[14] See further 7.2.3.2.
[15] Art.9(1) of Reg. 17 reads: 'Subject to review of its decision by the Court of Justice, the Commission shall have sole power to declare Art.85(1) inapplicable pursuant to Art.85(3) of the Treaty.'

matter, presumably at the instigation of one of the parties, since there is no power for a direct reference from a national court to the Commission.

It is difficult to prescribe anything but a very limited role for article 85 as an instrument of merger control in national courts. Where the transaction amounts to a concentration then, whether it has a Community dimension or not, article 22(2) of Regulation 4064/89 will prevent reliance on article 85 EEC in national courts. In the case of other transactions, the absence of an effective exemption process, in the hands of the court dealing with the *prima facie* issue of infringement of article 85(1), makes it a cumbersome tool for such purposes. Nevertheless, for those seeking to resist those mergers and acquisitions still within its scope by obtaining an injunction from a national court on the basis of article 85 it may provide a useful spoiling tactic. If a *prima facie* case of infringement of article 85(1) is made out then a national court which believes that the merger should nevertheless be allowed to proceed has few options open to it. It may stay its proceedings pending the outcome of an investigation by the Community authorities, but that may have the same effect as an interlocutory injunction and may be enough to cause the parties to withdraw from the proposed merger. Alternatively, it may decide to take no action, on the ground that any harm to the complainant, should the merger prove to be prohibited, can be adequately compensated in damages.[16] Although the latter course of action would avoid the spoiling effect of a challenge to a merger which the court felt was entitled to an exemption, it may not be easy to find on the facts that damages would be an adequate remedy when any loss which might be caused to the complainant will inevitably be highly speculative and indefinite because it would arise out of a permanent change in the structure of the market. Thus, even if the Commission wishes to discourage the use of article 85 for merger control, it may be that those seeking to resist mergers, or to oppose the merging of competitors, will resort to proceedings in the national court as a spoiling tactic of the kind already familiar in takeover battles in the USA.

8.1.1.3 Limits on the direct effect of article 86 EEC

The application of article 86 in national courts suffers from no such constraints. Article 22(2) of Regulation 4064/89 is not thought to deprive article 86 EEC of direct effect,[17] although there is an unresolved question as to the effect and legality of article 22(1), which may prevent the application of article 86 to any concentration.[18] Moreover, the absence of a distinct exemption process means that permissible conduct by an undertaking in a dominant position must simply be held not to constitute an abuse;

---

[16] As in the *Garden Cottage Foods* case: supra note 12.
[17] 7.2.3.2.
[18] See 7.2.4.2.

correspondingly, conduct amounting to an abuse is by definition impermissible and no exemption is available. As a consequence, all the necessary decision-making power passes to the national court under the direct effect doctrine. Thus, the House of Lords in *Garden Cottage Foods Ltd* v *Milk Marketing Board*[19] was not prevented from considering every aspect of the case in determining whether an injunction or damages would be the appropriate remedy in the circumstances.

8.1.1.4 Direct effect and Regulation 4064/89

Regulation 4064/89 does not permit national courts to apply its provisions in the course of litigation before them. The Regulation is directly applicable under article 189(2) EEC, and its provisions appear to satisfy the test of direct effect of being clear and precise and requiring no further implementation. Nevertheless, article 21(1) provides:

'Subject to review by the Court of Justice, the Commission shall have sole jurisdiction to take the decisions provided for in this Regulation.'

This provision is similar to article 9(1) of Regulation 17, with the conspicuous difference that it embraces all decisions under the Regulation rather than discriminating between those decisions relevant to *prima facie* infringement and those relevant to exemption. This drafting may well result from the structure of article 2 of the Regulation, which combines both elements in a single paragraph,[20] rather than from any express design to eliminate the consequences of direct effect entirely, but the result is that the Regulation cannot be used in national courts.

8.1.1.5 Direct effect and the ECSC Treaty

There does not seem to be any scope for the application of article 66 ECSC in national courts. Under that provision 'concentration . . . whether it is effected by merger, acquisition of shares or parts of the undertaking or assets, loan, contract, or any other means of control' requires the prior authorisation of the Commission. Implicit in this requirement is the stipulation of an exclusive jurisdiction in these matters on the part of the Commission. Since article 65(4), paragraph 2 (which prohibits restrictive agreements), expressly provides that the Commission shall have sole jurisdiction,[21] it is perhaps a little surprising that the same formulation was not used in the case of concentrations. Nevertheless, the implied stipulation of exclusive jurisdiction is quite clear, and in any case the Court has never articulated a theory

---

[19] [1984] AC 130.
[20] Article 2 thus resembles article 86 EEC rather than article 85 EEC.
[21] In *SA Aciers Sidero* v *Fagerta Bruks Aktiebolag* [1973] CMLR 77 the Brussels Court of Appeal ruled that where the validity of an agreement was in issue in litigation before the national court, the proceedings must be stayed pending a ruling from the Commission.

of direct effect under the ECSC Treaty, although the concept, but not the term of art, of direct applicability is known in that context.[22]

8.1.2 Summary of the scope for national courts to apply EC merger rules in civil litigation

Article 85 EEC. This provision is of direct effect, but Regulation 17, article 9(3), prevents the application of article 85(3) by national courts. Consequently, national courts may impose the prohibition under article 85(1) in clear cases, and equally may declare it inapplicable in clear cases, but must defer their decision pending the Commission's ruling in cases where there is the possibility of an exemption. In the case of agreements giving rise to mergers which are found to infringe article 85(1), that fact may be used as a defence in a contract action, and may give rise to damages or an injunction, on the basis of a breach of statutory duty, where harm resulting from the agreement can be shown.

Article 86 EEC. This provision is of direct effect, and there is no restriction in Regulation 17 on its application by national courts which may, therefore, use it to full effect in civil litigation before them. In the UK, the House of Lords has held[23] (in interlocutory proceedings) that infringement is a breach of statutory duty which normally sounds in damages, and in default of which an injunction would be available under the usual rules.[24]

Regulation 4064/89. Although the Regulation is directly applicable and appears to satisfy the test for direct effect, article 20 gives exclusive jurisdiction over decisions in relation to its provisions to the Commission, subject to review by the Court of Justice. Consequently, although the validity of a merger under the Regulation might be relevant to the determination of domestic litigation, the only path open to the court would be to stay its proceedings pending the outcome of the Commission's appraisal.

Article 66 ECSC. Here too the Commission is granted exclusive jurisdiction, so that the only course open to a national court, for which the validity of a concentration under this provision is significant, appears to be to stay its proceedings pending the outcome of the Commission's investigation.

---

[22] Halsbury's Laws, 4th ed. (1986), Vol.51, paras 3.41–3.42; the editors attribute this omission to the limited nature of preliminary rulings under article 41 ECSC, but also raise the question whether developments under the EEC Treaty might be thought to have extended to ECSC matters.

[23] [1984] AC 130.

[24] Cf. *American Cynamid Co* v *Ethicon Ltd* [1975] AC 396; see *Sirdar Ltd* v *Les Fils de Louis Mulliez* (supra note 10).

8.2 COMMUNITY LAW AND NATIONAL SUPERVISION OF THE BID PROCESS

A second focus of the relationship between Community and national law is in the area of supervision of the mechanics of a takeover or merger, (i.e. the bid process). Here the functions of the Commission and the national regulatory body (if there is one) are separate but complementary: the Commission being concerned with competition, the national regulatory body with the treatment of shareholders and more generally with the proper conduct of the bid process.[25] It is generally accepted that supervision of the bid process is a matter more properly left to national authorities, since the legal and commercial institutions involved have quite distinct national characteristics to which any supervisory legislation must be carefully attuned.[26]

In the United Kingdom, supervision of takeovers conducted through the stock market is undertaken by a non-statutory system of self-regulation by the City Takeover Panel which seeks, *inter alia*, to ensure that parties to a bid comply with the principles set out in the City Code on Takeovers and Mergers. This Code seeks to ensure that the bid process is conducted fairly and that the shareholders of the target company are treated equally and are given sufficient time and information to consider any offer. At the same time the City Code requires that the target company is not exposed for an unduly long period to the commercial uncertainty and disruption which is likely to result from a bid. The operation of the Takeover Code overlaps with any form of merger control, whether carried out by national or Community authorities. As far as UK merger control is concerned, the Takeover Code now makes specific provision for intervention by the UK and EC competition law authorities.[27]

The result of the interplay of several bodies regulating different but related aspects of the same transaction (i.e. the competition aspects and the bid process) is that there is potential for an imperfect 'fit' between their respective procedures. Thus, a direct conflict could result between national rules governing the bid process and Community merger control rules. An encouraging aspect of the new Regulation is that it sets strict time limits for Commission determination of compatibility with the common market which, in the case of the UK, are generally consistent with the existing bid timetable under the City Code. The possibility that a delay in the Regulation's timetable would put the City Code's timetable in jeopardy has

---

[25] See the statement issued by the City Takeover Panel on 19th August 1988 in the context of the bid for Irish Distillers (1988/15).

[26] In this context the proposed 13th Company Law Directive (see further 8.2.2 below) provides no more than minimum standards which Member States are free to exceed.

[27] See the amendments to the Code introduced by the Takeover Panel on 21 September 1990 (1990/18).

been specifically addressed by the amendments to the City Code[28] introduced by the Takeover Panel in September 1990. These are now incorporated in a revised edition of the City Code.

8.2.1 The *Irish Distillers* case

At the time of the Commission's intervention in the *Irish Distillers*[29] case in July 1988, the absence of specific provisions in the City Code to address the 'fit' between Community competition law and national control of the bid process caused difficulty and highlighted the need for a better fit between the two.[30] In the Irish Distillers case, Allied-Lyons and Grand Metropolitan established a joint venture company (GC & C Brands)[31] which launched a bid for Irish Distillers. During the currency of the bid the Commission intervened under article 85 EEC on the grounds, *inter alia*, that the joint venture participants[32] should have been competing for control, rather than dividing it between them. A settlement was reached under which Grand Metropolitan was to take 100% control of the offeror (GC & C Brands) and was to be entitled to make a restructured bid. Under the terms of the settlement, the other participants in GC & C Brands were free to make counter-bids within a period of 28 days. The Panel decided that the restructured bid by GC & C Brands amounted to a new bid. As such the bid was caught by Rule 35 of the City Code, which provides that where an offer has been withdrawn or has lapsed, the offeror may not, save with the consent of the Panel, make a fresh bid for a period of twelve months. Thus, in the absence of the exercise of the Panel's discretion under Rule 35, GC & C Brands would not have been in a position to implement its settlement with the Commission by making the proposed restructured bid. The same was true of Allied-Lyons' and Guinness' entitlement to make counter bids. The Panel, while being anxious to limit the extent to which Irish Distillers was placed under siege, took the view that the interests of the shareholders required that they be given an opportunity to consider the restructured bid. In one sense the result was no more than an example of the flexible and essentially pragmatic workings of the Panel; but it did anticipate the requirement for a fit between Community competition law and domestic regulation of the bid process.

[28] See Note 4 on Rule 31.6 of the Code.
[29] (1988) 21 Bull of EC 7-8/34.
[30] The fit between national competition law and national control of the bid process was, of course, well established and expressly covered in the City Code.
[31] GC & C Brands was owned as to 50% by Gilbeys of Ireland Group Ltd (a subsidiary of Grand Metropolitan plc) and Cantrell & Cochrane Group Ltd. Cantrell & Cochrane was owned as to 50.4% by Hiram Walker — Allied Vintners (a subsidiary of Allied-Lyons plc) and as to 49.6% by the Guinness Group. Guinness maintained that its involvement in GC & C Brands (including its bid for Irish Distillers) was passive.
[32] Identified as Grand Metropolitan and Allied-Lyons; the Commission reserved its position in respect of Guinness' stated passive involvement in the bidding vehicle GC & C Brands.

8.2.2 The Takeover Directive

The Commission takes the view that the appropriate form of Community action in this field is harmonisation rather than direct legislation (as indeed it has in the majority of company law issues), and to that end it has proposed a thirteenth Company Law Directive 'concerning takeover and other general bids'.[33] Takeovers by share transaction, as opposed to 'legal' or 'asset' mergers, are a relatively recent phenomenon and are still uncommon in some Member States, so that there is no comprehensive, let alone uniform, pattern of regulation. The Directive will provide for the establishment of a Supervisory Authority charged with ensuring observance of a number of principles designed to guarantee fair treatment of all shareholders.[34] This is an area in which the United Kingdom may find itself unwilling to accept the proposed Community solution, since the call in the Directive for establishment of a Supervisory Authority would appear to imply implementation of that proposal by national legislation, while the United Kingdom will almost certainly want to retain its system of City self-regulation.

It should be possible, once the Thirteenth Directive is implemented in the Member States,[35] to achieve a standard rule for the interlock of bid-supervision and merger control regulations. Somewhat surprisingly, the present draft contains no provision expressly dealing with suspension or withdrawal of a bid in the event of a merger investigation being announced. Article 13(1)(d) provides that an offer may be withdrawn in the event of lack of authorisation by the merger control authorities. The accompanying notes make clear that this provision applies to the case of refusal, such as prohibition by merger control authorities. There is no provision for the withdrawal or suspension of an offer pending a merger investigation, and yet article 12(1) provides a maximum period for bid acceptances of ten weeks from publication of the offer document, which is no doubt shorter than the period likely to be necessary for a full investigation by the Commission.[36] Consequently, provision for suspension or lapsing of bids upon announcement of a full investigation by the Commission appears to be essential. It may

---

[33] COM(90) 416 final, OJ 1990 C240/7.
[34] The main principles cover: the threshold for launching a full bid; requirement of bidding for all the shares; specification of the minimum content of the offer document; withdrawal, revision, time periods for acceptance of offers; the offeree company report.
[35] It is difficult to predict with confidence when that will be achieved. Considerable emphasis was placed on the Directive during the French Presidency of the Council in the second half of 1989, in the hope of implementation before the end of 1992, but at the time of writing officials admit privately that a considerable amount remains to be done.
[36] No doubt many cases will be dealt with on an expedited process because it soon becomes apparent that no anti-competitive effect will be caused and clearance can be granted, but in cases of doubt the full economic analysis necessary is likely to take at least 3 months. Regulation 4064/89 article 10(3) sets a period of 4 months, which may well be extended where the Commission is not satisfied that it has been furnished with all necessary information. See further 4.4.

be that this is to be achieved under article 12(1) and (2), which allow modification of the acceptance period (of between four and ten weeks) with the authorisation of the supervisory authority. At this stage, however, the drafting of these provisions is far from satisfactory,[37] and it must be hoped that more specific provision for this eventuality will be included in the final draft of the Directive.

8.3 COMMUNITY SUPREMACY IN MATTERS OF MERGER CONTROL

The most serious problem arising out of the interface of Community law and national law in the field of merger control is that of the potential for conflict between Community measures applied by the Commission and national measures applied by the competition authorities in the individual Member States, some of which have their own merger control procedures. Such conflicts arise out of different views, at Community and national level respectively, in relation to the industrial policy which merger control should promote and in relation to the size criteria against which concentrations should be assessed. Although there is sometimes said to be a distinction between those Member States which favour using merger control as an instrument of industrial policy and those which wish it to be restricted to matters of competition policy, the debate is really between advocates of an interventionist, positive industrial policy and advocates of a laissez-faire, free market industrial policy. In the absence of a formal federal system which gives determinant power to the central authority, it is clearly desirable that as far as possible national policy should continue to be given a proper role in controlling mergers as it has in other aspects of competition policy. Equally, as with all aspects of Community activity, the founding principle must remain that, in situations of direct conflict, primacy is granted to the supra-national rules derived from the Treaties. While these principles can be easily stated, it is more difficult in practice to identify precisely the respective areas of competence of the Community and national authorities.

8.3.1 Merger control and the supremacy principle[38]

In matters of merger control it is most likely that there will not be legislative conflicts between Community law and national law, in that it is clearly Community policy that its competition rules should apply only within a defined 'supra-national' sector, and should principally be applied by Community authorities, leaving national competition rules free to be applied

---

[37] It is known that article 13 has been the subject of considerable discussion, and that it remains in its present form in part because of a failure to agree on proposed amendments.

[38] 106/77 *Amministrazione delle Finanze dell Stato* v *Simmenthal SpA (No2)* [1978] ECR 629, [1978] 3 CMLR 623; cf. Hartley 215–244.

by national authorities in the national context. Thus articles 85 and 86 apply only in the case of an effect on trade between Member States, and although they are of direct effect there is no obligation for national competition authorities to apply them in competition cases. On the contrary, they may not be applied once the Commission has initiated proceedings, and until that time there is a power but not an obligation to apply them.[39] Equally, article 21(1) of Regulation 4064/89 expressly excludes its application by national authorities. Consequently, since the Community does not seek to impose its rule on national authorities, the issue of legislative conflict will not normally arise.

However, it is possible that in the case of civil proceedings (not being anti-trust proceedings initiated by the state) such a conflict might arise. For example, if it were alleged that an individual enjoyed certain 'direct effect' rights in respect of an agreement which was part of a merger prohibited under Community law, but it was claimed by the other party that the agreement or merger would not be invalid under English law, then there would be a conflict between the legislative provisions. It is also quite possible that there might be a conflict between Community and national authorities in respect of decisions, whether judicial or quasi-judicial, affecting the same merger; the national court in civil proceedings might differ, in its application of the relevant rule to the facts, from the view taken by the Community authority in anti-trust proceedings. It is theoretically possible, of course, for jurisdiction in merger cases to be so carefully allocated between the potential controlling authorities that such conflicts cannot arise. In practice, however, it seems that such a level of precision will be difficult to achieve. The resolution of the potential conflicts emerging from such situations depends upon the supremacy principle.

8.3.2   The limits of Community supremacy in practice: jurisdiction

The Community approach to potential conflicts between Community merger law and national regulations is based upon both a practical division of jurisdiction between Community and national authorities and upon the constitutional principle of the supremacy of Community law. The approach seeks, therefore, to avoid such conflicts wherever possible, but where that cannot be achieved it resolves them in accordance with the supremacy principle. Nevertheless, the possible outcomes of a merger investigation are sufficiently varied for it to be impossible to state a categorical rule that the supremacy principle leads inevitably to the Community authority's conclusion prevailing. In some instances, the existence of a Community ruling will not prevent a contrary national ruling ultimately deciding the fate of the proposed merger. In practice, the most significant element of the

[39]   Art.88 EEC; art.9(3) Reg.17.

Community approach is the distinction which continues to be maintained between the respective fields of application of Community and national law. According to this distinction, Community law will only be applied to competition issues which are of concern at the Community level, however that may be defined. Matters which affect only national competition policy may then be left to national authorities. The difficulty, then, is only in drawing the dividing line. Although it is possible to draw the line in such a way as to satisfy the policy interests of the respective authorities in the majority of cases, it is impossible to avoid overlap in a number of instances, and in these cases other principles are called into play to resolve the conflicts.

8.3.2.1 Regulation 4064/89

Under the Regulation, demarcation between Community and national fields of operation is maintained by the concept of 'Community dimension' contained in article 1 and examined in detail in Chapter 2.[40] Here the extent of Community jurisdiction is narrowly defined. Instead of a broad test of effect upon trade between Member States, which the Court of Justice was able to use in the early years of the Community to expand the Commission's jurisdiction over anti-trust cases, there is a narrow definition based upon turnover and the geographical centre of business activity. This narrow definition of the ambit of the Community's jurisdiction under the Regulation is, moreover, supported by the reciprocal provision in article 21(2) reserving matters falling within the definition of Community dimension exclusively to the Community authority (subject to one exception considered elsewhere[41]). Furthermore, the narrow definition is kept secure by the provision in article 22(2) that the ordinary competition law of the Community (i.e. articles 85 and 86 EEC) shall not apply to concentrations as defined by the Regulation. It should be noted, however, that the Regulation does not prevent the application of the ordinary competition law to mergers which do not fall within the scope of that definition. This point is taken up below.[42]

8.3.2.2 Articles 85 and 86 EEC

In respect of articles 85 and 86 of the Treaty of Rome the essential demarcation between the Community sphere and the national sphere is made by the condition that the conduct must have an effect upon trade between Member States for it to fall within the terms of the article in question.[43] If this condition is not satisfied the Commission should grant a negative clearance, or where it is clear from the beginning that the condition will not be satisfied it should decline jurisdiction in the case. It should be noted, however, that

---

[40] See 2.2 et seq.
[41] See Regulation 4064/89, art.9: see 3.4 et seq.
[42] See 8.3.2.2.
[43] See Bellamy & Child 2-113, and see 6&7/73 Commercial Solvents v Commission [1974] ECR 223 at 252; 22/78 Hugin v Commission [1979] ECR 1869.

the reciprocal conclusion does not apply: the fact that an effect upon trade between Member States can be shown does not prevent national authorities also ruling upon a case, although there are some constraints upon their freedom to rule as they choose. Although the notion of affecting trade between Member States has been very widely interpreted by the Court of Justice, it is remarkable that resulting instances of conflict between national and Community law have been avoided. As far as merger control is concerned, in practice the breadth of the interpretation will not prove significant if the interpretation of Regulation 4064/89 considered in Chapter 7 is adopted, because neither article 85, nor 86 would be applied as a means of merger control except in a small minority of cases. Should article 85 or 86 become more prominent in merger control, however, there is no doubt that the Member States will be unhappy with the breadth of the interpretation, which allocates far greater scope to Community control than does the corresponding provision of Regulation 4064/89. The potential for conflict would then be high.

8.3.2.3   The ECSC Treaty
Under the ECSC Treaty these demarcation issues do not arise because the only jurisdiction in such cases lies with the Commission, and coal and steel matters are outside the scope of national merger control regulations.[44]

8.3.3   Loopholes in the demarcation system

The above outline of the demarcation between Community and national authorities makes clear that it is impossible to draw a clear line between their respective areas of competence. Under Regulation 4064/89 the demarcation is much more precisely defined than it is under the Treaty of Rome, and the respective areas of competence of Community and national authorities are exclusively allocated. As a consequence, the general problem of overlap which exists under articles 85 and 86 EEC should not arise. Nevertheless, it is possible to identify three potential loopholes in respect of the Regulation, in addition to the problem of overlap of jurisdiction in respect of articles 85 and 86 EEC.

8.3.3.1   Referral of concentrations relating to a distinct market to the Member State authority: article 9 of Regulation 4064/89
Article 9 gives the Commission power to refer to a Member State a concentration having a Community dimension (in order to ensure effective competition in a distinct market within that Member State[45]). This exception to the exclusive jurisdiction of the Commission over concentrations having a Community dimension is provided for by article 21(2) of Regulation

[44]   See 6.1.2.
[45]   See 3.4 *et seq.*

4064/89. Although the matter is not addressed expressly in Regulation 4064/89, it seems that the choices open to the Commission in deciding whether or not to refer a case to the competent authority of any Member State rule out the possibility of the Commission dealing with the matter itself and also allowing the Member State to deal with the matter.[46] Thus, unless the Court of Justice adopts a different interpretation of article 9(3) of Regulation 4064/89 there should be no conflict in this case.

8.3.3.2 Protection of a Member State's legitimate interests under article 21(3) of Regulation 4064/89

The second potential loophole by which a Member State might apply its law to a concentration having a Community dimension is expressly provided for under article 21(3) of the Regulation, which allows Member States to 'take appropriate measures to protect legitimate interests other than those taken into consideration by this Regulation'.[47] Although the Regulation identifies three such interests, it is very difficult to predict the precise ambit of this very loosely defined power. The only secure definition is by way of exclusion, since any matter which the Commission must take into account under article 2 of Regulation 4064/89 is excluded from consideration by Member States in the exercise of this power.[48] It is important to note that such measures must be compatible with other provisions of Community law, and so for example must not be discriminatory on grounds of nationality and may not be a disguised means of preventing the free movement of goods. This power granted to Member States does not grant exclusive jurisdiction over the merger concerned, so that it raises the possibility of a conflict with the Commission's own determination in respect of the same merger.[49]

8.3.3.3 Concentrations not having a Community dimension

The third potential loophole in the demarcation provided for by the Regulation lies in the possibility that the Commission might continue to use the existing competition law in the case of concentrations not falling within the definition of Community dimension in the Regulation. Although article 22(2) provides that the ordinary competition law[50] does not apply to concentrations as defined by article 3 of the Regulation,[51] and article 22(1) provides that only the new Regulation is to apply to concentrations as defined by article 3, there is some doubt as to whether the Regulation can legally exclude the continued

---

46   See 3.4.2.2.
47   See 2.4.2.
48   Perhaps this is the real reason for the inclusion in art.2(1)(b) of the development of technical and economic progress, since its inclusion there denies Member States the opportunity of applying it to undermine the Commission's determination.
49   See below 8.3.4.1 and 8.3.4.2.
50   Reg 17, Reg 1017/68, Reg 1017/68, Reg 4056/86 and Reg 3975/87 — all of which implement arts. 85 and 86 for specified purposes.
51   See 7.1 and 7.2.

application by the Commission of articles 85 and 86 EEC.[52] Consequently, despite the apparent intention that mergers not having a Community dimension should remain within national jurisdiction, the Regulation leaves open the possibility of applying either article 85 or article 86 in the way in which they have in the past been applied to mergers. In such a case there might be a conflict of a kind not easily resolved.

There is little doubt that at present the Commission would settle for control over the 'mega-mergers', and would not wish to spend time on lesser affairs. It will have some difficulty coping with the extra work that an aggregate turnover threshold of 5 billion ECU will bring.[53] However, the Commission's position cannot be given formal legal status within the Regulation, and the only withdrawal by the Commission of its potential jurisdiction over such issues has been made at the level of a statement entered in the Minutes of the Council at the time of the adoption of Regulation 4064/89[54] which is of uncertain legal effect and which does no more than reserve the Commission's position as to the future exercise of that jurisdiction.[55] It is conceivable that, should the Commission wish to widen its definition of Community dimension in order to extend its jurisdiction under the Regulation,[56] but meets with resistance in the Council, then it might well resort to article 85 both to extend its jurisdiction and to put pressure on the Council to comply with its wish. Equally, the Commission's exercise of its residual powers under articles 85 and 86 might be forced by a third party complainant.[57]

8.3.3.4 Overlap between national and Community jurisdiction in cases under articles 85 and 86 EEC

The problem of conflict is inevitably more acute in respect of articles 85 and 86 EEC, since the test of affecting trade between Member States is inherently imprecise. It is easy to imagine any number of situations in which both Community and national authorities would claim an interest in regulating whether a merger should be allowed to take place, and in which the non-exclusive jurisdiction rule for Community competence would be satisfied. For example, suppose that a German manufacturer which already has a significant presence on the British market acquires a minority interest in a British manufacturer of industrial chemicals which exports to all European countries. There can be little doubt that the United Kingdom authorities would regard such a takeover as falling within their competence, even if

---

[52] See 7.2.4 et seq.
[53] Generally accepted to be up to 50 mergers a year, but thought by some to be fewer than that.
[54] Published at [1990] 4 CMLR 314.
[55] See 7.2.4.3.
[56] See Regulation 4064/89, art.1(3).
[57] See 7.2.4.3.

the policy of the day was not to interfere in such transactions so long as competition on the market would not be eliminated. On the other hand, the Community authorities would argue that the transaction might affect trade between Member States, and so would also claim competence over it. Although it is far from inevitable that such authorities would determine the outcome in different ways, the potential for conflict then arises.[58]

It is clear, therefore, that under the ordinary competition law the demarcation system is only rudimentary, and that is largely attributable to the fact that, when the Community competence is called into play, there is no bar to a continuing Member State competence over the same matter. The Commission's response to this criticism has been to say that there is constant and fruitful cooperation at an administrative level between the Commission and Member State authorities which serves to avoid such conflicts.[59] Such cooperation is no doubt to be expected and welcomed, but the welcome is subject to two reservations. The first is that cooperation, without an established institutional framework of priorities, can only work up to the point of one of the parties placing a particular interest before the general interest in maintaining the relationship of cooperation. Thus, as soon as a Member State authority determines that its interest in regulating a particular merger is paramount, to the extent of refusing to concede jurisdiction to the Commission, the cooperative method of avoiding conflict will collapse, at least temporarily. The second is that, such cooperation being administrative and thus at the level of officials within the respective organisations, it will be entirely or almost entirely unpublished and so immune from comment or critique and inaccessible to those who may be affected by it. The requirement of legal security for parties who must carry out their commercial activities within the law is unlikely to be satisfied where the procedural details of the law are hidden within processes of administrative cooperation. Community law is in this respect subject to the criticism that its informal nature makes it very uncertain for those who wish to plan potential merger transactions in the light of all potentially applicable law.

8.3.4 Resolution of conflicts between Community and national rulings in respect of mergers and acquisitions

In circumstances in which a Member State's competition authority does apply its law to a merger upon which the Commission has already pronounced, or upon which the Commission subsequently pronounces, it will be necessary to determine how any resulting conflict would be resolved. The result will depend in part upon whether the ruling is in the form of a prohibition or an approval of the transaction in question.

58 For the resolution of such conflicts, see below 8.3.4.1 and 8.3.4.2.
59 6th Report on Competition Policy, paras. 114-116.

8.3.4.1 The consequences of Community prohibition

Here, at least from the Community perspective, it is possible to give a clear and straightforward answer. The general supremacy doctrine would result in the Community prohibition prevailing over any possible contrary national outcome, irrespective of whether the Community or national ruling came first in time.

Prohibition under articles 85 and 86 EEC This solution has long been established as far as article 85 EEC is concerned, and it must be assumed that the same rule would apply in the case of article 86. In *Wilhelm* v *Bundeskartellamt*[60] the German competition authorities sought a preliminary ruling from the Court of Justice in relation to the powers of the national authority to continue proceedings at a time when the same complaint was being investigated by the Commission. At the time when the ruling was sought the outcome of the Commission proceedings was unknown, and the Court's answer had to be given in contemplation of either a negative clearance or the grant of an exemption under article 85(3). The Court answered in terms unequivocally asserting the supremacy principle:

'conflicts between the rules of the Community and national rules in the matter of the law on cartels must be resolved by applying the principle that Community law takes precedence. . . should it prove that a decision of a national authority regarding an agreement would be incompatible with a decision adopted by the Commission at the culmination of the procedure initiated by it, the national authority is required to take proper account of the effects of the latter decision.'[61]

The principle is then explained in functional terms:

'the application of the national law may not prejudice the full and uniform application of Community law or the effects of measures taken or to be taken to implement it.'[62]

Where the Community has ruled against a merger under article 85, the only means of ensuring full application of the measure taken to implement Community law would be to prevent national law interfering in any way with the prohibition imposed. This conclusion from the *Wilhelm* case has been confirmed by the Court of Justice,[63] and is accepted by all leading commentators.[64] There is no reason to think that it would not also apply

[60] 14/68 [1969] ECR 1, [1969] CMLR 100.
[61] [1969] ECR 1 at 14.
[62] Ibid at 15.
[63] 45/85 *Verband der Sachversicherer* v *Commission* [1987] ECR 405.
[64] Bellamy & Child 1-086; Kerse 10.27; Goyder p. 348; Whish p. 40.

in the case of merger control under articles 85 and 86 EEC, whether in
a case of a merger not falling within the meaning of concentration or in
a case in which the Commission was exercising its residual powers under
article 89 EEC.[65]

Prohibition under Regulation 4064/89   There is no reason to suppose that
the principle laid down in the *Wilhelm* case in respect of article 85 and
article 86 should not also apply to Regulation 4064/89. In this case, of course,
the Regulation will for the most part avoid conflicts arising because article
21(2) prevents Member States from applying national legislation to mergers
having a Community dimension. The exception to this bar, under which
Member State authorities may be empowered to apply national law to protect
their legitimate interests,[66] will not apply to allow Member States to
undermine Commission prohibitions. In the Statement in the Minutes of
Council at the time of the adoption of Regulation 4064/89, in respect of
article 21(3) the Commission makes clear that it does not regard this procedure
as permitting Member States to authorise concentrations prohibited by the
Commission. Commission prohibitions under Regulation 4064/89 cannot,
therefore, be overcome by a ruling from the national authority.

8.3.4.2   The consequences of Community 'approval'
Where the Community authorities do not impose a prohibition on a merger
it is possible loosely to describe the merger as enjoying Community approval.
In practice, however, it is necessary to be more specific about the nature
of the Community's 'decision'. In the first place, it is necessary to distinguish
between categories of approval. It is possible to divide Community
competition policy into positive and negative elements: the negative element
is concerned with whether or not an agreement should be prohibited; the
positive element is concerned with the active encouragement of certain forms
of restrictive agreement. As a matter of policy it can be argued that the
scope for Member State law to apply, in circumstances where there has
been a Community ruling, ought to depend upon the nature of the approval
given. If it is in the form of an exemption given because the Commission's
assessment is that the merger will bring positive competitive (or other)
benefits, then it should not be open to national authorities to undermine
that assessment by imposing a prohibition on national grounds which conflict
with the Commission's assessment of policy in a Community merger.[67] If,
on the other hand, the approval is in the nature of a negative clearance,

---

[65]   See 7.2.4.3.
[66]   See 8.3.3.2.
[67]   Such an argument was pursued by British brewers wishing to overturn the Monopoly and
Merger Commission's divestiture ruling, on the ground that under the block exemption
(Reg. 1984/83) the practices condemned by M&MC are allowed by reference to art.85(3)
EEC. But on block exemptions see note 88 below.

which says no more than that no harmful Community impact has been identified, then it should probably be open to national authorities to take a stricter line if a national interest would be adversely affected.

It is also necessary to be precise about the legal status of the Community ruling. It has already been noted that the Commission, for reasons of its enormous workload and the desire for speed in competition and especially merger cases, often works at an informal level and does not issue actual decisions[68] but simply sends the parties what is known as a comfort letter. Since the Court of Justice has ruled that comfort letters are without legal status and do not amount to decisions,[69] Member States are free to apply their own law in a situation where the Commission's only action has been in this form.[70] The Court has suggested, however, that if the Member State court anticipates that its decision will be in conflict with the Commission's ruling as communicated in the comfort letter then it would be appropriate for the national court to stay its proceedings for a period in order to allow the Commission, should it so wish, to come to a formal decision.[71]

Finally, it is of course necessary to take into account whether the potential for conflict actually exists. The consequences of these factors will become apparent throughout the rest of this section, which will consider in turn the various approval rulings which may be in issue.

(a)   Commission rulings under article 6(1)(a) of Regulation 4064/89   Article 6(1)(a) provides that the Commission must decline jurisdiction in the case of a merger which does not fall within the scope of the Regulation.[72] In the normal course of events in such a case, therefore, any scrutiny of the proposed merger is the proper prerogative of the national authorities, and no question of conflict between a Community ruling and a national ruling should arise.

However, reference has already been made to the possibility that the Commission might apply the ordinary competition law to mergers falling outside the scope of the Regulation. In such a case there would be no conflict between a ruling under the Regulation and a ruling under national law, but there might be a conflict of any of categories (d) to (g) below, in which case the resolutions outlined there would apply. A further possibility is intervention by the Commission beyond the scope of the Regulation at the invitation of a Member State under article 22(3)–(5). In such a case there should not be a conflict between the Commission's ruling and a decision

[68]   See art.189 EEC and Hartley, pp. 99–102.
[69]   See the perfume cases: 253/78 *Procureur de la République* v *Giry and Guerlain* [1980] ECR 2327, [1981] 2 CMLR 99; 99/79 *Lancome* v *Etos* [1980] ECR 2511, [1981] 2 CMLR 164; 37/79 *Marty* v *Lauder* [1980] ECR 2481, [1981] 2 CMLR 143; 31/80 *L'Oreal* v *De Nieuwe AMCK* [1980] ECR 3775, [1981] 2 CMLR 235.
[70]   253/78 *Procureur de la République* v *Giry and Guerlain* [1980] ECR 2327, 2374–2375.
[71]   Ibid at 13.
[72]   See 3.2.1.

by the authority in the Member State. Nevertheless, there might be a conflict between the Commission's ruling and the ruling of a Member State other than the one inviting the Commission to intervene. However, the Commission's intervention would be restricted to effects within the territory of the requesting Member State,[73] and any other Member State would be able to come to conflicting conclusions with effect within its own territory. Consequently, there should be no reason to invoke the conflict rules.

(b) Commission rulings under article 8(2) of the Regulation Article 8(2) of the Regulation contains the approval provision in respect of concentrations which have a Community dimension but 'which do not create or strengthen a position as a result of which effective competition would be significantly impeded in the common market', as provided for in article 2(2). It presents Commission approval in the form of a negative clearance rather than a positive endorsement. In accordance with the general principle stated earlier, in the limited circumstances in which article 21(3) allows national rules to be applied to concentrations which have a Community dimension, a national prohibition would take precedence over the Commission's ruling of compatibility with the common market. Article 21(3) thus creates a loophole in the Regulation's demarcation rules which might allow a conflict between Community and national law in respect of the Member States' power to apply their own law in taking appropriate measures to protect legitimate interests. The Commission accepts that this provision gives the Member State the power to override its own approval of a proposed merger, or to impose more onerous conditions; but the Commission will argue that such power extends only to the territory of the Member State in question, and that beyond the bounds of that territory the Commission's approval takes precedence over the Member State's view. This very restrictive interpretation is not supported by the text of article 21(3), but it is consistent with the apparent purpose of that provision.

(c) Commission failure to comply with the Regulation's time-limits Article 10 lays down time limits for Commission action under the Regulation, and the power to extend these time-limits is very restricted. Where the Commission fails to comply with the time-limit, the Regulation provides that the concentration shall be deemed declared compatible with the common market. It seems that by comparison with the above category of case, this presents a stronger argument for the Member State ruling to prevail over the 'approval' given.[74]

---

[73] Regulation 4064/89, art.22(5).
[74] In respect of a previous draft (OJ 1988 C130/4), Hornsby (loc.cit. note 79 at 304) argues that such deemed authorisation cannot be regarded as positive action within the *Wilhelm* formulation, and so should not benefit from the Community supremacy principle.

The interface of Community law and national law

(d) Negative clearance under article 85(1)   Negative clearance is the means by which 'the Commission may certify that, on the basis of the facts in its possession, there are no grounds under article 85(1) . . . for action on its part in respect of an agreement.'[75] The effect of a negative clearance in the case of a merger, then, would be to state that there is no reason in Community law to prohibit the merger. As a consequence, there should be no reason to oppose the application of national law in such circumstances. In terms of the test laid down in *Wilhelm* v *Bundeskartellamt*,[76] a national prohibition could not 'prejudice the full and uniform application of Community law or the effects of measures taken or to be taken to implement it',[77] because only a negative implementation has taken place, and no Community policy is threatened. In this case there is no reason to distinguish between actual decisions and mere comfort letters; both are effective to indicate that the Commission does not propose to apply Community law, thus leaving the way clear for national law to be applied to the merger 'from the point of view of the restrictive effects it may produce nationally'. This much has been expressly stated by the Court of Justice in proceedings under article 177 which related to a negative clearance by way of a comfort letter.[78] The argument is *a fortiori* in the case of a formal decision. These conclusions are accepted by the majority of commentators,[79] and by the Commission.[80]

(e) Exemption under article 85(3) by Commission decision   The law on this issue is unclear.[81] There is no direct ruling on the matter by the Court of Justice.[82] The Commission strongly supports[83] an analysis which says that in such circumstances national law cannot be applied, because that would be to 'prejudice the full and uniform application of Community law or the effects of measures taken or to be taken to implement it'.[84] This argument is drawn from a very careful interpretation of the Court's words in *Wilhelm* v *Bundeskartellamt*, and in particular both the principle quoted above and the reference in that case to the power of 'Community authorities to carry out certain positive, though indirect action, with a view to promoting a harmonious development of economic activity within the whole Community

---

[75] Art.2, Reg.17.
[76] [1969] ECR 1, [1969] CMLR 100.
[77] Ibid at 15.
[78] 253/78 etc *Procureur de la République* v *Giry and Guerlain* [1980] ECR 2327 at 2375.
[79] Bellamy & Child 1-086; Kerse 10.28; Goyder p. 348; Hornsby, *National and Community control of concentrations in a single market* (1988) 13 ELRev 295 at 299.
[80] Cf. 10th Report on Competition Policy (1980) at 155.
[81] Bellamy & Child: 1-086.
[82] The issue was deliberately left open in *Procureur de la République* v *Giry and Guerlain* (supra note 78).
[83] 4th Report on Competition Policy (1975) 43–47, which accepts that the issue is not without difficulty.
[84] *Wilhelm* v *Bundeskartellamt* (supra note 76) at 15.

in accordance with article 2 of the Treaty.'[85] The reference to 'positive action' must be taken to mean the exemption process in pursuit of a positive policy under article 85(3). A decision to grant an exemption would then be a measure taken to implement Community law in respect of such policy, and national law is not permitted to interfere with that process.

Others support the view that article 85(3) is no more than a permissive measure, and not an instrument of positive policy implementation, which merely removes the general Community ban on restrictive agreements from a particular agreement for a limited period of time.[86] This view is not without merit, although it appears to be inconsistent with the spirit of the *Wilhelm* judgment, and does not find support in any other Court pronouncement.[87] Most commentators conclude, whichever theory they may actually prefer, that at least in the case of individual exemptions under article 85(3) it is most likely that when the Court eventually rules on the matter it will hold that they may not be contradicted by national competition authority rulings.[88]

(f)   Exemption under article 85(3) by comfort letter   There may be some doubt whether any approvals of this kind actually take place. Comfort letters are more usually associated with informal negative clearances, which fall within category (a) above. It has not been the practice of the Commission to issue exemption notices except by formal decision in respect of the usual application of article 85 to restrictive agreements.[89]

Two factors, however, lead to the possibility that some rulings communicated only by comfort letter will be more akin to exemptions than to negative clearances. The first is the emergence of a rule of reason in respect of agreements which are not in themselves restrictive but which contain restrictive ancillary terms. This development makes it more difficult in the case of comfort letters to distinguish between rulings based on the mere absence of adverse effect and those based on a positive policy of encouraging particular types of agreement. The second factor is the particular requirement of speed in merger scrutiny proceedings, which means that

[85]   Ibid at para 5.
[86]   Cf. Kerse 10.29-10.30; Hornsby, loc.cit. note 79 at 301-304. See also the submission of A-G Roemer in *Wilhelm* (supra note 76).
[87]   Hornsby (loc.cit. note 79 at 303) finds support in the grant of a power to impose stricter national conditions under certain block exemptions, but see note 88.
[88]   Many also conclude that in the case of block exemptions national authority rulings should prevail (e.g., Bellamy & Child: 1-090), presumably on the ground that these are not individual decisions where the specific facts have already been weighed and ruled upon by the Commission. Nevertheless, they appear to be measures implementing a positive Community policy. Since there is no block exemption under article 85(3) for mergers the point need not be pursued here. (But see the block exemption for R & D joint ventures: 5.3.5).
[89]   Article 9(1) of Reg.17 does not, however, appear completely to rule out such a means of proceeding. And see the Commission's treatment of the *GEC-Siemens/Plessey* takeover, where an informal decision not to intervene was taken on the ground that an article 85(3) individual exemption was almost certain to be granted.

under article 85 the Commission prefers to proceed by informal means rather than by the very slow formal decision process. If this trend continues it is quite possible that some rulings will be based on positive rather than negative factors of competition policy. Against this argument, it can be pointed out that nearly all of the Commission's rulings on mergers to date have been concerned with the question of appreciable effect on competition, and have been resolved either by abandonment of the proposal or by agreed modification of the terms of the agreement. In few cases has it appeared that the Commission was actively pursuing a positive policy of the kind encountered under article 85(3). Nevertheless, should such a case arise it is difficult to see that the outcome could be other than that national law would be allowed to take precedence over the Commission's informal ruling, for the sole reason of the absence of effective legal status of comfort letters.[90] This might, however, be a pyrrhic victory in the case of a notified agreement which could be re-opened before the Commission.

(g) *Approvals under article 86 EEC*   Under article 86, because of the absence of a positive clearance procedure, all decisions are in the form of a negative clearance; the prohibition contained in the article only applies in the case of abuse. Abusive conduct would never be entitled to be exempted, while non-abusive conduct does not require to be exempted. As a consequence, all article 86 rulings fall to be treated in the same way as article 85 negative clearances, as described in (d) above. In the absence of a measure implementing positive policy, national authorities are free to impose a stricter rule despite the Commission's approval of the merger. This conclusion is accepted by the Commission, which takes the view that 'if the Commission rules that a merger did not infringe article 86, it could not, in current circumstances of the law, raise any objections to any prohibition of that merger by a national authority based on stricter national law'.[91]

(h) *Decisions under article 66 ECSC*   Since there is exclusive jurisdiction in respect of coal and steel matters on the part of the Commission, there is no scope for conflicts in this area.[92] However, where some aspects of the merger concern matters outside the scope of the ECSC Treaty the national authorities may intervene in respect of those matters.[93]

[90] See *Procureur de la République* v *Giry and Guerlain* supra [1980] ECR 2327.
[91] 10th Report on Competition Policy (1980) at 155.
[92] See 8.1.1.5.
[93] See the account of *GKN/Sachs* in the 6th report on Competition Policy (1976) 110-113; German prohibition of activity authorised under art.66 ECSC and cleared by comfort letter under art.86 EEC did not raise a conflict with Community law. It must be assumed that the German competition authority did not claim jurisdiction over the ECSC matter.

8.4 CONCLUSIONS

The relationship between national law and Community law is one of the most difficult and most important elements of the Community legal order. In the present structure of the Community, peaceful coexistence and mutual cooperation are essential, whether viewed from the standpoint of officials trying to make the regulatory system work or businesses anxious to avoid the twin perils of double investigation and double jeopardy. Although it is possible to make certain predictions about the outcome of potential conflicts on the basis of a few fundamental principles of Community law, this is still to a considerable extent uncharted territory. It is necessary to proceed with caution, and to consult wherever possible with both national and Community officials. With Regulation 4064/89 finally in place, both Community and national authorities face a period of development and perhaps uncertainty, with the prospect, and certainly the goal, of achieving in the next few years a coherent system of merger control appropriate to the emerging single European market.

APPENDIX I

Council Regulation (EEC) No 4064/89 of 21 December 1989 on the control of concentration between undertakings OJ 1989 L395/1*

THE COUNCIL OF THE EUROPEAN COMMUNITIES,

Having regard to the Treaty established the European Economic Community, and in particular Articles 87 and 235 thereof,
Having regard to the proposal from the Commission[1],
Having regard to the opinion of the European Parliament[2],
Having regard to the opinion of the Economic and Social Committee[3],
Whereas, for the achievement of the aims of the Treaty establishing the European Economic Community, Article 3 (f) gives the Community the objective of instituting 'a system ensuring that competition in the common market is not distorted';
Whereas this system is essential for the achievement of the internal market by 1992 and its further development;
Whereas the dismantling of internal frontiers is resulting and will continue to result in major corporate re-organizations in the Community, particularly in the form of concentrations;
Whereas such a development must be welcomed as being in line with the requirements of dynamic competition and capable of increasing the competitiveness of European industry, improving the conditions of growth and raising the standard of living in the Community;
Whereas, however, it must be ensured that the process of re-organization does not result in lasting damage to competition; whereas Community law must therefore include provisions governing those concentrations which may significantly impede effective competition in the common market or in a substantial part of it;

---

* As corrected by the corrigendum published at OJ 1990 L257/13.

[1] OJ No C 130, 19.5.1988, p. 4.
[2] OJ No C 309, 5.12.1988, p. 55.
[3] OJ No C 208, 8.8.1988, p. 11.

Whereas Articles 85 and 86, while applicable, according to the case-law of the Court of Justice, to certain concentrations, are not, however, sufficient to cover all operations which may prove to be incompatible with the system of undistorted competition envisaged in the Treaty;

Whereas a new legal instrument should therefore be created in the form of a Regulation to permit effective control of all concentrations from the point of view of their effect on the structure of competition in the Community and to be the only instrument applicable to such concentrations;

Whereas this Regulation should therefore be based not only on Article 87 but, principally, on Article 235 of the Treaty, under which the Community may give itself the additional powers of action necessary for the attainment of its objectives, and also with regard to concentrations on the markets for agricultural products listed in Annex II to the Treaty;

Whereas the provisions to be adopted in this Regulation should apply to significant structural changes the impact of which on the market goes beyond the national borders of any one Member State;

Whereas the scope of application of this Regulation should therefore be defined according to the geographical area of activity of the undertakings concerned and be limited by quantitative thresholds in order to cover those concentrations which have a Community dimension; whereas, at the end of an initial phase of the application of this Regulation, these thresholds should be reviewed in the light of the experience gained;

Whereas a concentration with a Community dimension exists where the combined aggregate turnover of the undertakings concerned exceeds given levels worldwide and throughout the Community and where at least two of the undertakings concerned have their sole or main fields of activities in different Member States or where, although the undertakings in question act mainly in one and the same Member State, at least one of them has substantial operations in at least one other Member State; whereas that is also the case where the concentrations are effected by undertakings which do not have their principal fields of activities in the Community but which have substantial operations there;

Whereas the arrangements to be introduced for the control of concentrations should, without prejudice to Article 90 (2) of the Treaty, respect the principle of non-discrimination between the public and the private sectors; whereas, in the public sector, calculation of the turnover of an undertaking concerned in a concentration needs, therefore, to take account of undertakings making up an economic unit with an independent power of decision, irrespective of the way in which their capital is held or of the rules of administrative supervision applicable to them;

Whereas it is necessry to establish whether concentrations with a Community dimension are compatible or not with the common market from the point of view of the need to maintain and develop effective competition in the common market; whereas, in so doing, the Commission must place its appraisal within the general framework of the achievement of the fundamental objectives referred to in Article 2 of the Treaty, including that of strengthening the Community's economic and social cohesion, referred to in Article 130a;

Whereas this Regulation should establish the principle that a concentration with a Community dimension which creates or strengthens a position as result of which effective competition in the common market or in a substantial part of it is significantly impeded is to be declared incompatible with the common market;

Whereas concentrations which, by reason of the limited market share of the undertakings concerned, are not liable to impede effective competition may be presumed to be compatible with the common market; whereas, without prejudice to Articles 85 and 86 of the Treaty, an indication to this effect exists, in particular, where the market share of the undertakings concerned does not exceed 25% either in the common market or in a substantial part of it;

Whereas the Commission should have the task of taking all the decisions necessary to establish whether or not concentrations of a Community dimension are compatible with the common market, as well as decisions designed to restore effective competition;

Whereas to ensure effective control undertakings should be obliged to give prior notification of concentrations with a Community dimension and provision should be made for the suspension of concentrations for a limited period, and for the possibility of extending or waiving a suspension where necessary; whereas in the interests of legal certainty the validity of transactions must nevertheless be protected as much as necessary;

Whereas a period within which the Community must initiate proceedings in respect of a notified concentration and periods within which it must give a final decision on the compatibility or incompatibility with the common market of a notified concentration should be laid down;

Whereas the undertakings concerned must be afforded the right to be heard by the Commission when proceedings have been initiated; whereas the members of management and supervisory bodies and recognized workers' representatives in the undertakings concerned, together with third parties showing a legitimate interest, must also be given the opportunity to be heard;

Whereas the Commission should act in close and constant liaison with the competent authorities of the Member States from which it obtains comments and information;

Whereas, for the purposes of this Regulation, and in accordance with the case-law of the Court of Justice, the Commission must be afforded the assistance of the Member States and must also be empowered to require information to be given and to carry out the necessary investigations in order to appraise concentrations;

Whereas compliance with this Regulation must be enforceable by means of fines and periodic penalty payments; whereas the Court of Justice should be given unlimited jurisdiction in that regard pursuant to Article 172 of the Treaty;

Whereas it is appropriate to define the concept of concentration in such a manner as to cover only operations bringing about a lasting change in the structure of the undertakings concerned; whereas it is therefore necessary to exclude from the scope of this Regulation those operations which have as their object or effect the coordination of the competitive behaviour of undertakings which remain independent, since such operations fall to be examined under the appropriate provisions of Regulations implementing Article 85 or Article 86 of the Treaty; whereas it is appropriate to make this distinction specifically in the case of the creation of joint ventures;

Whereas there is no coordination of competitive behaviour within the meaning of this Regulation where two or more undertakings agree to acquire jointly control of one or more other undertakings with the object and effect of sharing amongst themselves such undertakings or their assets;

Whereas this Regulation should still apply where the undertakings concerned accept restrictions directly related and necessary to the implementation of the concentration;

Whereas the Commission should be given exclusive competence to apply this Regulation, subject to review by the Court of Justice;

Whereas the Member States may not apply their national legislation on competition to concentrations with a Community dimension, unless the Regulation makes provision therfor; whereas the relevant powers of national authorities should be limited to cases where, failing intervention by the Commission, effective competition is likely to be significantly impeded within the territory of a Member State and where the competition interests of that Member State cannot be sufficiently protected otherwise than by this Regulation; whereas the Member States concerned must act promptly in such cases; whereas this Regulation cannot, because of the diversity of national law, fix a single deadline for the adoption of remedies;

Whereas, furthermore, the exclusive application of this Regulation to concentrations with a Community dimension is without prejudice to Article 223 of the Treaty, and does not prevent the Member States from taking appropriate measures to protect legitimate interests other than those pursued by this Regulation, provided that such measures are compatible with the general principles and other provisions of Community law;

Whereas concentrations not covered by this Regulation come, in principle, within the jurisdiction of the Member States; whereas, however, the Commission should have the power to act, at the request of a Member State concerned, in cases where effective competition could be significantly impeded within that Member State's territory;

Whereas the conditions in which concentrations involving Community undertakings are carried out in non-member countries should be observed, and provision should be made for the possibility of the Council giving the Commission an appropriate mandate for negotiation with a view to obtaining non-discriminatory treatment for Community undertakings;

Whereas this Regulation in no way detracts from the collective rights of employees as recognized in the undertakings concerned,

HAS ADOPTED THIS REGULATION

Article 1

Scope

1. Without prejudice to Article 22 of this Regulation shall apply to all concentrations with a Community dimension as defined in paragraph 2.

2. For the purposes of this Regulation, a concentration has a Community dimension where:

(a)   the combined aggregate worldwide turnover of all the undertakings concerned is more than ECU 5 000 million, and

(b)   the aggregate Community-wide turnover of each of at least two of the undertakings concerned is more than ECU 250 million,

unless each of the undertakings concerned achieves more than two-thirds of its aggregate Community-wide turnover within one and the same Member State.

3. The thresholds laid down in paragraph 2 will be reviewed before the end of the fourth year following that of the adoption of this Regulation by the Council acting by a qualified majority on a proposal from the Commission.

Article 2

Appraisal of concentrations

1.   Concentrations within the scope of this Regulation shall be appraised in accordance with the following provisions with a view to establishing whether or not they are compatible with the common market.
In making this appraisal, the Commission shall take into account:

(a)   the need to maintain and develop effective competition within the common market in view of, among other things, the structure of all the markets concerned and the actual or potential competition from undertakings located either within or outwith the Community;
(b)   the market position of the undertakings concerned and their economic and financial power, the alternatives available to suppliers and users, their access to supplies or markets, any legal or other barriers to entry, supply and demand trends for the relevant goods and sevices, the interests of the intermediate and ultimate consumers, and the development of technical and economic progress provided that it is to consumers' advantage and does not form an obstacle to competition.

2.   A concentration which does not create or strengthen a dominant position as a result of which effective competition would be significantly impeded in the common market or in a substantial part of it shall be declared compatible with the common market.
3.   A concentration which creates or strengthens a dominant position as a result of which effective competition would be significantly impeded in the common market or in a substantial part of it shall be declared incompatible with the common market.

Article 3

Definition of concentration

1.   A concentration shall be deemed to arise where:

(a)   two or more previously independent undertakings merge, or
(b)   one or more persons already controlling at least one undertaking, or

— one or more undertakings
acquire, whether by purchase of securities or assets, by contract or by any other means, direct or indirect control of the whole or parts of one or more other undertakings.

2.   An operation, including the creation of a joint venture, which has as its object or effect the coordination of the competitive behaviour of undertakings which remain independent shall not constitute a concentration within the meaning of paragraph 1(b).
The creation of a joint venture performing on a lasting basis all the functions of an autonomous economic entity, which does not give rise to coordination of the competitive behaviour of the parties amongst themselves or between them and the joint venture, shall constitute a concentration within the meaning of paragraph 1(b).

3. For the purposes of this Regulation, control shall be constituted by rights, contracts or any other means which, either separately or in combination and having regard to the considerations of fact or law involved, confer the possibility of exercising decisive influence on an undertaking, in particular by:

(a) ownership or the right to use all or part of the assets of an undertaking;

(b) rights or contracts which confer decisive influence on the composition, voting or decisions of the organs of an undertaking.

4. Control is acquired by persons or undertakings which:

(a) are holders of the rights or entitled to rights under the contracts concerned; or

(b) while not being holders of such rights or entitled to rights under such contracts, have the power to exercise the rights deriving therefrom.

5. A concentration shall not be deemed to arise where:

(a) credit institutions or other financial institutions or insurance companies, the normal activities of which include transactions and dealing in securities for their own account or for the account of others, hold on a temporary basis securities which they have acquired in an undertaking with a view to reselling them, provided that they do not exercise voting rights in respect of those securities with a view to determining the competitive behaviour of that undertaking or provided that they exercise such voting rights only with a view to preparing the disposal or all or part of that undertaking or of its assets or the disposal of those securities and that any such disposal takes place within one year of the date of acquisition; that period may be extended by the Commission on request where such institutions or companies can show that the disposal was not reasonably possible within the period set;

(b) control is acquired by an office holder according to the law of a Member State relating to liquidation, winding up, insolvency, cessation of payments, compositions or analogous proceedings;

(c) the operations referred to in paragraph 1(b) are carried out by the financial holding companies referred to in Article 5 (3) of the Fourth Council Directive 78/660/EEC of 25 July 1978 on the annual accounts of certain types of companies[4], as last amended by Directive 84/569/EEC[5], provided however that the voting rights in respect of the holding are exercised, in particular in relation to the appointment of members of the management and supervisory bodies of the undertakings in which they have holdings, only to maintain the full value of those investments and not to determine directly or indirectly the competitive conduct of those undertakings.

Article 4

Prior notification of concentrations

1. Concentrations with a Community dimension defined in this Regulation shall be notified to the Commission not more than one week after the conclusion of the

---

[4]   OJ No L 222, 14.8.1978, p. 11.
[5]   OJ No L 314, 4.12.1984, p. 28.

agreement, or the announcement of the public bid, or the acquisition of a controlling interest. That week shall begin when the first of those events occurs.

2. A concentration which consists of a merger within the meaning of Article 3 (1) (a) or in the acquisition of joint control within the meaning of Article 3 (1) (b) shall be notified jointly by the parties to the merger or by those acquiring joint control as the case may be. In all other cases, the notification shall be effected by the person or undertaking acquiring control of the whole or parts of one or more undertakings.

3. Where the Commission finds that a notified concentration falls within the scope of this Regulation, it shall publish the fact of the notification, at the same time indicating the names of the parties, the nature of the concentration and the economic sectors involved. The Commission shall take account of the legitimate interest of undertakings in the protection of their business secrets.

Article 5

Calculation of turnover

1. Aggregate turnover within the meaning of Article 1 (2) shall comprise the amounts derived by the undertakings concerned in the preceding financial year from the sale of products and the provision of services falling within the undertakings' ordinary activities after deduction of sales rebates and of value added tax and other taxes directly related to turnover. The aggregate turnover of an undertaking concerned shall not include the sale of products or the provision of services between any of the undertakings referred to in paragraph 4.

Turnover, in the Community or in a Member State, shall comprise products sold and services provided to undertakings or consumers, in the Community or in that Member State as the case may be.

2. By way of derogation from paragraph 1, where the concentration consists in the acquisition of parts, whether or not constituted as legal entities, of one or more undertakings, only the turnover relating to the parts which are the subject of the transaction shall be taken into account with regard to the seller or sellers.

However, two or more transactions within the meaning of the first subparagraph which take place within a two-year period between the same persons or undertakings shall be treated as one and the same concentration arising on the date of the last transaction.

3. In place of turnover the following shall be used:

(a) for credit institutions and other financial institutions, as regards Article 1 (2) (a), one-tenth of their total assets.

As regards Article 1 (2) (b) and the final part of Article 1 (2), total Community-wide turnover shall be replaced by one-tenth of total assets multiplied by the ratio between loans and advances to credit institutions and customers in transactions with Community residents and the total sum of those loans and advances.

As regards the final part of Article 1 (2), total turnover within one Member State shall be replaced by one-tenth of total assets multiplied by the ratio between loans and advances to credit institutions and customers in transactions with residents of that Member State and the total sum of those loans and advances;

(b) for insurance undertakings, the value of gross premiums written which shall comprise all amounts received and receivable in respect of insurance contracts issued by or on behalf of the insurance undertakings, including also outgoing reinsurance premiums, and after deduction of taxes and parafiscal contributions or levies charged by reference to the amounts of individual premiums or the total volume of premiums; as regards Article 1 (2) (b) and the final part of Article 1 (2), gross premiums received from Community residents and from residents of one Member State respectively shall be taken into account.

4. Without prejudice to paragraph 2, the aggregate turnover of an undertaking concerned within the meaning of Article 1 (2) shall be calculated by adding together the respective turnovers of the following:

(a)   the undertaking concerned;
(b)   those undertakings in which the undertaking concerned, directly or indirectly:
— owns more than half the capital or business assets, or
— has the power to exercise more than half the voting rights, or
— has the power to appoint more than half the members of the supervisory board, the administrative board or bodies legally representing the undertakings, or
— has the right to manage the undertakings' affairs;
(c)   those undertakings which have in the undertaking concerned the rights or powers listed in (b);
(d)   those undertakings in which an undertaking as referred to in (c) has the rights or powers listed in (b);
(e)   those undertakings in which two or more undertakings as referred to in (a) to (d) jointly have the rights or powers listed in (b).

5.   Where undertakings concerned by the concentration jointly have the rights or powers listed in paragraph 4(b), in calculating the aggregate turnover of the undertakings concerned for the purposes of Article 1 (2):

(a)   no account shall be taken of the turnover resulting from the sale of products or the provision of services between the joint undertaking and each of the undertakings concerned or any other undertaking connnected with any one of them, as set out in paragraph 4 (b) to (e);
(b)   account shall be taken of the turnover resulting from the sale of products and the provision of services between the joint undertaking and any third undertakings. This turnover shall be apportioned equally amongst the undertakings concerned.

Article 6

Examination of the notification and initiation of proceedings

1.   The Commission shall examine the notification as soon as it is received.

(a)   Where it concludes that the concentration notified does not fall within the scope of this Regulation, it shall record that finding by means of a decision.
(b)   Where if finds that the concentration notified, although falling within the scope of this Regulation, does not raise serious doubts as to its compatibility with the common market, it shall decide not to oppose it and shall declare that it is compatible with the common market.
(c)   If, on the other hand, it finds that the concentration notified falls within

the scope of this Regulation and raises serious doubts as to its compatibility with the common market, it shall decide to initiate proceedings.

2. The Commission shall notify its decision to the undertakings concerned and the competent authorities of the Member States without delay.

Article 7

Suspension of concentrations

1. For the purposes of paragraph 2 a concentration as defined in Article 1 shall not be put into effect either before its notification or within the first three weeks following its notification.

2. Where the Commission, following a preliminary examination of the notification within the period provided for in paragraph 1, finds it necessary in order to ensure the full effectiveness of any decision taken later pursuant to Article 8 (3) and (4), it may decide on its own initiative to continue the suspension of a concentration in whole or in part until it takes a final decision, or to take other interim measures to that effect.

3. Paragraphs 1 and 2 shall not prevent the implementation of a public bid which has been notified to the Commission in accordance with Article 4 (1), provided that the acquirer does not exercise the voting rights attached to the securities in question or does so only to maintain the full value of those investments and on the basis of a derogation granted by the Commission under paragraph 4.

4. The Commission may, on request, grant a derogation from the obligations imposed in paragraphs 1, 2 or 3 in order to prevent serious damage to one or more undertakings concerned by a concentration or to a third party. That derogation may be made subject to conditions and obligations in order to ensure conditions of effective competition. A derogation may be applied for and granted at any time, even before notification or after the transaction.

5. The validity of any transaction carried out in contravention of paragraph 1 or 2 shall be dependent on a decision pursuant to Article 6 (1) (b) or Article 8 (2) or (3) or on a presumption pursuant to Article 10 (6).

This Article shall, however, have no effect on the validity of transactions in securities including those convertible into other securities admitted to trading on a market which is regulated and supervised by authorities recognized by public bodies, operates regularly and is accessible directly or indirectly to the public, unless the buyer and seller knew or ought to have known that the transaction was carried out in contravention of paragraph 1 or 2.

Article 8

Powers of decision of the Commission

1. Without prejudice to Article 9, all proceedings intitiated pursuant to Article 6 (1) (c) shall be closed by means of a decision as provided for in paragraphs 2 to 5.

2. Where the Commission finds that, following modification by the undertakings concerned if necessary, a notified concentration fulfils the criterion laid down in

Article 2 (2), it shall issue a decision declaring the concentration compatible with the common market.

It may attach to its decision conditions and obligations intended to ensure that the undertakings concerned comply with the commitments they have entered into *vis-à-vis* the Commission with a view to modifying the original concentration plan. The decision declaring the concentration compatible shall also cover restrictions directly related and necessary to the implementation of the concentration.

3. Where the Commission finds that a concentration fulfils the criterion laid down in Article 2 (3), it shall issue a decision declaring that the concentration is incompatible with the common market.

4. Where a concentration has already been implemented, the Commission may, in a decision pursuant to paragraph 3 or by a separate decision, require the undertakings or assets brought together to be separated or the cessation of joint control or any other action that may be appropriate in order to restore conditions of effective competition.

5. The Commission may revoke the decision it has taken pursuant to paragraph 2 where:

(a) the declaration of compatibility is based on incorrect information for which one of the undertakings concerned is responsible or where it has been obtained by deceit; or

(b) the undertakings concerned commit a breach of an obligation attached to the decision.

6. In the case referred to in paragraph 5, the Commission may take a decision pursuant to paragraph 3, without being bound by the deadline referred to in Article 10 (3).

Article 9

Referral to the competent authorities of the Member States

1. The Commission may, by means of a decision notified without delay to the undertakings concerned and the competent authorities of the other Member States, refer a notified concentration to the competent authorities of the Member State concerned in the following circumstances.

2. Within three weeks of the date of receipt of the copy of the notification a Member State may inform the Commission which shall inform the undertakings concerned that a concentration threatens to create or to strengthen a dominant position as a result of which effective competition would be significantly impeded on a market, within that Member State, which presents all the characteristics of a distinct market, be it a substantial part of the common market or not.

3. If the Commission considers that, having regard to the market for the products or services in question and the geographical reference market within the meaning of paragraph 7, there is such a distinct market and that such a threat exists, either:

(a) it shall itself deal with the case in order to maintain or restore effective competition on the market concerned; or

(b) it shall refer the case to the competent authorities of the Member State concerned with a view to the application of that State's national competition law.

If, however, the Commission considers that such a distinct market or threat does not exist it shall adopt a decision to that effect which it shall address to the Member State concerned.

4. A decision to refer or not to refer pursuant to paragraph 3 shall be taken where:

(a) as a general rule within the six-week period provided for in Article 10 (1), second subparagraph, where the Commission, pursuant to Article 6 (1) (b), has not initiated proceedings; or

(b) within three months at most of the notification of the concentration concerned where the Commission has initiated proceedings under Article 6 (1) (c), without taking the preparatory steps in order to adopt the necessary measures under Article 8 (2), second subparagraph, (3) or (4) to maintain or restore effective competition on the market concerned.

5. If within the three months referred to in paragraph 4 (b) the Commission, despite a reminder from the Member State concerned, has not taken a decision on referral in accordance with paragraph 3 nor has taken the preparatory steps referred to in paragraph 4 (b), it shall be deemed to have taken a decision to refer the case to the Member State concerned in accordance with paragraph 3 (b).

6. The publication of any report or the announcement of the findings of the examination of the concentration by the competent authority of the Member State concerned shall be effected not more than four months after the Commission's referral.

7. The geographical reference market shall consist of the area in which the undertakings concerned are involved in the supply of products or services, in which the conditions of competition are sufficiently homogeneous and which can be distinguished from neighbouring areas because, in particular, conditions of competition are appreciably different in those areas. This assessment should take account in particular of the nature and characteristics of the products or services concerned, of the existence of entry barriers or of consumer preferences, of appreciable differences of the undertakings' market shares between neighbouring areas or of substantial price differences.

8. In applying the provisions of this Article, the Member State concerned may take only the measures strictly necessary to safeguard or restore effective competition on the market concerned.

9. In accordance with the relevant provisions of the Treaty, any Member State may appeal to the Court of Justice, and in particular request the application of Article 186, for the purpose of applying its national competition law.

10. This Article will be reviewed before the end of the fourth year following that of the adoption of this Regulation.

Article 10

Time limits for initiating proceedings and for decisions

1. The decisions referred to in Article 6 (1) must be taken within one month at most. That period shall begin on the day following that of the receipt of a notification or, if the information to be supplied with the notification is incomplete, on the day following that of the receipt of the complete information.

That period shall be increased to six weeks if the Commission receives a request from a Member State in accordance with Article 9 (2).

2.   Decisions taken pursuant to Article 8 (2) concerning notified concentrations must be taken as soon as it appears that the serious doubts referred to in Article 6 (1) (c) have been removed, particularly as a result of modifications made by the undertakings concerned, and at the latest by the deadline laid down in paragraph 3.

3.   Without prejudice to Article 8 (6), decisions taken pursuant to Article 8 (3) concerning notified concentrations must be taken within not more than four months of the date on which proceedings are initiated.

4.   The period set by paragraph 3 shall exceptionally be suspended where, owing to circumstances for which one of the undertakings involved in the concentration is responsible, the Commission has had to request information by decision pursuant to Article 11 or to order an investigation by decision pursuant to Article 13.

5.   Where the Court of Justice gives a judgment which annuls the whole or part of a Commission decision taken under this Regulation, the periods laid down in this Regulation shall start again from the date of the judgment.

6.   Where the Commission has not taken a decision in accordance with Article 6 (1) (b) or (c) or Article 8 (2) or (3) within the deadlines set in paragraphs 1 and 3 respectively, the concentration shall be deemed to have been declared compatible with the common market, without prejudice to Article 9.

Article 11

Requests for information

1.   In carrying out the duties assigned to it by this Regulation, the Commission may obtain all necessary information from the Governments and competent authorities of the Member States, from the persons referred to in Article 3 (1) (b), and from undertakings and associations of undertakings.

2.   When sending a request for information to a person, an undertaking or an association of undertakings, the Commission shall at the same time send a copy of the request to the competent authority of the Member State within the territory of which the residence of the person or the seat of the undertaking or association of undertakings is situated.

3.   In its request the Commission shall state the legal basis and the purpose of the request and also the penalties provided for in Article 14 (1) (c) for supplying incorrect information.

4.   The information requested shall be provided, in the case of undertakings, by their owners or their representatives and, in the case of legal persons, companies or firms, or of associations having no legal personality, by the persons authorized to represent them by law or by their statutes.

5.   Where a person, an undertaking or an association of undertakings does not provide the information requested within the period fixed by the Commission or provides incomplete information, the Commission shall by decision require the information to be provided. The decision shall specify what information is required, fix an appropriate period within which it is to be supplied and state the penalties provided for in Articles 14 (1) (c) and 15 (1) (a) and the right to have the decision reviewed by the Court of Justice.

6.   The Commission shall at the same time send a copy of its decision to the

competent authority of the Member State within the territory of which the residence of the person or the seat of the undertaking or association of undertakings is situated.

Article 12

Investigations by the authorities of the Member States

1. At the request of the Commission, the competent authorities of the Member States shall undertake the investigations which the Commission considers to be necessary under Article 13 (1), or which it has ordered by decision pursuant to Article 13 (3). The officials of the competent authorities of the Member States responsible for conducting those investigations shall exercise their powers upon production of an authorization in writing issued by the competent authority of the Member State within the territory of which the investigation is to be carried out. Such authorization shall specify the subject matter and purpose of the investigation.

2. If so requested by the Commission or by the competent authority of the Member State within the territory of which the investigation is to be carried out, officials of the Commission may assist the officials of that authority in carrying out their duties.

Article 13

Investigative powers of the Commission

1. In carrying out the duties assigned to it by this Regulation, the Commission may undertake all necessary investigations into undertakings and associations of undertakings.

To that end the officials authorized by the Commission shall be empowered:

(a) to examine the books and other business records;
(b) to take or demand copies of or extracts from the books and business records;
(c) to ask for oral explanations on the spot;
(d) to enter any premises, land and means of transport of undertakings.

2. The officials of the Commission authorized to carry out the investigations shall exercise their powers on production of an authorization in writing specifying the subject matter and purpose of the investigation and the penalties provided for in Article 14 (1) (d) in cases where production of the required books or other business records is incomplete. In good time before the investigation, the Commission shall inform, in writing, the competent authority of the Member State within the territory of which the investigation is to be carried out of the investigation and of the identities of the authorized officials.

3. Undertakings and associations of undertakings shall submit to investigations ordered by decision of the Commission. The decision shall specify the subject matter and purpose of the investigation, appoint the date on which it shall begin and state the penalties provided for in Articles 14 (1) (d) and 15 (1) (b) and the right to have the decision reviewed by the Court of Justice.

4. The Commission shall in good time and in writing inform the competent authority of the Member State within the territory of which the investigation is

to be carried out of its intention of taking a decision pursuant to paragraph 3. It shall hear the competent authority before taking its decision.

5.   Officials of the competent authority of the Member State within the territory of which the investigation is to be carried out may, at the request of that authority or of the Commission, assist the officials of the Commission in carrying out their duties.

6.   Where an undertaking or association of undertakings opposes an investigation ordered pursuant to this Article, the Member State concerned shall afford the necessary assistance to the officials authorized by the Commission to enable them to carry out their investigation. To this end the Member States shall, after consulting the Commission, take the necessary measures within one year of the entry into force of this Regulation.

Article 14

Fines

1. The Commission may by decision impose on the persons referred to in Article 3 (1) (b), undertakings or associations of undertakings fines of from ECU 1 000 to 50 000 where intentionally or negligently:

(a)   they fail to notify a concentration in accordance with Article 4;

(b)   they supply incorrect or misleading information in a notification pursuant to Article 4;

(c)   they supply incorrect information in response to a request made pursuant to Article 11 or fail to supply information within the period fixed by a decision taken pursuant to Article 11;

(d)   they produce the required books or other business records in incomplete form during investigations under Article 12 or 13, or refuse to submit to an investigation ordered by decision taken pursuant to Article 13.

2.   The Commission may by decision impose fines not exceeding 10% of the aggregate turnover of the undertakings concerned within the meaning of Article 5 on the persons or undertakings concerned where, either intentionally or negligently, they:

(a)   fail to comply with an obligation imposed by decision pursuant to Article 7 (4) or 8 (2), second subparagraph;

(b)   put into effect a concentration in breach of Article 7 (1) or disregard a decision taken pursuant to Article 7 (2);

(c)   put into effect a concentration declared incompatible with the common market by decision pursuant to Article 8 (3) or do not take the measures ordered by decision pursuant to Article 8 (4).

3.   In setting the amount of a fine, regard shall be had to the nature and gravity of the infringement.

4.   Decisions taken pursuant to paragraphs 1 and 2 shall not be of criminal law nature.

Article 15

Periodic penalty payments

1. The Commission may by decision impose on the persons referred to in Article 3 (1) (b), undertakings or associations of undertakings concerned periodic penalty payments of up to ECU 25 000 for each day of delay calculated from the date set in the decision, in order to compel them:

(a) to supply complete and correct information which it has requested by decision pursuant to Article 11;
(b) to submit to an investigation which it has ordered by decision pursuant to Article 13.

2. The Commission may by decision impose on the persons referred to in Article 3 (1) (b) or on undertakings periodic penalty payments of up to ECU 100 000 for each day of delay calculated from the date set in the decision, in order to compel them:

(a) to comply with an obligation imposed by decision pursuant to Article 7 (4) or Article 8 (2), second subparagraph, or
(b) to apply the measures ordered by decision pursuant to Article 8 (4).

3. Where the persons referred to in Article 3 (1) (b), undertakings or associations of undertakings have satisfied the obligation which it was the purpose of the periodic penalty payment to enforce, the Commission may set the total amount of the periodic penalty payments at a lower figure than that which would arise under the original decision.

Article 16

Review by the Court of Justice

The Court of Justice shall have unlimited jurisdiction within the meaning of Article 172 of the Treaty to review decisions whereby the Commission has fixed a fine or periodic penalty payments; it may cancel, reduce or increase the fine or periodic penalty payments imposed.

Article 17

Professional secrecy

1. Information acquired as a result of the application of Articles 11, 12, 13 and 18 shall be used only for the purposes of the relevant request, investigation or hearing.
2. Without prejudice to Articles 4 (3), 18 and 20, the Commission and the competent authorities of the Member States, their officials and other servants shall not disclose information they have acquired through the application of this Regulation of the kind covered by the obligation of professional secrecy.
3. Paragraphs 1 and 2 shall not prevent publication of general information or

of surveys which do not contain information relating to particular undertakings or associations of undertakings.

Article 18

Hearing of the parties and of third persons

1. Before taking any decision provided for in Articles 7 (2) and (4), Article 8 (2), second subparagraph, and (3) to (5), and Articles 14 and 15, the Commission shall give the persons, undertakings and associations of undertakings concerned the opportunity, at every stage of the procedure up to the consultation of the Advisory Committee, of making known their views on the objections against them.

2. By way of derogation from paragraph 1, a decision to continue the suspension of a concentration or to grant a derogation from suspension as referred to in Article 7 (2) or (4) may be taken provisionally, without the persons, undertakings or associations of undertakings concerned being given the opportunity to make known their views beforehand, provided that the Commission gives them that opportunity as soon as possible after having taken its decision.

3. The Commission shall base its decision only on objections on which the parties have been able to submit their observations. The rights of the defence shall be fully respected in the proceedings. Access to the file shall be open at least to the parties directly involved, subject to the legitimate interest of undertakings in the protection of their business secrets.

4. Insofar as the Commission or the competent authorities of the Member States deem it necessary, they may also hear other natural or legal persons. Natural or legal persons showing a sufficient interest and especially members of the administrative or management bodies of the undertakings concerned or the recognized representatives of their employees shall be entitled, upon application, to be heard.

Article 19

Liaison with the authorities of the Member States

1. The Commission shall transmit to the competent authorities of the Member States copies of notifictions within three working days and, as soon as possible, copies of the most important documents lodged with or issued by the Commission pursuant to this Regulation.

2. The Commission shall carry out the procedures set out in this Regulation in close and constant liaison with the competent authorities of the Member States, which may express their views upon those procedures. For the purposes of Article 9 it shall obtain information from the competent authority of the Member State as referred to in paragraph 2 of that Article and give it the opportunity to make known its views at every stage of the procedure up to the adoption of a decision pursuant to paragraph 3 of that Article; to that end it shall give it access to the file.

3. An Advisory Committee on concentrations shall be consulted before any decision is taken pursuant to Article 8 (2) to (5), 14 or 15, or any provisions are adopted pursuant to Article 23.

4. The Advisory Committee shall consist of representatives of the authorities of the Member States. Each Member State shall appoint one or two representatives;

if unable to attend, they may be replaced by other representatives. At least one of the representatives of a Member State shall be competent in matters of restrictive practices and dominant positions.

5. Consultation shall take place at a joint meeting convened at the invitation of and chaired by the Commission. A summary of the case, together with an indication of the most important documents and a preliminary draft of the decisions to be taken for each case considered, shall be sent with the invitation. The meeting shall take place not less than 14 days after the invitation has been sent. The Commission may in exceptional cases shorten that period as appropriate in order to avoid serious harm to one or more of the undertakings concerned by a concentration.

6. The Advisory Committee shall deliver an opinion on the Commission's draft decision, if necessary by taking a vote. The Advisory Committee may deliver an opinion even if some members are absent and unrepresented. The opinion shall be delivered in writing and appended to the draft decision. The Commission shall take the utmost account of the opinion delivered by the Committee. It shall inform the Committee of the manner in which its opinion has been taken into account.

7. The Advisory Committee may recommend publication of the opinion. The Commission may carry out such publication. The decision to publish shall take due account of the legitimate interest of undertakings in the protection of their business secrets and of the interest of the undertakings concerned in such publication's (sic) taking place.

Article 20

Publication of decisions

1. The Commission shall publish the decisions which it takes pursuant to Article 8 (2) to (5) in the Official Journal of the European Communities.

2. The publication shall state the names of the parties and the main content of the decision; it shall have regard to the legitimate interest of undertakings in the protection of their business secrets.

Article 21

Jurisdiction

1. Subject to review by the Court of Justice, the Commission shall have sole jurisdiction to take the decisions provided for in this Regulation.

2. No Member State shall apply its national legislation on competition to any concentration that has a Community dimension.

The first subparagraph shall be without prejudice to any Member State's power to carry out any enquiries necessary for the application of Article 9 (2) or after referral, pursuant to Article 9 (3), first subparagraph, indent (b), or (5), to take the measures strictly necessary for the application of Article 9 (8).

3. Notwithstanding paragraphs 1 and 2, Member States may take appropriate measures to protect legitimate interests other than those taken into consideration by this Regulation and compatible with the general principles and other provisions of Community law.

Public security, plurality of the media and prudential rules shall be regarded as legitimate interests within the meaning of the first subparagraph.

Any other public interest must be communicated to the Commission by the Member State concerned and shall be recognized by the Commission after an assessment of its compatability with the general principles and other provisions of Community law before the measures referred to above may be taken. The Commission shall inform the Member State concerned of its decision within one month of that communication.

Article 22

Application of the Regulation

1. This Regulation alone shall apply to concentrations as defined in Article 3.

2. Regulations No 17[6], (EEC) No 1017/68[7], (EEC) No 4056/86[8] and (EEC) No 3975/87[9] shall not apply to concentrations as defined in Article 3.

3. If the Commission finds, at the request of a Member State, that a concentration as defined in Article 3 that has no Community dimension within the meaning of Article 1 creates or strengthens a dominant position as a result of which effective competition would be significantly impeded within the territory of the Member State concerned it may, insofar as the concentration affects trade between Member States, adopt the decisions provided for in Article 8 (2), second subparagraph, (3) and (4).

4. Articles 2 (1) (a) and (b), 5, 6, 8 and 10 to 20 shall apply. The period within which the proceedings may be initiated pursuant to Article 10 (1) shall begin on the date of the receipt of the request from the Member State. The request must be made within one month at most of the date on which the concentration was made known to the Member State or effected. This period shall begin on the date of the first of those events.

5. Pursuant to paragraph 3 the Commission shall take only the measures strictly necessary to maintain or restore effective competition within the territory of the Member State at the request of which it intervenes.

6. Paragraphs 3 to 5 shall continue to apply until the thresholds referred to in Article 1(2) have been reviewed.

Article 23

Implementing provisions

The Commission shall have the power to adopt implementing provisions concerning the form, content and other details of notifications pursuant to Article 4, time limits pursuant to Article 10, and hearings pursuant to Article 18.

Article 24

Relations with non-member countries

1. The Member States shall inform the Commission of any general difficulties

---

6   OJ No 13, 21.2.1962, p, 204/62.
7   OJ No L 175, 23.7.1968, p. 1.
8   OJ No L 378, 31.12.1986, p. 4.
9   OJ No L 374, 31.12.1987, p. 1.

encountered by their undertakings with concentrations as defined in Article 3 in a non-member country.

2. Initially not more than one year after the entry into force of this Regulation and thereafter periodically the Commission shall draw up a report examining the treatment accorded to Community undertakings, in the terms referred to in paragraphs 3 and 4, as regards concentrations in non-member countries. The Commission shall submit those reports to the Council, together with any recommendations.

3. Whenever it appears to the Commision, either on the basis of the reports referred to in paragraph 2 or on the basis of other information, that a non-member country does not grant Community undertakings treatment comparable to that granted by the Community to undertakings from that non-member country, the Commission may submit proposals to the Council for an appropriate mandate for negotiation with a view to obtaining comparable treatment for Community undertakings.

4. Measures taken under this Article shall comply with the obligations of the Community or of the Member States, without prejudice to Article 234 of the Treaty, under international agreements, whether bilateral or multilateral.

Article 25

Entry into force

1. This Regulation shall enter into force on 21 September 1990.

2. This Regulation shall not apply to any concentration which was the subject of an agreement or announcement or where control was acquired within the meaning of Article 4 (1) before the date of this Regulation's entry into force and it shall not in any circumstances apply to any concentration in respect of which proceedings were initiated before that date by a Member State's authority with responsibility for competition.

This Regulation shall be binding in its entirety and directly applicable in all Member States.

Done at Brussels, 21 December 1989.

For the Council
The President
E. CRESSON

APPENDIX II

Commission Regulation (EEC) No 2367/90 of 25 July 1990 on the notifications, time limits and hearings provided for in Council Regulation (EEC) No 4064/89 on the control of concentrations between undertakings OJ 1990 L219/5 including Annex I (Form CO)

THE COMMISSION OF THE EUROPEAN COMMUNITIES,

Having regard to the Treaty establishing the European Economic Community,

Having regard to Council Regulation (EEC) No 4064/89 of 21 December 1989 on the control of concentrations between undertakings[1], and in particular Article 23 thereof,

Having regard to Council Regulation No 17 of 6 February 1962, First Regulation implementing Articles 85 and 86 of the Treaty [2], as last amended by the Accession of Spain and Portugal, and in particular Article 24 thereof,

Having regard to Council Regulation (EEC) No 1017/68 of 19 July 1968 applying rules of competition to transport by rail, road and inland waterway[3], as last amended by the Act of Accession of Spain and Portugal, and in particular Article 29 thereof,

Having regard to Council Regulation (EEC) No 4056/86 of 22 December 1986 laying down detailed rules for the application of Articles 85 and 86 of the Treaty to maritime transport[4], and in particular Article 26 thereof,

Having regard to Council Regulation (EEC) No 3975/87 of 14 December 1987

---

[1]   OJ No L 395, 30.12.1989, p. 1.
[2]   OJ No 13, 21.2.1962, p. 204/62.
[3]   OJ No L 175, 23.7.1968, p. 1.
[4]   OJ No L 378, 31.12.1986, p. 4.

laying down detailed rules for the application of the competition rules to undertakings in air transport[5], and in particular Article 19 thereof,

Having consulted the Advisory Committee on Concentrations, as well as the Advisory Committees on Restrictive Practices and Monopolies in the Transport Industry, in Maritime Transport and in Air Transport,

1. Whereas Article 23 of Regulation (EEC) No 4064/89 empowers the Commission to adopt implementing provisions concerning the form, content and other details of notifications pursuant to Article 4, time limits pursuant to Article 10, and hearings pursuant to Article 18;

2. Whereas Regulation (EEC) No 4064/89 is based on the principle of compulsory notification of concentrations before they are put into effect; whereas, on the one hand, a notifiction has important legal consequences which are favourable to the parties, while, on the other hand, failure to comply with the obligation to notify renders the parties liable to a fine and may also entail civil law disadvantages for them; whereas it is therefore necessary in the interests of legal certainty to define precisely the subject matter and content of the information to be provided in the notification;

3. Whereas it is for the parties concerned to make full and honest disclosure to the Commission of the facts and circumstances which are relevant for taking a decision on the notified concentration;

4. Whereas in order to simplify and expedite examination of the notification it is desirable to prescribe that a form be used;

5. Whereas since notification sets in motion legal time limits for initiating proceedings and for decisions, the conditions governing such time limits and the time when they become effective must also be determined;

6. Whereas rules must be laid down in the interests of legal certainty for calculating the time limits provided for in Regulation (EEC) No 4064/89; whereas in particular the beginning and end of the period and the circumstances suspending the running of the period must be determined; whereas the provisions should be based on the principles of Regulation (EEC, Euratom) No 1182/71 of 3 June 1971 determining the rules applicable to periods, dates and time limits[6], subject to certain adaptations made necessary by the exceptionally short legal time limits referred to above;

7. Whereas the provisions relating to the Commission's procedure must be framed in such way as to safeguard fully the right to be heard and the rights of defence;

8. Whereas the Commission will give the parties concerned, if they so request, an opportunity before notification to discuss the intended concentration informally and in strict confidence; whereas in addition it will, after notification, maintain close contact with the parties concerned to the extent necessary to discuss with them any practical or legal problems which it discovers on a first examination of the case and if possible to remove such problems by mutual agreement;

9. Whereas in accordance with the principle of the right to be heard, the parties concerned must be given the opportunity to submit their comments on all the objections which the Commission proposes to take into account in its decisions;

10. Whereas third parties having sufficient interest must also be given the opportunity of expressing their views where they make a written application;

11. Whereas the various persons entitled to submit comments should do so in writing, both in their own interest and in the interest of good administration, without

---

[5] OJ No L 374, 31.12.1987, p. 1.
[6] OJ No L 124, 8.6.1971, p. 1.

prejudice to their right to request an oral hearing where appropriate to supplement the written procedure; whereas in urgent cases, however, the Commission must be able to proceed immediately to oral hearings of the parties concerned or third parties; whereas in such cases the persons to be heard must have the right to confirm their oral statements in writing;

12.   Whereas it is necessary to define the rights of persons who are to be heard, to what extent they should be granted access to the Commission's file and on what conditions they may be represented or assisted;

13.   Whereas it is also necessary to define the rules for fixing and calculating the time limits for reply fixed by the Commission;

14.   Whereas the Advisory Committee on Concentrations shall deliver its opinion on the basis of a preliminary draft decision; whereas it must therefore be consulted on a case after the inquiry in to that case has been completed; whereas such consultation does not, however, prevent the Commission from re-opening an inquiry if need be,

HAS ADOPTED THIS REGULATION:

SECTION I

NOTIFICATIONS

Article 1

Persons entitled to submit notifications

1.   Notifications shall be submitted by the persons or undertakings referred to in Article 4 (2) of Regulation (EEC) No 4064/89.

2.   Where notifications are signed by representatives of persons or of undertakings, such representatives shall produce written proof that they are authorized to act.

3.   Joint notifications should be submitted by a joint representative who is authorized to transmit and to receive documents on behalf of all notifying parties.

Article 2

Submission of notifications

1.   Notifications shall be submitted in the manner prescribed by form CO as shown in Annex I. Joint notifications shall be submitted on a single form.

2.   Twenty copies of each notifiction and fifteen copies of the supporting documents shall be submitted to the Commission at the address indicated in form CO.

3.   The supporting documents shall be either originals or copies of the originals; in the latter case the notifying parties shall confirm that they are true and complete.

4.   Notifications shall be in one of the official languages of the Community. This language shall also be the language of the proceeding for the notifying parties. Supporting documents shall be submitted in their original language. Where the original language is not one of the official languages, a translation into the language of the proceeding shall be attached.

Article 3

Information to be provided

1. Notifications shall contain the information requested by form CO. The information must be correct and complete.

2. Material changes in the facts specified in the notification which the notifying parties know or ought to have known must be communicated to the Commission voluntarily and without delay.

3. Incorrect of misleading information shall be deemed to be incomplete information.

Article 4

Effective date of notifications

1. Subject to paragraph 2 notifications shall become effective on the date on which they are received by the Commission.

2. Subject to paragraph 3, where the information contained in the notification is incomplete in a material respect, the Commission shall without delay inform the notifying parties or the joint representative in writing and shall fix an appropriate time limit for the completion of the information; in such cases, the notification shall become effective on the date on which the complete information is received by the Commission.

3. The Commission may dispense with the obligation to provide any particular information requested by form CO where the Commission considers that such information is not necessary for the examination of the case.

4. The Commission shall without delay acknowledge in writing to the notifying parties or the joint representative receipt of the notification and of any reply to a letter sent by the Commission pursuant to paragraph 2 above.

Article 5

Conversion of notifications

1. Where the Commission finds that the operation notified does not constitute a concentration within the meaning of Article 3 of Regulation (EEC) No 4064/89 it shall inform the notifying parties or the joint representative in writing. In such a case, the Commission may, if requested by the notifying parties, as appropriate and subject to paragraph 2 below, treat the notification as an application within the meaning of Article 2 or a notification within the meaning of Article 4 of Regulation No 17, as an application within the meaning of Article 12 or a notification within the meaning of Article 14 of Regulation (EEC) No 1017/68, as an application within the meaning of Article 12 of Regulation (EEC) No 4056/86 or as an application with the meaning of Article 3 (2) or of Article 5 of Regulation (EEC) No 3975/87.

2. In cases referred to in paragraph 1, second sentence, the Commission may require that the information given in the notification be supplemented within an appropriate time limit fixed by it in so far as this is necessary for assessing the operation on the basis of the abovementioned Regulations. The application or

notification shall be deemed to fulfil the requirements of such Regulations from the date of the original notification where the additional information is received by the Commission within the time limit fixed.

SECTION II

TIME LIMITS FOR INITIATING PROCEEDINGS AND FOR DECISIONS

Article 6

Beginning of the time limit

1. The periods referred to in Article 10 (1) of Regulation (EEC) No 4064/89 shall start at the beginning of the day following the effective date of the notification, within the meaning of Article 4 (1) and (2) of this Regulation.
2. The period referred to in Article 10 (3) of Regulation (EEC) No 4064/89 shall start at the beginning of the day following the day on which proceedings were initiated.
3. Where the first day of a period is not a working day within the meaning of Article 19, the period shall start at the beginning of the following working day.

Article 7

End of the time limit

1. The period referred to in the first subparagraph of Article 10 (1) of Regulation (EEC) No 4064/89 shall end with the expiry of the day which in the month following that in which the period began falls on the same date as the day from which the period runs. Where such a day does not occur in that month, the period shall end with the expiry of the last day of that month.
2. The period referred to in the second sub-paragraph of Article 10 (1) of Regulation (EEC) No 4064/89 shall end with the expiry of the day which in the sixth week following that in which the period began is the same day of the week as the day from which the period runs.
3. The period referred to in Article 10 (3) of Regulation (EEC) No 4064/89 shall end with the expiry of the day which in the fourth month following that in which the period began falls on the same date as the day from which the period runs. Where such a day does not occur in that month, the period shall end with the expiry of the last day of that month.
4. Where the last day of the period is not a working day within the meaning of Article 19, the period shall end with the expiry of the following working day.
5. Paragraphs 2 to 4 above shall be subject to the provisions of Article 8.

Article 8

Addition of holidays

Where public holidays or other holidays of the Commission as defined in Article 19 fall within the periods referred to in Article 10 (1) and in Article 10 (3) of Regulation (EEC) No 4064/89, these periods shall be extended by a corresponding number of days.

Article 9

Suspension of the time limit

1. The period referred to in Article 10 (3) of Regulation (EEC) No 4064/89 shall be suspended where the Commission, pursuant to Articles 11 (5) or 13 (3) of the same Regulation, has to take a decision because:

(a) Information which the Commission has requested pursuant to Article 11 (2) of Regulation (EEC) No 4064/89 from an undertaking involved in a concentration is not provided or not provided in full within the time limit fixed by the Commission;

(b) an undertaking involved in the concentration has refused to submit to an investigation deemed necessary by the Commission on the basis of Article 13 (1) of Regulation (EEC) No 4064/89 or to cooperate in the carrying out of such an investigation in accordance with the abovementioned provision;

(c) the notifying parties have failed to inform the Commission of material changes in the facts specified in the notification.

2. The period referred to in Article 10 (3) of Regulation (EEC) No 4064/89 shall be suspended:

(a) in the cases referred to in subparagraph 1 (a) above, for the period between the end of the time limit fixed in the request for information and the receipt of the complete and correct information required by decision;

(b) in the cases referred to in subparagraph 1 (b) above, for the period between the unsuccessful attempt to carry out the investigation and the completion of the investigation ordered by decision;

(c) in the cases referred to in subparagraph 1 (c) above, for the period between the occurrence of the change in the facts referred to therein and the receipt of the complete and correct information requested by decision or the completion of the investigation ordered by the decision.

3. The suspension of the time limit shall begin on the day following that on which the event causing the suspension occurred. It shall end with the expiry of the day on which the reason for suspension is removed. Where such day is not a working day within the meaning of Article 19, the suspension of the time limit shall end with the expiry of the following working day.

Article 10

Compliance with the time limit

The time limits referred to in Article 10 (1) and (3) of Regulation (EEC) No 4064/89 shall be met where the Commission has taken the relevant decision before the end of the period. Notification of the decision to the undertakings concerned must follow without delay.

SECTION III

HEARING OF THE PARTIES AND OF THIRD PARTIES

Article 11

Decisions on the suspension of concentrations

1. Where the Commission intends to take a decision under Article 7 (2) of Regulation (EEC) No 4064/89 or a decision under Article 7 (4) of that Regulation which adversely affects the parties, it shall, pursuant to Article 18 (1) of that Regulation, inform the parties concerned in writing of its objections and shall fix a time limit within which they may make known their views.

2. Where the Commission pursuant to Article 18 (2) of Regulation (EEC) No 4064/89 has taken a decision referred to in paragraph 1 provisionally without having given the parties concerned the opportunity to make known their views, it shall without delay and in any event before the expiry of the suspension send them the text of the provisional decision and shall fix a time limit within which they make known their views.

Once the parties concerned have made known their views, the Commission shall take a final decision annulling, amending or confirming the provisional decision. Where the parties concerned have not made known their view within the time limit fixed, the Commission's provisional decision shall become final with the expiry of that period.

3. The parties concerned shall make known their views in writing or orally within the time limit fixed. They may confirm their oral statements in writing.

Article 12

Decisions on the substance of the case

1. Where the Commission intends to take a decision pursuant to Article 8(2), second subparagraph, Article 8 (3) (4) and (5), Article 14 or Article 15 of Regulation (EEC) No 4064/89, it shall, before consulting the Advisory Committee on Concentrations, hold a hearing of the parties concerned pursuant to Article 18 of that Regulation.

2. The Commission shall inform the parties concerned in writing of its objections. The communication shall be addressed to the notifying parties or to the joint representative. The Commission shall, when giving notice of objections, fix a time limit within which the parties concerned may inform the Commission of their views.

3. Having informed the parties of its objections, the Commission shall upon request give the parties concerned access to the file for the purposes of preparing their observations. Documents shall not be accessible in so far as they contain business secrets of other parties concerned or of third parties, or other confidential information including sensitive commerical information the disclosure of which would have a significant adverse effect on the supplier of such information or where they are internal documents of the authorities.

4. The parties concerned shall, within the time limit fixed, make known in writing their views on the Commission's objections. They may in their written comments set out all matters relevant to the case and may attach any relevant documents in

proof of the facts set out. They may also propose that the Commission hear persons who may corroborate those facts.

Article 13

Oral hearings

1. The Commission shall afford parties concerned who have so requested in their written comments the opportunity to put forward their arguments orally, if those persons show a sufficient interest or if the Commission proposes to impose a fine or periodic penalty payment on them. It may also in other cases afford the parties concerned the opportunity of expressing their views orally.
2. The Commission shall summon the persons to be heard to attend on such date as it shall appoint.
3. It shall forthwith transmit a copy of the summons to the competent authorities of the Member States, who may appoint an official to take part in the hearing.

Article 14

Hearings

1. Hearings shall be conducted by persons appointed by the Commission for that purpose.
2. Persons summoned to attend shall either appear in person or be represented by legal representatives or representatives authorized by their constitution. Undertakings and associations of undertakings may be represented by a duly authorized agent appointed from among their permanent staff.
3. Persons heard by the Commission may be assisted by lawyers or university teachers who are entitled to plead before the Court of Justice of the European Communities in accordance with Article 17 of the Protocol on the Statute (EEC) of the Court of Justice, or by other qualified persons.
4. Hearings shall not be public. Persons shall be heard separately or in the presence of other persons summoned to attend. In the latter case, regard shall be had to the legitimate interest of the undertakings in the protection of their business secrets.
5. The statements made by each person heard shall be recorded.

Article 15

Hearing of third parties

1. If natural or legal persons showing a sufficient interest, and especially members of the administrative or management organs of the undertakings concerned or recognized workers' representatives of those undertakings, apply in writing to be heard pursuant to the second sentence of Article 18 (4) of Regulation (EEC) No 4064/89, the Commission shall inform them in writing of the nature and subject matter of the procedure and shall fix a time limit within which they may make known their views.
2. The third parties referred to in paragraph 1 above shall make known their views in writing or orally within the time limit fixed. They may confirm their oral statements in writing.

3.   The Commission may likewise afford to any other third parties the opportunity of expressing their views.

SECTION IV

MISCELLANEOUS PROVISIONS

Article 16

Transmission of documents

1.   Transmission of documents and summonses from the Commission to the addressees may be effected in any of the following ways:

(a)   delivery by hand against receipt;
(b)   registered letter with acknowledgement of receipt;
(c)   telefax with a request for acknowledgement of receipt;
(d)   telex.

2.   Subject to Article 18 (1), paragraph 1 above also applies to the transmission of documents from the parties concerned or from third parties to the Commission.
3.   Where a document is sent by telex or by telefax, it shall be presumed that it has been received by the addressee on the day on which it was sent.

Article 17

Setting of time limits

1.   In fixing the time limits provided for in Articles 4 (2), 5 (2), 11 (1) and (2), 12 (2) and 15 (1), the Commission shall have regard to the time required for preparation of statements and to the urgency of the case. It shall also take account of public holidays in the country of receipt of the Commission's communication.
2.   The day on which the addressee received a communication shall not be taken into account for the purpose of fixing time limits.

Article 18

Receipt of documents by the Commission

1.   Subject to Article 4 (1), notifications must be delivered to the Commission at the address indicated in form CO or have been dispatched by registered letter before expiry of the period referred to in Article 4 (1) of Regulation (EEC) No 4064/89. Additional information requested to complete notifictions pursuant to Article 4 (2) or to supplement notifications pursuant to Article 5 (2) of this Regulation must reach the Commission at the aforesaid or have been dispatched by registered letter before the expiry of the time limit fixed in each case. Written comments on Commission communications pursuant to Articles 11 (1) and (2), 12 (2) and 15 (1) must be delivered to the Commission at the aforesaid address before the time limit fixed in each case.
2.   Where the last day of a period referred to in paragraph 1 is a day by which

documents must be received and that day is not a working day within the meaning of Article 19, the period shall end with the expiry of the following working day.

3. Where the last day of a period referred to in paragraph 1 is a day by which documents must be dispatched and that day is a Saturday, Sunday or public holiday in the country of dispatch, the period shall end with the expiry of the following working day in that country.

Article 19

Definition of Commission working days

The term 'working days' in Articles 6 (3), 7 (4), 9 (3) and 18 (2) means all days other than Saturdays, Sundays, public holidays set out in Annex II and other holidays as detemined by the Commission and published in the *Official Journal of the European Communities* before the beginning of each year.

Article 20

Entry into force

This Regulation shall enter into force on 21 September 1990.

This Regulation shall be binding in its entirety and directly applicable in all Member States.

Done at Brussels, 25 July 1990.

For the Commission
Leon BRITTAN
Vice-President

ANNEX I

FORM CO RELATING TO THE NOTIFICATION OF A CONCENTRATION PURSUANT TO COUNCIL REGULATION (EEC) No 4064/89

A   Introduction

This form specifies the information to be provided by an undertaking or undertakings when notifying the Commission of a concentration with a Community dimension. A 'concentration' is defined in Article 3 and 'Community dimension' by Article 1 of Regulation (EEC) No 4064/89.

Your attention is particularly drawn to Regulation (EEC) No 4064/89 and to Commission Regulation (EEC) No 2367/90. In particular you should note that:

(a)   all information requested by this form must be provided. However, if, in good faith, you are unable to provide a response to a question or can only respond to a limited extent on the basis of available information, indicate this and give reasons. If you consider that any particular information requested by this form may not be necessary for the Commission's examination of the case, you may ask the Commission to dispense with the obligation to provide that information, under Article 4(3) of Regulation (EEC) No 2367/90;

(b)   unless all sections are completed in full or good reasons are given explaining why it has not been possible to complete unanswered questions (for example, because of the unavailability of information on a target company during a contested bid) the notification will be incomplete and will only become effective on the date on which all the information is received. The notification will be deemed to be incomplete if information is incorrect or misleading;

(c)   incorrect or misleading information where supplied intentionally or negligently could make you liable to a fine.

B   Who must notify

In the case of a merger (within the meaning of Article 3 (1) (a) of Regulation (EEC) No 4064/89 or the acquisition of joint control in an undertaking within the meaning of Article 3 (1) (b) of Regulation (EEC) No 4064/89, the notification shall be completed jointly by the parties to the merger or by those acquiring joint control as the case may be.

In the case of the acquisition of a controlling interest in an undertaking by another, the acquirer must complete the notification.

In the case of a public bid to acquire an undertaking, the bidder must complete the notification.

Each party completing the notification is responsible for the accuracy of the information which it provides.

For the purposes of this form 'the parties to the concentration' ('the parties') includes the undertaking in which a controlling interest is being acquired or which is the subject of a public bid.

C Supporting documentation

The completed notification must be accompanied by the following:

(a) copies of the final or most recent versions of all documents bringing about the concentration, whether by agreement between the parties concerned, acquisition of a controlling interest or a public bid;

(b) in a public bid, a copy of the offer document. If unavailable on notification it should be submitted as soon as possible and not later than when it is posted to shareholders;

(c) copies of the most recent annual reports and accounts of all the parties to the concentration;

(d) copies of reports of analyses which have been prepared for the purposes of the concentration and from which information has been taken in order to provide the information requested in sections 5 and 6;

(e) a list and short description of the contents of all other analyses, reports, studies and surveys prepared by or for any of the notifying parties for the purposes of assessing or analysing the proposed concentration with respect to competitive conditions, competitors (actual and potential), and market conditions. Each item in the list must include the name and position held of the author.

D How to notify

The notification must be completed in one of the offical languages of the European Community. This language shall thereafter be the language of the proceedings for all notifying parties.

The information requested by this form is to be set out using the sections and paragraph numbers of the form.

Supporting documents shall be submitted in their original language; where this is not an official language of the Community they shall be translated, into the language of the proceeding (Article 2 (4) of Regulation (EEC) No 2367/90).

The supporting documents may be originals or copies of the originals. In the latter case the notifying party shall confirm that they are true and complete.

The financial data requested in Section 2.4 below must be provided in Ecus at the average conversion rates prevailing for the years or other period in question.

Twenty copies of each notification and fifteen copies of all supporting documents must be provided.

The notification should be sent to:

Commission of the European Communities,
Directorate General for Competition (DG IV),
Merger Task Force (Cort. 150),
200, rue de la Loi,
B-1049 Brussels;

or be delivered by hand during normal Commission working hourse at the following address:

Commission of the European Communities,
Directorate General for Competition (DG IV),
Merger Task Force,
150, avenue de Cortenberg,
B-1040 Brussels.

E Secrecy

Article 214 of the Treaty and Article 17 (2) of Regulation (EEC) No 4064/89 require the Commission and the Member States, their officials and other servants not to disclose information they have acquired through the application of the Regulation of the kind covered by the obligation of professional secrey. The same principle must also apply to protect confidentiality as between notifying parties.

If you believe that your interests would be harmed if any of the information you are asked to supply was to be published or otherwise divulged to other parties, submit this information separately with each page clearly marked 'Business secrets'. You should also give reasons why this information should not be divulged or published.

In the case of mergers or joint acquisitions, or in other cases where the notification is completed by more than one of the parties, business secrets may be submitted under separate cover, and referred to in the notification as an annex. In such cases the notification will be considered complete on receipt of all the annexes.

F References

All references contained in this form are to the relevant articles and paragraphs of Council Regulation (EEC) No 4064/89.

SECTION 1

1.1   *Information on notifying party (or parties)*
      Give details of:
1.1.1 name and address of undertaking,
1.1.2 nature of the undertaking's business,
1.1.3 name, address, telephone, fax and/or telex of, and position held by, the person to be contacted.
1.2   *Information on other parties to the concentration*[7]([8])
      For each party to the concentration (except the notifying party) give details of:
1.2.1 name and address of undertaking,
1.2.2 nature of the undertaking's business,
1.2.3 name, address, telephone, fax and/or telex of, and position held by, the person to be contacted.
1.3   *Address for service*
      Give an address in Brussels if available to which all communications may be made and documents delivered in accordance with Article 1 (4) of Commission Regulation (EEC) No 2367/90.

[7]   A concentration is defined in Article 3.
[8]   This includes the target company in the case of a contested bid, in which case the details should be completed as far as is possible.

1.4   *Appointment of representatives*
Article 1 (2) of Commission Regulation (EEC) 2367/90 states that where notifications are signed by representatives of undertakings, such representatives shall produce written proof that they are authorized to act. Such written authorization must accompany the notification and the following details of the representatives of the notifying party or parties and other parties to the concentration are to be given below:

1.4.1 is this a joint notification?
1.4.2 if 'yes', has a joint representative been appointed?
       if 'yes', please give details requested in 1.4.3 to 1.4.6 below;
       if 'no', please give details of the representatives who have been authorized to act for each of the parties to the concentration indicating who they represent;
1.4.3 name of representative;
1.4.4 address of representative;
1.4.5 name of person to be contacted (and address if different from 1.4.4);
1.4.6 telephone, telefax and/or telex.

SECTION 2

Details of the concentration

2.1   Briefly describe the nature of the concentration being notified. In doing so state:

— whether the proposed concentration is a full legal merger, an acquisition, a concentrative joint venture or a contract or other means conferring direct or indirect control within the meaning of Article 3 (3);
— whether the whole or parts of parties are subject to the concentration;
— whether any public offer for the securities of one party by another has the support of the former's supervisory boards of management or other bodies legally representing the party concerned.

2.2   List the economic sectors involved in the concentration.
2.3   Give a brief explanation of the economic and financial details of the concentration. In doing so provide, where relevant, information about the following:

— any financial or other support received from whatever source (including public authorities) by any of the parties and the nature and amount of this support,
— the proposed or expected date of any major events designed to bring about the completion of the concentration,
— the proposed structure of ownership and control after the completion of the concentration.

2.4   For each of the parties, the notifying party shall provide the following data for the last three financial years;

2.4.1 worldwide turnover[9],

2.4.2 Community-wide turnover[9] [10],

2.4.3 turnover in each Member State[9] [10],

2.4.4 the Member State, if any, in which more than two-thirds of Community-wide turnover is achieved[9] [10],

2.4.5 profits before tax worldwide[11],

2.4.6 number of employees worldwide[12].

SECTION 3

Ownership and control[13]

For each of the parties provide a list of all undertakings belonging to the same group. This list must include:

3.1   all undertakings controlled by the parties, directly or indirectly, within the meaning of Article 3 (3);

3.2   all undertakings or persons controlling the parties directly or indirectly within the meaning of Article 3 (3);

3.3   for each undertaking or person identified in 3.2 above, a complete list of all undertakings controlled by them directly or indirectly, within the meaning of Article 3 (3).

For each entry to the list the nature and means of control shall be specified;

3.4   provide details of acquisitions made during the last three years by the groups identified above, of undertakings active in affected markets as defined in section 5 below.

The information sought in this section may be illustrated by the use of charts or diagrams where this helps to give a better understanding of the pre-concentration structure of ownership and control of the undertakings.

---

[9] See Artice 5 for the definition of turnover and note the special provisions for credit, insurance, other financial institutions and joint undertakings.

   For insurance undertakings, credit and other financial institutions, Community-residents and residents of a Member State are defined as natural or legal persons having their residence in a Member State, thereby following the respective national legislation. The corporate customer is to be treated as resident in the country in which it is legally incorporated.

   For the calculation of turnover, the notifying party should also refer to the examples: guidance note I for credit and other financial institutions: guidance note II for insurance undertakings: guidance note III for joint undertakings.

[10] See guidance note IV for the calculation of turnover in one Member State with respect to Community-wide turnover.

[11] 'Profits before tax' shall comprise profit on ordinary activities before tax on profit.

[12] Employees shall comprise all persons employed in the enterprise who have a contract of employment and receive remuneration.

[13] See Article 3 (3) to (5).

SECTION 4

Personal and financial links

With respect to each undertaking or person disclosed in response to Section 3 provide:

4.1   a list of all other undertakings which are active on affected markets (affected markets are defined in section 5) in which the undertakings of the group hold individually or collectively 10% or more of the voting rights or issued share capital. In each case state the percentage held;

4.2   a list of all other undertakings which are active on affected markets in which the persons disclosed in response to Section 3 hold 10% or more of the voting rights or issued share capital. In each case state the percentage held;

4.3   a list for each undertaking of the members of their boards of management who are also members of the boards of management or of the supervisory boards of any other undertaking, which is active on affected markets; and (where applicable) for each undertaking a list of the members of their supervisory boards who are also members of the boards of management of any other undertaking which is active on affected markets;

in each case stating the name of the other undertaking and the position held.

Information provided here may be illustrated by the use of charts or diagrams where this helps to give a better understanding.

SECTION 5

Information on affected markets

The notifying party shall provide the data requested having regard to the following definitions:

PRODUCT MARKETS

A relevant product market comprises all those products and/or services which are regarded as interchangeable or substitutable by the consumer, by reason of the products' characteristics, their prices and their intended use.

A relevant product market may in some cases be composed of a number of individual product groups. An individual product group is a product or small group of products which present largely identical physical or technical characteristics and are fully interchangeable. The difference between products within the group will be small and usually only a matter of brand and/or image. The product market will usually be the classification used by the undertaking in its marketing operations.

RELEVANT GEOGRAPHIC MARKET

The relevant geographic market comprises the area in which the undertakings concerned are involved in the supply of products or services, in which the conditions of competition are sufficiently homogenous and which can be distinguished from neighbouring areas because, in particular, conditions of competition are appreciably different in those areas.

Factors relevant to the assessment of the relevant geographic market include the nature and characteristics of the products or services concerned, the existence of entry barriers or consumer preferences, appreciable differences of the undertakings' market shares between neighbouring areas or substantial price differences.

AFFECTED MARKETS

Affected markets consist of relevant product markets or individual product groups, in the Common Market or a Member State or, where different, in any relevant geographic market where:

(a)   two or more of the parties (including undertakings belonging to the same group as defined in Section 3) are engaged in business activities in the same product market or individual product group and where the concentration will lead to a combined market share of 10% or more. These are horizontal relationships; or

(b)   any of the parties (including undertakings belonging to the same group as defined in Section 3) is engaged in business activities in a product market which is upstream or downstream of a product market or individual product group in which any other party is engaged and any of their market shares in 10% or more, regardless of whether there is or is not any existing supplier/customer relationship between the parties concerned. These are vertical relationships.

I   Explanation of the affected relevant product markets

5.1   Describe each affected relevant product market and explain why the products and/or services in these markets are included (and why others are excluded) by reason of their characteristics, their prices and their intended use.

5.2   List the individual product groups defined internally by your undertaking for marketing purposes which are covered by each relevant product market described under 5.1 above.

II   Market data on affected markets

For each affected relevant product market and, where different, individual product group, for each of the last three financial years:

(a)   for the Community as a whole;

(b)   individually for each Member State where the parties (including undertakings belonging to the same group as defined in Section 3) do business;

(c)   and where different, for any relevant geographic market,

provide the following:

5.3   an estimate of the value of the market and, where appropriate, of the volume (for example in units shipped or delivered) of the market[14]. If available, include statistics prepared by other sources to illustrate your answers. Also provide a forecast of the evolution of demand on the affected markets;

5.4   the turnover of each of the groups to which the parties belong (as defined in Section 3);

5.5   an estimate of the market share of each of the groups to which the parties belong;

5.6   an estimate of the market share (in value and where appropriate volume) of

---

[14]   The value and volume of a market should reflect output less exports plus imports for the geographic market under consideration.

all competitors having at least 10% of the geographic market under consideration. Provide the name, address and telephone number of these undertakings;

5.7   a comparison of prices charged by the groups to which the parties belong in each of the Member States and a similar comparison of such price levels between the Community and its major trading partners (eg the United States, Japan and EFTA);

5.8   an estimate of the value (and where appropriate volume) and source of imports to the relevant geographic market;

5.9   the proportion of such imports that are derived from the groups to which the parties belong;

5.10   an estimate of the extent to which any of these imports are affected by any tariff or non-tariff barriers to trade.

III   Market data on conglomerate aspects

In the absence of horizontal or vertical relationships, where any of the parties (including undertakings belonging to the same group as defined in Section 3) holds a market share of 25% or more for any product market or individual product group, provide the following information:

5.11   a description of each relevant product market and explain why the products and/or services in these markets are included (and why others are excluded) by reason of their characteristics, their prices and their intended use;

5.12   a list of the individual product groups defined internally by your undertaking for marketing purposes which are covered by each relevant product market described;

5.13   an estimate of the value of the market and the market shares of each of the groups to which the parties belong for each affected relevant product market and, where different, individual product group, for the last financial year:

(a)   for the Community as a whole;

(b)   individually for each Member State where the groups to which the parties belong do business;

(c)   and where different, for any relevant geographic market.

In each response in Section 5 the notifying party shall explain the basis of the estimates used or assumptions made.

SECTION 6

General conditions in affected markets

The following information shall be provided in relation to the affected relevant product markets and, where different, affected individual product groups:

RECORD OF MARKET ENTRY

6.1   Over the last five years (or a longer period if this is more appropriate) has there been any significant entry to these markets in the Community? If the answer is 'yes', provide information on these entrants, estimating their current market shares.

6.2   In the opinion of the notifying pary are there undertakings (including those at present operating only in extra-Community markets) that could enter the Community's markets? If the answer is 'yes', provide information on these potential entrants.

6.3   In the opinion of the notifying party what is the likelihood of significant market entry over the next five years?

FACTORS INFLUENCING MARKET ENTRY

6.4   Describe the various factors influencing entry into affected markets that exist in the present case, examining entry from both a geographical and product viewpoint. In so doing take account of the following where appropriate:

— the total costs of entry (capital, promotion, advertising, necessary distribution systems, servicing etc.) on a scale equivalent to a significant viable competitor, indicating the market share of such a competitor;
— to what extent is entry to the markets influenced by the requirement of government authorization or standard setting in any form? Are there any legal or regulatory controls on entry to these markets?
— to what extent is entry to the markets influenced by the availability of raw materials?
— to what extent is entry to the markets influenced by the length of contracts between an undertaking and its suppliers and/or customers?
— describe the importance of licensing patents, know-how and other rights in these markets.

VERTICAL INTEGRATION

6.5   Describe the nature and extent of vertical integration of each of the parties.

RESEARCH AND DEVELOPMENT

6.6   Give an account of the importance of research and development in the ability of a firm operating on the relevant market to compete in the long term. Explain the nature of the research and development in affected markets carried out by the undertakings to the concentration.

In so doing take account of the following where appropriate:
— the research and development intensities[15] for these markets and the relevant research and developmenmt intensities for the parties concerned;
— the course of technological development for these markets over an appropriate time period (including developments in products and/or services, production processes, distribution systems etc.);
— the major innovations that have been made in these markets over this time period and the undertakings responsible for these innovations;
— the cycle of innovation in these markets and where the parties are in this cycle of innovation;
— describe the extent to which the parties concerned are licensees or licensors of patents, know-how and other rights in affected markets.

---

[15]   Research and development intensity is defined as research and development expenditure as a proportion of turnover.

DISTRIBUTION AND SERVICE SYSTEMS

6.7   Explain the distribution channels and service networks that exist on the affected markets. In so doing take account of the following where appropriate:

— the distribution systems prevailing on the market and their importance. To what extent is distribution performed by third parties and/or undertakings belonging to the same group as the parties as disclosed in Section 3?

— the service networks (for example maintenance and repair) prevailing and their importance in these markets. To what extent are such services performed by third parties and/or undertakings belonging to the same group as the parties as disclosed in Section 3?

COMPETITIVE ENVIRONMENT

6.8   Give details (names, addresses and contacts) of the five largest suppliers to the notifying parties and their individual share of the purchases of the notifying parties.

6.9   Give details (names, addresses and contacts) of the five largest customers of the notifying parties and their individual share of the sales of the notifying parties.

6.10   Explain the structure of supply and demand in affected markets. This explanation should allow the Commission further to appreciate the competitive environment in which the parties carry out their business. In so doing take account of the following where appropriate:

— the phases of the markets in terms of, for example, take-off, expansion, maturity and decline. In the opinion of the notifying party, where are the affected products in these phases?

— the structure of supply. Give details of the various identifiable categories that comprise the supply side and describe the 'typical supplier' of each category;

— the structure of demand. Give details of the various identifiable groups that comprise the demand side and describe the 'typical customer' of each group;

— whether public authorities, government agencies or state enterprises or similar bodies are important participants as sources of supply or demand. In any instance where this is so give details of this participation;

— the total Community-wide capacity for the last three years. Over the period what proportion of this capacity is accounted for by the parties and what have been their rates of capacity utilization?

COOPERATIVE AGREEMENTS

6.11   To what extent do cooperative agreements (horizontal and/or vertical) exist in the affected markets?

6.12   Give details of the most important cooperative agreements engaged in by the parties in the affected markets, such as licensing agremeents, research and development, specialization, distribution, long-term supply and exchange of information agreements.

TRADE ASSOCIATIONS

6.13   List the names and addresses of the principal trade associations in the affected markets.

WORLDWIDE CONTEXT

6.14   Describe the worldwide context of the proposed concentration indicating the position of the parties in this market.

SECTION 7

General matters

7.1   Describe how the proposed concentration is likely to affect the interests of intermediate and ultimate consumers, and the development of technical progress.

7.2   In the event that the Commissioner finds that the operation notified does not constitute a concentration within the meaning of Article 3 of Regulation (EEC) No 4064/89, do you request that it be treated as an application within the meaning of Article 2 or a notification within the meaning of Article 4 of Regulation No 17, as an application within the meaning of Article 12 or a notification within the meaning of Article 14 of Regulation (EEC) No 1017/68, as an application within the meaning of Article 12 of Regulation (EEC) No 4056/86 or as an application within the meaning of Article 3 (2) or Article 5 of Regulation (EEC) No 3975/87?

SECTION 8

Declaration

The notification must conclude with the following declaration which is to be signed by or on behalf of all the notifying parties.

The undersigned declare that the information given in this notification is correct to the best of their knowledge and belief, that all estimates are identified as such and are their best estimates of the underlying facts and that all the opinions expressed are sincere.

They are aware of the provisions of Article 14 (1) (b) of Regulation (EEC) No 4064/89.

Place and date:
Signatures:

GUIDANCE NOTE I*

CALCULATION OF TURNOVER FOR CREDIT AND OTHER FINANCIAL INSTITUTIONS

(Article 5 (3) (a))

For the calculation of turnover for credit institutions and other financial institutions, we give the following example (proposed merger between bank A and bank B)

I Consolidated balance sheets

(in million ecu)

Assets	Bank A		Bank B	
Loans and advances to credit institutions	20 000		1 000	
— to credit institutions within the Community:		(10 000)		(500)
— to credit institutions within one (and the same) Member State X:		(5 000)		(500)
Loans and advances to customers	60 000		4 000	
— to Community residents;		(30 000)		(2 000)
— to residents of one (and the same) Member State X:		(15 000)		(500)
Other assets:	20 000		1 000	
Total assets:	100 000		6 000	

II Calculation of turnover

In place of turnover, the following figures shall be used:

	Bank A	Bank B

1 Aggregate worldwide turnover

is replaced by one-tenth of total assets: 10 000   600
the total sum of which is more the ECU 5 000 million.

2 Community-wide turnover

is replaced by, for each bank, one-tenth of total assets multiplied by the ratio between loans and advances to credit institutions and customers within the Community; to the total sum of loans and advances to credit institutions and customers.

---

*   In the following guidance notes, the terms 'institution' or 'undertaking' are used subject to the exact definition in each case.

	Bank A	Bank B
This is calculated as follows:		
one-tenth of total assets:	10 000	600

which is multiplied for each bank by the ratio
between:

	Bank A	Bank B
loans and advances to credit institutions and customers	10 000	500
within the Community	30 000	2 000
	40 000	2 500

and
the total sum of loans and advances to credit

	Bank A	Bank B
institutions	20 000	1 000
and customers	60 000	4 000
	80 000	5 000

For
Bank A: 10 000 multiplied by (40 000:80 000) = 5 000
Bank B: 600 multiplied by (2 500: 5 000) =   300
which exceeds ECU 250 million for each of the banks.

3 *Total turnover within one (and the same) Member State X*

	Bank A	Bank B
is replaced by one-tenth of total assets:	10 000	600

which is multiplied for each bank by the ratio between loans and advances to credit institutions and customers within one and the same Member State X; to the total sum of loans and advances to credit institutions and customers.

	Bank A	Bank B
This is calculated as follows:		
loans and advances to credit institutions and customers	5 000	500
within one (and the same) Member State X	15 000	500
	20 000	1 000

and
the total sum of loans and advances to

	Bank A	Bank B
credit institutions and customers	80 000	5 000

For
Bank A: 10 000 multiplied by (20 000:80 000) = 2 500
Bank B: 600 multiplied by (1 000: 5 000) =   120
Result:
50% of bank A's and 40% of bank B's Community-wide turnover are achieved in one (and the same) Member State X.

III Conclusion

Since

(a) the aggregate worlwide turnover of bank A plus bank B is more than ECU 5 000 million;
(b) the Community-wide turnover of each of the banks is more than ECU 250 million; and
(c) each of the banks achieve less than two-thirds of its Community-wide turnover in one (and the same) Member State,

the proposed merger would fall under the scope of the Regulation.

GUIDANCE NOTE II

CALCULATION OF TURNOVER FOR INSURANCE UNDERTAKINGS

(Article 5 (3) (a))

For the calculation of turnover for insurance undertakings, we give the following example (proposed concentration between insurances A and B):

I Consolidated profit and loss account

(in million ecu)

Income	Insurance A	Insurance B
Gross premiums written — gross premiums received from Community residents: — gross premiums received from residents of one (and the same) Member State X: Other income:	5 000 (4 500) (3 600) 500	300 (300) (270) 50
Total income:	5 500	350

II Calculation of turnover

1 Aggregate worldwide turnover
is replaced by the value of gross premiums written worldwide, the sum of which is ECU 5 300 million.

2 Community-wide turnover
is replaced, for each of the insurance undertakings, by the value of gross premiums written with Community residents. For each of the insurance undertakings, this amount is more than ECU 250 million.

3   Turnover within one (and the same) Member State X
is replaced, for insurance undertakings, by the value of gross premiums written
with residents of one (and the same) Member State X.
For insurance A, it achieves 80% of its gross premiums written with Community
residents within Member State X, whereas for insurance B, it achieves 90% of
its gross premiums written with Community residents in that Member State X.

III   Conclusion
Since

(a)   the aggregate worldwide turnover of insurances A and B, as replaced by the
value of gross premiums written worldwide, is more than ECU 5 000 million;
(b)   for each of the insurance undertakings, the value of gross premiums written
with Community residents is more than ECU 250 million; but
(c)   each of the insurance undertakings achieves more than two-thirds of its gross
premiums written with Community residents in one (and the same) Member State X,

the proposed concentration would not fall under the scope of the Regulation.

GUIDANCE NOTE III

CALCULATION OF TURNOVER FOR JOINT UNDERTAKINGS

A   CREATION OF A JOINT UNDERTAKING (Article 3 (2))

In a case where two (or more) undertakings create a joint undertaking that constitutes
a concentration, turnover is calculated for the undertakings concerned.

B   EXISTENCE OF A JOINT UNDERTAKING (Article 5 (5))

For the calculation of turnover in case of the existence of a joint undertaking C
between two undertakings A and B concerned in a concentration, we give the following
example:

I   Profit and loss accounts

(in million ecu)

Turnover	Undertaking A	Undertaking B
Sales revenues worldwide	10 000	2 000
— Community	(8 000)	(1 500)
— Member State Y	(4 000)	(900)

(in million ecu)

Turnover	Joint undertaking C
Sales revenues worldwide — with undertaking A — with undertaking B	100 (20) (10)
Turnover with third undertakings — Community-wide — in Member State Y	70 (60) (50)

II Consideration of the joint undertaking

(a) The undertaking C is jointly controlled (in the meaning of Article 3 (3) and (4)) by the undertakings A and B concerned by the concentration, irrespective of any third undertaking participating in that undertaking C.

(b) The undertaking C is not consolidated by A and B in their profit and loss accounts.

(c) The turnover of C resulting from operations with A and B shall not be taken into account.

(d) The turnover of C resulting from operations with any third undertaking shall be apportioned equally amongst the undertakings A and B, irrespective of their individual shareholdings in C.

(e) Any joint undertaking existing between one of the undertakings concerned and any third undertaking shall (unless already consolidated) not be taken into account.

III Calculation of turnover

(a) Undertaking A's aggregate worldwide turnover shall be calculated as follows: ECU 10 000 million and 50% of C's worldwide turnover with third undertakings (i.e. ECU 35 million), the sum of which is ECU 10 035 million.

Undertaking B's aggregate worldwide turnover shall be calculated as follows: ECU 2 000 million and 50% of C's worldwide turnover with third undertakings (i.e. ECU 35 million), the sum of which is ECU 2 035 million.

(b) The aggregate worldwide turnover of the undertakings concerned is ECU 12 070 million.

(c) Undertaking A achieves ECU 4 025 million within Member State Y (50% of C's turnover in this Member State taken into account), and a Community-wide turnover of ECU 8 030 million (including 50% of C's Community-wide turnover); and undertaking B achieves ECU 925 million within Member State Y (50% of C's turnover in this Member State taken into account), and a Community-wide turnover of ECU 1 530 million (including 50% of C's Community-wide turnover).

IV   Conclusion

Since

(a)   the aggregate worldwide turnover of undertakings A and B is more than
ECU 5 000 million,

(b)   each of the undertakings concerned by the concentration achieves more than
ECU 250 million within the Community,

(c)   each of the undertakings concerned (undertaking A 50,1% and undertaking
B 60,5%) achieves less than two-thirds of its Community-wide turnover in one (and
the same) Member State Y,

the proposed concentration would fall under the scope of the Regulation.

GUIDANCE NOTE IV

APPLICATION OF THE TWO-THIRDS RULE

(Article 1)

For the application of the two-thirds rule for undertakings, we give the following
examples (proposed concentration between undertakings A and B):

I   Consolidated profit and loss accounts

EXAMPLE 1

(in million ecu)

Turnover	Undertaking A	Undertaking B
Sales revenues worldwide	10 000	500
— within the Community:	(8 000)	(400)
— in Member State X:	(6 000)	(200)

EXAMPLE 2 (a)

(in million ecu)

Turnover	Undertaking A	Undertaking B
Sales revenues worldwide	4 800	500
— within the Community:	(2 400)	(400)
— in Member State X:	(2 100)	(300)

EXAMPLE 2 (b)

Same figures as in example 2 (a), BUT undertaking B achieves ECU 300 million in Member State Y.

II   Application of the two-thirds rule

EXAMPLE 1

1 *Community-wide turnover*
   is, for undertaking A, ECU 8 000 million and for undertaking B ECU 400 million.

2 *Turnover in one (and the same) Member State X*
   is, for undertaking A (ECU 6 000 million), 75% of its Community-wide turnover and is, for undertaking B (ECU 200 million), 50% of its Community-wide turnover.

3 *Conclusion*
   In this case, although undertaking A achieves more than two-thirds of its Community-wide turnover in Member State X, the proposed concentration would fall under the scope of the Regulation due to the fact that undertaking B achieves less than two-thirds of its Community-wide turnover in Member State X.

EXAMPLE 2 (a)

1 *Community-wide turnover*
   of undertaking A is ECU 2 400 million and of undertaking B, ECU 400 million.

2 *Turnover in one (and the same) Member State X*
   is, for undertaking A, ECU 2 100 million (i.e. 87.5% of its Community-wide turnover); and, for undertaking B ECU 300 million (i.e. 75% of its Community-wide turnover).

3 *Conclusion*
   In this case, each of the undertakings concerned achieves more than two-thirds of its Community-wide turnover in one (and the same) Member State X; the proposed concentration would not fall under the scope of the Regulation.

EXAMPLE 2 (b)

Conclusion

In this case, the two-thirds rule would not apply due to the fact that undertakings A and B achieve more than two-thirds of their Community-wide turnover in different Member States X and Y. Therfore, the proposed concentration would fall under the scope of the Regulation.

ANNEX II

Holidays in 1990*

			B	DK	D	GR	E	F	IRL	I	L	NL	P	UK
New Year:	1.	1.	X	X	X	X	X	X	X	X	X	X	X	X
New Year:	2.	1.												X[1]
Carnival Monday:	26.	2.			X									
St. Patrick:	19.	3.							X					X[2]
Maundy Thursday:	12.	4.		X				X						
Good Friday:	13.	4.		X	X	X	X		X			X	X	X
Easter Monday:	16.	4.	X	X	X	X		X	X	X	X	X		X
Anniversary of the Liberation:	25.	4.								X				
Liberty Day:	25.	4.										X		
The Queen's Birthday:	30.	4.										X		
Labour Day:	1.	5.	X		X	X	X	X		X	X		X	
May holiday:	7.	5.												X
Armistice 1945:	8.	5.						X						
General Prayer Day:	11.	5.		X										
Ascension:	24.	5.	X	X	X			X			X	X		
Spring holiday:	28.	5.												X
Whit Monday:	4.	6.	X	X	X	X		X	X		X	X		
Constitution Day:	5.	6.		X										
Corpus Christi:	14.	6.			X[3]							X		
Orangeman's Day:	12.	7.												X[2]
St. James:	24.	7.					X							
First Monday in August:	6.	8.							X					X[1]
Friedensfest:	8.	8.			X[4]									
Assumption:	15.	8.	X		X[5]	X	X			X	X		X	
Summer Bank holiday:	27.	8.												X
Republic Day:	5.	10.											X	
National holiday:	12.	10.					X							
Bank holiday:	29.	10.							X					
All Saints:	1.	11.	X		X[6]		X	X		X	X		X	
All Souls:	2.	11.	X											
Dynasty Day:	15.	11.	X											
Repentance Day:	21.	11.			X									
Constitution Day:	6.	12.					X							
Christmas:	25.	12.	X	X	X	X	X	X	X	X	X	X	X	X
Second day of Christmas:	26.	12.	X	X	X	X			X	X	X	X		X

*   These dates may change from year to year, but the left-hand column is included as a guide.
[1]   Scotland.
[2]   Northern Ireland.
[3]   Baden-Württemberg, Bayern, Hessen, Nordrhein-Westfalen, Rheinland-Pfalz, Saarland.
[4]   City of Augsburg (Bayern).
[5]   Saarland and Bayern, Bayern, public holiday in administrative districts with a predominantly Catholic population.
[6]   Baden-Württemberg, Bayern, Nordrhein-Westfalen, Rheinland-Pfalz, Saarland.

Commission

New Year's Day	1 January
Day after New Year's Day	2 January
Holy/Maundy Thursday	12 April
Good Friday	13 April
Easter Monday	16 April
Labour Day	1 May
Anniversary of the declaration by Robert Schuman	9 May
Ascension Day	24 May
Day after Ascension Day	25 May
Whit Monday	4 June
Assumption Day	15 August
All Saints Day	1 November
All Souls Day	2 November
Christmas	24 December
	25 December
	26 December
	27 December
	28 December
	29 December
	30 December
	31 December

APPENDIX III

Commission notice regarding the concentrative and cooperative operations under Council Regulation (EEC) No 4064/89 of 21 December 1989 on the control of concentrations between undertakings[1] (90/C 203/06) OJ 1990 C 203/10

I Introduction

1. Article 3 (1) of Council Regulation (EEC) No 4064/89 ('the Regulation') contains an exhaustive list of the factual circumstances which fall to be considered as concentrations. In accordance with the 23rd recital, this term refers only to operations that lead to a lasting change in the structures of the participating undertakings.

By contrast, the Regulation does not deal with operations whose object or effect is the coordination of the competitive activities of undertakings that remain independent of each other. Situations of this kind are cooperative in character. Accordingly, they fall to be assessed under the provisions of Regulations (EEC) No 17[2], (EEC) No 1017/68[3], No 4056/86[4] or No 3975/87[5]. The same applies to an operation which includes both a lasting structural change and the coordination of competitive behaviour, where the two are inseperable.

If the structural change can be separated from the coordination of competitive behaviour, the former will be assessed under the Regulation and the latter, to the extent that it does not amount to an ancillary restriction within the meaning of Article 8 (2), second subparagraph of the Regulation, falls to be assessed under the other Regulations implementing Articles 85 and 86 of the EEC Treaty.

2. The purpose of this notice is to define as clearly as possible, in the interests

[1] OJ No L 395, 30.12.1989, p. 1.
[2] OJ No 13, 21.2.1962, p 204/62.
[3] OJ No L 175, 23.7.1968, p. 1.
[4] OJ No L 378, 31.12.1986, p. 4.
[5] OJ No L 374, 31.12.1987, p. 1.

of legal certainty, concentrative and cooperative situations. This is particularly important in the case of joint ventures. The same issue is raised in other forms of association between undertakings such as unilateral or reciprocal shareholdings and common directorships, and of certain operations involving more than one undertaking, such as unilateral or reciprocal transfers of undertakings or parts of undertakings, or joint acquisition of an undertaking with a view to its division. In all these cases, operations may not fall within the scope of the Regulation, where their object or effect is the coordination of the competitive behaviour of the undertakings concerned.

3. This notice sets out the main considerations which will determine the Commission's view to what extent the aforesaid operations are or are not caught by the Regulation. It is not concerned with the assessment of these operations, whether under the Regulation or any other applicable provisions, in particular Articles 85 and 86 of the EEC Treaty.

4. The principles set out in this notice will be followed and further developed by the Commission's practice in individual cases. As the operations considered are generally of a complex nature, this notice cannot provide a definitive answer to all conceivable situations.

5. This notice is without prejudice to the interpretation which may be given by the Court of Justice or the Court of First Instance of the European Communities.

II Joint Ventures within Article 3 of the Regulation

6. The Regulation in Article 3(2) refers to two types of joint venture: those which have as their object or effect the coordination of the competitive behaviour of undertakings which remain independent (referred to as 'cooperative joint ventures') and those which perform on a lasting basis all the functions of an autonomous economic entity and which do not give rise to coordination amongst themselves or between them and the joint venture (referred to as 'concentrative joint ventures'). The latter are concentrations and as such are caught by the Regulation. Cooperative joint ventures fall to be considered under other regulations implementing Articles 85 and 86[6].

A Concept of joint venture

7. To define the term 'joint venture' within the meaning of Article 3 (2), it is necessary to refer to the provision of Article 3 (1) (b) of the Regulation. According to the latter, JVs are undertakings that are jointly controlled by several other undertakings, the parent companies. In the context of the Regulation the term JV thus implies several characteristics:

1 Undertaking

8. A JV must be an undertaking. That is to be understood as an organized assembly of human and material resources, intended to pursue a defined economic purpose on a long-term basis.

---

[6] See footnotes 2 to 5 on the previous page.

2   Control by other undertakings

9.   In the context of the Regulation, a JV is controlled by other undertakings. Pursuant to Article 3 (3) of the Regulation, control means the possibility of exercising, directly or indirectly, a decisive influence on the activities of the JV; whether this condition is fulfilled can only be decided by reference to all the legal and factual circumstances of the individual case.

10.   Control of a JV can be based on legal, contractual or other means, within which the following elements are especially important:

— ownership or rights to the use of all or some of the JV's assets,
— influence over the composition, voting or decisions of the managing or supervisory bodies of the JV,
— voting rights in the managing or supervisory bodies of the JV,
— contracts concerning the running of the JV's business.

3   Joint control

11.   A JV under the Regulation is jointly controlled. Joint controls exists where the parent companies must agree on decisions concerning the JV's activities, either because of the rights acquired in the JV or because of contracts or other means establishing the joint control. Joint control may be provided for in the JV's constitution (memorandum or articles of association). However, it need not be present from the beginning, but may also be established later, in particular by taking a share in an existing undertaking.

12.   There is no joint control where one of the parent companies can decide alone on the JV's commercial activities. This is generally the case where one company owns more than half the capital or assets of the undertaking, has the right to appoint more than half of the managing or supervisory bodies, controls more than half of the votes in one of those bodies, or has the sole right to manage the undertaking's business. Where the other parent companies either have completely passive minority holdings or, while able to have a certain influence on the undertaking, cannot, individually or together, determine its behaviour, a relative majority of the capital or of the votes or seats on the decision-making bodies will suffice to control the undertaking.

13.   In many cases, the joint control of the JV is based on agreements or concertation between the parent companies. Thus, a majority sharehoder in a JV often extends to one or more minority shareholders a contractual right to take part in the control of the JV. If two undertakings each hold half of a JV, even if there is no agreement between them, both parent companies will be obliged permanently to cooperate so as to avoid reciprocal blocking votes on decisions affecting the JV's activity. The same applies to JVs with three or more parents, where each of them has a right of veto. A JV can even be controlled by a considerable number of undertakings that can together muster a majority of the capital or the seats or votes on the JV's decision-making bodies. However, in such cases, joint control can be presumed only if the factual and legal circumstances — especially a convergence of economic interests — support the notion of a deliberate common policy of the parent companies in relation to the JV.

14.   If one undertaking's holding in another is, by its nature or its extent, insufficient to establish sole control, and if there is no joint control together with

third parties, then there is no concentration within the meaning of Article 3 (1) (b) of the Regulation. Article 85 or 86 of the EEC Treaty may however by applicable on the basis of Regulation (EEC) No 17 or other implementing Regulations (see III.1).

B Concentrative joint ventures

15. For a joint venture to be regarded as concentrative it must fulfil all the conditions of Article 3 (2), subparagraph 2, which lays down a positive condition and a negative condition.

1 Positive condition: joint ventures performing on a lasting basis all the functions of an autonomous economic entity

16. To fulfil this condition, a JV must first of all act as an independent supplier and buyer on the market. JVs that take over from their parents only specific partial responsibilities are not to be considered as concentrations where they are merely auxiliaries to the commercial activities of the parent companies. This is the case where the JV supplies its products or services exclusively to its parent companies, or when it meets its own needs wholly from them. The independent market presence can even be insufficient if the JV achieves the majority of its supplies or sales with third parties, but remains substantially dependent on its parents for the maintenance and development of its business.

17. A JV exists on a lasting basis if it is intended and able to carry on its activity for an unlimited, or at least for a long, time. If this is not the case there is generally no long-term change in the structures of the parent companies. More important than the agreed duration are the human and material resources of the JV. They must be of such nature and quantity as to ensure the JV's existence and independence in the long term. This is generally the case where the parent companies invest substantial financial resources in the JV, transfer an existing undertaking or business to it, or give it substantial technical or commercial know-how, so that after an intitial starting-up period it can support itself by its own means.

18. A decisive question for assessing the autonomous character of the JV is whether it is in a position to exercise its own commercial policy. This requires, within the limits of its company objects, that it plans, decides and acts independently. In particular, it must be free to determine its competitive behaviour autonomously and according to its own economic interests. If the JV depends for its business on facilities that remain economically integrated with the parent companies' businesses, that weakens the case for the autonomous nature of the JV.

19. The JV's economic independence will not be contested merely because the parent companies reserve to themselves the right to take certain decisions that are important for the development of the JV, namely those concerning alterations of the objects of the company, increases or reductions of capital, or the application of profits. However, if the commercial policy of the JV remains in the hands of the parent undertakings, the JV may take on the aspect of an instrument of the parent undertakings' market interests. Such a situation will usually exist where the JV operates in the market of the parent undertakings. It may also exist where the JV operates in markets neighbouring, or upstream or downstream of, those of the parent undertakings.

2 Negative condition: absence of coordination of competitive behaviour

20.   Subject to what is said in the first paragraph of this notice a JV can only be considered to be concentrative within the meaning of Article 3 (2), subparagraph 2 of the Regulation, if it does not have as its object or effect the coordination of the competitive behaviour of undertakings that remain independent of each other. There must not be such coordination either between the parent companies themselves or between any or all of them on the one hand and the JV on the other hand. Such coordination must not be an object of the establishment or operation of the JV, nor may it be the consequence thereof. The JV is not to be regarded as concentrative if as a result of the agreement to set up the JV or as a result of its existence or activities it is reasonably foreseeable that the competitive behaviour of a parent or of the JV on the relevant market will be influenced. Conversely, there will normally be no foreseeable coordination when all the parent companies withdraw entirely and permanently from the JV's market and do not operate on markets neighbouring those of the JV's.

21.   Not every cooperation between parent companies with regard to the JV prevents a JV from being considered concentrative. Even concentrative JVs generally represent a means for parent companies to pursue common or mutually complementary interests. The establishment and joint control of a JV is, therefore, inconceivable without an understanding between the parent companies as concerns the pursuit of those interests. Irrespective of its legal form, such a concordance of interests is an essential feature of a JV.

22.   As regards the relations of the parent undertakings, or any one of them, with the JV, the risk of coordination within the meanding of Article 3 (2) will not normally arise where the parent undertakings are not active in the markets of the JV or in neighbouring or upstream or downstream markets. In other cases, the risk of coordination will be relatively small where the parents limit the influence they exercise to the JV's strategic decisions, such as those concerning the future direction of investment, and when they express their financial, rather than their market-oriented, interests. The membership of the JV's managing and supervisory bodies is also important. Common membership of the JV's and the parent companies' decision-making bodies may be an obstacle to the development of the JV's autonomous commercial policy.

23.   The dividing line between the concordance of interests in a JV and a coordinatin of competitive behaviour that is incompatible with the notion of concentration cannot be laid down for all conceivable kinds of case. The decisive factor is not the legal form of the relationship between the parent companies and between them and the JV. The direct or indirect, actual or potential effects of the establishment and operation of the JV on market relationships, have determinant importance.

24.   In assessing the likelihood of coordination of competitive behaviour, it is useful to consider some of the different situations which often occur:

(a)   JVs that take over pre-existing activities of the parent companies;
(b)   JVs that undertake new activities on behalf of the parent companies;
(c)   JVs that enter the parent companies' markets;
(d)   JVs that enter upstream, downstream or neighbouring markets.

(a) JVs that take over pre-existing activities of the parent companies

25. There is normally no risk of coordination where the parent companies transfer the whole of certain business activities to the JV and withdraw permanently from the JV's market so that they can remain neither actual nor potential competitors — of each other nor of the JV. In this context, the notion of potential competition is to be interpreted realistically, according to the Commission's established practice[7]. A presumption of a competitive relationship requires not only that one or more of the parent companies could re-enter the JV's market at any time; this must be a realistic course in the light of all objective circumstances.

26. Where the parent companies transfer their entire business activities to the JV, and thereafter act only as holding companies, this amounts to complete merger from the economic viewpoint.

27. Where the JV takes on only some of the activities that the parent companies formerly carried on independently, this can also amount to a concentration. In this case, the establishment and operation of the JV must not lead to a coordination of the parent companies' competitive behaviour in relation to other activities which they retain. Coordination of competitive behaviour between any or all of the parent companies and the JV must also be excluded. Such coordination is likely where there are close economic links between the areas of activity of the JV on one side and of the parent companies on the other. This applies to upstream, downstream and neighbouring product markets.

28. The withdrawal of the parent companies need not be simultaneous with the establishment of the JV. It is possible — so far as necessary — to allow the parent companies a short transitional period to overcome any starting-up problems of the JV, especially bottlenecks in production or supplies. This period should not normally exceed one year.

29. It is even possible for the establishment of a JV to represent a concentration situation where the parent companies remain permanently active on the JV's product or service market. In this case, however, the parent companies' geographic market must be different from that of the JV. Morover, the markets in question must be so widely separated, or must present structures so different, that, taking account of the nature of the goods or services concerned and of the cost of (first or renewed) entry by either into the other's market, competitive interaction may be excluded.

30. If the parent companies' markets and the JV's are in different parts of the Community or neighbouring third countries, there is a degree of probability that either, if it has the necessary human and material resources, could extend its activities from the one market to the other. Where the territories are adjacent or very close to each other, this may even be assumed to be the case. At least in this last case, the actual allocation of markets gives reason to suppose that it follows from a coordination of competitive behaviour between parent companies and the JV.

(b) JVs that undertake new activities on behalf of the parent companies

31. There is normally no risk of coordination in the sense described above where the JV operates on a product or service market which the parent companies individually have not entered and will not enter in the foreseeable future, because they lack the organizational, technical or financial means or because, in the light of all the

---

[7] See the Thirteenth Report (1983) on Competition Policy, point 55.

objective circumstances, such a move would not represent a commercially reasonable course. An individual market entry will also be unlikely where, after establishing the JV, the parent companies no longer have the means to make new investments in the same field, or where an additional individual operation on the JV's market would not make commercial sense. In both cases there is no competitive relationship between the parent companies and the JV. Consequently, there is no possibility of coordination of their competitive behaviour. However, this assessment is only true if the JV's market is neither upstream nor downstream of, nor neighbouring, that of the parent companies.

32. The establishment of a JV to operate in the same product or service market as the parent companies but in another geographic market involves the risk of coordination if there is competitive interaction between the parent companies' geographic market and that of the JV.

(c)   JVs that enter the parent companies' market

33. Where the parent companies, or one of them, remain active on the JV's market or remain potential competitors of the JV, a coordination of competitive behaviour between the parent companies or between them and the JV must be presumed. So long as this presumption is not rebutted, the Commission will take it that the establishment of the JV does not fall under Article 3 (2), subparagraph 2 of the Regulation.

(d)   JVs that operate in upstream, downstream or neighbouring markets

34. If the JV is operating in a market that is upstream or downstream of that of the parent companies, then, in general, coordination of purchasing or, as the case may be, sales policy between the parent companies is likely where they are competitors on the upstream or downstream market.

35. If the parent companies are not competitors, it remains to be examined whether there is a real risk of coordination of competitive behaviour between the JV and any of the parents. This will normally be the case where the JV's sales or purchases are made in substantial measure with the parent companies.

36. It is not possible to lay down general principles regarding the likelihood of coordination of competitive behaviour in cases where the parent companies and the JV are active in neighbouring markets. The outcome will depend in particular on whether the JV's and the parent companies' products are technically or economically linked, whether they are both components of another product or are otherwise mutually complementary, and whether the parent companies could realistically enter the JV's market. If there are no concrete opportunities for competitive interaction of this kind, the Commission will treat the JV as concentrative.

III   Other links between undertakings

1   Minority shareholdings

37. The taking of a minority shareholding in an undertaking can be considered a concentration within the meaning of Article 3 (1) (b) of the Regulation if the new shareholder acquires the possibility of exercising a decisive influence on the undertaking's activity. If the acquisition of a minority shareholding brings about

a situation in which there is an undertaking jointly controlled by two or more others, the principles described above in relation to JVs apply.

38. As long as the threshold of individual or joint decisive influence has not been reached, the Regulation is not in any event applicable. Accordingly, the assessment under competition law will be made only in relation to the criteria laid down in Articles 85 and 86 of the EEC Treaty and on the basis of the usual procedural rules for restrictive practices and abuses of dominant position[8].

39. There may likewise be a risk of coordination where an undertaking acquires a majority or minority interest in another in which a competitor already has a minority interest. If so, this acquisition will be assessed under Articles 85 and 86 of the EEC Treaty.

2   Cross-shareholding

40. In order to bring their autonomous and hitherto separate undertakings or groups closer together, company owners often cause them to exchange shareholdings in each other. Such reciprocal influences can serve to establish or to secure industrial or commercial cooperation between the undertakings or groups. But they may also result in establishing a 'single economic entity'. In the first case, the coordination of competitive behaviour between independent undertakings is predominant; in the second, the result may be a concentration. Consequently, reciprocal directorships and cross-shareholdings can only be evaluated in relation to their foreseeable effects in each case.

41. The Commission considers that two or more undertakings can also combine without setting up a parent-subsidiary relationship and without either losing its legal personality. Article 3 (1) of the Regulation refers not only to legal, but also to economic concentrations.

The condition for the recognition of a concentration in the form of a combined group is, however, that the undertakings or groups concerned are not only subject to a permanent, single economic management, but are also amalgamated into a genuine economic unit, characterised internally by profit and loss compensation between the various undertakings within the groups and externally by joint liability.

3   Representation on controlling bodies of other undertakings

42. Common membership of managing or supervisory boards of various undertakings is to be assessed in accordance with the same principles as cross-shareholdings.

43. The representation of one undertaking on the decision-making bodies of another is usually the consequence of an existing shareholding. It reinforces the influence of the investing undertaking over the activities of the undertaking in which it holds a share, because it affords it the opportunity of obtaining information on the activities of a competitor or of taking an active part in its commercial decisions.

44. Thus, common membership of the respective boards may be the vehicle for the coordination of the competitive behaviour of the undertakings concerned, or for a concentration of undertakings within the meaning of the Regulation. This will depend on the circumstances of the individual case, among which the economic

---

[8]   Judgment of the Court of Justice of the European Communities in Joined Cases 142 and 156/84 BAT and Reynolds ECR 1987, pp. 4566 and 4577.

link between the shareholding and the personal connection must always be examined. This is equally true of unilateral and reciprocal relationships between undertakings.

45. Personal connections not accompanied by shareholdings are to be judged according to the same criteria as shareholding relationships between undertakings. A majority of seats on the managing or supervisory board of an undertaking will normally imply control of the latter; a minority of seats at least a degree of influence over its commercial policy, which may further entail a coordination of behaviour. Reciprocal connections justify a presumption that the undertakings concerned are coordinating their business conduct. A very wide communality of membership of the respective decision-making bodies — that is, up to half of the members or more — may be an indication of a concentration.

4 Transfers of undertakings or parts of undertakings

46. A transfer of assets or shares falls within the definition of a concentration, according to Article 3 (1) (b) of the Regulation, if it results in the acquirer gaining control of all or of part of one or more undertakings. However, the situation is different where the transfer conferring control over part of an undertaking is linked with an agreement to coordinate the competitive behaviour of the undertakings concerned, or where it necessarily leads to or is accompanied by coordination of the business conduct of undertakings which remain independent. Cases of this kind are not covered by the Regulation: they must be examined according to Articles 85 and 86 of the EEC Treaty and under the appropriate implementing Regulations.

47. The practical application of this rule requires a distinction between unilateral and reciprocal arrangements. A unilateral acquisition of assets or shares strongly suggests that the Regulation is applicable. The contrary needs to be demonstrated by clear evidence of the likelihood of coordination of the parties' competitive behaviour. A reciprocal acquisition of assets or shares, by contrast, will usually follow an agreement between the undertakings concernd as to their investments, production or sales, and thus serves to coordinate their competitive behaviour. A concentration situation does not exist where a reciprocal transfer of assets or shares forms part of a specialization or restructuring agreement or other type of coordination. Coordination presupposes in any event that the parties remain at least potential competitors after the exchange has taken place.

5 Joint acquisition of an undertaking with a view to its division

48. Where several undertakings jointly acquire another, the principles for the assessment of a joint venture are applicable, provided that within the acquisition operation, the period of joint control goes beyond the very short term. In this case the Regulation may or may not be applicable, depending on the concentrative or cooperative nature of the JV. If, by contrast, the sole object of the agreement is to divide up the assets of the undertaking and this agreement is put into effect immediately after the acquisition, then, in accordance with the 24th recital, the Regulation applies.

APPENDIX IV

Commission notice regarding restrictions ancillary to concentrations (90/C 203/05) OJ 1990 C203/5

I Introduction

1. Council Regulation (EEC) No 4064/89 of 21 December 1989 on the control of concentrations between undertakings ('the Regulation')[1] states in its 25th recital that its application is not excluded where the undertakings concerned accept restrictions which are directly related and necessary to the implementation of the concentration, hereinafter referred to as 'ancillary restrictions'. In the scheme of the Regulation, such restrictions are to be assessed together with the concentration itself. It follows, as confirmed by Article 8 (2), second subparagraph, last sentence of the Regulation, that a decision declaring the concentration compatible also covers these restrictions. In this situation, under the provisions of Article 22, paragraphs 1 and 2, the Regulation is solely applicable, to the exclusion of Regulation No 17[2] as well as Regulations (EEC) No 1017/68[3], (EEC) No 4056/86[4] and (EEC) No 3975/87[5]. This avoids parallel Commission proceedings, one concerned with the assessment of the concentration under the Regulation, and the other aimed at the application of Articles 85 and 86 to the restrictions which are ancillary to the concentration.

2. In this notice, the Commission sets out to indicate the interpretation it gives to the notion of 'restrictions directly related and necessary to the implementation of the concentration'. Under the Regulation such restrictions must be assessed in relation to the concentration, whatever their treatment might be under Articles 85 and 86 if they were to be considered in isolation or in a different economic context. The Commission endeavours, within the limits set by the Regulation, to take the greatest account of business practice and of the conditions necessary for the implementation of concentrations.

This notice is without prejudice to the interpretation which may be given by the Court of Justice of the European Communities.

[1]   OJ No L 395, 30.12.1989, p. 1.
[2]   OJ No 13, 12.2.1962, p. 204/62.
[3]   OJ No L 175, 23.7.1968, p. 1.
[4]   OJ No L 378, 31.12.1986, p. 4.
[5]   OJ No L 374, 31.12.1987, p. 1.

II Principles of evaluation

3. The 'restrictions' meant are those agreed on between the parties to the concentration which limit their own freedom of action in the market. They do not include restrictions to the detriment of third parties. If such restrictions are the inevitable consequence of the concentration itself, they must be assessed together with it under the provisions of Article 2 of the Regulation. If, on the contrary, such restrictive effects on third parties are separable from the concentration they may, if appropriate, be the subject of an assessment of compatability with Articles 85 and 86 of the EEC Treaty.

4. For restrictions to be considered 'directly related' they must be ancillary to the implementations of the concentration, that is to say subordinate in importance to the main object of the concentration. They cannot be substantial restrictions wholly different in nature from those which result from the concentrations itself. Neither are they contractual arrangements which are among the elements constituting the concentration, such as those establishing economic unity between previously independent parties, or organizing joint control by two undertakings of another undertaking. As integral parts of the concentration, the latter arrangements constitute the very subject matter of the evaluation to be carried out under the Regulation.

Also excluded, for concentrations which are carried out in stages, are the contractual arrangements relating to the stages before the establishment of control within the meaning of Article 3, paragraphs 1 and 3 of the Regulation. For these, Articles 85 and 86 remain applicable as long as the conditions set out in Article 3 are not fulfilled.

The notion of directly related restrictions likewise excludes from the application of the Regulation additional restrictions agreed at the same time which have no direct link with the concentration. It is not enough that the additional restrictions exist in the same context as the concentration.

5. The restrictions must likewise be 'necessary to the implementation of the concentration', which means that in their absence the concentration could not be implemented or could only be implemented under more uncertain conditions, at substantially higher cost, over an appreciably longer period or with considerably less probability of success. This must be judged on an objective basis.

6. The question of whether a restriction meets these conditions cannot be answered in general terms. In particular as concerns the necessity of the restriction, it is proper not only to take account of its nature, but equally to ensure, in applying the rule of proportionality, that its duration and subject matter, and geographic field of application, do not exceed what the implementation of the concentration reasonably requires. If alternatives are available for the attainment of the legitimate aim pursued, the undertakings must choose the one which is objectively the least restrictive of competition.

These principles will be followed and further developed by the Commission's practice in individual cases. However, it is already possible, on the basis of past experience, to indicate the attitude the Commission will take to those restrictions most commonly encountered in relation to the transfer of undertakings or parts of undertakings, the division of undertakings or of their assets following a joint acquisition of control, or the creation of concentrative joint ventures.

III Evaluation of common ancillary restrictions in cases of the transfer of an undertaking

A Non-competition clauses

1. Among the ancillary restrictions which meet the criteria set out in the Regulation are contractual prohibitions on competition which are imposed on the vendor in the context of a concentration achieved by the transfer of an undertaking or part of an undertaking. Such prohibitions guarantee the transfer to the acquirer of the full value of the assets transferred, which in general include both physical assets and intangible assets such as the goodwill which the vendor has accumulated or the know-how he has developed. These are not only directly related to the concentration, but are also necessary for its implementation because, in their absence, there would be reasonable grounds to expect that the sale of the undertaking or part of an undertaking could not be accomplished satisfactorily. In order to take over fully the value of the assets transferred, the acquirer must be able to benefit from some protection against competitive acts of the vendor in order to gain the loyalty of customers and to assimilate and exploit the know-how. Such protection cannot generally be considered necessary when *de facto* the transfer is limited to physical assets (such as land, buildings or machinery) or to exclusive industrial and commerical property rights (the holder of which could immediately take action against infringements by the transferor of such rights).

However, such a prohibition on competition is justified by the legitimate objective sought of implementing the concentration only when its duration, its geographical field of application, its subject matter and the persons subject to it do not exceed what is reasonably necessary to that end.

2. With regard to the acceptable duration of a prohibition on competition, a period of five years has been recognized as appropriate when the transfer of the undertaking includes the goodwill and know-how, and a period of two years when it includes only the goodwill. However, these are not absolute rules; they do not preclude a prohibition of longer duration in particular circumstances, where for example the parties can demonstrate that customer loyalty will persist for a period longer than two years or that the economic life cycle of the products concerned is longer than five years and should be taken into account.

3. The geographic scope of the non-competition clause must be limited to the area where the vendor had established the products or services before the transfer. It does not appear objectively necesary that the acquirer be protected from competition by the vendor in territories which the vendor had not previously penetrated.

4. In the same manner, the non-competition clause must be limited to products and services which form the economic activity of the undertaking transferred. In particular, in the case of a partial transfer of assets, it does not appear that the acquirer needs to be protected from the competition of the vendor in the products or services which constitute the activities which the vendor retains after the transfer.

5. The vendor may bind himself, his subsidiaries and commercial agents. However, an obligation to impose similar restrictions on others would not qualify as an ancillary restriction. This applies in particular to clauses which would restrict the scope for resellers or users to import or export.

6. Any protection of the vendor is not normally an ancillary restriction and is therefore to be examined under Articles 85 and 86 of the EEC Treaty.

B   Licences of industrial and commercial property rights and of know-how

1.   The implementation of a transfer of an undertaking or part of an undertaking generally includes the transfer to the acquirer, with a view to the full exploitation of the assets transferred, of rights to industrial or commercial property or know-how. However, the vendor may remain the owner of the rights in order to exploit them for activities other than those transferred. In these cases, the usual means for ensuring that the acquirer will have the full use of the assets transferred is to conclude licensing agreements in his favour.

2.   Simple or exclusive licences of patents, similar rights or existing know-how can be accepted as necessary for the completion of the transaction, and likewise agreements to grant such licences. They may be limited to certain fields of use, to the extent that they correspond to the activities of the undertaking transferred. Normally it will not be necessary for such licences to include territorial limitations on manufacture which reflect the territory of the activity transferred. Licences may be granted for the whole duration of the patent or similar rights or the duration of the normal economic life of the know-how. As such licences are economically equivalent to a partial transfer of rights, they need not be limited in time.

3.   Restrictions in licence agreements, going beyond what is provided above, fall outside the scope of the Regulation. They must be assessed on their merits according to Article 85(1) and (3). Accordingly, where they fulfil the conditions required, they may benefit from the block exemptions provided for by Regulation (EEC) No 2349/84 on patent licences[6] or Regulation (EEC) No 559/89 on know-how licences[7]

4.   The same principles are to be applied by analogy in the case of licences of trademarks, business names or similar rights. There may be situations where the vendor wishes to remain the owner of such rights in relation to activities retained, but the acquirer needs the rights to use them to market the products constituting the object of the activity of the undertaking or part of an undertaking transferred.

In such circumstances, the conclusion of agreements for the purpose of avoiding confusion between trademarks may be necessary.

C   Purchase and supply agreements

1.   In many cases, the transfer of an undertaking or part of an undertaking can entail the disruption of traditional lines of internal procurement and supply resulting from the previous integration of activities within the economic entity of the vendor. To make possible the break up of the economic unity of the vendor and the partial transfer of the assets to the acquirer under reasonable conditions, it is often necessary to maintain, at least for a transitional period, similar links between the vendor and the acquirer. This objective is normally attained by the conclusion of purchase and supply agreements between the vendor and the acquirer of the undertaking or part of an undertaking. Taking account of the particular situation resulting from the break up of the economic unity of the vendor such obligations, which may lead to restrictions of competition, can be recognized as ancillary. They may be in favour of the vendor as well as the acquirer.

2.   The legitimate aim of such obligations may be to ensure the continuity of supply to one or other of the parties of products necessary to the activities retained

---

[6]   OJ No L 219, 16.8.1984, p. 15.
[7]   OJ No L 61, 4.3.1989, p. 1.

(for the vendor) or taken over (for the acquirer). Thus, there are grounds for recognizing for a transitional period, the need for supply obligations aimed at guaranteeing the quantities previously supplied within the vendor's integrated business or enabling their adjustment in accordance with the development of the market.

Their aim may also be to provide continuity of outlets for one or the other of the parties, as they were previously assured within the single economic entity. For the same reason, obligations providing for fixed quantities, possibly with a variation clause, may be recognized as necessary.

3. However, there does not appear to be a general justification for exclusive purchase or supply obligations. Save in exceptional circumstances, for example resulting from the absence of a market or the specificity of products, such exclusivity is not objectively necessary to permit the implementation of a concentration in the form of a transfer of an undertaking or part of an undertaking.

In any event, in accordance with the principle of proportionality, the undertakings concerned are bound to consider whether there are no alternative means to the ends pursued, such as agreements for fixed quantities, which are less restrictive than exclusivity.

4. As for the duration of procurement and supply obligations, this must be limited to a period necessary for the replacement of the relationship of dependency by autonomy in market. The duration of such a period must be objectively justified.

IV   Evaluation of ancillary restrictions in the case of a joint acquisition

1. As set out in the 24th recital, the Regulation is applicable when two or more undertakings agree to acquire jointly the control of one or more other undertakings, in particular by means of a public tender offer, where the object or effect is the division among themselves of the undertakings or their assets. This is a concentration implemented in two successive stages; the common strategy is limited to the acquisition of control. For the transaction to be concentrative, the joint acquisition must be followed by a clear separation of the undertakings or assets concerned.

2. For this purpose, an agreement by the joint acquirers of an undertaking to abstain from making separate competing offers for the same undertaking, or otherwise acquiring control, may be considered an ancillary restriction.

3. Restrictions limited to putting the division into effect are to be considered directly related and necessary to the implementation of the concentration. This will apply to arrangements made between the parties for the joint acquisition of control in order to divide among themselves the production facilities or the distribution networks together with the existing trademarks of the undertaking acquired in common. The implementation of this division may not in any circumstances lead to the coordination of the future behaviour of the acquiring undertakings.

4. To the extent that such a division involves the break up of a pre-existing economic entity, arrangements that make the break up possible under reasonable conditions must be considered ancillary. In this regard, the principles explained above in relation to purchase and supply arrangements over a transitional period in cases of transfer of undertakings should be applied by analogy.

V   Evaluation of ancillary restrictions in cases of concentrative joint ventures within the meaning of Article 3 (2) subparagraph 2 of the Regulation

This evaluation must take account of the characteristics peculiar to concentrative joint ventures, the constituent elements of which are the creation of an autonomous economic entity exercising on a long-term basis all the functions of an undertaking, and the absence of coordination of competitive behaviouur between the parent undertakings and between them and the joint venture. This condition implies in principle the withdrawal of the parent undertakings from the market assigned to the joint venture and, therefore, their disappearance as actual or potential competitors of the new entity.

A   Non-competition obligations

To the extent that a prohibition on the parent undertakings competing with the joint venture aims at expressing the reality of the lasting withdrawal of the parents from the market assigned to the joint venture, it will be recognized as an integral part of the concentration.

B   Licences for industrial and commercial property rights and know-how

The creation of a new autonomous economic entity usually involves the transfer of the technology necessary for carrying on the activities assigned to it, in the form of a transfer of rights and related know-how. Where the parent undertakings intend nonetheless to retain the property rights, particularly with the aim of exploitation in other fields of use, the transfer of technology to the joint venture may be accomplished by means of licences. Such licences may be exclusive, without having to be limited in duration or territory, for they serve only as a substitute for the transfer of property rights. They must therefore be considered necessary to the implementation of the concentration.

C   Purchase and supply obligations

If the parent undertakings remain present in a market upstream or downstream of that of the joint venture, any purchase and supply agreements are to be examined in accordance with the principles applicable in the case of the transfer of an undertaking.

Index